GCSE
Geography
for WJEC B

Andy Owen, Andy Leeder
& Glyn Owen

Second Edition

DYNAMIC LEARNING

HODDER EDUCATION
AN HACHETTE UK COMPANY

Acknowledgements

Text extracts and screenshots

p.82 Weather forecast for Snowdonia, 19 August 2009, © Crown copyright 2010, the Met Office; **p.94** Rainfall and discharge data for River Llobregat, Barcelona (May 2007-May 2008), Agencia Catalana de L'Aigua, *http://aca.gencat.net:2020/sdim/visor.do*; **p.97** Diet in the delta before and after the cyclone, and percentage of deaths by age and gender, *Post Nargis Joint Assessment by the Tripartite Core Group* (July 2008), Government of the Union of of Myanmar, United Nations and ASEAN; **p.109** UNICEF, development data for selected Pacific region countries; **p.110** Exports of timber from Solomon Islands to China, *http://www.globaltimber.org.uk/ solomonislands.htm*, reproduced by permission; **p.115** Protected areas in Central America and Mexico, Earthlands/Institute of Environmental Awareness; **p.132** UNICEF, website extract describing the reaction to the Niger food crisis in 2005; **pp.156-157** Plan of the Boscastle flood defences designed by the Environment Agency, reproduced by permission of Cornwall Council; **p.158** Screenshot from the Environment Agency website - Your flood plan, *www.environment-agency.gov.uk*; **p.160** Screenshot for the Environment Agency flood maps, *www.environment-agency.gov.uk*; **p.161** Department for Business Information & Skills, screenshot from Future flooding report, *www.foresight.gov.uk/Flood%20and%20Defence/Chapter4a.pdf*, reproduced by permission; **p.171** Predicted change in sea level in south-west England and Wales, Department for Environment Food & Rural Affairs; **p.177** St. Osyth local government website extract describing the flood of 1953, *http://www.stosyth.gov. uk/default.asp?calltype=greatflood* (October/ November 2000), reproduced by permission of St. Osyth Parish Council; **p.178** Screenshot from Environment Agency website showing areas close to Jaywick that are at risk of coastal flooding; **p.181** Toni O'Loughlin, 'Climate change threatens Australia's coastal lifestyle, report warns', *The Guardian* (28 October, 2009), copyright Guardian News & Media Ltd 2009, reproduced by permission of the publisher; **p.183** 'Beach war' hotels probed over sand theft, *Metro* (31 July, 2009); **p.185** Cost of flood damage in 2050 after a flood similar to the 1953 storm surge, 'Safecoast - trends in flood risk', *www.safecoast.org* (July 2008), reproduced by permission of Rijkswaterstaat-Centre for Water Management; **p.189** World Bank, data on male population in Mali, and changing employment structure by sector; **p.191** Eurostat, percentage of the population of Europe with internet access (2007); **p.192** Data on jobs gained or lost in the West Midlands, 2000-2005, reproduced by permission of West Midlands Regional Observatory; **p.195** Daouda Ballo, 'Waste recycling; an example of informal work', *www.oxfam.org.uk/ coolplanet* (Oxfam, 2007), reproduced with the permission of Oxfam GB, Oxfam House, John Smith Drive, Cowley, Oxford OX4 2JY, UK, www.oxfam.org.uk/ education; **p.197** World Bank report, Rural Women in the Sahel and their Access to Agricultural extension: Overview of Five Country Studies (1994); **p.200** 'A national issue', *The Guardian* (23 June, 2008); **p.202** Redrawn maps of the increase/decrease in audiences of regional programmes, 1998-2003, *www.ofcom.org.uk*; **p.203**: James Purnell, MP, 'Making Britain the world's creative hub', Institute for Public Policy Research speech (June, 2005); **p.212** Colm Regan, 'Dear George, here we are in the middle of things having a great time…' cartoon, *Thin Black Lines: Political Cartoons & Development Education* (Teachers in Development Education, 1988); **p.214** Origin of visitors to Lebanon, June 2009 and Number of visitors to Lebanon (six-month totals from January to June), Lebanon Tourist Board; **p.215** Land use zones in Tyre Coast Reserve, Destination Lebanon; **p.216** Recycle Wales logo; Municipal recycling/composting rate (per cent) from 1998/99 and Local Authority Municipal Waste reuse/recycling/composting rate since 2003/04, StatsWales website, reproduced by permission of Waste Awareness Wales, Welsh Local Government Association, www.wasteawarenesswales.org.uk; **p.217** Jackie Bow, '£400m giant waste incinerator bid for Ffos-y-fran', *Merthyr Extress* (5 February, 2009), © Media Wales, reproduced by permission; **p.225** Dr Malcolm Ramsay, © Jim Metzner Productions, Inc.; **p.226**: Computer models from the Intergovernmental Panel on Climate Change (IPCC), based on Climate Change 2007: Synthesis Report. Contribution of Working Groups I, II and III to the Intergovernmental Panel on Climate Change, Table SPM.6. IPCC, Geneva, Switzerland, reproduced by permission of IPCC; **p.232** Colm Regan, Man thinking about car and woman thinking about shoes, cartoon, *Thin Black Lines: Political Cartoons & Development Education* (Teachers in Development Education, 1988); **p.235** Colm Regan, Man eating the world that someone else is holding, cartoon, *Thin Black Lines: Political Cartoons & Development Education* (Teachers in Development Education, 1988); **p.251** Ndaba Dlamini, 'Jo'burg advertises its successes', *www.joburg.org.za*; **p.253** Hydrograph (data), Center for Sustainability & The Global Environment, *www.sage.wisc.edu/riverdata/index. php?qual=256*; **p.259** Forbes 2000 list, *Forbes Magazine* (2008); **p.262** Screenshot map of Coca-Cola plants in South Asia, *www.coca-colaindia.com*; **p.263** Campaign to hold Coca-Cola accountable, India Resource Centre website; **p.267** International Cocoa Organization (ICCO), data on cocoa supply and demand, 2007/2008, *Quarterly Bulletin of Cocoa Statistics*, Volume XXXIV, No. 2.

Crown copyright material is reproduced under the terms of the Open Government Licence.

Every effort has been made to track and acknowledge ownership of copyright. The publishers will be glad to rectify any omissions brought to their notice at the earliest opportunity.

Although every effort has been made to ensure that website addresses are correct at time of going to press, Hodder Education cannot be held responsible for the content of any website mentioned in this book. It is sometimes possible to find a relocated web page by typing in the address of the home page for a website in the URL window of your browser.

Hachette UK's policy is to use papers that are natural, renewable and recyclable products and made from wood grown in sustainable forests. The logging and manufacturing processes are expected to conform to the environmental regulations of the country of origin.

Orders: please contact Bookpoint Ltd, 130 Milton Park, Abingdon, Oxon OX14 4SB.
Telephone: (44) 01235 827720. Fax: (44) 01235 400454. Lines are open 9.00–5.00, Monday to Saturday, with a 24-hour message answering service. Visit our website at www.hoddereducation.co.uk

© Andy Owen, Andy Leeder and Glyn Owen 2012
First published in 2009
This second edition published in 2012 by
Hodder Education,
An Hachette UK company
338 Euston Road
London NW1 3BH

Impression number   5 4 3 2 1

Year   2014 2013 2012

Cover photo © Mira/Alamy
Illustrations by Oxford Illustrators, Barking Dog and DC Graphic Design Ltd
Typeset in 11.5 Times by DC Graphic Design Limited, Swanley Village, Kent
Printed in Italy

A catalogue record for this title is available from the British Library

ISBN: 978 14441 87250

Contents

Introduction

The main features of the book

This book includes the following features which have been designed to try to help you make the most of your course. These are:

- GIS panels which explain how digital technology is used to store and retrieve geographical information.
- Advice on how to develop your geographical skills
- Sections in which you are asked to predict what might happen to geography in 20, 50 or 100 years in the future.
- Case studies of real places to illustrate the concepts you have studied
- Going Further panels which will stretch and challenge the most able students

Places and case studies

South Africa

Geography is the study of places. Most pages in this book illustrate the processes, issues or concepts of geography by using a particular place. In that way the geography is kept real. You need a detailed and thorough knowledge of some places if you want to be a successful geographer. We call these more detailed studies 'case studies'. The table on page v shows you which of the places, described in this book, could become your case studies.

Geographical Information Systems (GIS)

A Geographical Information System (GIS) is a way of storing digital geographical data on a computer or server. Most GIS systems will allow the user to interact with the data to produce a custom-made table, graph or map. Some companies sell GIS programmes that will allow you to collect, store and process data on your school's computer system. However, not every school has these programmes, so the GIS panels in this book give you the web addresses of some useful GIS sites that are available for free on the internet. These sites will allow you to view and process the data that they have collected, but, in most cases, you cannot add data of your own.

Geographical skills

Geographers need certain skills in order to be able to process information from maps, graphs or text extracts. These skills include, for example, being able to read an OS map or describe the trend on a graph. The Geographical Skills panels in this book will help you develop these important skills and will also help you to tackle the activities on each page.

Theme	Geographical Skills panels	Pages
1	Describing locations	7
	Bi-polar surveys	13
	Describing distributions	29
	Making comparisons	33
2	Describing a climate graph	81
	Diamond ranking	131
	Labelling and annotation	142
	Recognising patterns	144
	Using geographical terms	151
3	Locating places on an OS map	199

Geographical Futures

An exciting recent development in geographical education has been the idea that we should be able to use our understanding of geographical processes and patterns to predict what might happen in the future. The more you think about it, the more it makes sense to plan for the future, so Geographical Futures pages address issues such as climate change, coastal management and the best ways to improve our airports to cope with future growth in air traffic.

Going Further

Going Further panels cover some interesting issues that are not essential to your understanding of GCSE Geography but might lead you into new areas of research. Geography is a popular choice at AS level. Going Further might just get you thinking about this next step.

Case studies matrix

Specified case study		Page in specification	Scale	Case study in revised edition	pages	Alternative case study in revised edition	pages
1	Housing	14	L–R	Cardiff	8–11	Nairobi, Kenya	12–18
2	Retail distribution & change	14	L–R	Shrewsbury	24–25	Cardiff	20–22
3	Access to services	14	L	Barcelona	28–33		
4	Urban – rural migration	15	L–R	Limpopo to Johannesburg	40–45		
5	Planning issue	15	L	Housing, Suffolk	50–55	New runway, Heathrow	60–61
6	Leisure use of rural environment	15	L	West Fjords, Iceland	72–78	Ynyslas, mid Wales	69–71
7	Extreme weather event	16	L–R	Hurricane in Burma	96–97	Drought in Catalonia	94–95
8	Ecosystem	16	L–R	Rainforest, Solomon Islands	108–111	Rainforest Costa Rica	114–115
9	Desertification	17	R	Sahel	120–128	Northern Ghana	126–131
10	River flooding	18	R	River Severn 2007, UK	153–154	River Valency, 2004	148–151
11	River Management	18	L	River Valency, Boscastle, UK	156–157	River Severn, Shrewsbury	159–163
12	Coasts	19	R	Cerdigion, Wales	174–176	Essex, UK	177–179 & 184–186
13	Changing industrial location	20	R	TV and media, London/ Salford Quays	200–203	Tourism in Cancun, Mexico	204–208
14	MNC	20	R / N / I	Nokia	209–211		
15	Impact of economic activity	21	L	Acid rain in Chinese cities	212–213	Barnes Elms Reservoirs, London	218–219
16	Climate change	21	L / N / I	UK	230–231	Iceland	226–227
17	Trans-boundary water issue	22	N / I	Lesotho Hills Water Project	246–249	Dams on River Mekong	254–257
18	Aid	23	I	Short / long term aid to Mali	132–133		

Photo acknowledgements

The Publishers would like to thank the following for permission to reproduce copyright material.

p.1 © Fotograferen.net/Alamy; **p.2** © Andy Owen; **p.4** © Andy Owen; **p. 6** *all* © Andy Owen; **p.8** *all* © Andy Owen; **p.11** © Andy Owen; **p.12** *t* © dbimages/Alamy, *b* © George Philipas/Alamy; **p.14** © Sean Sprague/Alamy; **p.19** © Andy Owen; **p.20** *all* © Andy Owen; **p.21** *all* © Andy Owen; **p.24** © Andy Owen; **p.25** logo © All The Little Shops; **p.26** © Rex Features/Ray Tang; **p.27** © Rex Features/Dimitris Legakis; **p.30** © Alamy/Tony Vilches; **p.36** *all* © Andy Owen; **p.38** © Andy Owen; **p.39** *tl* © Andy Owen, *tr* © Rex Features/Kevin Foy, *b* © Sodapix; **p.47** *tl* © So-Shan Au, *tr* © Alamy/PhotoSpin, Inc., *bl* © dav820-Fotolia.com, *br* © Getty Images/George Doyle/Stockdisc; **p.56** © Raf Makda/View Pictures/Rex Features; **p.64** *l* © Getty Images/Maeers/Hulton, *r* © Still Pictures/Paul Glendell; **p.67** © Andy Owen; **p.68** © Chris Howes/Wild Places Photography/Alamy; **p.69** *l* © Andy Owen, *r* © The Photolibrary Wales/Alamy; **p.70** © Andy Owen ; **p.71** *t* © Keith Burdett/Alamy, *b* © Andy Owen; **p.72** *all* © Andy Owen; **p.73** *t* © Andy Owen, *b* © Ferðakort & Landmælingar Íslands; **p.74** *all* © Andy Owen; **p.75** © Andy Owen; **p.76** © Andy Owen; **p.77** *t* © Rex Features/SplashDownDirect/Heimir Harar, *b* © Andy Owen; **p.78** © Nick Cobbing/Alamy; **p.79** © FLPA/David Burton; **p.80** © David Forster/Alamy; **p.82** © The Photolibrary Wales/Alamy; **p.83** © NASA; **p.84** © Space Science and Engineering Center, University of Wisconsin, Madison; **p.85** © Imagebroker/Alamy; **p.86** © Andy Owen; **p.89** © NASA/Image Courtesy GOES Project Science Office; **p.92** © http://visibleearth.nasa.gov/view_detailphp?id=6204: Jacques Descloitres, MODIS Rapid Response Team, NASA/GSFC 6204; **p.94** © JOSEP LAGO/AFP/Getty Images; **p.98** © *tl and tr* © Andy Owen, *br* © Photoshot/NHPA/Martin Harvey; **p.100** *all* © Andy Owen; **p.101** *tr* FLPA/Paul Hobson, *all others* © Andy Owen; **p.102** © FLPA/Tui De Roy/Minden Pictures; **p.103** © FLPA/Tui De Roy/Minden Pictures; **p.104** *tl* © Getty Images/Ben Cranke, *tr* © Corbis/Royalty-Free; **p.105** © FLPA/Gerry Ellis/Minden Pictures; **p.106** © Photoshot Holdings Ltd/Alamy; **p.107** © blickwinkel/Alamy; **p.108** © Corbis/Wolfgang Kaehler; **p.109** © Panos/Natalie Behring; **p.110** *all* © Forests Monitor; **p.111** © Panos/Natalie Behring; **p.112** © Jacqui Owen; **p.114** © NASA/Goddard Space Flight Centre; **p.115** © Alamy/Celia Mannings; **p.119** © Jeff Rotman/Oxford Scientific/Getty Images; **p.124** © Ian Nellist/Alamy; **p.125** © Neil Cooper/Alamy; **p.129** © Joerg Boethling/Alamy; **p.130** © Mark Newham/Eye ubiquitous/Hutchinson; **p.131** © Practical Action; **p.133** © Panos Pictures/Crispin Hughes; **p.135** © Andy Owen; **p.136** © Andy Owen; **p.137** © Andy Owen; **p.138** © Colin Lancaster; **p.139** *t* © Colin Lancaster, *b* © Andy Owen; **p.140** © Andy Owen; **p.141** © Andy Owen; **p.142** © Andy Owen; **p.143** *all* © Andy Owen; **p.144** *all* © Andy Owen; **p. 145** *all* © Andy Owen; **p.146** © PA Images; **p.147** © Simon Robinson; **p.155** *all* © Keith Morris/Alamy; **p.156** © Andy Owen; **p.157** *all* © Andy Owen; **p.158** © geogphotos/Alamy; **p.159** *t* © Richard Stanton/UPPA/Photoshot, *b* © Andy Owen; **p.164** *all* © Andy Owen; **p.165** © Andy Owen; **p.166** © Andy Owen; **p.167** *all* © Andy Owen; **p.168–9** © *t* © Alamy/Jeremy Moore/PhotolibraryWales, *b* © Andy Owen; **p.170** © Andy Owen; **p.173** *all* © Andy Owen; **p.174** © Andy Owen; **p.175** © Andy Owen; **p.177** © Getty Images/Jason Hawkes; **p.179** © GeoPerspectives; **p.180** © Bruce Miller/Alamy; **p.183** © PA Images/AP/Israel Leal; **p.184** © Getty Images/Jason Hawkes; **p.187** © Joerg Boethling/Alamy; **p.188** © *tl* © Alamy/Jim West, *tr* © Alamy/David Pearson, *bl* © PA Images/Thomas Kienzle/AP, *br* © PurestockX; **p.191** © Photos 12/Alamy; **p.192** *t* © The Potteries Museum & Art Gallery, Stoke-on-Trent, *b* © Andy Owen; **p.194** *t* © Panos Pictures/Dieter Telemans, *bl* © Panos Pictures/Crispin Hughes, *br* © Getty Images/Seyllou/AFP; **p.195** © Alamy/James Hawkins; **p.197** © The International Women's Tribune Centre; **p.201** © Barrie Harwood/Alamy; **p.202** *l* BBC One logo reproduced by permission, *r* ITV 1 logo reproduced by permission of ITV Network Ltd; **p.204** *l* © Rex Features/The Travel Library, *r* © Rex Features/The Travel Library; **p.205** © Andy Owen; **p.206** *bl* © Alamy/Travelwide; **p.207** © Andy Owen; **p.208** © Andy Owen; **p.209** © Corbis/Andreas Gebert/DPA; **p.212** © Getty Images/Goh Chai Hin/AFP; **p.213** © NASA/Goddard Space Flight Center Scientific Visualization Studio; **p.216** logo © recycle for Wales; **p.219** *all* © Andy Owen; **p.220** © Rex Features/James D. Morgan; **p.222** © Nick Cobbing/Alamy; **p.224** *tr* © Rex Features/Sipa Press, *c* © Corbis/Arko Data/Reuters, *bl* © Skyscan/Corbis; **p.226** © Getty Images/Photographer's Choice; **p.229** © Eduardo Abad/epa/Corbis; **p.232** © Panos Pictures/Christien Jaspars; **p.241** © Panos Pictures/Alfredo Caliz; **p.242** © Andy Owen; **p.244** *l* © Olivier Asselin/Alamy, *r* © Gary Whitton/Alamy; **p.249** © Friedrich Stark/Alamy; **p.250** © Getty Images/Mark Peters, logo © Google; **p.253** © International Water Management; **p.255** © Richard T. Nowitz/CORBIS; **p.258** *tl* © Still Pictures/Rom Giling, *tr* © Getty Images/Raveendran/AFP, *bl* © PETER PARKS/AFP/Getty Images; **p.259** © Stuart Freedman/Panos Pictures; **p.260** © Rex Features; **p.262** © Getty Images/Raveendran/AFT; **p.264** © Corbis/Flip Schulke; **p.265** *r* © Corbis/Reinhard Krause/Reuters, *l* © Christian Aid/Andrew Pendleton, *b* © Panos Pictures/Karen Robinson; **p.268** © Fairtrade®; **p.269** © Panos Pictures/Karen Robinson

The Barcelona Museum of Contemporary Art is in the district of El Raval. This district has undergone a process of gentrification in recent years. Several old apartment buildings were demolished here to create space for the museum and a large open square.

Chapter 1
Variation in quality of life and access to housing

Investigating housing tenure in the UK

Most people in the UK live in a home that they rent from someone else, one that they own, or one that they buy with the help of a mortgage.

The financial and legal relationships of a householder are described as **housing tenure**.

Owner occupation

In order to access this part of the housing market you need a large lump sum of money (perhaps an inheritance) to buy your house outright. Alternatively, you need a regular wage so that you can convince the mortgage lender you will be able to make the regular repayments on your mortgage. If you fail to keep up with the repayments you can lose your home. This is known as **repossession**. There are approximately 14.7 million owner occupied households in the UK.

Renting from a private landlord

Renting from a private landlord suits a wide range of people because this sector of the housing market contains a very wide range of properties from luxury penthouses to tiny bedsits. In many cases, the landlord makes an agreement to let the property for only six months. This suits people who are expecting to move again soon, like a student or a young professional seeking a new job, but is less desirable for families wishing to settle down. Around 2.7 million households rent from a private landlord.

Renting from a social landlord

An alternative to renting from private landlords is to rent from **social landlords**. These are not-for-profit organisations such as a housing association or the local authority. People who apply to a social landlord are put on a waiting list and allocated points depending on their housing need. People waiting for **social housing** have relatively little choice about where they live as this decision is made by the housing officer. Around 3.8 million households rent their home from a social landlord.

Figure 1 Flats for sale and for rent from a private landlord in the Riverside district of Cardiff

Housing tenure		% of all households			
		1981		2007	
Owner occupiers	Owned outright	25	57	31	70
	Buying with a mortgage or loan	32		39	
Tenants renting from a social landlord	Rented from local council	30	32	11	18
	Rented from housing association	2		7	
Tenants renting from a private landlord	Unfurnished	9	11	9	12
	Furnished	2		3	

Figure 2 Changing housing tenure in the UK

Figure 3 The advantages and disadvantages of each type of tenure

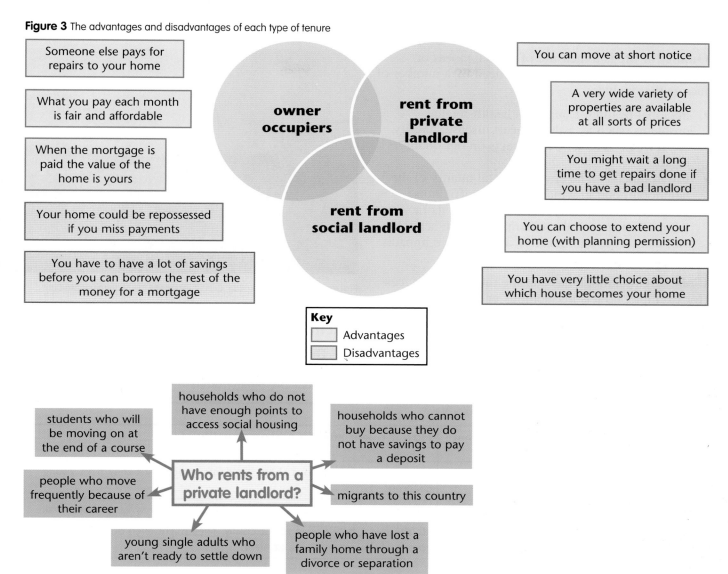

Figure 4 The private rented sector meets a variety of people's housing needs

Activities

1 **a)** Choose a suitable technique to show the data in Figure 2 on a graph.
   b) Describe the changes in this data.

2 Make a copy of the Venn diagram in Figure 3. Discuss the statements provided and add them to your diagram in the area where they fit best.

3 Study Figures 3 and 4. Describe the advantages and disadvantages of renting from:
   a) a private landlord
   b) a social landlord.

How does the urban environment affect quality of life?

Quality of life is a measure of the happiness or contentment we feel and is influenced by a number of factors that include:

*   Personal health – Long term health-related problems, such as asthma, heart disease, obesity or HIV can have serious impacts on our quality of life.
*   Environment – The environmental quality of the neighbourhood in which we live (traffic noise, congestion, air quality, vandalism) and its facilities (shops, transport links, cinema, chemist, schools etc) can create both positive and negative impacts on quality of life.

If our neighbourhood has a crime rate, poor services (for example, no leisure facilities or green spaces) and there is a busy road outside the front door, we might experience a relatively poor quality of life.

Figure 5 Homes in Riverside, Cardiff, opposite the Millennium Stadium

Activity

1 Discuss the housing shown in Figure 5. How might the River Taff and Millennium Stadium affect the quality of life of the residents here?

Figure 6 How does the urban environment affect quality of life?

Features of the urban environment that may affect quality of life	How it might affect a person's quality of life
Living next to a very busy road	He/she might feel anxious about accidents, especially if they have young children.
Living under the flight path of an airport	The noise from aeroplanes could be annoying and may keep them awake.
Living next to empty buildings that have been burnt or vandalised	He/she might be worried about crime. They might even be too afraid to go out of their own house at night.

Investigating spheres of influence

Each feature of the urban environment has a sphere of influence – an area within which the quality of life of residents may be affected in either a good or bad way. A good primary school, for example, will have a benefit for all families who are living within the local neighbourhood that is the catchment area for that school.

Most features of the urban environment have only a very local effect on quality of life. For example, a town centre pub or nightclub can be very rowdy at closing time. Local residents complain about noise, bad language and drunken fights on the streets, especially at the weekend. The worst affected properties are next to the pub. People in houses further away hear less of the noise. Geographers call this the 'friction of distance' and its effect is shown in Figure 7.

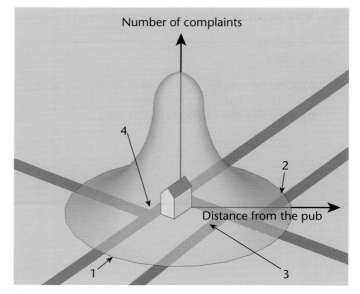

Figure 7 Friction of distance creates a sphere of influence

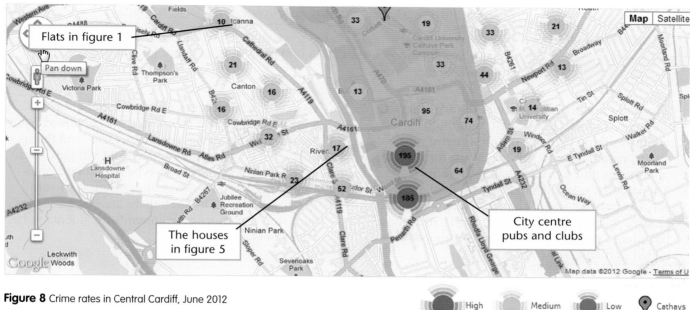

Figure 8 Crime rates in Central Cardiff, June 2012

High   Medium   Low   Cathays

Figure 9 How do different features of the urban environment affect your quality of life?

	Where would you want each of these urban features?				
	Next door	In the same street	In the same neighbourhood	In a different part of the town/city	In a different town/city
Takeaway					
Premiership football ground					
Skate park					
Dual carriageway					
Secondary school					
Cemetery					
Petrol station					
Canal					
A&E (accident and emergency)					
Nuclear power station					
Sewage works					
Fire station					
Parks and gardens					

Activities

2 Study Figure 7. Copy the diagram and match the following statements to the correct numbered arrows.
  A Most complaints about noise are from people living closest to the pub.
  B People living in the next street sometimes complain about noise from the pub.
  C People living in this neighbourhood are hardly ever disturbed by noise.
  D The outer limit of complaints. Everyone living inside this line is within the sphere of influence.

3 **a)** Describe the distribution of crimes shown in Figure 8.
  b) How might this affect quality of life?

4 **a)** Work in pairs to discuss the urban features listed in Figure 9. From the point of view of a teenager, sort the features into those that you think would have a positive effect on quality of life and those that would have a negative effect.
  b) Sort the list again, this time from the point of view of a retired couple. Is this list different to **a)**? If so, why?
  c) Make a copy of Figure 9 and place a tick to show where you would want each feature in your perfect urban environment. Use this table to explain why some urban features have a larger sphere of influence than others.

Comparing quality of life in different urban zones

<table>
<tr><td>Newcastle-under-Lyme</td><td>Newcastle-under-Lyme is a large town in Staffordshire in the West Midlands. It has a population of around 125,000 people. Like many UK towns, it can be divided into three zones:</td></tr>
</table>

- The inner urban area – A zone of older housing and more modern flats. Most households are within walking distance of town centre jobs, shops, entertainment, schools, sixth form centres or colleges and services such as libraries.
- The suburbs – Residential areas. There are local schools but few shops and few other services. Houses were first built here in the 1930s. These have large gardens. Other neighbourhoods were added in the period 1950–1990.

- The commuter villages – These are about 6 to 8 km from the town centre and are separated from the suburban housing estates by farm land that is protected as **green belt**. Once rural villages, these have grown into suburban-type neighbourhoods containing large housing estates built between 1980 and 2010. Although there are bus routes to the town, it is more convenient for residents to be car owners.

A Inner urban housing in Cross Heath

B Baldwin's Gate, a commuter village in Loggerheads ward

Figure 10 How does the urban environment influence quality of life?

Activities

1 Describe the location of Newcastle-under-Lyme.

2 Study Figure 10. For each photo, suggest one way in which the situation of the house might affect quality of life. Remember, the effect could be positive or negative.

Simple statement	so	which means that
Houses in A are close to a busy road		
Houses in B are opposite a park		

3 a) Use Figure 12 to describe the distribution of wards with:
   i) significantly lower life expectancy
   ii) significantly higher life expectancy.

b) Study Figures 11 and 12.
   i) Compare the distribution of areas that have significantly lower life expectancy to the manufacturing and mining zones within the town.
   ii) Suggest reasons for the patterns you have described.

4 Use all the information on pages 6–7. Decide where you would advise each of the following groups of people to live in Newcastle-under-Lyme. You must be able to justify your decision.
   a) A family with two teenage children. Both parents are in professional occupations.
   b) A single parent of a young child. The parent has two part-time jobs, both are semi-routine occupations.
   c) A retired couple who have sold a house for £450,000 and have no mortgage.
   d) A single university graduate who has a professional occupation and is thinking of changing jobs in two years.

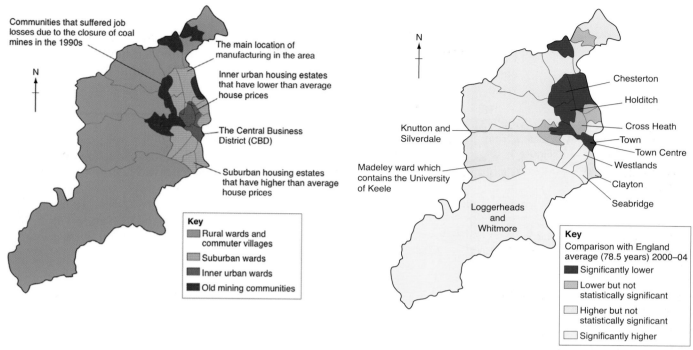

Figure 11 Different urban zones within Newcastle-under-Lyme

Figure 12 Variations in life expectancy in Newcastle-under-Lyme

Figure 13 Available housing in the inner urban and suburban wards, August 2012

		Town ward	Westlands ward	Baldwin's Gate
Houses available for sale	Price range £	99,000–700,000	52,000–475,000	190,000–900,000
	Average price £	132,000	260,000	385,000
Houses available for private rent	Price range (£ per calendar month)	400–1,300	450–2,000	1,900
	Number of properties available	66	10	1

GEOGRAPHICAL SKILLS

Describing locations

To describe a location means to be able to pinpoint somewhere on a map or to describe where a place is compared to other significant features on a map. Describing a location on an OS map can be easily done by giving a grid reference. However, describing a location on a map that has no grid lines requires a different technique.

First, you need to give a broad indication of location by describing in which part of the map the viewer should be looking. Always use geographical terms, such as 'in the West Midlands', rather than 'at the bottom of the map' or 'near to Wales'.

Then, to describe the exact location of a place, you should use other significant places on the map; places that really stand out, such as Manchester

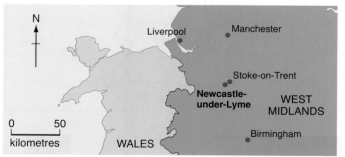

Figure 14 The location of Newcastle-under-Lyme

or Birmingham. Use a combination of two facts to pinpoint a specific location, for example, using this map:

- the distance from Manchester using kilometres
- the direction from Manchester using points of the compass.

Investigating quality of life in Cardiff

Cardiff

Cardiff is the capital of Wales. It has an estimated population of 346,000 (2011). Like Newcastle-under-Lyme (see pages 6–7) it can be divided into zones. In this case study, we will investigate variations of quality of life within the inner urban zone.

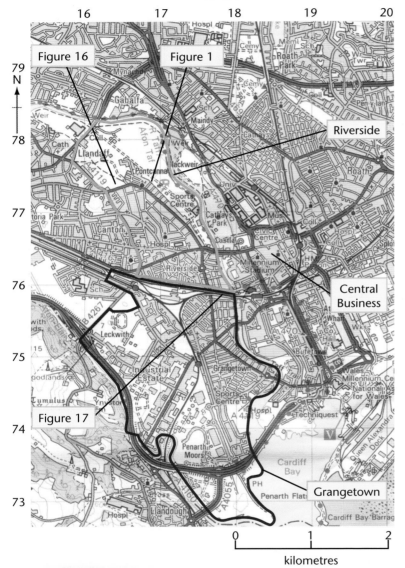

Activities

1 Study Figure 15. Match the following four-figure grid references to features on the map a–d:

   1774   1873   1677   1876

   a) Open space in Llandaff (Figure 16)
   b) Civic Centre, in the central business district (CBD)
   c) Cardiff Bay
   d) Sports Centre (Grangetown)

2 a) Describe the location of:
      i) Riverside   ii) Grangetown
   b) Suggest the advantages of each location for local residents.

3 Suggest how the features in Figures 15, 16 and 17 would influence quality of life for local residents. Use grid references when describing evidence on the map.

Figure 15 An Ordnance Survey extract showing central Cardiff. Scale 1:50,000. Sheet 171. Numbered boxes refer to photograph figure numbers. Riverside is shown with a pink boundary. Grangetown is shown in dark blue. © Crown Copyright and/or database right. All rights reserved. Licence number 100036470

Figure 16 Victorian terraced housing overlooking Llandaff Field (LSOA RIV04. See page 10)

Figure 17 Mixed urban land uses: terraced housing, modern flats, petrol station and Millennium Stadium on the southern boundary of Riverside. (LSOA RIV02. See page 10)

Which groups of people live in this area of Cardiff?

Planners, politicians and retailers are just a few groups who are interested in what geographers call **socio-economic groups**. These are groups of people who have distinct social and economic characteristics. A number of factors influence which socio-economic group we belong to, including age, education, income, ethnicity and race. The UK National Statistics Office categorises people by job type, as you can see in Figure 18.

Different groups of people need different kinds of housing and services. For example, a single person needs a one room apartment whereas a family with teenage children need a home with three or more bedrooms. Some people have special housing needs, for example a wheelchair user will need ground floor accommodation.

Figure 18 Socio-economic groups (in percentages by job type) in inner urban Cardiff (2001 census)

People aged 16–74 in employment working as:	Grangetown Ward	Riverside Ward	Cardiff Unitary Authority	Wales Country
Managers and senior officials	12.07	12.44	13.43	12.24
Professional occupations	11.36	23.24	15.47	10.43
Associate professional and technical occupations	13.71	20.48	15.96	12.8
Administrative and secretarial occupations	12.87	10.3	14.52	12.15
Skilled trades occupations	10.18	6.82	8.5	13.44
Personal service occupations	5.96	4.77	6.01	7.44
Sales and customer service occupations	9.99	6.65	8.97	7.98
Process, plant and machine operatives	9.21	4.52	5.79	10.2
Elementary occupations	14.65	10.78	11.35	13.33

Activities

4 **a)** Use Figure 18 to compare the socio-economic groups living in Grangetown and Riverside. Prepare a short report that highlights the most significant differences. Include at least one graph.

   b) Use the National Statistics website to research the 2011 census data. Search for occupations in Grangetown and Riverside in 2011. Have they changed much since 2001?

5 Discuss the following socio-economic groups before completing this table:

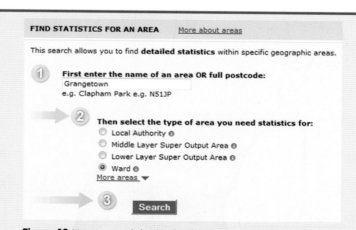

Figure 19 How to search for the data shown in Figure 18 using http://www.neighbourhood.statistics.gov.uk/dissemination

Socio-economic group	Housing need	Housing want	Features that would be needed in the neighbourhood
Low income families with young children		A large garden	
Students	One room apartment		
Single OAPs			Doctor's surgery
Couples with no children, each in a professional job			

Measuring standard of living and deprivation

Standard of living is a measure of the relative wealth of individuals or families. It can be measured using household income figures. A person's level of qualifications or occupation can also be an indicator of income. In regions where unemployment figures are high, or jobs are part time or low paid, the number of households living in **poverty** can be high.

Deprivation is a more complex way of measuring poverty. The Welsh Government monitors deprivation across the whole of Wales. They use eight factors (shown in Figure 20) to measure levels of deprivation. So how deprived are the inner urban areas of Cardiff?

Figure 20 Eight factors used by the Welsh Government when measuring deprivation. The weightings show that, for example, income is considered to be almost five times more important than physical environment when calculating overall deprivation.

Factor	% weighting
Employment	23.5
Income	23.5
Education, Skills and Training	14
Health	14
Geographical Access to Services	10
Community Safety	5
Housing	5
Physical Environment	5

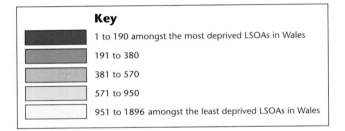

Key

	1 to 190 amongst the most deprived LSOAs in Wales
	191 to 380
	381 to 570
	571 to 950
	951 to 1896 amongst the least deprived LSOAs in Wales

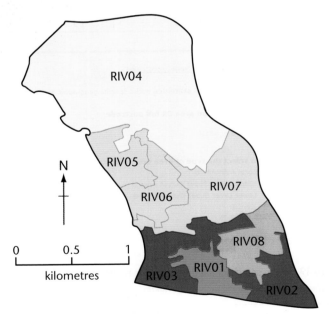

Figure 21 Deprivation in Riverside (2011). There are 1896 Lower Super Output Areas (LSOAs) in Wales. The Welsh government has put all of these small districts into rank order of deprivation. The map shows five categories of deprivation (by rank order).

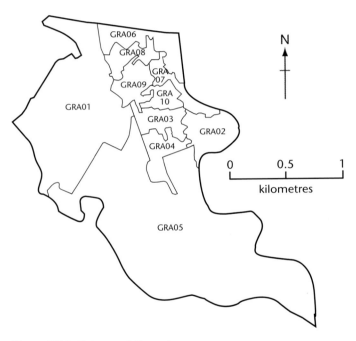

Figure 22 Outline map of Grangetown

Figure 23 Deprivation in Grangetown

LSOA in Grangetown	Overall deprivation
GRA01	886
GRA02	493
GRA03	212
GRA04	106
GRA05	503
GRA06	396
GRA07	553
GRA08	264
GRA09	381
GRA10	354

Ethnic minorities in Cardiff

Cardiff is a multicultural city. A total of 8 per cent of the population are members of ethnic minorities. The Somali population in Cardiff has a population estimated to be a little under 10,000. Most of them live in a relatively small neighbourhood within the inner urban area in the districts of Grangetown and Riverside. Some are retired sailors who worked on boats and in the docks up until the 1980s. But many of the younger Somalis are refugees who have arrived

in the UK since the collapse of the Somali government in 1991 and the resulting civil war. Somalis choose to live in this district to be close to other family members and to use specialist food shops and mosques that exist here (Cardiff has 32 mosques, of which nine are in Grangetown and Riverside). This district also has a wide variety of different sized houses and flats for both rent and sale at a variety of prices.

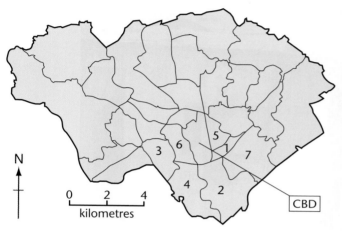

Figure 24 Outline map of the wards of Cardiff

Figure 25 Wards with significant ethnic populations

Map reference	Ward	Black	Asian	Mixed ethnicity
1	Adamsdown	3.4	5.8	3.5
2	Butetown	13.4	8.1	8.3
3	Canton	0.8	4.7	1.8
4	Grangetown	4.2	13.2	3.8
5	Plasnewydd	1.5	9.5	1.7
6	Riverside	2.8	15.6	2.4
7	Splott	1.8	3.3	2.9

Figure 26 A shop in Riverside selling halal meat

Activities

1 a) Describe the pattern of deprivation in Riverside.
 b) Use evidence from Figures 15, 16 and 17 to help explain the pattern on Figure 21.
 c) Does it surprise you that standard of living can vary so much within one small area? Work in groups to plan an investigation into standard of living and quality of life in a neighbourhood close to your school. What questions would you want answered? How would you structure your investigation?

2 a) Make a copy of Figure 22. Use the data in Figure 22 to create a choropleth (a map like Figure 21).
 b) How does Riverside compare to Grangetown? Describe the main similarities and differences.

3 Describe the distribution of wards which have a significant ethnic population within Cardiff.

What kind of housing is available in Nairobi?

Nairobi is the capital city of Kenya. It has a population of just over 3 million people. Like all African cities it has some neighbourhoods of wealthy residents who live in formal housing, and other neighbourhoods of poorer residents, some of whom live in **informal housing**.

The suburb of Karen, to the west of the city centre, is a suburban neighbourhood of high-income housing. Many residents are descended from European families who moved to Nairobi in the mid twentieth century. In 2012, detached houses in this suburb cost between £240,000 and £280,000 (for a four bedroom bungalow with a ¼ acre garden surrounded by an electrified perimeter fence).

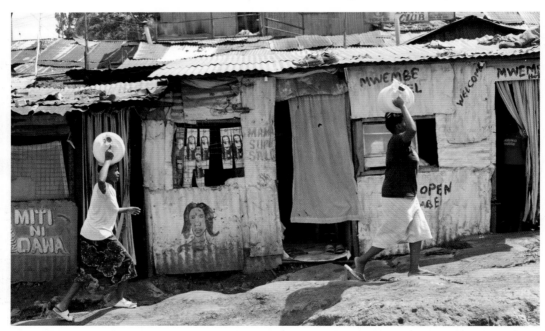

Figure 27 Informal housing in Kibera, Nairobi, Kenya

Figure 28 Formal housing in Karen patrolled by a security company

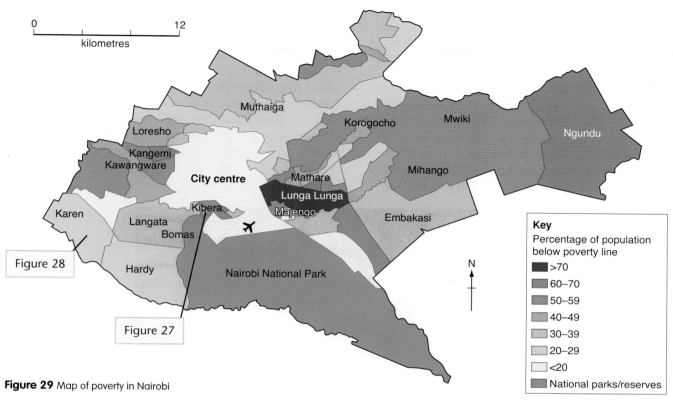

Figure 29 Map of poverty in Nairobi

Key
Percentage of population below poverty line
- >70
- 60–70
- 50–59
- 40–49
- 30–39
- 20–29
- <20
- National parks/reserves

GEOGRAPHICAL SKILLS

Bi-polar surveys

Geographers often use pairs of descriptive words to record their impressions of an urban environment. This is called a bi-polar survey. You can use bi-polar surveys during fieldwork, or when doing 'virtual' fieldwork using urban images on a site such as Google Street View or www.geograph.org.uk. Place a cross in the box on each row that best shows your feelings about the place.

clean					dirty
healthy					unhealthy
safe					unsafe
well planned					badly planned
spacious					cramped
quiet					noisy
pleasant					unpleasant
distinctive					ordinary
cared for					uncared for

Activities

1 Study Figures 27 and 28. Make a copy of the bi-polar table above and place crosses of two different colours in the boxes to show how you feel about each place.

2 Imagine you live in Kibera.
   a) Describe what you think are the most important issues that face your community.
   b) You live in informal housing. Discuss who you can ask for help with these issues. What would you do?

3 Write an estate agent's advert for the home in Figure 28.

4 Use Figure 29 to
   a) Describe the location of the informal settlement at Kibera.
   b) Describe the distribution of districts where:
      i) more than 50 per cent of residents live in poverty
      ii) less than 29 per cent of residents live in poverty.

What kind of housing?

Many people in poorer countries do not have a legal right to their home. They live in **informal housing**, which is housing that does not have planning permission. People who live in informal housing do not own the land where they live. They usually pay rent to a landlord, but they don't pay council tax and their homes are often ignored by the local authority. These residents could be thrown out of their homes at any time by the police if the local authority chooses to do so. We say they have no **security of tenure**.

Very few people in the UK live in informal housing, but the situation is quite different at a global scale. It is estimated that at least 1 billion people around the world live in informal housing. Most of these 1 billion people live in poverty. They have poorly paid or unregulated jobs (read more about **informal jobs** on page 194). Most informal housing is in the rapidly growing cities of the world's poorest countries.

Figure 30 The informal settlement of Kibera, Nairobi

Activities

1 Study Figure 30 and make a copy of Figure 32. Discuss each statement before completing the table to show how the quality of life of residents of Kibera is affected.

2 Study Figure 31. Explain how three of these statements could affect quality of life in Kibera.

3 **a)** Work in groups to draw a series of graphs to represent the data in Figure 33.
   b) Discuss how Nairobi's climate might affect quality of life in Kibera. Focus on:
   i) the condition of alleyways
   ii) rubbish and human/animal waste
   iii) weather hazards and the safety of buildings in the settlement.

Living in Kibera

People have lived in an informal settlement in Kibera since around 1904. At that time, Kenya was governed by the British. One British regiment, the King's African Rifles (KAR), had a training ground close to Kibera. The British recruited Nubian soldiers from northern Sudan and allowed the families of these soldiers to settle here. As the settlement grew, homes were built by Nubian landlords, who then rented the rooms to local people.

Kenya became independent of British rule in 1963. The new government made informal settlements, such as the one at Kibera, illegal. Consequently, most homes in Kibera do not have a piped water supply, sewers and safe levels of **sanitation**, paved roads, street lighting, or electricity connected to their home.

Despite these issues, the settlement has continued to grow. Some people have claimed that 1 million people live in Kibera and it has been described as the 'largest slum in Africa'. However, in 2010, a mapping project estimated the population to be between 235,000 and 270,000.

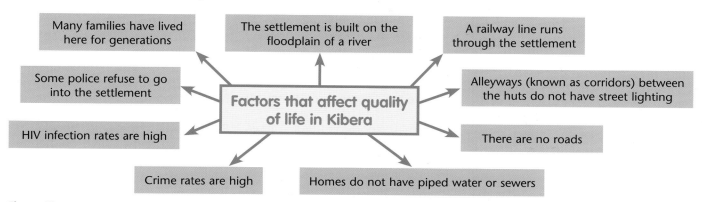

Figure 31 Factors that affect quality of life in Kibera

Figure 32 Explaining quality of life in Kibera

	So ...	which means that ...
There are no roads for vehicles ...	emergency vehicles cannot quickly get into the settlement	
Human and animal waste lies in open gutters in the footpaths ...		
Many huts are built at the foot of steep slopes. They have no foundations and are built on layers of rubbish ...		
People cook on charcoal stoves ...		people suffer from lung and throat conditions.

Figure 33 Climate in Nairobi

Month:	Jan	Feb	Mar	Apr	May	Jun	Jul	Aug	Sep	Oct	Nov
Max temperature in °C	24.5	25.6	25.6	24.1	22.6	21.5	20.6	21.4	23.7	24.7	23.1
Min temperature in °C	11.5	11.6	13.1	14	13.2	11	10.1	10.2	10.5	12.5	13.1
Total rainfall in mm	64.1	56.5	92.8	219.4	176.6	35	17.5	23.5	28.3	55.3	154.2
Total number of rainy days	4	5	9	16	13	5	3	4	4	7	15
Chances of rain %	12.9	17.2	29.0	53.3	41.9	16.7	9.7	12.9	13.3	22.6	50.0

Who makes decisions in Kibera?

The local authority, police and residents of informal settlements are all involved in decision making. However, the residents have no security of tenure. In other words, they have no legal right to live there and could be evicted at any time. It is this insecurity, as well as poverty, that prevent people from improving their homes.

WHERE THE SIDEWALKS END:
HOW THE POOR COMBAT POVERTY DAILY

Molly O'Meara Sheehan

On city maps, the location of this settlement – called 'Mtumba' by the 6,000 people who live there – shows up as prime habitat for rhino and giraffe. That's because this unsanctioned community lies on the edge of Nairobi National Park. Mtumba is only one of the many slums around Nairobi. In fact, more than half of the residents of Kenya's capital city cannot afford to live in 'formal' housing, and have been forced to find shelter in slums like this one.

'We can't depend on the government for anything,' says Castro as we walk through the settlement. He points out a water tap – one of two small spigots that supply water for the entire settlement. But no city water is piped here. Instead, these taps are fed by private companies that truck in tanks. And they sell their water at a premium. As of yet, no company has seen fit to establish any sort of business setting up toilets or sewers. Instead the 6,000 people who live here share three flimsy pit latrines.

Informal communities have certain advantages. Rents are lower than in formal housing. There are no property taxes. Residents can skirt cumbersome zoning laws that separate housing from businesses, and set up shop inside their homes or just outside. Mtumba's commercial strip boasts rows of brightly painted storefronts, each about one metre wide. There are produce stands, coffee shops, a 'movie house' showing videos, a barber shop, and an outfit that collects old newspapers.

But … slums are often located in a city's least-desirable locations – situated on steep hillsides, on flood plains, or downstream from industrial polluters – leaving residents vulnerable to disease and natural disasters.

'Land is the key to implement any project for development,' says a Mtumba woman who is involved in the community's self-run school. She explains that the people of her community have difficulty convincing themselves – let alone anyone else – to invest in water, toilets, or any sort of improvement. Why bother if the neighbourhood could be bulldozed the next day? Indeed, a central obstacle to any sort of 'self-help' in many slums is that in the eyes of the law the residents do not belong on the land where they live.

Figure 34 Extract from *Global Urban Development* magazine, describing the Mtumba informal settlement in Nairobi, Kenya

Activity

1 Read Figure 34 which describes Mtumba, a small informal settlement in southern Nairobi.
   a) Describe two advantages of living here.
   b) Explain why residents in Mtumba are at risk of both natural disasters and poor health.

2 a) Who is making decisions about planning issues and the provision of services in Mtumba? Explain what each of the following groups is doing:
   i) The residents.
   ii) Officials of the city authority such as planners.
   iii) Local businesses.
   b) How does this differ to planning decisions that are made about your own community?

3 Explain what is preventing the residents of Mtumba from improving their homes.

Should the people of Kibera be rehoused?

The Kenyan government and United Nations have jointly agreed to try to rehouse people from Kibera in modern blocks of flats. But the Nubian landlords who 'own' homes in the settlement believe the land belongs to them. To rehouse everyone will cost an estimated $1.2 billion and will take at least nine years. People will be moved to apartments and the new community will include schools and shops. The first 1500 people to be rehoused were moved into 300 newly constructed two room apartments in September 2009. These flats have an affordable monthly rent of around $10 (average wages for Kibera residents are $2 per day).

> When we have cleared other informal settlements there have been problems. Some families share their new two room apartment with another family to help pay the rent. This makes them very over-crowded. There is no privacy for anyone and infectious diseases spread easily.

An urban planner

> We are opposed to enforced evictions. We demand that the government consult the people of Kibera and work with them to improve housing, services and roads in the settlement.

Spokesperson for Amnesty International

> The land of Kibera belongs to the Nubian people of Nairobi. It was given to us by the British. We will fight this rehousing project in the courts to protect our land and income.

A Nubian landlord

> Many of the homes in Kibera are owned by a handful of rich and powerful landlords who rent their tiny homes to powerless families living in poverty. These 'slumlords' can own as many as 1000 properties. These landlords oppose the rehousing project because they do not want to lose their income. They don't care about the terrible conditions that their tenants live in.

Spokesperson for Umande Trust, an NGO working in Kibera to provide clean water and sanitation

> When a home is damaged by a rainstorm the residents usually camp on top of the remains of their home until repairs can be made. Building materials cannot be left unattended otherwise they are stolen. Theft is a serious problem that prevents the existing homes in Kibera from being upgraded.

A spokesperson for an NGO working in Kibera

> The problem in Kibera is just too big and the government has been slow to act. At the current rate it will take 1,178 years to complete the rehousing project!

A government spokesman

Figure 35 Stakeholder views on the rehousing of people from Kibera

Activities

4 Discuss Figure 35.
  a) Use these stakeholder views to outline:
     i) the arguments for clearing Kibera and providing government built houses
     ii) the arguments against clearing Kibera.
  b) State whether or not you think residents of Kibera should be rehoused. Explain your decision.

5 Watch the video 'The women of Kibera' on the Amnesty International website: http://www.amnesty.org/en/news-and-updates/video-and-audio/video-women-kibera-kenya-20090306
  a) Describe three ways that quality of life could be improved for teenage girls in Kibera.
  b) Produce a poster or leaflet that shows how Kibera could be improved for teenagers.

Self-help in Nairobi through micro-credit schemes

The Population Council is an international, not-for-profit NGO. In Kenya the Population Council decided to introduce a **micro-credit** scheme for young women. The scheme is called TRY.

If you earn less than US$1 a day, how can you save even small amounts of money so that you can start your own business? Traditional banks are unlikely to lend you any money because you do not own a house or have some other guarantee that you can repay the loan. So micro-credit loans are now being used to support new businesses in the world's poorest communities. Micro-credit is where small loans are given to entrepreneurs who are too poor to qualify for traditional bank loans.

The TRY micro-credit scheme provides small loans to young women living in the squatter settlements of Nairobi. The girls receive basic financial training and are then grouped into teams of five. Each girl agrees to save a minimum of 50 Kenyan shillings (about US$0.65) each week.

The girls meet once a week. At these meetings they collect and record their savings and are given business advice. Many of these young women become great friends and use the meeting as an opportunity to share concerns about their relationships with partners or parents as well as their money worries. After saving for eight weeks, each team of five girls decides which two of its members are going to receive the first loan. These loans are in the order of 10,000 Kenyan shillings (US$130). Making this decision can be difficult, but it is based on the strength of each girl's business plan. Other members of the group can only receive their loans after the first two loans have been paid back. This arrangement creates a strong sense of responsibility: none of the girls wants to let down other members of the group.

The young women have used their loans in all sorts of businesses such as hairstyling, tailoring or running a market stall. Other girls have taken up jobs in welding or as mechanics. Some create new businesses, others expand existing businesses.

Not only has the scheme helped poor young women to set up businesses and earn money, it has also helped them to save. Before joining the scheme each girl had average savings of just US$43. After three years each member has average savings of US$95.

Activity

1 Define the term micro-credit.

2 Suggest why micro-credit schemes loan money to women and the poorest members of society.

Going further

The Grameen Bank

The Grameen Bank (which means 'Bank of the Villages') was founded in 1983 by Muhammad Yunus. It makes micro-credit loans to the poorest people of Bangladesh.
It has been so successful that it has inspired the development of micro-credit schemes in many other developing countries, including Kenya. Muhammad Yunus was awarded the Nobel Peace Prize in 2006.

www.grameen–info.org/
The official Grameen Bank website gives more information about micro-credit loans in Bangladesh.

www.grameenfoundation.org/
The website of a non-profit making organisation set up to reproduce the success of the Bangladesh Grameen Bank in other countries.

Activities

3 From the homepage www.grameen-info.org/ click on the link to the Grameen Bank and click the drop-down menu under 'Methodology' in the top bar to find the link to 'Ten Indicators'. What do these indicators tell you about the way in which poverty is measured in Bangladesh compared to the UK?

4 Use the Grameen Foundation website to produce a map of countries in which micro-credit schemes are supported by the Foundation. Explain why micro-credit schemes are necessary in relatively wealthy countries such as the USA.

Chapter 2
Access to services and changing service provision

Geographical concepts of retailing

Imagine you need to go and buy some basic, everyday items of shopping. How far would you go to get a newspaper, some milk or a loaf of bread? These items are relatively cheap and there is no real benefit to you, the consumer, if you shop around to get the best price because your time is probably more valuable to you than any cost savings you might make. In other words, consumers of these **convenience goods** tend to buy them from a shop that is close to home or close to their workplace.

On the other hand, more expensive items are usually worth shopping around for to try to find a bargain. Consumers like to compare the price of shoes or clothing or 'white goods' such as fridges and washing machines. We buy these **comparison goods** less frequently than everyday convenience goods and we are prepared to travel further to find the best bargain.

Figure 1 District shopping centre, Riverside, Cardiff

Activity

1   Study Figures 1 and 2. Put the shops in Figure 1 into rank order according to the probable size of their catchment areas.

Understanding consumer behaviour is important when it comes to locating a new shop or retail service. A corner shop selling everyday grocery items will attract customers from a relatively small **catchment area** – perhaps an area containing a few neighbouring streets. But a specialist shop, selling comparison goods, could attract customers from a much larger catchment area – perhaps the whole city.

Another concept that retailers use when deciding where to locate a shop is the **threshold** of a good or service. By this they mean the minimum population size you need before there is a demand for that item. For example, all consumers need a haircut every few weeks, but consumers only buy a new television every few years. The hairdresser has a low threshold population and a small catchment area, so even a small town may have more than one hairdresser. A television retailer has a much larger threshold population and a larger catchment area, so would not locate a new shop in a small town or village.

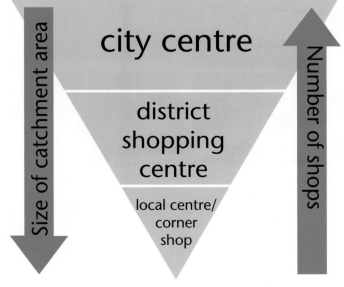

Figure 2 Retail hierarchy

Cardiff

What are the current patterns of retailing in UK cities?

The retail hierarchy shown in Figure 2 (see page 19) means that similar types of shops are commonly found in similar locations within all UK towns and cities. This pattern is shown in Figure 3. How far does this pattern of urban retailing reflect what can be found in your nearest town or city? What are the similarities and what are the differences?

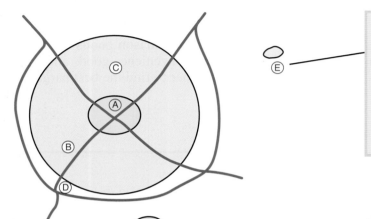

Fact box for zone E
- In small settlements outside the urban area, shopping services have suffered in recent years.
- Often coinciding with the closure of the village post office, village stores cannot compete with supermarkets, which are used by residents while commuting to work in the city or town.
- A recent trend has been the growth of farmers' markets at weekends.

⬭	:	Central Business District
⬭	:	Urban area
Ⓐ – Ⓔ	:	Typical retail zones within the city
—	:	Main roads

Figure 3 Typical pattern of retailing in UK cities

Figure 5 (a)

Figure 5 (b)

Figure 4

Figure 7

Figure 6

- Large covered shopping centres or 'malls' contain mainly chain stores.
- Department stores are a feature.
- Limited parking can be a significant problem, especially on busy roads.
- Parking close to the shops can be expensive and difficult to find.
- There are large car parks which are usually free.
- Good road access makes deliveries easy.
- There are lots of fast food outlets and shops catering for ethnic groups.
- Electrical superstores, DIY superstores and furniture warehouses dominate.
- Newsagents, off licenses and takeaways are all common.

- Many independently owned butchers and grocers have closed due to competition.
- There are a lot of 'pound shops' and charity shops.
- These sites are a relatively recent feature – developed from the 1990s to the present day.
- Most of the shops in this area are open long hours, including Sundays.

Figure 8 Features of retailing in UK cities

Activities

1 Study Figure 3. It shows the location of four retail zones in a typical city, and one in a nearby village. A description of the retailing in the village has been given. Copy and complete the table below using the photographs in Figures 4–7 and the statements in Figure 8. You may use each statement more than once.

	City centre shops (CBD)	District shopping centres	Local cornershops	'Out-of-town' retailing
Location on Figure 3	A	B	C	D
Photograph that best represents this zone				
Description that fits this zone				
Probable size of catchment area (large, medium or small)				

2 Discuss what you consider to be the advantages and disadvantages of shopping in the city centre before completing the following table.

	Advantages	Disadvantages
For a teenage shopper		
For a retailer		

Where does retailing occur in Cardiff?

The photographs on pages 20–21 were all taken in Cardiff. Study the map below and compare the four locations to the typical pattern for UK cities shown in Figure 3.

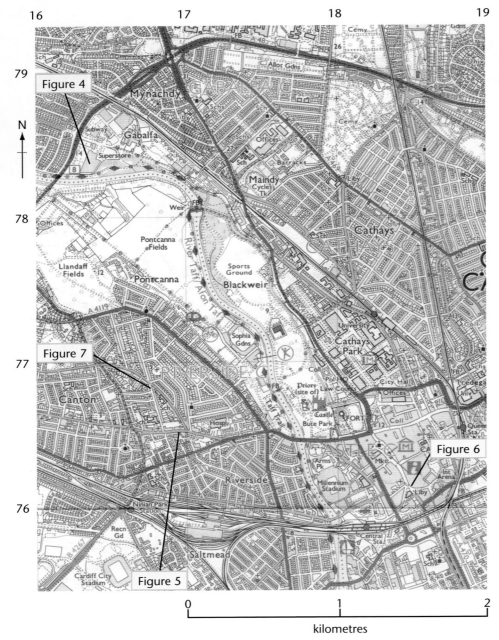

Figure 9 Extract from an Ordnance Survey map. Scale 1:25,000. Sheet 151. © Crown Copyright and/or database right. All rights reserved. Licence number 100036470

Activity

Use Figure 9.

1 **a)** Describe the location of Figure 6 using a grid reference.
   b) Describe the location of each of the other retail zones in relation to the CBD (Figure 6).

2 Use map evidence to explain why the location of Figure 4 is ideal for a large superstore.

Different opinions on retail change

Stories like the news headline in Figure 10 are common in our local newspapers. Retail change always creates a range of opinion. Some people are very happy about what is happening in our towns and cities, whilst others are saddened by events. The range of views expressed in Figure 11 show how different people in different circumstances react to the events around them.

New site for superstore meets local opposition

The local planning authority has confirmed that it has over 100 letters of opposition to the proposed supermarket planned for the old cattle market site in East Street. Most opposition is based on the way the supermarket will kill local businesses. We already have enough ...

Figure 10 News headline about a proposed new site for a superstore

Figure 11 Different views on retail change

Elderly lady – lives in the suburbs

> I used to shop locally. All the shopkeepers knew me and I used to chat with them. The butcher and fishmonger closed when they opened the big supermarket a mile away. I can't get to the supermarket easily as I don't drive. Things are a bit cheaper if you buy in bulk. I don't need to, there's only me.

Young mother – lives in a village

> I was pleased when they opened the new shopping mall in the city centre. It's weatherproof and I can comfortably take my two young girls around with me. There are lifts and toilets and even a roundabout inside the main hall. Parking can be a problem and expensive, but I don't mind as it's just once a week.

Professional man – lives in the suburbs

> I must admit I've got mixed feelings about the new retail park on the edge of town. I did find it convenient when I furnished my flat and decorated and upgraded all the kitchen equipment. I have a heavy heart though, as my father ran his own DIY store in the town centre. You could get everything there. Sadly he had to close because of the expensive rates and the competition from the huge superstores.

Environmentalist – lives in the inner suburbs

> All around us we are saving up problems for the future. We are forcing people into their cars to shop out of town on land that was once green fields. There was nothing wrong with shopping locally. Things may have been more expensive in the corner shops, but they were an important part of the community. The town centre looks increasingly run down. On some streets there is a spiral of decline when key shops move out. It just seems to be banks and building societies mixed with charity shops and pound shops. I hate the shopping malls, they burn electricity day and night, not least for the air conditioning.

Activity

1 Ask your parents what they think about the changes to shopping patterns over the last 30 years. Record their feelings as positive and negative. Share the outcome in class to create a complete list.

2 In addition to the changes already mentioned on these two pages, there are a number of other changes taking place in our lives that have an impact on shopping provision.
   a) Read the information on the right, select one of the changes and suggest how local events/examples could enable you to gain a greater understanding and awareness of the issue.
   b) Alternatively, after some initial research, suggest up to five websites that would allow students in your class to investigate the issue/change on a national or European scale.

- Post offices are being closed across the country. What is the reason, and how does the closure affect different groups of people?
- People are becoming more aware of 'food miles'. Should we be concerned about the distance some of our food travels before we buy it? What could be done to reduce food miles?
- New sites for superstores/retail parks are always being sought. Local authorities have a duty to promote the use of brownfield sites in the first instance. Why are greenfield sites favoured by store owners?
- Using the internet to shop is becoming increasingly popular. To what extent do your family and friends use it? What are the implications (good and bad) for this trend?

Can the town centre fight back?

Figure 12 The historic shopping heart of Shrewsbury

Shrewsbury typifies retail patterns and trends in most UK cities. The traditional shopping area can be found in the historic heart of the town, situated within the great loop of the river Severn. In recent years two shopping malls have been built and some areas in the centre have been pedestrianised. Where Shrewsbury bucks the trend is that it has retained many of the older independent shops, avoiding being labelled a **clone town**. In this section we look at how the local planners, working with partners in retailing, are attempting to re-invigorate the centre. Shops in Shrewsbury were affected by the 2008/09 recession and, as you might expect, there is an ongoing debate within the town about the negative impacts on the town centre of developing suburban retail parks.

Over the last few years, residents of Shrewsbury have voiced their opinions on the increasing number of online forums and weblogs available to them. Shopping provision in the town has been a recurring theme on the forum.

The examples in Figure 14 are typical of the range of views.

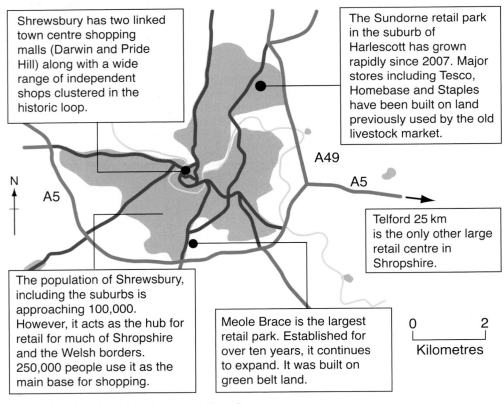

Shrewsbury has two linked town centre shopping malls (Darwin and Pride Hill) along with a wide range of independent shops clustered in the historic loop.

The Sundorne retail park in the suburb of Harlescott has grown rapidly since 2007. Major stores including Tesco, Homebase and Staples have been built on land previously used by the old livestock market.

A49

A5

N

A5

Telford 25 km is the only other large retail centre in Shropshire.

The population of Shrewsbury, including the suburbs is approaching 100,000. However, it acts as the hub for retail for much of Shropshire and the Welsh borders. 250,000 people use it as the main base for shopping.

Meole Brace is the largest retail park. Established for over ten years, it continues to expand. It was built on green belt land.

0   2
Kilometres

'Trouble is, Tesco Extra is just that. It's more than just a supermarket. The new hypermarket (which it technically will be) will be a town centre in itself. This is wonderful for North Shrewsbury, but maybe not for Shrewsbury town centre.'

'I feel sorry for the smaller traders in town, but in today's world of economics they just can't survive!'

'Parking in the town centre is so expensive, that's why I'm definitely going to use the new retail park.'

'At least Shrewsbury is an interesting place to shop. I went to Telford last week and I could have been anywhere in the UK. It's just a clone town in my view.'

Figure 13 The location of the retail areas in Shrewsbury

Figure 14 Viewpoints of Shrewsbury residents

Can Shrewsbury attract shoppers back to the town centre?

All local authorities face the same issue: they have to meet the needs of the consumers and respond to companies who wish to invest in their towns and cities – hence the development of out-of-town retail parks. On the other hand, the planners don't want to damage the town centre as a vibrant place to visit and shop. The planners in Shrewsbury are working hard to support the smaller independent retailers and the larger stores that wish to remain in the town centre. An initiative that started in Shrewsbury is now being copied across the country. Figure 15 shows how smaller shopkeepers can work together, using modern approaches to retailing. A monthly promotional e-newspaper helps trade and encourages new members to join.

In recent years the planners have worked with shop owners in Shrewsbury. Their aim is to make the town centre a more attractive place in which to shop. Their ideas are wide ranging and efforts will need to continue if Shrewsbury is to fight off competition from the services provided in Telford and beyond. The list below summarises some of the ongoing projects:

- improved town centre signage
- improved parking provision without penalising car owners
- better use of public open space and the promotion of a continental style cafe culture
- more public toilets
- an increase in Sunday trading opportunities
- lower rates to encourage new owners into empty shop units
- joined-up thinking in terms of all infrastructure and services, including public transport.

Activity

1 The news article in Figure 16 is based on the comments made by Sir Stuart Rose, executive of Marks and Spencer, in support of the Shrewsbury town centre forum. How far do you agree with him? Do you support the reasons he gives, that the future for town centres is bright?

2 List five things that you think could be done to reinvigorate town centre shopping areas. Rank the list in order of priority and share the list with your class. Collate the responses and try to rank the top ten ideas.

Figure 15 All The Little Shops scheme

All The Little Shops/ Shrewsbury has been sponsored by *Shropshire Enterprise Partnership and BeVivid* to help the independent retailers of Shrewsbury. Funding has meant all independent retailers and businesses in this region can create their own webpage, display up to 30 products and, if they wish, trade online – totally free.

It is easy for a retailer to set up a shop on this website and just as easy for visitors to the website to see the diverse independent retailers on offer in Shrewsbury, browse a wide range of products, plan their shopping trip, see what else there is to do 'Whilst in Town'.

We hope that All the Little Shops/Shrewsbury will encourage local shopping and increase visits into the shops – but some visitors will be from far away, so we have created a 'secure single payment gateway' which means a visitor can buy a range of products from different shops and pay by credit card – with just one payment.

This important initiative is a first for All the Little Shops – the pilot scheme has been successful and the scheme is now rolling out across the country. It is hoped that by helping local independent retailers – the soul of our town centres in the UK – they will take advantage of this great opportunity and allow the internet to help build awareness of their business and encourage more people into their shops.

Go to: **www.allthelittleshops.co.uk** for more information

There are good times ahead for town centres across the UK. Rising fuel costs will draw people back into accessible town centres. Out-of-town centres have reached their peak and local authorities will increasingly refuse planning permission under new government legislation. The timeless, ageless appeal of town centres will attract people out of the concrete malls into the social, spiritual and attractive space that historic town centres provide.

Figure 16 Good times ahead?

The rise and rise of internet sales

As well as being hit hard by out-of-town superstores and retail parks, town centre high streets have suffered from the rise and rise of internet shopping. Some of the empty shop units that we see in our high streets can be explained by the closure of shops such as those selling CDs and DVDs. These stores have faced stiff opposition from internet downloads of music and the steady rise of companies such as Amazon, the online book and music sales company.

Figure 17 Zavvi had closed most of its stores by 2009

Figure 18 shows the huge increase in internet use (for shopping) in the period 2001–6.

- UK shoppers spent £3.8 billion online in August 2009, 16 per cent higher than the same month in 2008.
- In total, online sales in the UK were worth £43.8 billion in 2008.
- Online sales at Marks and Spencer rose by 30 per cent in 13 weeks leading up to September 2009.
- John Lewis sales rose by 11.6 per cent to reach £151.5 million for the year up to August 2009.

An interesting fact is that the online shopping revolution has had an impact on different groups of people. The so-called 'silver surfers' – that is, people aged over 65 – are not getting left behind. In fact they accounted for the biggest percentage rise in internet banking users in 2009, with a staggering 275 per cent increase on the previous year. Younger shoppers are embracing the idea too. Advertisers target social networking sites such as Facebook and Twitter, particularly with a view to increasing sales of computer hardware and computer games.

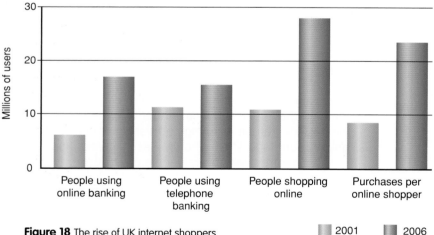

Figure 18 The rise of UK internet shoppers

2001   2006

Activity

1 Conduct a survey within your class and at home to find out the online shopping habits in your area. Discuss the questions you need to ask collectively, to enable you to build up a picture of who is buying online and what they are buying.

2 List the positive and negative impacts that the rise and rise of internet shopping is having. Try to think of social, economic and environmental impacts.

Silver surfer

Since I bought a computer, I haven't looked back. I love shopping online. I don't have transport and I'm a bit frail now. It saves me the worry and hassle of having to go to the shops as everything is delivered to my door. Things are a bit cheaper online as well – that's important if you only get a pension. When my local post office closed I decided to get my pension paid straight into my online bank account.

Dell has been delighted by the advertising campaign launched through Twitter. In 2008/9 we have generated sales of over £1.8 million, with people clicking directly from 'tweets'.

Spokesperson for Dell

Figure 19 All ages are embracing the internet sales revolution

Amazon locates new warehouse in Swansea

Swansea

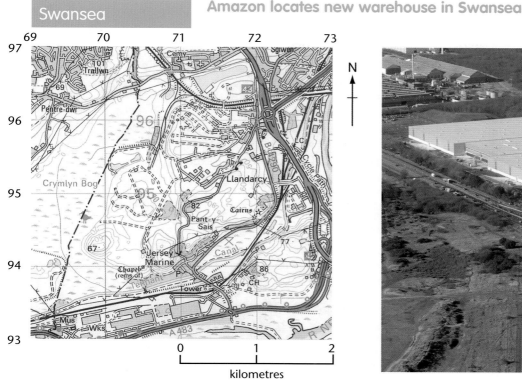

Figure 20 An Ordnance Survey extract showing the location of the Amazon warehouse. Scale 1:50,000 Sheet 170. The centre of the warehouse is at 711934 © Crown copyright and/or database right. All rights reserved. Licence number 100036470

Figure 21 The huge Amazon warehouse near Swansea

Amazon is one of the leading online retailers in the UK. In 2008 it opened its fourth distribution warehouse in the UK. Situated at Jersey Marine to the east of Swansea, it occupies land where the former Delta Compton aluminium works was once located (see Figure 20). Other UK warehouse locations include Glenrothes in Fife, Gourock in Inverclyde, and Milton Keynes, Buckinghamshire. The site at Swansea employs 1,200 full-time workers and covers a land area equivalent to 10 football pitches.

When the warehouse was opened in 2008, it received positive support from most people, but there were a few negative comments. Look at the range of views expressed below:

- 'This is a powerful shot in the arm for the Welsh economy. It's about jobs for the future.'
- 'The construction jobs alone will create jobs for years.'
- 'It's not just warehouse workers and delivery drivers. There will be jobs for management and jobs in IT support.'
- 'The new link road to the M4 motorway will improve road links for all the other industries nearby.'

- 'To have such a big name in e-commerce will put the region on the map – it's bound to attract other industries.'
- 'We're losing manufacturing jobs and becoming a nation of service workers; this can't be good in the long run.'
- 'Most of the jobs will be low pay – that's hardly a boost for the economy.'
- 'It's places like this that are killing our high street. It's not going to help us regenerate the city centre shopping area of Swansea.'

Activity

3 Look at Figures 20 and 21. Suggest why this is an ideal site for the warehouse.

4 Use a map of the UK and locate all of the Amazon warehouses. Describe the distribution of the warehouses and suggest reasons why Amazon selected these sites.

5 Consider the views on the opening of the new warehouse. In your class, debate if this factory and the rise of internet shopping as a whole, is largely good for the UK.

What do we mean by urban services?

Barcelona

One advantage of living in a large urban area is that you can get access to a range of useful services:

- Leisure and sports facilities such as swimming pools or tennis courts.
- Cultural venues such as museums, galleries and theatres.
- Health services such as clinics and hospitals.
- A range of schools, colleges and universities providing parents with choice.
- Places of worship for a variety of faiths.
- Specialist shops and services such as travel agents and solicitors.
- A variety of public transport services including bus, train and underground.

GIS Activity: Barcelona city council website

http://w20.bcn.cat:1100/GuiaMap
Barcelona is a large city in Catalonia on the North East coast of Spain. The city council has an excellent GIS on its website. You can view a map of the whole city or use the zoom function to view individual streets in great detail.

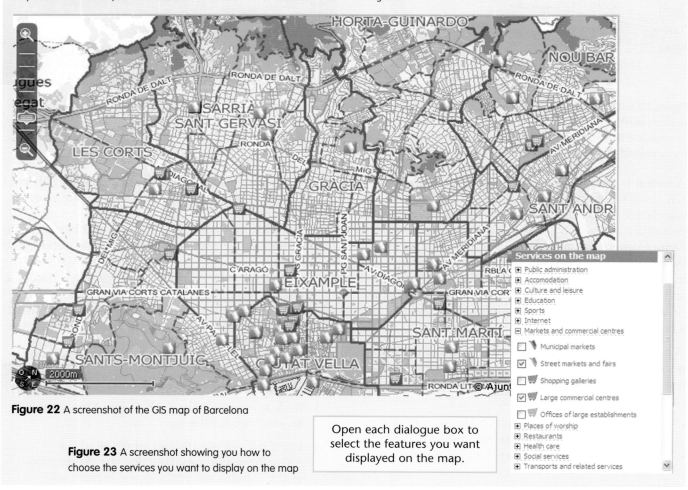

Figure 22 A screenshot of the GIS map of Barcelona

Figure 23 A screenshot showing you how to choose the services you want to display on the map

Open each dialogue box to select the features you want displayed on the map.

Does everyone have equal access to urban services?

People living in larger cities such as Barcelona have more choice of services than people living in the countryside: but do all city dwellers have equal access to urban services? In this case study we will see that some groups of people have better access to urban services than others. This may be for one of two reasons:

- The services are not distributed evenly through the urban area. So, for example, people living in a central district may have better access to theatres and museums than people living in a distant suburb of the city.
- Some services are more expensive than others, and not all groups of people can afford them.

GEOGRAPHICAL SKILLS

Describing distributions

To describe a distribution is to describe how similar features are spread across a map. Geographers are interested in the distribution of natural features such as forests or other habitats, as well as human features such as settlements, hospitals or sporting facilities.

Describing a distribution requires you to do two things.

1   You need to describe where on the map the features are located. For example, a lot of the street markets marked on Figure 22 are in the Ciutat Vella (or old city of Barcelona), whereas there are very few in Sants-Montjuïc.
2   You need to describe any pattern the features might make. These distribution patterns are shown in Figure 24:

- **Regular**, where the features are more or less equally spaced.
- **Random**, where the features are scattered across the map at irregular distances from each other.
- **Clustered**, where the features are grouped together into only one part of the map.
- **Linear**, where the features all fall along a line.

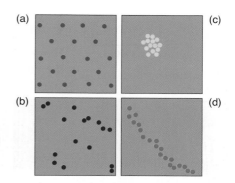

Figure 24 Distribution patterns

Activity

1   **a)** Match the following services to their likely distribution pattern:
- motorway service stations • clustered
- high-street banks in a town • regular linear
- primary schools in a large town • regular

b) Suggest reasons why these services are distributed in this way.

2   Match the four distribution patterns shown in Figure 24 to the following terms:
- random • regular
- linear • clustered

3   **a)** Describe the distribution of large commercial centres on Figure 22.

b) Suggest why so many are on major roads such as Av. Diagonal.

4   **a)** Compare the distribution of these larger centres to the street markets and fairs.

b) Give reasons for the differences you have noticed.

Barcelona

Figure 25 The location of Barcelona

Multicultural Barcelona and the distribution of services for ethnic groups

Barcelona is a large city with a population of more than 1.5 million people. The surrounding districts are also urban, so its overall size is greater than 4 million people. The city grew rapidly during the 1970s and 1980s, attracting migrants from Spain and abroad. Like many large European cities, it has a diverse multicultural population, and the city has sizeable populations of people descended from:

- Mexico and other Spanish-speaking Central and South American countries
- parts of Asia, especially Pakistan and China
- various African countries, but especially Morocco
- other European countries.

Barcelona's ethnic groups tend to be concentrated in the **inner urban** districts of the city. The district of El Raval, in the Ciutat Vella (the old city centre), has a sizeable immigrant population: 27.6 per cent of the population are foreign migrants compared with 7.2 per cent for Barcelona as a whole. Muslims from Morocco and Pakistan may choose to live here because they have better access to particular services that are also clustered in this part of Barcelona. For example, Ciutat Vella has ten of Barcelona's sixteen mosques, and three of these are in El Raval. The district also has many shops catering for the Muslim population such as halal butchers and stores offering internet or telephone connections to all parts of the globe. It also has video rental stores that specialise in Asian films.

However, an alternative explanation for the concentration of Moroccans and Pakistanis in El Raval is that this is one of the cheapest districts of Barcelona in which to live. Many immigrants from these countries do poorly paid work and cannot afford to live in other, more expensive, parts of the city.

Figure 26 Halal butchers in El Raval provide a service for the Muslim population of the district

Activity

1 Describe the distribution of mosques in Figure 27. Make sure you use the relevant words from the following list:
   - regular
   - random
   - linear
   - clustered
   - distribution.

Figure 27 The distribution of mosques in Barcelona

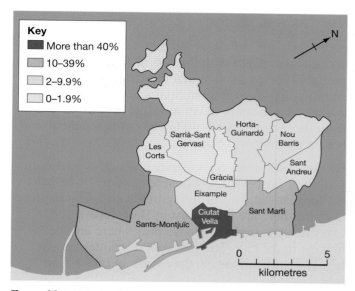

Figure 28 Pakistani and Moroccan population of Barcelona (% of total in each district)

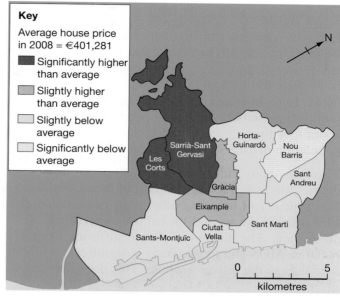

Figure 29 Average house prices (euros) 2008

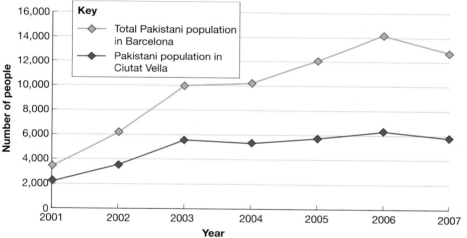

Figure 30 The Pakistani population of Barcelona

	Moroccan population in Ciutat Vella	Total Moroccan population in Barcelona
2001	3,019	7,165
2002	3,645	9,751
2003	4,061	11,985
2004	4,247	13,594
2005	4,390	14,508
2006	4,468	15,522
2007	3,887	12,816

Figure 31 The Moroccan population of Barcelona

Activity

2 Explain why there are so many mosques in Ciutat Vella.

3 Give three reasons why Pakistani and Moroccan immigrants might choose to live in El Raval.

4 Use Figures 28 and 29.
   a) Compare the distribution of Barcelona's Muslim population with the pattern of house prices.
   b) What does this suggest about the income of Pakistani and Moroccan immigrants?

5 Study Figure 30.
   a) Describe the trend shown on both lines.
   b) Use the graph to explain whether Barcelona's Pakistani population is getting more or less concentrated into Ciutat Vella.

6 a) Use the data in Figure 31 to draw another pair of lines on a line graph.
   b) Compare this graph with Figure 30. What are the main similarities and differences?

Do Barcelona's wealthier districts have better access to some services?

El Raval is an inner urban district within the Ciutat Vella (or old city). The district has narrow streets set out during the medieval development of the city, so it is not easy for modern traffic. Most of the housing is in six- to eight-storey apartment buildings. The **population density**, at 34,445 people per km^2, is about four times greater than London's average population density of 8,860 people per km^2.

There are many indicators that suggest that this district has both a lower standard of living, and a lower quality of life, than other parts of Barcelona. El Raval has the second-lowest **life expectancy** of all districts. The number of people suffering from malaria, AIDS and tuberculosis is significantly higher here than in the city as a whole. This does not

necessarily mean that the district has poor healthcare services compared with the rest of Barcelona. It is probably due to the fact that these diseases are more common in Africa than in Spain, and the district has a large Moroccan population. Most people suffering from these diseases would have contracted them before migrating to Spain.

By contrast, Sarrià-Sant Gervasi, which is a western suburb of Barcelona, is home to residents who have the highest standard of living in the city. Population densities here are the lowest in Barcelona and life expectancy is highest. House prices here are the highest in the city. 36.7 per cent of residents have higher qualifications, so they work in better-paid jobs.

Figure 32 Distribution of badminton courts in Barcelona

Activity

1 Use Figure 32.
   a) Describe the distribution of badminton courts in Barcelona.
   b) List the districts which have no badminton courts. Using Figure 33, state whether each of these districts has house prices that are above or below Barcelona's average.

   c) Assuming that customers have to pay a membership or court fee to play badminton, explain why the badminton courts are located only in certain districts.
   d) What groups of people have poor access to these sports facilities?

GEOGRAPHICAL SKILLS

Making comparisons

Making comparisons about two different places is an important skill. In order to compare two places successfully you must link a statement about one to the other with a connective in the same sentence. Connectives are words such as 'however', 'whereas' and 'similarly' (more are given in Figure 34).

Connectives to highlight difference
... unlike ...
... whereas ...
... though ...
... conversely ...
... is much greater than ...
... is much smaller than ...
... is significantly larger than ...

Connectives to highlight similarity
... like ...
... similarly ...
... equally ...
... identically ...
... likewise ...
... in common with ...

Figure 34
Connectives that can be used for comparison

	Density (persons per km²) 2004	Life expectancy 2006	Persons with higher qualifications (%) 2006	Immigrant population (%) 2007	Average house price (euros) 2008
Ciutat Vella	23,943	73.2	11.4	44.1	331,346
Eixample	34,863	79.7	23.9	16.3	459,624
Sants-Montjuïc	8,246	78.4	11.1	17.9	315,813
Les Corts	13,718	80.4	26.9	10.9	566,689
Sarrià-Sant Gervasi	6,900	80.5	36.7	11.0	832,854
Gràcia	28,477	79.2	21.6	14.1	409,216
Horta-Guinardó	14,197	79.0	12.1	11.8	333,214
Nou Barris	20,572	78.2	6.2	15.2	267,952
Sant Andreu	21,504	79.1	10.5	12.0	328,427
Sant Marti	20,192	78.9	10.6	13.8	359,966
Barcelona	15,635	78.5	16.5	100*	401,281

Figure 33 Standard of living and quality of life indicators for Barcelona's main districts

* 100% of the immigrants living in the city live in Barcelona. This includes 4.6 per cent who have no fixed address

Activity

2 Study Figure 33. Choose one column that shows standard of living and one that shows quality of life. Explain the difference between these two concepts.

3 Use Figures 33 and 34.
   a) Compare the quality of life in Les Corts with Sarrià-Sant Gervasi.
   b) Compare the standard of living in Eixample with Nou Barris.

Chapter 3
Urbanisation

Global patterns of urban development

The United Nations estimates that by 2008 more than half of the world's population will be living in **urban** areas: larger towns and cities. The **urban population**, which is the percentage of people living in towns and cities, has grown steadily since the 1950s:

- 30 per cent in 1950.
- 47 per cent in 2000.
- It is estimated that it will reach 60 per cent by 2030.

The process by which the population of a country becomes more urban and less rural is known as **urbanisation**. Urbanisation causes the physical and human growth of towns and cities. Urbanisation is caused by a combination of two factors:

- The migration of people from rural to urban areas.
- The **natural increase** of the urban population due to there being more births than deaths.

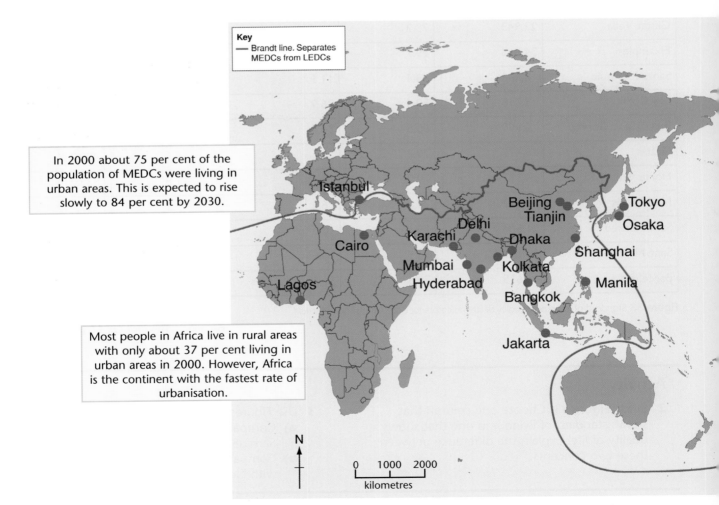

Key
— Brandt line. Separates MEDCs from LEDCs

In 2000 about 75 per cent of the population of MEDCs were living in urban areas. This is expected to rise slowly to 84 per cent by 2030.

Most people in Africa live in rural areas with only about 37 per cent living in urban areas in 2000. However, Africa is the continent with the fastest rate of urbanisation.

Figure 1 Map showing the location of those cities that are forecast to be mega-cities by 2015

Urbanisation is currently much more rapid in the **Less Economically Developed Countries (LEDCs)** than in **More Economically Developed Countries (MEDCs)**. LEDCs tend to have faster-growing populations than MEDCs and they also have a larger number of people moving from rural to urban areas.

People move for a variety of reasons. Conflicts and natural disasters may force people to move, in which case the migrants may be described as **refugees**. However, in most cases people migrate out of choice rather than because of violence or disaster. People generally move because they want to improve their standard of living by finding a better-paid job. A migrant who moves in order to find work is described as an **economic migrant**. Many migrants also expect that moving to the city will improve their quality of life, perhaps by giving them better access to clean water or healthcare facilities.

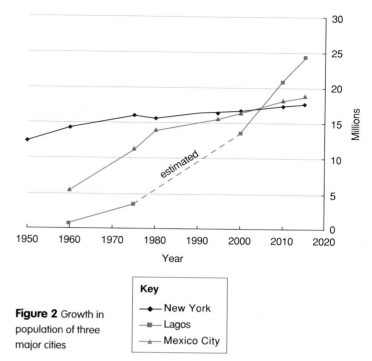

Figure 2 Growth in population of three major cities

Key
New York
Lagos
Mexico City

Activity

1 Use Figure 1 to complete the following:

    MEDCs have a *larger / smaller* proportion of people living in urban areas than LEDCs. Of the less economically developed regions:
    • .... is the most urbanised
    • .... is experiencing the most rapid urbanisation.

2 Use the text on these pages to make your own definitions for urbanisation, refugees and economic migrant.

3 Explain the two factors that led to the more rapid urbanisation in LEDCs.

4 **a)** Describe the likely distribution of the world's mega-cities in 2015.
   b) Use Figure 2 to describe and explain the trend of each graph.

Los Angeles

New York

Brandt line

Mexico City

Rio de Janeiro

São Paulo

Buenos Aires

The urban population of LEDCs should reach 50 per cent by 2020.

South America and the Caribbean are the most urbanised part of the less economically developed world with about 75 per cent of the population living in urban areas.

Ipswich

Re-urbanisation

During the 1970s and 80s, it became unfashionable to live in the inner urban area of many UK towns and cities. People didn't really want to live in older urban areas, especially those that had run-down industrial buildings, such as the docks and waterfronts of the UK's ports. However, in recent years, these **brownfield sites** have been redeveloped with new homes and people are moving back in. This process is known as **re-urbanisation**.

Ipswich is one of the fastest growing towns in the UK. Figure 3 shows the predicted growth of the town and the number of new dwellings required to meet this increase. Like many of the towns and cities in the south-east, Ipswich is partly growing through natural population increase but also through significant inward migration of people.

Figure 3 Population growth of Ipswich and housing need

	Population			Estimated number of new dwellings required
	2001 Census	2021 (predicted)	Change	
Suffolk as a whole	670,200	733,600	+ 63,400	61,700
Ipswich	117,400	138,700	+ 21,300	15,400

The Waterfront vision

The Waterfront is the biggest regeneration project in the East of England. Formerly an industrial dock area with warehouses and factory sites, the site had become increasingly derelict since the 1970s. Ipswich Borough Council, working in partnership with a number of developers, created a vision where new residences would blend with culture, business, and a range of leisure and education opportunities. The best of the old would be retained and striking new designs would show the ambition of the town as it moved into the twenty-first century. Sadly, due to economic difficulties, many apartments are still incomplete in 2012. The website at www.ipswich.gov.uk (use the search facility within this site) provides you with more detail on each aspect of the scheme.

Figure 4 An Ordnance Survey extract of the location of Ipswich Waterfront. Scale 1:25,000 Sheet 197 © Crown Copyright and/or database right. All rights reserved. Licence number 100036470

Figure 5 The vision becomes reality

Looking west across the new marina towards the high-rise apartments

Re-using the old to create new leisure opportunities amongst the apartments

The few remaining warehouses await development

An A level Geography student undertaking an investigation into the Waterfront interviewed more than 50 residents of the new apartments surrounding the dock and 30 visitors who were enjoying many of the bars and restaurants in the area. From the responses, the development is clearly very popular!

The location is superb. I can walk to my office in the town centre in a matter of minutes and I no longer need to use my car during the week.

I have all the entertainment I need on my doorstep. The bars are lively at night and on a sunny day you can sit and watch the activity in the marina whilst enjoying a latte.

Whilst the rents are not cheap, my apartment has all I need. The small kitchen/diner is fitted out with brand-new appliances and the two bedrooms mean that I can have friends staying over.

This is my first visit to Ipswich. I'm amazed how modern everything looks, but they have done really well to keep some of the old buildings to add character. The four-star hotel I'm staying in was once an old flour mill.

I think they have a really nice balance of places to work, such as the law firms and the estate agents, along with the leisure facilities like the dance studio and the art gallery – and best of all there's a variety of flats and apartments. It would be great to live here.

I love the brave architectural styles and colours of the new university buildings. When the halls of residence are completed, this would be a fantastic place to be a student.

Figure 6 The views of residents and visitors

Is it all good news?

With such positive reports, it is difficult to find any opposition to what the planners have achieved in Ipswich. However, one letter, written to the editor of the local newspaper, does voice some concerns …

Dear Sir

Once again your newspaper reports the Waterfront development in a positive way. Was your journalist wearing rose-tinted spectacles when he wrote the feature article in last night's edition of the paper (4 February 2010)? Hasn't he heard that the local council has failed to include enough affordable housing in their plans? I know that the local Labour and Liberal Party are most upset by this oversight. How do you explain that some of the expensive apartments remain empty?

Perhaps the biggest problems have yet to arise. I cannot be alone in thinking that a traffic management scheme for the area has been forgotten. The increase in residents and businesses in the area has choked the already congested road system. I understand that the local roads are now designated as an Air Quality Management Area due to the fumes from stationary cars.

I have no doubt that the council will have to build a new river crossing to ease the traffic flow. To do this it will have to use its powers of compulsory purchase. As always, someone will lose out. They won't think twice about an opportunity to move out one of the few boat repair yards left in the area.

Mr G Dixie
resident of Ipswich

Figure 7 A letter to the editor …

Activity

1 Study Figure 3. What factors create the need for so many new dwellings in Ipswich?

2 Discuss why the development of sustainable communities needs to include facilities for housing, work and leisure.

3 For a new development close to your school, design a table which has two columns featuring positive and negative aspects of the scheme. Try to consider social, economic and environmental factors when you review the successes and failures of the scheme.

Barcelona

Gentrification of El Raval, Barcelona

The rapid growth of Barcelona's population during the last 80 years has put tremendous pressure on housing, transport systems and other services in the city. By 1980, 4 per cent of people lived in homes unfit for human habitation and 16 per cent lived in housing areas with serious deficiencies. El Raval, a large residential area near to the city's port, suffered severe problems of overcrowding. Many families lived in old apartment blocks that needed repair. The streets were narrow and congested. High crime rates meant that many residents felt unsafe. Drug dealing and prostitution were common. Tourists were warned not to visit the area.

Activity

1 Study the list of principles used by Barcelona planners set out in Figure 11. Select two from the list and explain why you think the principle is important.

FRANCE
N
ANDORRA
PYRENEES
SPAIN
Figueras
Catalonia
Lérida
Barcelona
Tarragona
Mediterranean Sea
0
100
kilometres

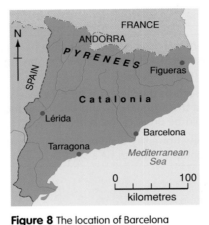

Figure 8 The location of Barcelona

	Population of the metropolitan area	Size of the metropolitan area (km^2)
1930	500,000	60
1950	800,000	125
1970	1,500,000	250
1990	4,000,000	500
2020 (est)	4,200,000	500

Figure 9 The growth of Barcelona

Figure 10 The regeneration of the old coastal industrial area – now called Vila Olimpica

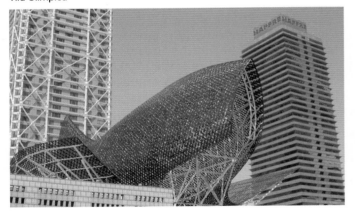

By tackling these problems, Barcelona's planners developed a reputation for effective urban regeneration. Cities across Europe have copied its methods. In the 1980s the planners dealt with huge brownfield sites, such as the decaying industrial areas adjacent to the port. The 1992 Olympic site was an ideal place for the planners to flex their muscles.

Into the twenty-first century, the planners have moved to a policy of **gentrification**. This means making existing residential neighbourhoods better places in which to live. Figure 11 shows some of the principles that underpin the work of Barcelona planners.

Figure 11 Planning in Barcelona – how to revive an urban area

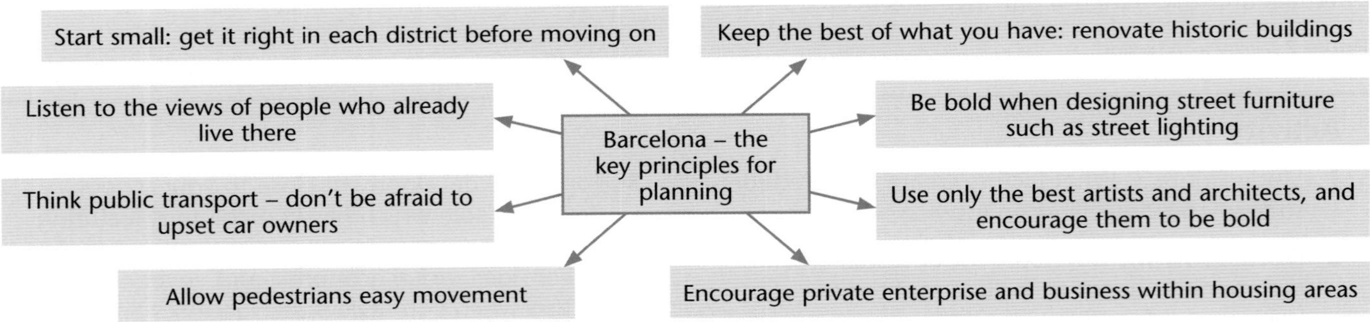

Barcelona – the key principles for planning
Start small: get it right in each district before moving on
Keep the best of what you have: renovate historic buildings
Listen to the views of people who already live there
Be bold when designing street furniture such as street lighting
Think public transport – don't be afraid to upset car owners
Use only the best artists and architects, and encourage them to be bold
Allow pedestrians easy movement
Encourage private enterprise and business within housing areas

In the district of El Raval, the planners have demolished some of the old apartment blocks. The population density of the district has fallen but quality of life for remaining residents has improved. Demolition of buildings has made the streets wider and created open spaces for people to sit or enjoy a pavement café. Parks and gardens have been created as well as skateboard parks. New museums and art galleries that celebrate the city's culture and heritage have opened.

The area had a long history of crime

Today it is vibrant, particularly at night

Figure 12 Rejuvenating the problem district of El Raval

Solve one problem, create another!

Barcelona is now a favourite destination for short breaks. Guide books are crammed with information on how to enjoy the history, art and culture of this exciting city. Some books include an honest assessment of some of the problems you may encounter. In rejuvenated districts like El Raval the vibrant atmosphere at night can be threatening to some visitors and a nightmare for local people who want to catch some sleep.

The city authorities have hit back. In 2006, new by-laws were introduced with on-the-spot fines for:

- noisy revellers, especially in alleys, and in streets with balconies
- the inappropriate consumption of alcohol in public places
- graffiti
- the inappropriate use of public areas and street furniture.

Street signs have been posted in problem areas such as El Raval, and buses carry adverts to encourage bikers to move around quietly!

Figure 14 Thousands of motos are used by young people causing disturbance to residents

Every night the city streets are hosed down, the unpleasant contribution from countless dogs is made worse through drunken humans adding to the stench with rivers of pee. Noise pollution is also a problem in El Raval. The screaming and shouting of revellers combined with the menace of motos leads to sleepless nights for residents. It seems that the youths deliberately alter the muffles on their exhaust system to create maximum noise nuisance. Locals put up signs on balconies demanding quiet. The local authority has started to revoke licences for breaking noise pollution rules.

Damien Simonis – Lonely Planet

Figure 13 Extract from the *Lonely Planet Guide: Barcelona*

Activity

2 In a class discussion, identify areas that suffer from anti-social behaviour. Suggest how the local authority might reduce the problem.

3 The following websites provide you with more information on how Barcelona is leading the way to rejuvenate problem city areas. Study the information and use the links, then list five things that you think British planners should incorporate in their work.

http://w3.bcn.es

www.guiabcn.cat/guiaturistica/
en_ordinance.html

Investigating rural to urban migration in South Africa

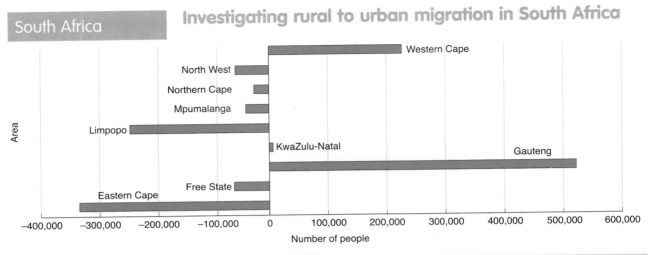

Figure 15 Total population gains and losses due to migration in 2005

Gauteng is South Africa's most urban province and contains three major cities of more than one million people: Johannesburg, Pretoria and Soweto. By contrast, the largest city in the neighbouring province of Limpopo has only 90,000 people and more than 90 per cent of the population lives in rural areas. In this case study we will investigate the reasons for migration between Limpopo and Gauteng, and also examine the effects of this migration on rural communities.

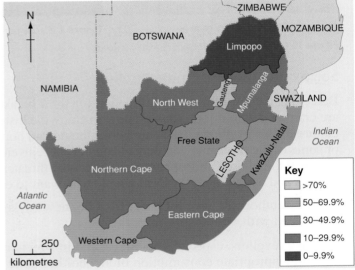

Figure 16 Urban population in South Africa's provinces (estimate based on population living in settlements greater than 20,000 people)

Activity

1 Use Figures 15 and 16 to complete the following:

The two most urban provinces are:
i) .... which gained .... migrants during 2005 and;
ii) .... which gained .... migrants in 2005.

The more rural provinces, such as ...., gained / lost population during the year.

2 Study Figure 17. Choose from the following phrases to describe the flow of migrants from Limpopo:

Most migrants migrate short / long distances. Most / all migrants move to provinces that are less rural than Limpopo. Some / many migrants move to the most urban provinces of South Africa.

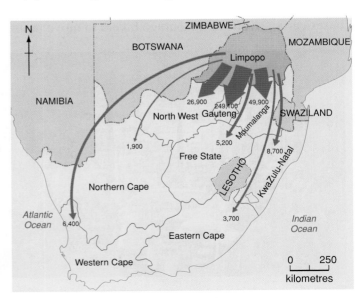

Figure 17 Migration from Limpopo province during 2005

What are the push/pull factors for rural to urban migration in South Africa?

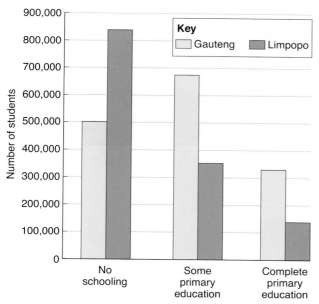

Figure 18 Comparing education in Limpopo with Gauteng

People living in rural areas such as Limpopo are attracted by the jobs and better opportunities available in cities such as Johannesburg. The possibility of better healthcare and schools for their children are **pull factors** that encourage migrants to leave their rural homes. At the same time, migrants are often dissatisfied with life in the countryside. Few rural houses have a connection to the national electricity grid. Most people do not own an electric cooker, let alone a computer or television. Lack of money, poor job opportunities and relatively low quality of life are all **push factors** that can force people to move away from rural areas.

People living in the province of Limpopo rely on either farming or tourism for their income. The region has a seasonal wet/dry tropical **climate** and a **savanna ecosystem**. Rural population densities are relatively high and farm sizes small.

Most households in Limpopo earn a little less than 1,000 Rand a month, whereas average household income in Johannesburg is 7,175 Rand a month. The **poverty line** in South Africa is defined at 1,100 Rand (about US$150) a month. Of people in Limpopo, 60 per cent live below this poverty line compared with only 20 per cent of people in Gauteng province.

Activity

3 Based on the evidence in Figures 15, 16 and 17:
   a) suggest why so few migrants move from Limpopo to Western Cape
   b) suggest which regions are losing migrants to Western Cape and give reasons for your answer.

4 Use Figure 18. How many students in each province:
   a) have no schooling
   b) complete primary education?

5 Explain how each of the following might be push factors that contribute to migration from rural areas of Limpopo.
   • The rural areas are densely populated.
   • Rainfall is low and unpredictable.
   • Rural communities are isolated from services such as schools and healthcare.

6 List the reasons for rural to urban migration using this table:

	Push factors	Pull factors
Economic reasons		
Education		
Quality of life		

The percentage of Johannesburg residents who:
• own an electric stove in the home: 77.86 per cent
• own a fridge or freezer: 87.26 per cent
• own a dishwasher: 5.24 per cent
• own a vacuum cleaner: 31.35 per cent
• own a television: 89.53 per cent
• own a hi-fi or music centre: 73.61 per cent
• own a personal computer: 17.86 per cent
• have a telephone connection: 57.65 per cent
• have eaten in a restaurant in the last month: 44.1 per cent
• bought a take-away meal in the last month (from a permanent establishment, not a street hawker): 55.26 per cent
• hired a video or DVD in the last month: 13.65 per cent.

Figure 19 Some lifestyle statistics for Johannesburg, drawn from the annual All Media Products Survey (AMPS)

7 Study Figure 19 taken from a South African website. Suggest how the internet and advertising might accidentally encourage further migration into Johannesburg.

What are the consequences of rural to urban migration?

What effect does migration have on the rural areas that the migrants leave behind? Does the loss of so many people cause economic and social problems in the countryside? Or does migration create benefits for rural areas? Research suggests that the consequences of migration are very complex. They include:

- **Brain drain** – the loss of some of the most skilled workers.
- **Remittances** – the money sent back by workers to support their families.
- Information and ideas – new technologies and skills learned in the city flow back into the country where they are used to support local businesses.

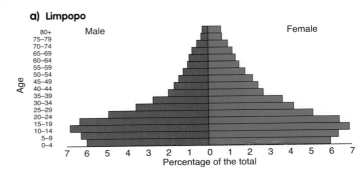

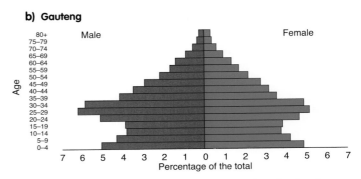

Figure 20 Population pyramids for a) Limpopo (a rural province) and b) Gauteng (a neighbouring urban province)

www.statssa.gov.za/census2001/digiatlas/index.html
This site uses to display an online atlas of South Africa. It uses data from the most recent census which can be displayed in either map or graph form.

Activity

1 Compare the population pyramids in Figure 20. Focus on the differences/similarities in the following parts of each graph:
   a) The percentage of the population aged 0 to 19.
   b) The percentage of the population aged 25 to 34.

   c) The balance between males and females.

2 Use Figure 21 to suggest reasons for the differences you noticed between the population pyramids.

3 Explain whether each of the following is an advantage or disadvantage to a rural area that is losing migrants:
   a) brain drain
   b) remittances
   c) information and ideas.

Studies in South Africa show that:
- those aged between 15 and 35 are the most likely to migrate
- more males migrate than females, but an increasing number of females are migrating
- female migrants are slightly younger than male migrants
- circular migration (see page 43) is more common than permanent migration
- some rural migrants move to large urban areas such as Johannesburg, but many rural migrants move to smaller towns
- an increasing number of rural migrants move to other rural areas.

Figure 21 Key points of migration in South Africa

Circular migration

Many migrants do not make a permanent move to the city. It is common for people to leave the countryside when there are few farming jobs and return at busier times of the year, for example, at harvest. This temporary form of rural to urban migration is known as **circular migration**.

Circular migration brings both benefits and problems to rural communities. Migrants earn money which can be sent to the rural family and invested in improving the farm: repairing terraces and in tree-planting schemes. Circular migrants also reduce demand on village food and water supplies. This is particularly helpful in Limpopo which has a long dry season.

However, circular migration is almost certainly one of the reasons for the spread of AIDS and other sexually transmitted diseases. Studies in South Africa suggest that migrants are three times more likely to be infected with HIV than non-migrants. A returning migrant who is unaware that he or she is HIV positive could then infect a partner in the rural home. It is more difficult to treat rural AIDS sufferers because of their isolation from health clinics.

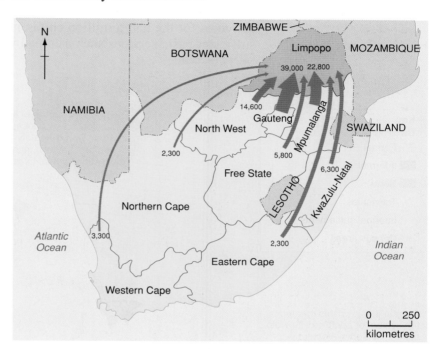

Figure 22 Migration into Limpopo, 2005

Activity

4 Define circular migration.

5 Use Figure 22.
   a) How many migrants returned from provinces that are mostly urban?
   b) Compare this map with Figure 17 on page 40. What are the similarities and differences?

6 Use the text and your own ideas to complete the following table about the advantages and disadvantages of circular migration:

	Advantages to the rural area	Disadvantages to the rural area
Economic		
Social		

7 Explain why circular migration is likely to be more beneficial to rural areas than permanent migration.

Johannesburg

Investigating urban change in Johannesburg

Johannesburg is South Africa's biggest city. It has a population of more than 1.5 million. On the edge of the city is the settlement of Soweto. Soweto is a black township with another 1 million people. It grew up during the apartheid era when black Africans were forced to live in locations separate from white South Africans. Approximately 12 per cent of the housing in Soweto is informal.

Quality of life in Soweto for many residents is poor. The population has grown quickly and the housing density is very high. There is little space for leisure activities for the half a million children who live here. The township lacks sufficient basic services such as piped water, sanitation and waste collection.

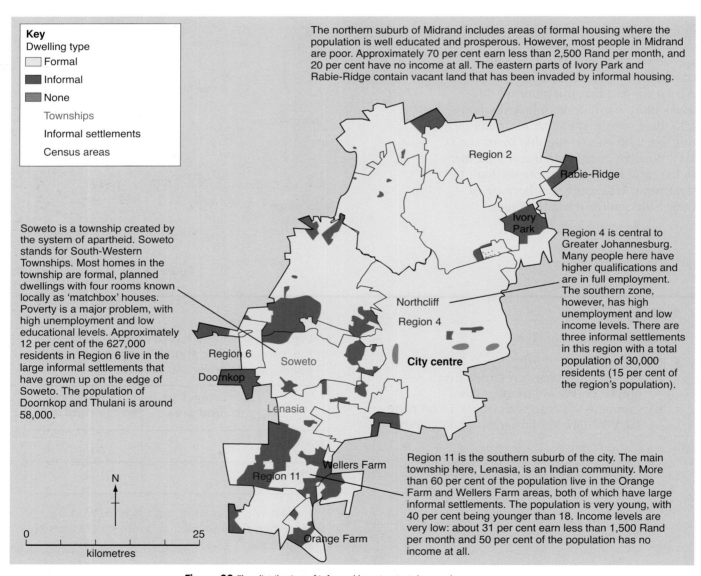

Key

Dwelling type

☐ Formal
■ Informal
■ None

Townships

Informal settlements

Census areas

The northern suburb of Midrand includes areas of formal housing where the population is well educated and prosperous. However, most people in Midrand are poor. Approximately 70 per cent earn less than 2,500 Rand per month, and 20 per cent have no income at all. The eastern parts of Ivory Park and Rabie-Ridge contain vacant land that has been invaded by informal housing.

Soweto is a township created by the system of apartheid. Soweto stands for South-Western Townships. Most homes in the township are formal, planned dwellings with four rooms known locally as 'matchbox' houses. Poverty is a major problem, with high unemployment and low educational levels. Approximately 12 per cent of the 627,000 residents in Region 6 live in the large informal settlements that have grown up on the edge of Soweto. The population of Doornkop and Thulani is around 58,000.

Region 4 is central to Greater Johannesburg. Many people here have higher qualifications and are in full employment. The southern zone, however, has high unemployment and low income levels. There are three informal settlements in this region with a total population of 30,000 residents (15 per cent of the region's population).

Region 11 is the southern suburb of the city. The main township here, Lenasia, is an Indian community. More than 60 per cent of the population live in the Orange Farm and Wellers Farm areas, both of which have large informal settlements. The population is very young, with 40 per cent being younger than 18. Income levels are very low: about 31 per cent earn less than 1,500 Rand per month and 50 per cent of the population has no income at all.

Figure 23 The distribution of informal housing in Johannesburg

Figure 24a Racial structure of the population

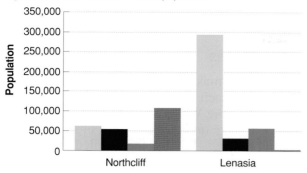

Districts of Johannesburg

Key		Northcliff	Lenasia
	African	59,484	292,880
	Mixed race	53,363	30,760
	Indian	17,238	54,457
	White	107,514	443

Figure 24b Occupations (number of people employed)

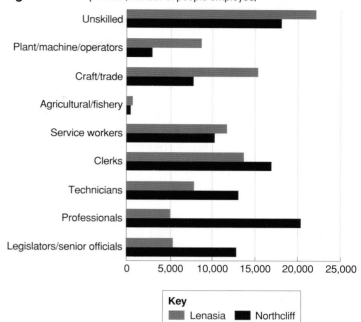

Key
Lenasia   Northcliff

Figure 24c Housing type

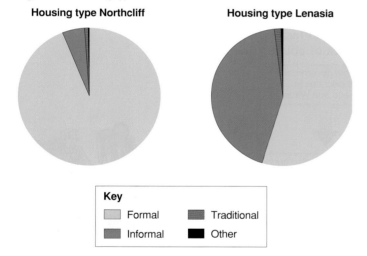

Key
Formal   Traditional
Informal   Other

Households	Northcliff		Lenasia	
	number of houses	%	number of houses	%
Formal	75,603	94.0	60,093	54.8
Informal	3,726	4.6	47,499	43.3
Traditional	924	1.1	1,587	1.4
Other	141	0.2	444	0.4
Total households	80,394		109,623	

Activity

1 Use Figure 23 to describe the location of Soweto.

2 Use Figure 23 to describe the distribution of informal settlements in Johannesburg.

3 Using evidence from Figure 24, compare the human geography of Lenasia with Northcliff. Use the following headings as a structure for three short paragraphs:

Racial structure   Occupations   Housing type

4 Using evidence from the graphs, suggest which of the two regions has the higher standard of living. Give at least two reasons for your answer.

Understanding the planning system in England and Wales

The planning system in England and Wales involves three tiers of decision making. The national government sets overall targets for things such as housing, new schools and transport. Each Regional Assembly then has to produce a **Regional Spatial Strategy** (in Wales this document is called the Wales Spatial Plan). The planners need to consider the impact that the need for new housing will have on other elements of the plan, such as new roads, schools, better waste management or conservation projects. Finally, the detailed plans for each local area are produced by local authorities. They must plan within the guidelines provided by the Regional Spatial Strategy. They consult local people in order to produce a **Local Development Framework (LDF)**. These three tiers of decision making are illustrated in Figure 1.

Who is involved in planning decisions?

The answer is all of us! We are all **stakeholders** – in other words, everyone has a view on the planning issues that affect their community. A key element of the planning process is that all stakeholders can become involved. They can respond to the ideas being put forward by the three tiers of the planning process, i.e. national government, Regional Assemblies and local authorities. The aim is that all individuals and groups who may be touched by planning decisions will feel that they can contribute to the policy and help to shape it. Stakeholders come in all shapes and sizes, they might be:

- an individual householder who is concerned that a proposed new road will disturb their peaceful home
- a parish council that is keen to see an increase in playground facilities in its area
- a pressure group that is lobbying to protect a specific area of countryside
- development consultants working on behalf of a large landowner who hopes to build a large sports complex.

We can all play a part in the planning process, sometimes promoting new developments, sometimes trying to stop planning proposals.

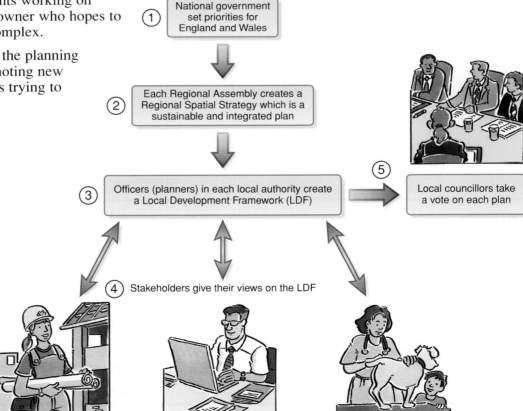

① National government set priorities for England and Wales

② Each Regional Assembly creates a Regional Spatial Strategy which is a sustainable and integrated plan

③ Officers (planners) in each local authority create a Local Development Framework (LDF)

⑤ Local councillors take a vote on each plan

④ Stakeholders give their views on the LDF

Figure 4 The three tiers of decision making in the planning process

Who would be a planner?

Planners make bold statements about the future. In England and Wales they work with elected councillors to produce a Local Development Framework (LDF). They offer solutions to solve existing problems and develop ideas for a better future. The statements below are typical of what appears in many LDFs.

Our vision is to improve the quality of life for all who live in, work in, learn in and visit the city, by supporting growth and making sure that development happens in a sustainable way so that the facilities enjoyed by local people are not harmed and the town is improved.

By 2025 we will live in a more vibrant, active and attractive modern city which successfully combines modern development with historic character. It will be a place where people want to live, work, learn, visit and invest – and it will have a reduced carbon footprint.

Figure 2 A planner introducing the LDF

The spider diagram (Figure 3) shows just a small number of the factors that planners need to consider when shaping the LDF. An important part of the process is to consult with local people about their feelings.

Public open space

Landscape and wildlife issues

Work and employment issues

Housing needs

Cultural provision

Transport issues

What do planners need to consider when shaping their LDF?

Waste disposal

Crime/Policing issues

Shopping services

Education opportunities

National and regional government plans

Leisure facilities

Figure 3 What do planners need to consider when shaping their LDF?

Activity

1 What would you say to your local planners to make sure that the views of teenagers are represented in the LDF? As a starting point, use the ideas put forward by teenagers in a Newport school (Figure 4) when planners visited their geography class.

The facilities in the local park are poor. Why don't you build things like a skateboard park?

We need more CCTV in some areas of the town to protect us, particularly at night.

Why don't you provide more sports areas in the middle of housing estates? It would be great if they were caged and had floodlights.

You need to put more cycle lanes on our roads. You want us to cycle to school, but we don't feel safe.

Figure 4 Ideas suggested by teenagers in a Newport school for their LDF

Is the UK suffering a housing crisis?

The UK is experiencing a housing crisis. It is estimated that at least an extra 223,000 new houses or flats are needed every year to meet demand. The government has set the building industry a target: by the year 2016 it wants to see 240,000 homes being built every year. That's an extra 3 million homes between 2007 and 2020. But where should these new homes be built? The greatest demand is in the South East of England. The economy is strongest in the South East, so this is an area where many younger people are moving to from other parts of the UK and from other EU countries.

Figure 5 Number of new homes needed by 2026 in each of the Regional Assemblies in England

Key
Number of new houses that need to be built by 2026

- more than 700,000
- 600,000 – 699,000
- 500,000 – 599,000
- 400,000 – 499,000
- 300,000 – 399,000
- less than 300,000

Brownfield or greenfield?

A lot of new house building took place after the Second World War. New suburban homes were built on the edges of UK cities and the term **urban sprawl** was used to describe the resulting uncontrolled growth. UK planners at the time were so concerned about the loss of countryside that they prevented further loss by creating green belts: wide zones around many UK cities within which new developments were restricted. Green belts currently occupy 13 per cent of total land area in England. Many people living in smaller towns and rural areas of the South East are reluctant to see new housing development on any **greenfield site** whether it is on existing green belt land or any other farmland. An alternative is to use a **brownfield site**. In other words, new homes could be built on derelict sites within cities. Apart from preventing the loss of green spaces this has other advantages which make this a more sustainable option:

- Residents will use existing services such as public transport, schools and shops, which helps to maintain demand for these services and keeps them running.
- The city remains compact rather than sprawling outwards. This reduces commuting distances from home to work.

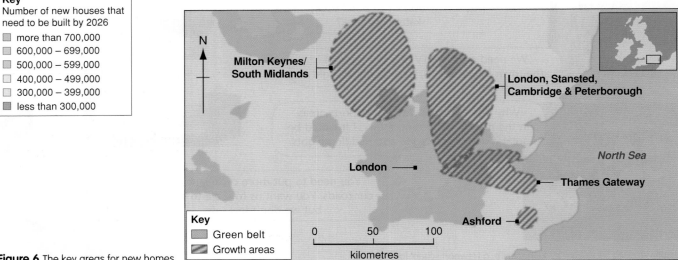

Key
- Green belt
- Growth areas

0   50   100
kilometres

Figure 6 The key areas for new homes

Figure 7 Why do we need so many new houses in the East and South East regions?

We are living longer: In 2003, the population over 65 was 11 million people: by 2026 it is estimated that this will increase to 13 million people. With better health, more elderly people are staying in their home, which means property is not freed up for the next generation.

Population increase: With a combination of natural increase (more births than deaths), migration into the region from other parts of the UK and immigration (e.g. economic migrants from Eastern Europe), the population of the East is expected to grow by 10 per cent (compared with the UK growth rate of 6.7 per cent).

Increasing number of people living alone: A lot of young adults choose to live alone. Also more marriages are breaking up, so there is a need for more homes to accommodate the split families (the divorce rate has actually slowed in recent years).

Why do we need so many new houses in the East and South East?

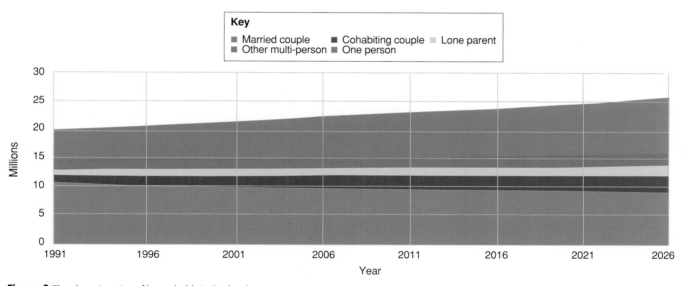

Figure 8 The changing size of households in England

Activity

1 Use Figure 5.
  a) Describe the pattern in England. Which regions will need to provide most new housing?
  b) Suggest why some regions need more new homes than others.

2 a) List five groups who might oppose plans for new housing and five who might benefit from it.
  b) Explain why many people will be concerned that new homes are being planned for green belt areas.

3 Use Figure 8.
  a) Roughly how many households were in each category in 1991 and how many will there be in 2026?
  b) Compare the trend in married couples with one-person households over this period.
  c) Use Figure 7 to explain the trends you can see in Figure 8.

4 Write a short article for your local newspaper explaining why new homes are needed. Keep your article factual and between 300 and 500 words long.

Suffolk

Recognising conflicting viewpoints – a planning dilemma

In 2004 the draft East of England Plan recognised the need for nearly 500,000 new homes to be built in the East of England by the year 2021. The plan required 58,000 of these to be built in Suffolk with a minimum of 10,000 to be constructed in Suffolk Coastal District.

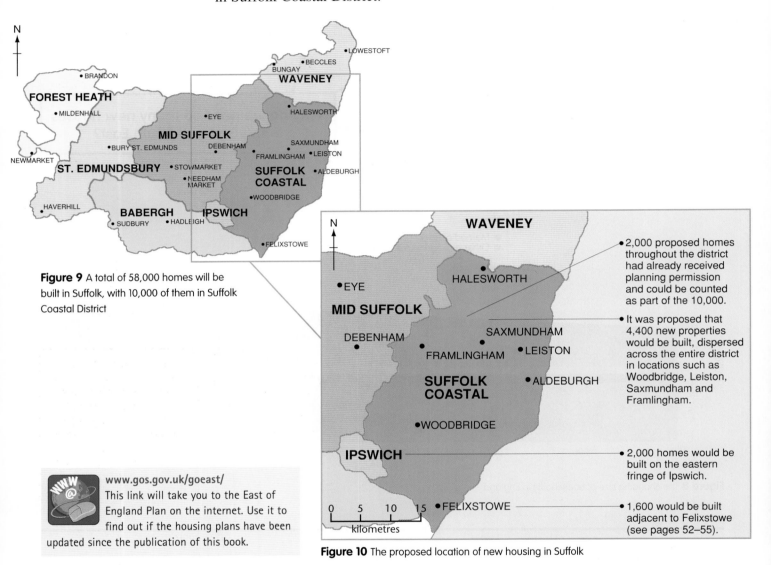

Figure 9 A total of 58,000 homes will be built in Suffolk, with 10,000 of them in Suffolk Coastal District

www.gos.gov.uk/goeast/
This link will take you to the East of England Plan on the internet. Use it to find out if the housing plans have been updated since the publication of this book.

- 2,000 proposed homes throughout the district had already received planning permission and could be counted as part of the 10,000.
- It was proposed that 4,400 new properties would be built, dispersed across the entire district in locations such as Woodbridge, Leiston, Saxmundham and Framlingham.
- 2,000 homes would be built on the eastern fringe of Ipswich.
- 1,600 would be built adjacent to Felixstowe (see pages 52–55).

Figure 10 The proposed location of new housing in Suffolk

Activity

1 Copy and complete the following description:

Suffolk Coastal District is west/east of Ipswich. It is one of six/seven rural districts in the county of Suffolk. The largest settlement in SCDC is Felixstowe which is approx ...... km to the north/north-west/south-east of Ipswich.

2 **a)** Describe the distribution of proposed new housing in Figure 10.
   b) Suggest reasons why the largest clusters are close to Ipswich and Felixstowe.
   c) Suggest why so many houses will be dispersed across the district.
   d) Suggest who might object to building these new houses, and who might support their construction.

How influential are the views of stakeholders?

Stakeholders are invited to participate in this planning process. They can attempt to persuade local authorities to change their plans. Sometimes they offer new, alternative ideas. After the consultation period is over, the planners will state their preferred options and publish definite plans. Even at this point, stakeholders can comment in the hope of affecting decisions. After all the stakeholder views are taken into account, the final decision is made by the elected council.

You will recognise that the views of some stakeholders might be taken more seriously than others. Some people try to prevent change because of the effect it will have on their own home or quality of life. They have what is called a 'not-in-my-back-yard' (**NIMBY**) attitude. Planners listen to such viewpoints but they must balance any negative social, economic or environmental impacts of a scheme against the needs identified in the LDF. In fact, most of the power is in the hands of two groups:

- the officers employed by the Planning Authorities who prepare the LDF
- the local councillors who vote on each plan.

However, if the councillors make unpopular decisions, anyone aged 18 or over can vote against them next time there is a local election.

Figure 11 Examples of views of different stakeholders considering change in South Suffolk

Councillor	**Business owner – haulier**	**Elderly lady**	**Environmentalist**
I am a parish councillor and I speak on behalf of the village community. We are keen to increase the number of play facilities in our growing village. We want a small park for the younger children with swings and slides, and a floodlit all-weather football pitch for the teenagers. We have to persuade the council to build on the old derelict recreation ground.	I own a large fleet of lorries taking goods in and out of the port. My drivers complain that there is a lack of rest places along the feeder roads. The authority needs to create lorry parks that have toilet and refreshment facilities.	I've lived in this quiet village for 50 years and now I hear that they want to build 30 affordable houses. It will change the character of the village. I must try to stop the plans.	I've no objection to new housing, not least the building of affordable homes for local people. However, they must select a brownfield site, not an area of green belt where we stand to lose more countryside.

Activity

3 Discuss the views expressed in Figure 11.
   a) Identify one NIMBY point of view.
   b) Identify one view that is considering a sustainable future.
   c) Of the four views, which views would you take more seriously, and why?

4 Using the search engine of your local newspaper, find examples of pressure groups, individuals and stakeholders who have participated in the consultation process outlined in a local LDF.

Investigating the options around Felixstowe

Suffolk Coastal District Council (SCDC) needed to consider the views of stakeholders in the communities where houses might be built. To do this they produced sketch maps showing the possible location of the new housing. Figure 12 is an example of one of these sketch maps. It shows the five potential sites that could be used to accommodate 1,600 homes and the associated community facilities close to Felixstowe. SCDC says that the proposals in their Local Development Framework:

- are for sustainable housing communities
- guarantee that one third of the houses will be 'affordable'
- are sensitive to reducing any social, economic and environmental impacts.

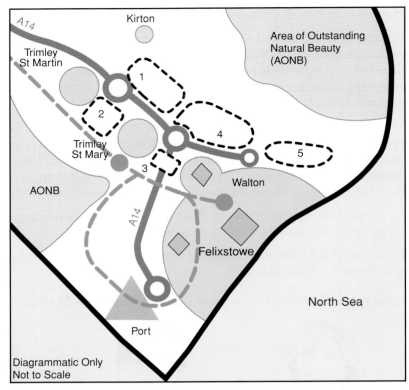

Figure 12 Planners' sketch map of five possible sites for the housing near Felixstowe

Figure 13 The fields at site 2 between the two Trimley communities

Activity

1 Study Figures 12, 13 and 14.
   a) Suggest three possible reasons why people living in Trimley St Mary and Trimley St Martin might object to sites 2 or 3.
   b) Explain what is meant by a sustainable housing community.

Figure 14 Ordnance Survey extract of the Trimley area, showing the areas where development is possible. Scale 1:25,000, Sheet 197. © Crown Copyright and/or database right. All rights reserved. Licence number 1000036470

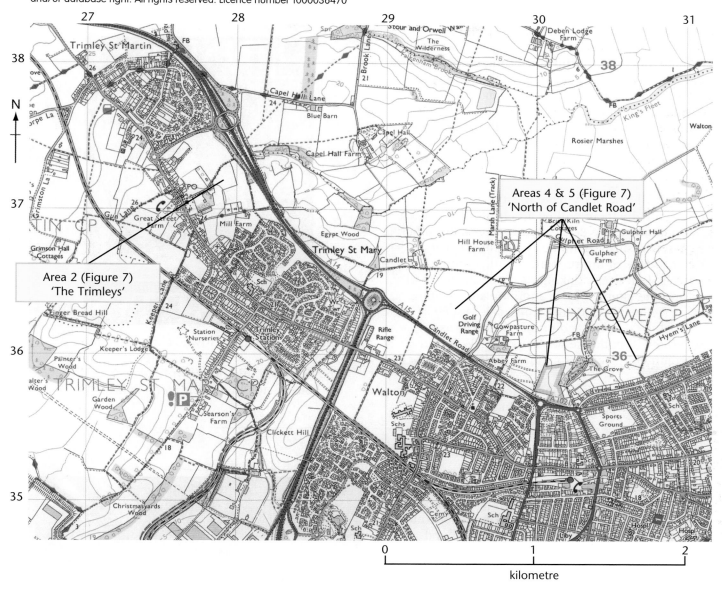

Activity

2 a) Use Figures 13 and 14 to choose adjectives that describe this landscape from the following pairs:

peaceful _ _ _ _ _ busy
natural _ _ _ _ _ artificial
modern _ _ _ _ _ traditional
friendly _ _ _ _ _ hostile

b) Use these and other adjectives to write a 200-word document that summarises a sense of place for this part of Suffolk.

3 a) Describe the feature found at each of the following six-figure grid references:

281361   296362   305355
291354   271377   277357

b) Use this and other evidence to write a 300-word document supporting the view that this area has sufficient transport, education and leisure facilities to be described as a sustainable community.

c) If 1,600 extra homes are built here, what additional services or transport links do you think will be needed? Justify your choice using evidence from the map.

What do the stakeholders think of the proposed development?

Figure 15 Stakeholder concerns about the development of Area 2

STAG is an informal group of like-minded villagers (from Trimley St Martin and Trimley St Mary). They have used the consultation period to voice their concerns about developing land between the two existing villages. The main fear is that the 'village-style life', enjoyed by both communities, will be lost when the area becomes a suburban landscape linked to Felixstowe and possibly to Ipswich in future years.

- We will lose our village lifestyle.
- Eventually there will be a Felixstowe–Ipswich continuum. We don't want to live in the suburbs.
- We will suffer building chaos for 20 years.
- The value of our properties will go down.
- The High Road, linking the two villages, will become jammed every morning and evening.
- There are not enough local services such as doctors, dentists and primary schools as it is.
- Who will build the new services? Will our community charges go up in order to pay for them?
- There will be disruption to local roads when they put in new power, water and telephone services.
- The A14 is already crowded and dangerous. Most of the new people will commute into Ipswich.
- They should build on brownfield sites or disperse the houses, not build them in one place.

Figure 16 Stakeholder concerns about the development of Areas 4 & 5

The 'Save Felixstowe Countryside' group is made up of a range of individuals, from all walks of life, who live in the Felixstowe area. Their single aim is to preserve the remaining countryside around Felixstowe for the benefit of local people, tourists and future generations.

- This is a high-quality rural landscape. It is valuable for walking, cycling and birdwatching. Local people and visitors alike enjoy it.
- It is a natural barrier between the Area of Outstanding Beauty and the town.
- Buildings will create light pollution that will disturb precious birds like kingfishers, marsh harriers and spotted woodpeckers.
- Further wildlife disturbance to brown hares and otters will be caused by noise and the presence of domestic cats and dogs.
- Most of the land is valuable Grade 2 agricultural land. We need this land for growing food for future generations.
- The Council talks about the need to include services and amenities as well as houses. How large will this area eventually be?
- Who will pay for the new power and drainage systems required – the hard-pressed ratepayers?
- Where will the allotment holders go?

Your decision

You have joined the planning team at SCDC for two weeks as part of your school's work experience programme. The senior manager wants you to have a taste of the problems and issues faced by planners who work for local authorities.

You are only working for two weeks at the planning office, so the planners have not given you the thousands of responses they have received following the draft proposals published in the LDF. They want you just to focus on the responses received about areas 2, 4 and 5. If the planning issue were this simple, which of the two sites would you recommend as a way of moving forward?

Make a copy of the matrix and use it to organise your initial ideas. On the matrix you should select a maximum of five issues from Figures 15 and 16. Try to select a range as some of the concerns overlap. Suggest if the issue relates to a social (SO), economic (EC) or environmental (EN) concern. Some of the issues may overlap these concerns. State why you think the issue relates to sustainability. Two rows have been completed for you.

Group	Issue selected from Figures 10 and 11	Social (SO)? Economic (EC)? Environmental (EN)?	Why is this a concern in terms of a sustainable future?
STAG (Save Trimley Against Growth)	We will suffer building chaos for 20 years	SO + EC	Villagers might decide to leave the area, splitting up friends and neighbours and forcing them to sell their houses cheaply.
SFC (Save Felixstowe Countryside)	We will lose an area of high-quality rural landscape	EN + EC	People need places for leisure as well as houses. If we build here local people have nowhere to walk dogs, and tourists will stop coming to Felixstowe, causing job losses.

What is a sustainable community?

The BedZED community shown in Figure 17 is a **sustainable community** of 82 homes built in Beddington, Surrey by a housing association called the Peabody Trust. The homes use green technologies to reduce their energy consumption. The development only uses renewable energy sources: solar energy and woodchips. A boiler uses waste woodchips to create both heat and power for all the homes. The Trust claim that BedZED is a **carbon-neutral development** – in other words, the homes do not add any extra carbon dioxide emissions to the atmosphere.

The houses have created a lot of media interest and the residents are proud of their 'green' homes. The UK needs many more new homes and, because of problems created by **climate change**, the government wants many more carbon-neutral schemes to be built. In fact, the government says 3 million new homes will be needed in the UK by 2020. But building so many new houses is bound to create conflict as local residents often object to new housing being built close to their homes. A priority for both the government and the developers is that any new housing developments are seen by local communities as sustainable. They should:

- create a better quality of life for people living there today
- use resources in such a way that future generations can also have a decent quality of life.

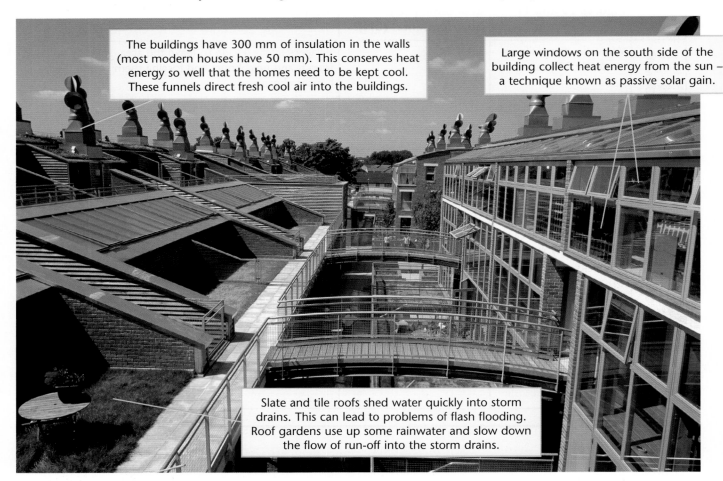

The buildings have 300 mm of insulation in the walls (most modern houses have 50 mm). This conserves heat energy so well that the homes need to be kept cool. These funnels direct fresh cool air into the buildings.

Large windows on the south side of the building collect heat energy from the sun – a technique known as passive solar gain.

Slate and tile roofs shed water quickly into storm drains. This can lead to problems of flash flooding. Roof gardens use up some rainwater and slow down the flow of run-off into the storm drains.

www.peabody.org.uk/
The Peabody Trust is a Housing Association providing social housing at a fair rent to its tenants. It is responsible for the BedZED development shown in Figure 12. Follow the links to new developments to read more.

www.eco-schools.org.uk/
This site describes how to audit your own school so that you can see how green it is.

Figure 17 The Beddington Zero Energy Development (BedZED) is the UK's largest carbon-neutral eco-community – the first of its kind in the UK

Figure 18 Web extract from the Peabody Trust

What are the features of BedZED?

The design is to a very high standard and is used to enhance the environmental dimensions, with strong emphasis on roof gardens, sunlight, solar energy, reduction of energy consumption and waste water recycling.

BedZED provides 82 residential homes with a mixture of tenures, 34 for outright sale, 23 for shared ownership, 10 for key workers and 15 at affordable rent for social housing – with a further 14 galleried apartments for outright sale.

The homes are a mixture of sizes and the project also includes buildings for commercial use, an exhibition centre, a children's nursery and a show flat so that visitors may see what it is like to live at BedZED.

Using renewable materials

Where possible, BedZED is built from natural, recycled or reclaimed materials. All the wood used has been approved by the Forest Stewardship Council or comparable internationally recognised environmental organisations, to ensure that it comes from a sustainable source.

Space heating

Through the innovative design and construction, heat from the sun and heat generated by occupants and everyday activities such as cooking are sufficient to heat BedZED homes to a comfortable temperature. The need for space heating, which accounts for a significant part of the energy demand in conventional buildings, is therefore reduced or completely eliminated.

Green transport plan

Transport energy accounts for a large proportion of the energy consumption of any development.

A green transport plan promotes walking, cycling and use of public transport. A car pool for residents has been established, and all these initiatives have helped to provide a strategic and integrated approach to transport issues.

The BedZED project shows that it is possible to reduce reliance on cars and it introduced the first legally binding Green Transport Plan as a condition of planning permission.

BedZED's target is a 50 per cent reduction in fossil-fuel consumption by private car use over the next ten years compared with a conventional development.

Figure 19 Possible features of a sustainable community

Activity

1 Discuss the features in Figure 17.
   Use this and the eco-schools website (www.eco-schools.org.uk/) to audit (list the good and bad features of) your own school. How could your community be more sustainable?

2 Study Figure 18. Explain how the BedZED development:
   a) caters for at least three different groups of people
   b) reduces carbon emissions in three different ways
   c) reduces people's use of cars.

3 Discuss Figure 19.
   a) For each feature in the diagram, suggest how it might be sustainable.
   b) Suggest at least two of the features that might be controversial. Which groups of people might come into conflict over these suggestions?
   c) Suggest at least two more features that you think are necessary in a new sustainable community.

Planning sustainable residential areas to combat climate change

Climate change could have serious effects in large cities where heatwaves could become much more common. During heatwaves there are more days when people suffer from the uncomfortable effects of heat stress. In severe conditions, heatwaves can cause death, especially in the very young and very old. During the heatwave of August 2003, the temperature in central London was 9°C higher than the surrounding countryside. Paris too was exceptionally hot and the extreme conditions caused at least 14,000 deaths in France.

The buildings and traffic in a large city influence the local climate, an effect known as **urban micro-climate**. One of the main impacts that a city has on the local climate is to create temperatures that are warmer than in the surrounding rural area. This is known as the **urban heat island.** The city acts like a massive storage heater, transferring heat from buildings and cars to the dome of air that covers the city.

- During the day, concrete, brick and tarmac absorb heat from the sun. This heat is then radiated into the atmosphere during the evening and at night.
- Buildings that are badly insulated lose heat energy, especially through roofs and windows. Heat is also created in cars and factories and this heat is also lost to the air from exhausts and chimneys.

Scientists know that the combination of climate change and the urban heat island are causing stress in some cities in the northern hemisphere. Figure 22 provides evidence of rising heat island effects in New York, Paris and Tokyo.

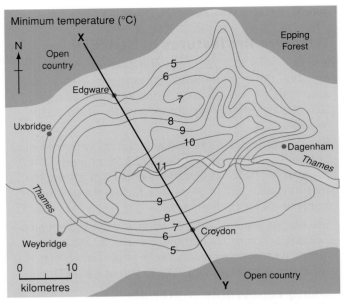

Figure 20 London's urban heat island, night-time temperatures in mid-May

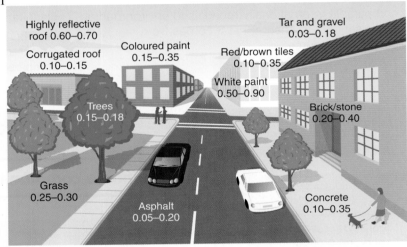

Figure 21 How the urban environment reflects the sun's energy. The closer the number to 1.0 the more energy is reflected. Surfaces with very low numbers are absorbing more of the sun's energy. They then emit this heat at night

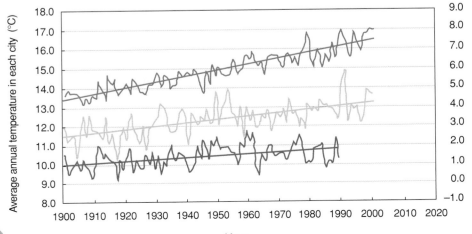

Figure 22 Trends in average urban temperatures in Tokyo, New York and Paris

What can be done about the urban heat island?

As temperatures rise more people install air-conditioning in their homes, but air-conditioning uses a lot of electrical energy. The production of more electricity creates the greenhouse gases that are causing climate change. It is estimated that the use of an air-conditioner for just one year in a hot climate such as Florida produces more CO_2 than a person in Cambodia produces in a lifetime. Figure 23 examines how the impact of the urban heat island could be reduced in the future.

> We need to reduce energy use. All new buildings must be well insulated to reduce heat loss. We need to design cars and air-conditioning that use less energy and have low emissions of greenhouse gases.

Engineer

Scientist

> We should create a network of parks so that the wind can blow through our cities and remove some of the heat. Cold groundwater can be pumped through pipes in our underground train stations. That would cool the air. The roofs of buildings can be coated in light-coloured materials to reflect sunshine.

> We need more green spaces. Parks reflect more of the sun's energy. More trees must be planted. The shade from trees reduces air temperatures. Trees soak up carbon dioxide and pollution from traffic.

Urban planner

Politician

> People need to change their lifestyles. People should take long holidays away from the city in the summer. We need to cut traffic by encouraging car users to switch to public transport. We can do this by congestion charging, as in Central London.

Figure 23 Possible ways of reducing the urban heat island

Activity

1 Use Figure 20.
   a) Describe the location of the area of highest temperatures in London.
   b) Describe the distribution of places with lower temperatures.
   c) Suggest reasons for the pattern shown on the map.

2 Use Figure 20 to draw a cross section of London's urban heat island along the line x–y.

3 a) Use Figure 22 to compare the urban temperatures in each city.
   b) Use the trend to predict the urban temperatures in each city by 2020.

4 Use Figures 21 and 23 to explain how the creation of more parks, woodlands and lakes in our cities might:
   a) affect the urban micro-climate
   b) make urban areas more sustainable in the future.

5 Use Figure 23 to outline the arguments for and against each of the following:

Strategy to reduce the urban heat island	Arguments for	Arguments against	Who might oppose this plan
Create more green spaces			
Reduce number of cars			
Design better homes			

Geography Futures

A planning conflict. Do we need another airport?

The growth of air travel, for business and tourism, has economic and environmental impacts. Environmental campaigners are concerned about the emission of carbon dioxide from air travel which adds to the **greenhouse effect**. They also oppose the expansion of airports. Those who work in the aviation industry point out that the growth in the number of flights is good for the UK economy as more foreign tourists visit the UK. They say we need new runways so that more planes can use UK airports.

Figure 24 The number of passengers (millions) travelling through UK airports, 1950–2007

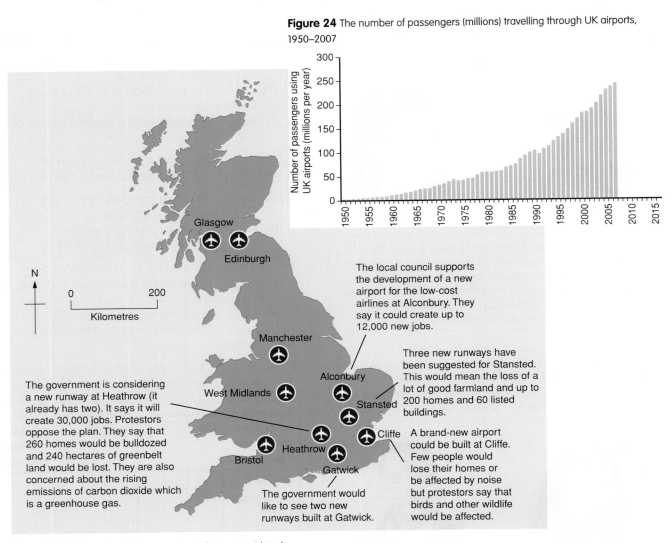

Figure 25 UK airports where expansion is being considered

The local council supports the development of a new airport for the low-cost airlines at Alconbury. They say it could create up to 12,000 new jobs.

Three new runways have been suggested for Stansted. This would mean the loss of a lot of good farmland and up to 200 homes and 60 listed buildings.

The government is considering a new runway at Heathrow (it already has two). It says it will create 30,000 jobs. Protestors oppose the plan. They say that 260 homes would be bulldozed and 240 hectares of greenbelt land would be lost. They are also concerned about the rising emissions of carbon dioxide which is a greenhouse gas.

A brand-new airport could be built at Cliffe. Few people would lose their homes or be affected by noise but protestors say that birds and other wildlife would be affected.

The government would like to see two new runways built at Gatwick.

Activity

1 Study Figure 24.
   a) Describe how the number of people using UK airports changed:
      i) between 1950 and 1983
      ii) between 1983 and 2007.
   b) Use evidence from the graph to predict how many passengers could be using UK airports by 2015.

Local resident, close to Heathrow

We are angry and depressed. It's as if our community has been on death row for six years while government considers the third runway plan. We will fight these plans in the courts.

The growth of air traffic in the UK is undermining the government target to reduce carbon emissions. Here at Plane Stupid we believe that the planned new runway at Heathrow should be scrapped. Internal flights should also be banned and people encouraged to use railways instead.

Climate change protester

Estate agent

Noise from landing and take-off already affects thousands of home-owners. This can have a negative affect on house prices. No one wants to risk buying a house in an area where an airport may be expanded.

The continued growth of air travel is essential, so we need to expand our airports. We need better airports so that more tourists visit the UK. We believe that carbon dioxide from aircraft can be reduced in the future by use of better technology such as cleaner, more efficient aircraft engines.

Government minister

Figure 26 Opposing views on the growth of air travel and the expansion of UK airports

Airport	2005	2015	2030
Heathrow	65	80	135
Gatwick	35	35	40
Stanstead	20	35	55
Luton	10	15	15
London City	2	4	5
Total for all London airports	**132**	**169**	**250**
Other UK airports	93	139	203
Total for all UK airports	**225**	**308**	**453**

Figure 27 Predicted growth in the number of passengers using UK airports (millions of people per year). Source: www.dft.gov.uk/pgr/aviation/atf/co2forecasts09/co2forecasts09.pdf

Activity

2 Study Figures 25 and 27.
  a) Draw a sketch map of south-east England and show the location of the airports.
  b) Use the information in Figure 27 to add symbols and labels to your map to show by how much each airport is likely to expand.
  c) Suggest how this expansion might affect local communities.

Activity

3 Study Figures 25 and 26.
  a) Outline the arguments for and against expanding existing airports.
  b) Sort your arguments under these headings:
     Environmental   Economic   Social

4 Would it be better to expand Heathrow or build a new airport to the east of London? Use the resources here, and the internet, to research these options. Create a poster that persuades people to support whichever you think is the better idea.

GIS Activity: Eurostat and Defra

http://epp.eurostat.ec.europa.eu

Eurostat is the official website for statistics that cover the members of the EU. Use this weblink to go to the home page. Then, on the right of the screen, follow the link to Country Profiles (which has a thumbnail map of the EU) to get to the GIS. Figure 28 is an example of the kind of map you can produce.

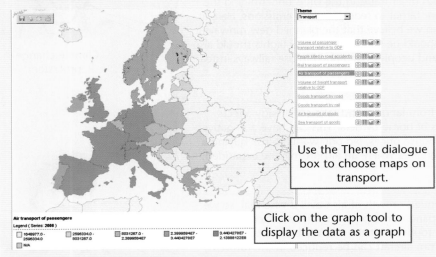

Use the Theme dialogue box to choose maps on transport.

Click on the graph tool to display the data as a graph

Figure 28 Map of air transport created by the Eurostat GIS

Activity

1 Use the website to investigate the following hypotheses:
   a) Air transport of passengers has grown fastest in eastern European countries.
   b) Data for air transport of passengers shows evidence that the growth of this industry is now slowing.

GIS Activity: Defra Noise Mapping England website

http://services.defra.gov.uk/wps/portal/noise

Researching noise nuisance

Noise is a nuisance to people living under flight paths close to airports. The government believes that noise levels will stay similar to those of today, even as the number of planes increases, because newer planes are quieter. Defra, which is a government department, has mapped noise levels around the airports of England. Figure 29 shows the area immediately to the east of Heathrow.

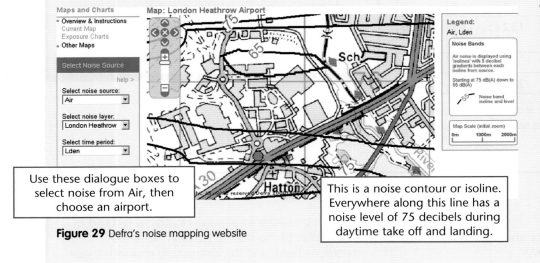

Use these dialogue boxes to select noise from Air, then choose an airport.

This is a noise contour or isoline. Everywhere along this line has a noise level of 75 decibels during daytime take off and landing.

Figure 29 Defra's noise mapping website

Activity

2 Use this GIS to compare the area affected by noise under Birmingham International Airport and Heathrow. Consider the number and size of residential areas that are affected by 60 decibels or more.

Chapter 5
Rural change and planning issues

Moving in or moving out?

Urban and rural are at different ends of a sliding scale known as the rural-urban continuum. The rural regions of Europe fall in different places on this continuum. Some are relatively accessible to large cities while others are extremely remote. Kent and Cambridgeshire in England, for example, contain many villages and small rural towns. But these rural communities are close to major transport routes, allowing them access to work, shops, education and entertainment available in London. The population of accessible rural areas such as this is growing. This process is known as **counter-urbanisation**. It is not possible to **commute** easily from the more remote regions of Europe. In some of these regions **rural depopulation** is occurring, as people leave the countryside to seek work in the city. In this chapter we will examine both of these trends, and the issues they create for rural communities.

| cities | urban-rural fringe | accessible rural region | remote rural region |

Figure 1 The rural-urban continuum

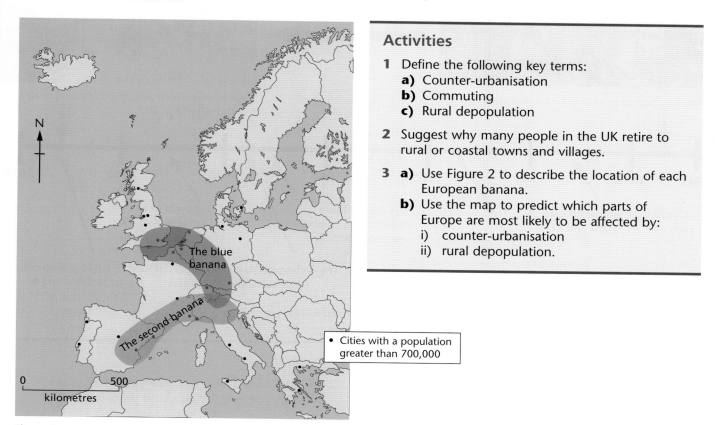

Figure 2 Europe's bananas. The two regions of Europe in which urban economies have grown fastest in the last 20 years and in which there is the most counter-urbanisation.

Activities

1 Define the following key terms:
   a) Counter-urbanisation
   b) Commuting
   c) Rural depopulation

2 Suggest why many people in the UK retire to rural or coastal towns and villages.

3 **a)** Use Figure 2 to describe the location of each European banana.
   b) Use the map to predict which parts of Europe are most likely to be affected by:
      i)   counter-urbanisation
      ii) rural depopulation.

Why do people want to move from the city to the country in MEDCs?

The migration of people from larger cities into towns and villages in the countryside is a process known as counter urbanisation. This process has created enormous change in the rural areas of many MEDCs, especially in western Europe. Cities are often seen as stressful places in which to live and work. The cost and difficulty of commuting through rush hour traffic; the lack of open space and places for children to play safely; noise; pollution and rising crime are all given as reasons for leaving the city. By contrast, life in a smaller town or village has many attractions. People are drawn to the peace and quiet; access to open countryside can reduce stress and tension; and lower numbers of cars may seem safer for parents who have young children.

How has technology contributed to change in the countryside?

The move from town to country first became popular in the UK in the 1960s and 70s. This was a period of rising car ownership and expansion of the motorway network. It became possible to commute from a home in the country to a job in the city. Since then, massive changes in communication technology have made it possible for increasing numbers of people to work from a home in the country. Writers, researchers and business consultants can spend most of the working week at a computer at home and only need to commute to the office for the occasional meeting. This type of work is known as **teleworking** or tele-cottaging.

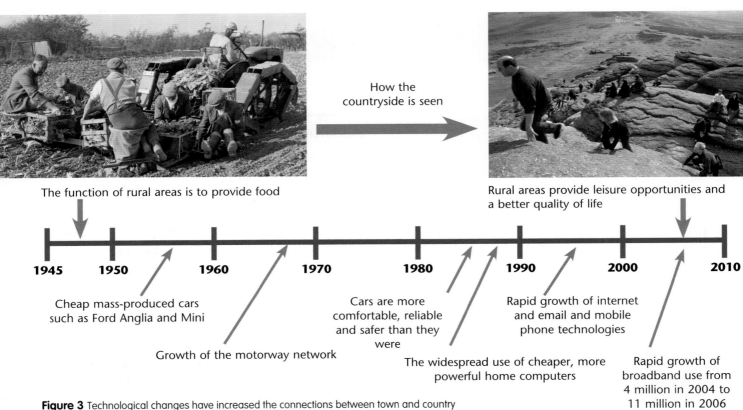

How the countryside is seen

The function of rural areas is to provide food

Rural areas provide leisure opportunities and a better quality of life

1945   1950   1960   1970   1980   1990   2000   2010

Cheap mass-produced cars such as Ford Anglia and Mini

Growth of the motorway network

Cars are more comfortable, reliable and safer than they were

The widespread use of cheaper, more powerful home computers

Rapid growth of internet and email and mobile phone technologies

Rapid growth of broadband use from 4 million in 2004 to 11 million in 2006

Figure 3 Technological changes have increased the connections between town and country

Activity

1 Study Figure 3. Use it to explain how technology has allowed:
   a) greater commuting
   b) greater use of the countryside for leisure
   c) more opportunities to move to the country and work from home.

2 Using Figure 3, suggest how you imagine the countryside might change 20 years from now.

Shropshire

How are rural populations changing?

In South Shropshire, in the West Midlands, the relatively high quality of life in the countryside appeals to a wide range of people including young professionals, families and the retired. What these people have in common is the ability to pay the relatively high prices of rural homes. However, the countryside doesn't appeal to everyone. Many teenagers living in this area move to cities elsewhere in the UK when they leave school. The lack of jobs, leisure facilities, shops, theatres and cinemas in the countryside are push factors, while the chance to go to university and the greater choice of jobs are pull factors for moving to a city. In addition, the cost of buying a house in the countryside is likely to prevent young people on lower incomes from staying in a rural area. So, newcomers to rural life often have different social and economic (or socio-economic) backgrounds from the local people they replace.

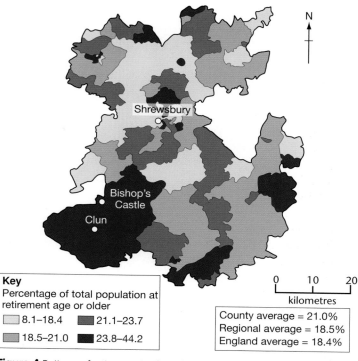

Figure 4 Patterns of retirement in Shropshire in different wards

Key
Percentage of total population at retirement age or older
□ 8.1–18.4 ■ 21.1–23.7
■ 18.5–21.0 ■ 23.8–44.2

0   10   20
kilometres

County average = 21.0%
Regional average = 18.5%
England average = 18.4%

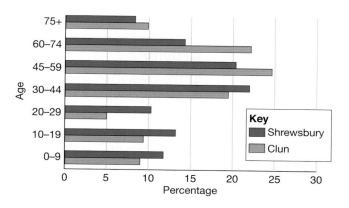

Figure 5 Comparing population structures in Shrewsbury and Clun

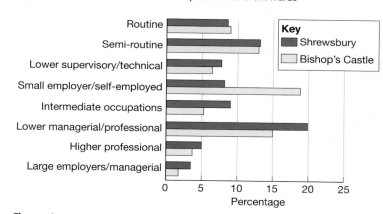

Figure 6 Comparing occupations in Shrewsbury and Bishop's Castle (Source: 2001 Census)

Activity

3 Use Figure 4 to describe the distribution of wards that have more than 23.8 per cent retired population.

4 Use Figure 5.
   a) Compare the population structure of Clun to that of Shrewsbury.
   b) Suggest two reasons for the differences you have noticed.

5 Use Figure 6.
   a) Compare occupations in Bishop's Castle and Shrewsbury.
   b) Use this evidence to explain why some younger adults are leaving south Shropshire.

6 Draw up a table like the one below. Add to the push and pull factors that cause movements in and out of rural areas like Shropshire.

Retired professional moving out of larger towns and into the countryside		Young adult moving out of the countryside and into larger towns	
Push factors	Pull factors	Push factors	Pull factors
	Peace and quiet	Few full-time jobs	

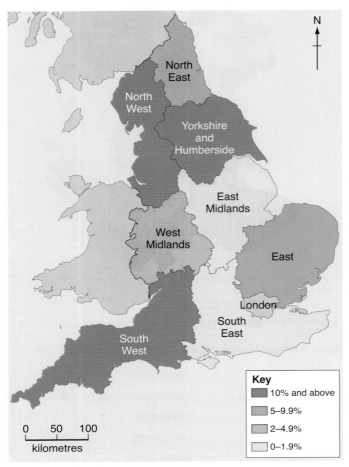

Figure 8 The percentage of homes in hamlets and isolated villages that are unoccupied because they are either second homes or rented out as holiday homes

Key
- 10% and above
- 5–9.9%
- 2–4.9%
- 0–1.9%

Change can lead to conflict: the lack of affordable homes

- Is it true that many young rural people can no longer afford to stay in the countryside because there is a lack of **affordable homes**?
- Is it true that too little new social housing is being built and that the sale of owner-occupied housing to newcomers is forcing up the price of rural homes?

Newcomers to a rural area often commute to a full-time job outside the rural area, whereas local residents may work locally. Commuters may do their shopping in a large retail park on the edge of the city where they work because by the time they get home the village shops have closed for the day. The result is that, as a village attracts more commuters, its shops may get fewer customers. Village pubs close and are converted to homes, bus services are axed, and local shops and banks may also close. The rise of internet banking has also badly affected small rural branches.

Activity

1 Give two different reasons for the closure of some rural banks and building societies.

2 Study Figure 7. Identify two main causes for the lack of affordable housing in rural areas.

3 Describe and explain the point of view expressed in the song lyrics in Figure 9.

4 Suggest why some rural areas have more second homes than others. Consider the effect of:
   a) distance from larger cities
   b) the attractiveness of the countryside.

5 Use an atlas or the internet to find a map of England's National Parks. Compare this map with Figure 8.

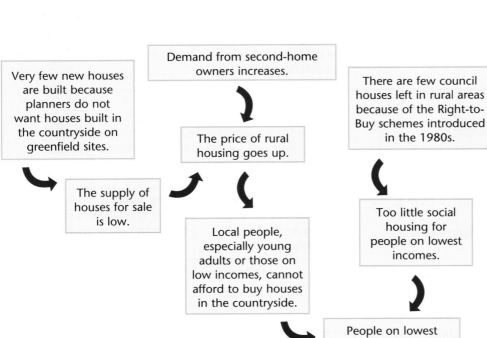

Figure 7 Rural housing issues

The second homes issue

The lack of affordable housing in rural areas is often linked to the sale of rural houses as **second homes** or holiday cottages. When a rural house is sold to be used as a second home at weekends or during holidays there are two effects:

1 One less house is available to local people. As we have seen, increasing demand for rural homes forces up rural house prices.
2 Even more village services are likely to close. Owners of second homes may spend only a few weeks of each year in their village home, so have little use for village services.

Figure 10 suggests that there are many different views about the function of the UK's countryside. This is partly because rural areas in the UK are so varied:

- Many small towns in the south-east have become commuter villages.
- Large parts of the south-east and east are used for growing cereal crops.

- Many coastal areas in the south-west are used for tourism.

Most second homes tend to be in the most scenic parts of England, especially in Devon, Cornwall, Cumbria and parts of Yorkshire. These areas are shown in Figure 8.

Within these large regions there is huge variation. The average number of second homes for England is 0.6 per cent, but this rises to as much as 12.6 per cent among isolated homes and tiny hamlets in north-west England. The Lake District National Park has an unusually high number of second homes. In the area surrounding the village of Hawkshead, seen in the centre of Figure 10, it is estimated that 40 per cent of all homes are second homes or holiday cottages.

Figure 9 An extract from the lyrics of Country Life by folk group Show of Hands

> *And the red brick cottage where I was born*
> *Is the empty shell of a holiday home.*
> *Most of the year there's no one there,*
> *The village is dead and they don't care.*
> *Now we live on the edge of town.*
> *Haven't been back since the pub closed down.*
> *One man's family pays the price*
> *For another man's vision of country life.*

A safe place for wildlife?

A place to retire?

Homes for commuters?

Farming and food production?

A holiday retreat?

Somewhere to go walking, riding and fishing?

Figure 10 What is the countryside for?

How recreation can damage our countryside

The increased leisure use of rural areas can cause conflict with local people or conservationists. Visitors may disturb the peace of local residents, park in gateways, leave gates open, drop litter or allow their dogs to chase farm animals or scare ground nesting birds. These problems can become severe if the visitors are concentrated into one geographical area, perhaps somewhere that is particularly accessible and scenic. Such places are known as **honeypot sites**. In some instances, the environment of honeypot sites is physically damaged by visitor pressure. For example, in some parts of Snowdonia or the Peak District, footpaths have become eroded, leaving scars in the landscape.

Figure 11 Footpath erosion in the Lake District. The sign asks walkers to keep to the footpath.

Figure 12 Causes of footpath erosion

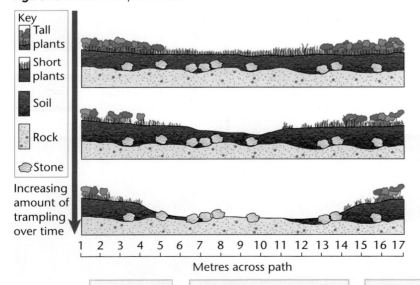

Key
- Tall plants
- Short plants
- Soil
- Rock
- Stone

Increasing amount of trampling over time

1 2 3 4 5 6 7 8 9 10 11 12 13 14 15 16 17
Metres across path

| Plants die | Soil is exposed to rainwater | Soil is eroded by rain splash and gulley erosion |

| The path becomes wider and wider | Plants are short and stunted where they have been trampled |

| Walkers avoid the central muddy section of path so walk at the edge | Stones are exposed as soil is eroded |

Activity

1 **a)** Make a copy of Figure 12.
  b) Add a suitable label for each stage of the diagram.
  c) Copy the statements and put them in order to show why the path gets wider over time.

2 **a)** Why does the sign in Figure 11 ask walkers to keep to the path, even though the path is already damaged?
  b) Suggest why it is difficult to manage environments like the one in Figure 11.

Ynyslas

How can rural environments under pressure from visitors be managed?

Figure 13 A view across the Ynyshir nature reserve looking north-west over the estuary towards Aberdyfi

Figure 14 The Countryside Council for Wales says the dunes have a strong sense of place. The 'everchanging landforms as well as distinct vegetation patterns provide constant interest. Views in all directions from higher dunes provide constant drama'

The Dyfi estuary is a beautiful rural environment that attracts many visitors each year. People visit this part of West Wales for relaxation on the beach or in the dunes or to enjoy a number of leisure activities that include walking, riding, sailing and birdwatching.

The Dyfi estuary was classed as a Site of Special Scientific Interest (SSSI) in the 1950s. This was because the Dyfi was seen to be one of the best, most unspoilt estuaries in the west of Britain. Much of the estuary, including the sand dunes at Ynyslas at the mouth of the estuary, became a National Nature

Reserve (NNR) in 1969. An OS map that includes this part of the Reserve can be seen on page 175. The area is managed by the Countryside Council for Wales (CCW). This organisation has two main aims:

- 'to protect, maintain and, if possible, to enhance the wildlife of the reserves and their outstanding physical features'
- 'to allow as much public access as is compatible with the primary aims of conservation and research'.

There is a natural tension between these two aims. If too many people visit a site such as Ynyslas they could disturb wildlife or even damage fragile physical features such as the sand dunes themselves.

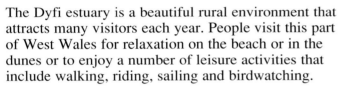

Figure 15 Results of a survey of 224 visitors to Ynyslas sand dunes

Trip purpose	Number
Informal visit to relax	94
To walk dog	56
Walk	49
Landscape appreciation	36
Family outing	25
Active sport	18
Nature watching	13
Picnic	11
Educational visit	9
Specialist interest	2
Other	18

Activity

3 a) The CCW describes the sand dunes as 'attractive, exposed and wild'. Discuss and choose three words to sum up the landscape in Figure 13.
   b) Read the caption to Figure 14. What would you say are the distinctive characteristics of the estuary as a whole?

4 a) Choose a suitable graphical technique to represent the data in Figure 15.
   b) Suggest which, if any, of these reasons for visiting the reserve might conflict with the aim of:
      i) conserving wildlife
      ii) conserving landscape features.

Changing styles of management at Ynyslas

Conservation management of the sand dunes at Ynyslas began in 1969 when the area was designated as a National Nature Reserve. During the 1960s some parts of the dune system had been damaged by off-road vehicles. In some places the marram grass, the roots of which help to bind the loose sand, had been destroyed by people driving into and parking in the dunes. The wind had then eroded huge hollows in the **windward** slopes of the dune system creating ugly scars known as blow-outs. The management strategies used by wardens at Ynyslas have gradually changed since 1969. These changes are summarised in Figure 16.

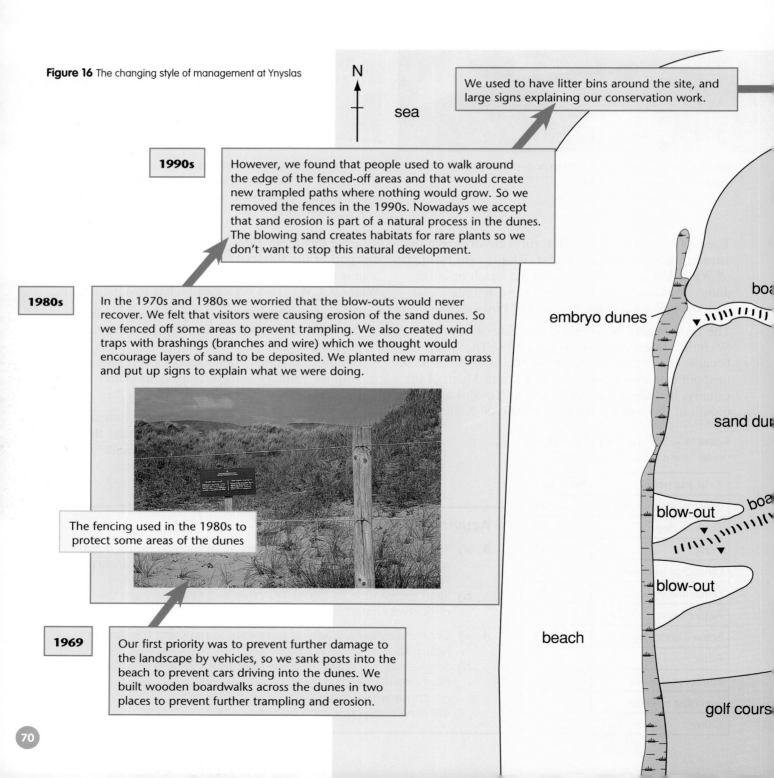

Figure 16 The changing style of management at Ynyslas

N

sea

1990s

We used to have litter bins around the site, and large signs explaining our conservation work.

However, we found that people used to walk around the edge of the fenced-off areas and that would create new trampled paths where nothing would grow. So we removed the fences in the 1990s. Nowadays we accept that sand erosion is part of a natural process in the dunes. The blowing sand creates habitats for rare plants so we don't want to stop this natural development.

1980s

In the 1970s and 1980s we worried that the blow-outs would never recover. We felt that visitors were causing erosion of the sand dunes. So we fenced off some areas to prevent trampling. We also created wind traps with brashings (branches and wire) which we thought would encourage layers of sand to be deposited. We planted new marram grass and put up signs to explain what we were doing.

The fencing used in the 1980s to protect some areas of the dunes

1969

Our first priority was to prevent further damage to the landscape by vehicles, so we sank posts into the beach to prevent cars driving into the dunes. We built wooden boardwalks across the dunes in two places to prevent further trampling and erosion.

embryo dunes

boa

sand du

blow-out

boa

blow-out

beach

golf cours

Activity

1 Study Figure 16. Use it to complete the following table. You should be able to identify at least four issues.

Issue	Management strategy	Evaluation of strategy
1		
2		

2 Produce a short report on management at Ynyslas. In it you must identify:
a) why people visit
b) the two main aims of the wardens
c) how and why management strategies have changed
d) how you think management of the dunes should change in future.

A lot of rabbits live in the dunes. They keep the grass short and stop it from choking the less competitive flowering plants. The rabbit dung makes the soil much more fertile and as many as 40 different species of flowering plants can grow in just 1 square metre. Also some birds nest in the abandoned rabbit burrows. So we like to have a healthy population of rabbits. However, our neighbour is the golf course. They don't want too many rabbits burrowing into the putting greens and creating damage. So we erected a rabbit-proof fence along our southern boundary. The problem is that this fence now has holes in it and will be costly to maintain.

We found that the litter bins used to overflow and rubbish blew about, so we got rid of all the bins.

2000s

Lots of song birds live in the dunes including linnet, stonechat, skylark and meadow pipit. We have one area where ringed plovers breed. These small birds nest on the ground and are easily disturbed. So we have fenced off the shingle area where they nest.

-out

parking area

posts to prevent cars driving into the dunes

visitor centre

In recent years we have enlarged and improved the visitor centre and the boardwalks. Now anyone can easily cross the site to get to the beach. Wheelchair users can access the visitor centre along the boardwalks.

The boardwalk and visitor centre

road

caravan park

One of our biggest management problems today is dog fouling. People are banned from walking their dogs in the summer months on Borth beach to the south. So they come up to Ynyslas to walk their dogs. The problem is that there are very few bacteria in the sandy soil so the dog excrement does not bio-degrade. It lies around for ages and is a nuisance for other visitors.

2009

Pyramidal orchids

71

Iceland

How is leisure use affecting rural Iceland?

Iceland has only one major city, the capital Reykjavik. Many wealthy residents of Reykjavik own second homes in the countryside so they can get away from the city at the weekend. This is a form of counter-urbanisation. Most second homes are located in the 'Golden Circle' region: a rural area about one hour's drive to the east of Reykjavik. This area contains many of Iceland's most popular attractions such as Geysir and Gullfoss.

The construction of second homes and the growth of tourism are changing this rural community and these changes could create conflict. Locals could feel swamped by newcomers: Grimsnes (in grid square 0221), just one housing development in the Golden Circle, has more than 1,500 holiday homes but has only 356 permanent residents.

The recreational use of rural areas by visitors from Reykjavik is also causing conflict. Off-road driving in the rural regions of Iceland is popular, but the tyre tracks and deep ruts are scarring the landscape. The Environment and Food Agency of Iceland is so concerned about this damage that most off-road driving has been banned since 1999.

Figure 17 There are more than 1,500 holiday homes like this in Grimsnes

Figure 18 The construction of new holiday homes in Selfoss (grid ref: 0118 in Figure 20) creates valuable local employment

Activity

1 Use Figure 20.
   a) Give a four-figure grid reference for Geysir (north-east corner of the map).
   b) Use the map to give directions and approximate distances to travel from Grimsnes to Geysir.
   c) Give four pieces of evidence that the area is heavily used by tourists.

2 Describe two ways in which counter-urbanisation could create conflict in Iceland's rural regions.

3 Suggest the arguments for and against the building of more second homes and holiday homes in Grimsnes.

4 Study Figure 19. Give three reasons why soils in Iceland are at great risk of erosion.

5 Suggest why wilderness regions, such as Figure 19, are so attractive to visitors.

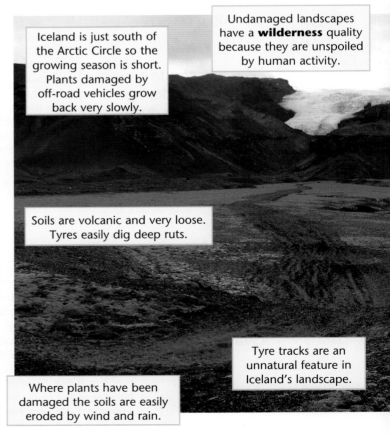

Iceland is just south of the Arctic Circle so the growing season is short. Plants damaged by off-road vehicles grow back very slowly.

Undamaged landscapes have a **wilderness** quality because they are unspoiled by human activity.

Soils are volcanic and very loose. Tyres easily dig deep ruts.

Tyre tracks are an unnatural feature in Iceland's landscape.

Where plants have been damaged the soils are easily eroded by wind and rain.

Figure 19 Illegal off-road driving in Skaftafell National Park has left these tyre tracks

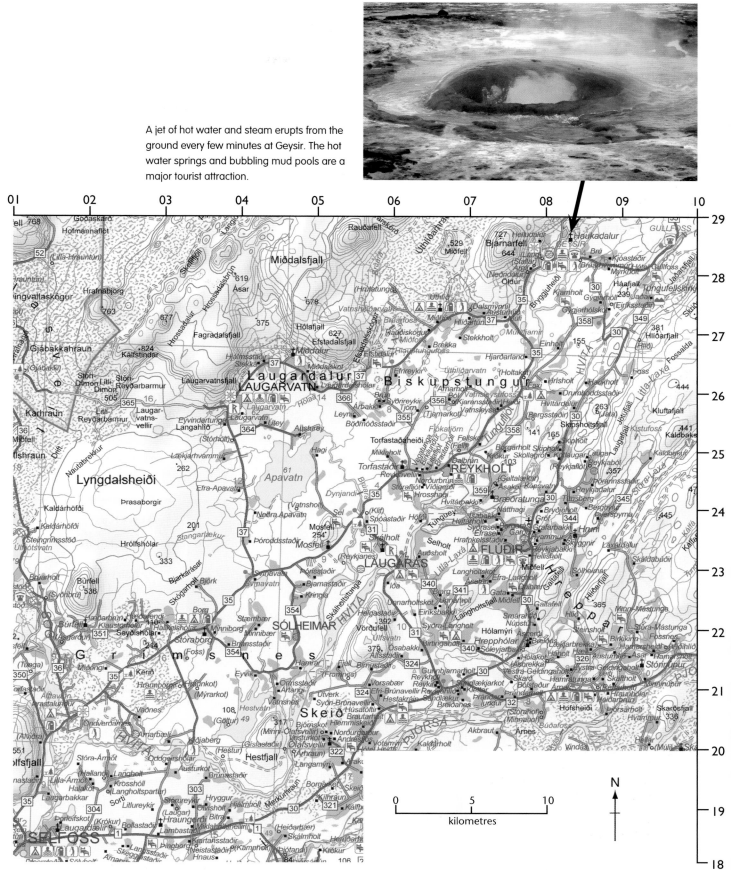

A jet of hot water and steam erupts from the ground every few minutes at Geysir. The hot water springs and bubbling mud pools are a major tourist attraction.

Figure 20 The Golden Circle region, east of Reykjavik. Grimsnes is in the south-west portion of the map (Scale 1:250,000)

Iceland

Is tourism good or bad for Iceland?

The waterfall at Gullfoss (which means 'Golden Falls') is one of Iceland's main tourist attractions. It has more than 300,000 visitors a year. Gullfoss and nearby Geysir are a little over one hour from Reykjavik by road. Many people come by coach as part of a tour of the 'Golden Circle' region. There is no fee to visit the waterfall itself, but visitors contribute in many ways to the local economy by:

- spending money in the large café and gift shop
- paying for a coach trip from Reykjavik (about £49 in 2012)
- hiring a car to visit the area
- staying overnight in one of the many local hotels and guesthouses
- eating in a local restaurant
- paying for a flight over the falls in a light aircraft
- paying for a local leisure activity such as whitewater rafting or horse riding.

All of this creates a lot of employment and business opportunities for local people. For example, many local farmers have converted their buildings to large guesthouses or have opened riding stables. The money earned by local people is then spent in local shops and businesses. This is an example of the **positive multiplier effect**.

Figure 21 A light aircraft takes tourists for a sightseeing flight over Gullfoss waterfall

Figure 22 Tourists at Gulfoss waterfall

Activity

1 Use Figures 21 and 22. Work in pairs to make a list of ten words that describe how people might be affected by experiencing this landscape.

Not all of the impacts of tourism are good for Iceland and its people. The peak of the tourist season to Iceland's rural areas is from June to August. Fewer people visit in the winter when it is only light for a few short hours. Employment in the hotels is seasonal and most people need a second job when there are fewer tourists.

The sheer number of visitors can also cause problems such as footpath erosion at honeypot sites such as Gullfoss. Steps and paths have to be managed carefully if they are to be safe and not look an eyesore.

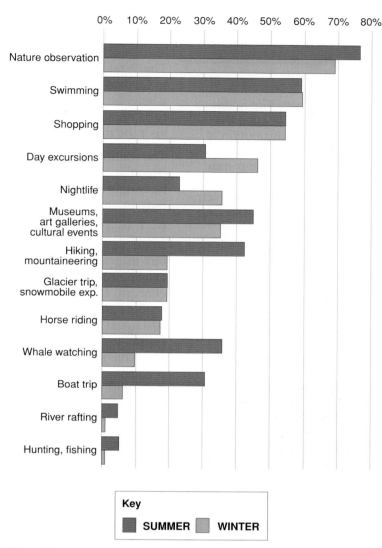

Figure 23 Main leisure activities of tourists to Iceland

| Steps are eroded by walkers |
| An ugly scar is eroded |
| Summers are short |
| Plants grow slowly |
| Rainfall is heavy |
| People walk to the edge of the steps |
| The path becomes dangerous |
| Soil is easily eroded in steep slopes |

Figure 24 Footpath erosion at Seljalandsfoss, another tourist attraction in the Golden Circle

Activity

2 Use Figure 23.
   a) Suggest why nightlife and day excursions (coach trips to places like Gullfoss) are more popular in winter.
   b) Suggest why whale watching and boat trips are more popular in summer.
   c) List the leisure activities that are linked to landscape.

3 Use the statements in Figure 24 to explain why the footpath in this honeypot site has been eroded.

4 Explain why it is important for Iceland's government to protect the country's dramatic landscape.

Iceland

Can sustainable futures be created from tourism in rural Iceland?

Activity

1 Study Figure 26.
   a) Describe the distribution of regions that have lost most people.
   b) Describe which parts of Iceland are gaining population.
   c) Explain the pattern you have identified in answers a) and b).

The West Fjords is the most remote part of Iceland from Reykjavik. Most tourists to Iceland visit Reykjavik, where nightclubs are an attraction, or the South West where the main attraction is the Blue Lagoon spa. Many tourists also visit the rural area known as the 'Golden Circle' in the south region. Far fewer tourists visit the more remote parts of Iceland.

The traditional rural economy of the West Fjords is in decline. Fishing has always been the biggest employer, but the government has cut the number of fish that can be caught in order to conserve fish stocks in the sea. Sheep farming is the second biggest employer, but it is unprofitable and unpopular among the young.

Each year the rural regions of Iceland receive some migrants and lose others. In some regions more people leave the region than move in, a situation known as **net out-migration**. The loss of people by migration, combined with low birth rates, is causing rural depopulation. Depopulation of the West Fjords is causing serious concern. If rural populations become too small then essential services such as schools and doctors' clinics become increasingly inefficient and expensive to sustain. If a doctor's surgery closes, local people find that they are further and further away from health care. Rural communities could become unsustainable and have no future.

Figure 25 A derelict trawler on a beach in the West Fjords

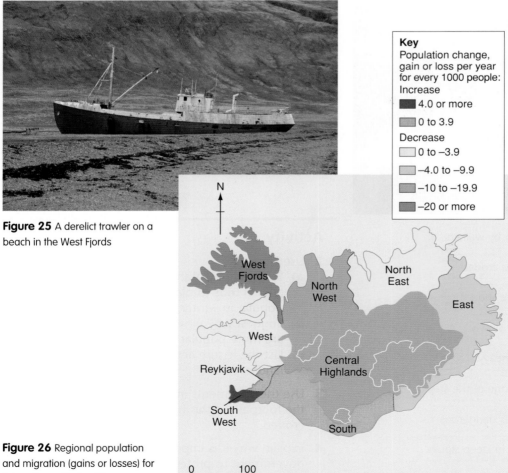

Key
Population change, gain or loss per year for every 1000 people:
Increase
- 4.0 or more
- 0 to 3.9

Decrease
- 0 to −3.9
- −4.0 to −9.9
- −10 to −19.9
- −20 or more

Figure 26 Regional population and migration (gains or losses) for the regions of Iceland (average figures for 2001–5)

1986	14.1
1987	17.8
1988	31.1
1989	27.7
1990	18.4
1991	23.4
1992	9.8
1993	16.0
1994	28.6
1995	47.9
1996	40.7
1997	44.6
1998	39.4
1999	43.5
2000	29.1
2001	21.2
2002	23.0
2003	16.7
2004	27.6
2005	39.2
2006	33.4

Figure 27 Net out-migration from West Fjords, 1986–2006 (figures per 1,000 population)

Whale watching creates jobs and can continue without damaging the environment, so it is an example of a sustainable development for rural communities in Iceland. Iceland has a long tradition of whale hunting but many people support an end to whaling if jobs are created in nature-based tourism instead. Apart from whale watching, the West Fjords has much to offer tourists interested in the natural environment:

- sea or river fishing
- bird watching
- kayaking, horse riding and hiking in the summer and skiing in winter.

Iceland's government believes that new industries such as tourism must be encouraged in order to **diversify** the rural economy. The West Fjords Development Agency (Atvest) is attempting to diversify the rural economy by promoting tourism to the region as well as trying to attract high-tech industries such as data processing, specialised food processing and fishing-related industries. The Northern Periphery Programme gives European Union money to projects in the remote regions of Arctic countries. One of its projects is called Saga Lands. This project is being used in the West Fjords to develop facilities for tourists who are interested in the Viking heritage and culture of the region.

Figure 28 Whale watching helps to sustain rural communities in Iceland

Activity

2 Explain how depopulation can affect rural services such as clinics, schools and post offices.

3 **a)** Choose a suitable technique to graphically represent the data in Figure 27.
   b) Is the depopulation issue getting worse? Use evidence from your graph.

4 Use Figure 29 and an atlas.
   a) Name four countries.
   b) Describe the distribution of these countries.

5 Explain how projects such as Saga Lands (Viking culture) or whale watching create jobs both directly and indirectly in the rural community.

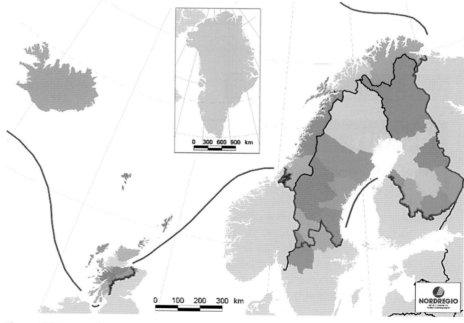

Figure 29 A map of the region that qualifies for development assistance from the Northern Periphery Programme

Creating sustainable rural communities

Figure 30 A minke whale caught by a whaling boat from Isafjordur in 2003

Year	Number of tours
1995	2,200
1996	9,700
1997	20,540
1998	30,330
1999	32,250
2000	45,400
2001	60,550
2002	62,050

Figure 31 The growth in the number of whale-watching tourists in Iceland

i) Specialised agriculture and breeding

a) Excellent water supply

ii) Ecotourism

b) Knowledge of fisheries-related industries

iii) Remote data processing (using the internet to transfer and process databases, software and spreadsheets)

c) Unused industrial and farm buildings

iv) Film production

d) Relatively cheap, renewable sources of electricity

v) Production of fresh water and marine foods (e.g. fish farming)

e) Long coastline with sheltered **fjords**

f) Highly educated and skilled workforce

vi) Industry that requires up to 30 megawatts of power

vii) Fisheries-related industry

g) Magnificent and clean environment

viii) Activity and adventure holidays

h) Excellent mobile communications and high usage of home computers

Figure 32 The resources of the West Fjords, and industries that could be developed as the economy diversifies

Activity

1 a) Choose an appropriate graphical technique to represent the data in Figure 31.
   b) Describe the trend of your graph.
2 Suggest the point of view of each of the following to both whale hunting and whale watching:
   a) A member of Greenpeace in the UK.
   b) The owner of a whaling boat in Isafjordur, which is the largest settlement in the West Fjords.
   c) The owner of a hotel in Isafjordur.

3 Explain why it is important for the rural economy of Iceland to diversify.
4 Study Figure 32.
   a) Match the West Fjords' resources a)–h) to potential industries that could be attracted to the region i)–viii).
   b) Use your list to describe how you think the West Fjords should diversify its economy. Suggest the possible advantages of your scheme compared with alternative types of diversification.

Placing boulders on the beach to repair the sea defences at Happisburgh, Norfolk. The cliffs here are not very resistant to erosion and would erode rapidly if it weren't for coastal defenses such as this.

Investigating global patterns of climate

From the icy cold of the Arctic to the tropical heat and intense rainstorms of the equator, different regions of the world have very different and distinctive climates. Figure 1 shows a bus fording a river to reach a campsite at Landmannalaugar in central Iceland. Buses make the trip once every day between mid-June and mid-September. However, the unsurfaced roads in central Iceland are impassable in winter because of the snow and ice. In summer, the snow melts and the rivers fill with **meltwater**. Iceland, on the edge of the Arctic Circle, has a seasonal climate with cold winters and cool summers. By contrast, the latitudes between the tropics remain hot throughout the year. Figure 2 explains why latitude affects temperature.

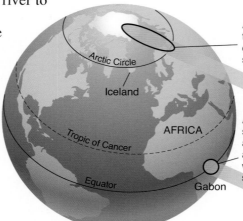

Figure 2 Solar heating of the Earth varies with latitude

At the Arctic Circle solar energy strikes the ground at a low angle and is spread over a large area. Each m² within this **solar footprint** is heated only gently.

At 0° latitude solar energy strikes the ground at almost a right angle. Energy is concentrated into a small footprint and each m² within that footprint is heated strongly.

Figure 1 Crossing central Iceland. How does the Icelandic climate affect people?

Activity

1 Read about the transport difficulties of reaching Landmannalaugar at http://www.landmannalaugar.info
   a) Use Figure 1 and the website to explain why motorists have to check the weather forecast before travelling to Landmannalaugar.
   b) Explain why it is difficult to reach Landmannalaugar by bicycle.

GEOGRAPHICAL SKILLS

Describing a climate graph

Each climate graph has four features that you need to describe. Study the graph and ask yourself:

1 What is the total annual rainfall? This is calculated by adding all of the values for the rainfall bars together.
2 Are there distinctive wet or dry seasons? If so, when are they, and how long does each last?
3 What is the annual temperature range? This is the difference in temperature between the hottest and coldest times of the year.
4 Does the temperature show a distinctive seasonal pattern? If so, at what time of year are the hot and cold seasons?

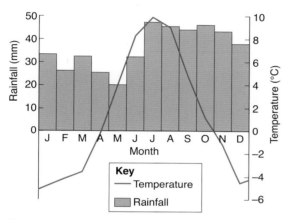

Figure 3 Climate graph for Reykjahlid in northern-central Iceland

Describing the climate of Reykjahlid, Iceland

1 Reykjahlid has a rather dry climate with a total annual rainfall of only around 430 mm.
2 Between December and April the precipitation is very low and, because temperatures are below freezing, would fall as snow. Monthly rainfall in the summer is slightly higher than in winter.
3 The annual temperature range is around 15°C which is large.
4 The months from June to August are cool, with temperatures just below 10°C. The months from December to March are cold with temperatures in the range 0 to –4°C during this winter period.

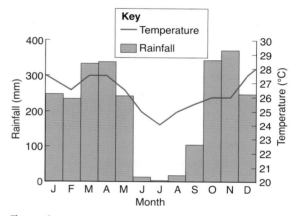

Figure 4 Climate graph for Gabon, equatorial Africa

Activity

2 Study Figure 2 and read the geographical skills section on climate graphs before copying and completing the following:
   a) Iceland is just south of ...... whereas Gabon is on the ....
   b) The sun strikes the ground in Iceland at ......, whereas in Gabon this angle is much .... This means that the sun's energy is more ...... in Gabon.
   c) The annual temperature ...... is the difference between maximum and ...... temperatures.

   d) **In Reykjahlid the maximum temperature is ...... °C and the minimum is ...... °C.**

3 Use the geographical skills advice to describe the climate pattern in Gabon shown in Figure 4.

4 Using the following headings, describe the main differences between the climate in Iceland and Gabon.
   • Total rainfall
   • Seasonal rainfall pattern
   • Temperature range

How does altitude affect temperature?

Moutainous regions are much colder than lowlands. Temperatures decrease by 1°C for every 100 m in height. This is because solar radiation (heat from the sun) passes directly through the atmosphere, heating the Earth's surface. Warm air rises from the Earth's surface as convection currents. As the air rises it then cools.

Snowdonia

Wednesday

Weather

Cloudy with occasional outbreaks of rain or drizzle during the morning. Some drier, brighter spells are likely to the lee of high ground. During the afternoon rain and drizzle will turn more persistent and heavier later.

Visibility

The visibility will be good at lower levels, but moderate in rain and poor in hill fog.

Hill fog

Hill fog will be patchy with cloud bases around 600 to 700 metres during the morning. Cloud bases will lower to 300 to 400 metres in the west later as rain becomes heavier.

Maximum winds above 500 metres

Strong to gale southerly winds with speeds 30 to 40 mph will gust to 50 or 60 mph at times over exposed peaks and ridges.

Temperature

Valleys	Plus 20 degrees Celsius
900 metres	Plus 12 degrees Celsius
Freezing level	Will be above the peaks.

Source: Met Office

Figure 5 Weather forecast for Snowdonia, 19 August 2009

Activity

1 a) Use Figure 5 to describe how altitude affects the weather in Snowdonia.
   b) Suggest how a walker visiting the mountain should prepare for their walk.

2 The highest mountain in Britain is Ben Nevis at 1,344 m. What should the temperature difference be between the summit and sea level?

Figure 6 The summit of Snowdon in winter

How does the sea affect temperatures?

Ocean currents are able to transfer heat from warm latitudes to cooler ones. The west coast of Britain is kept much warmer in winter than other places in similar latitudes by one such current of warm water, the North Atlantic Drift (also known as the Gulf Stream). The sea is also able to retain its heat in winter and cools down very slowly. Places towards the centre of Europe and so further away from the sea have much colder winters. For example, Plymouth and Prague are at the same latitude (50°N), but have very different winter temperatures. The warming effect of the sea has a big impact on coastal regions, giving them what is called a **maritime climate**. Places with a maritime climate tend to have quite a lot of precipitation, mild (rather than cold) winters and warm (rather than hot) summers.

Average temperature °C	Plymouth	Prague
January	6	-2·5
July	16	18

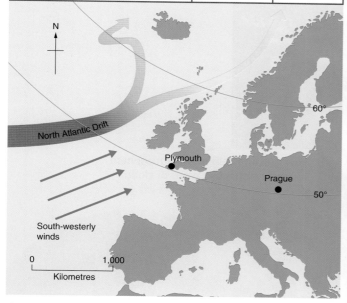

Figure 8 Comparing Plymouth and Prague

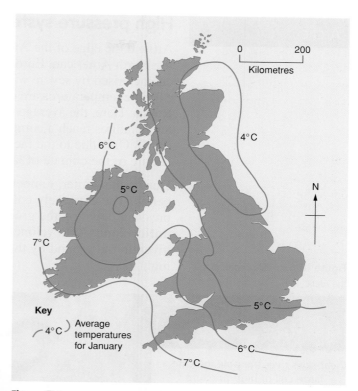

Figure 7 Average temperatures for January

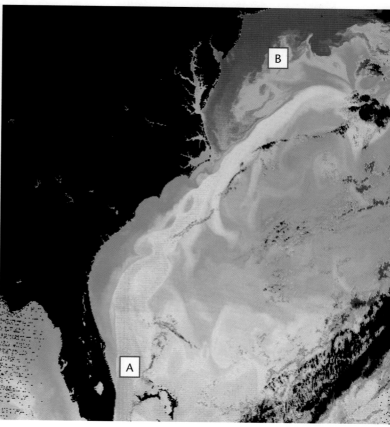

Figure 9 Satellite image of the Gulf Stream. The orange colours show warm water. Cold water is blue. Land is black

Activity

3 **a)** Use Figure 7 to describe the January temperature pattern for the British Isles.
   b) The lines on the map are called *isotherms*. Suggest a definition for this term.

4 Study Figure 9. Describe what is happening at A and B.

Arctic

High pressure systems and the continental climate

Around the edge of the Arctic region, between 60°N and 70°N, are large parts of the North American, European and Asian land masses. The climate here is characterised by severe winters and relatively short, cool summers. The most extreme temperatures are experienced in places far from the sea such as Norilsk in Russia. Here, the average winter temperature is -32°C whereas summer temperatures reach a comparatively high 15°C. This enormous **temperature range** (of 47°C) is due to the fact that continents heat up and cool down very quickly. This feature of the climate of large land masses is known as **continentality**.

During the winter, temperatures in Russia and Canada can fall to –20°C and below. The extremely cold ground chills the air above it. The cold air sinks, pressing down on the ground creating a high pressure system known as an **anticyclone**. Anticyclones are characterised by clear, cloudless skies. Any heat given to the ground by the weak winter sunshine is quickly lost in the cloudless night sky.

Figure 10 A satellite image of the Arctic

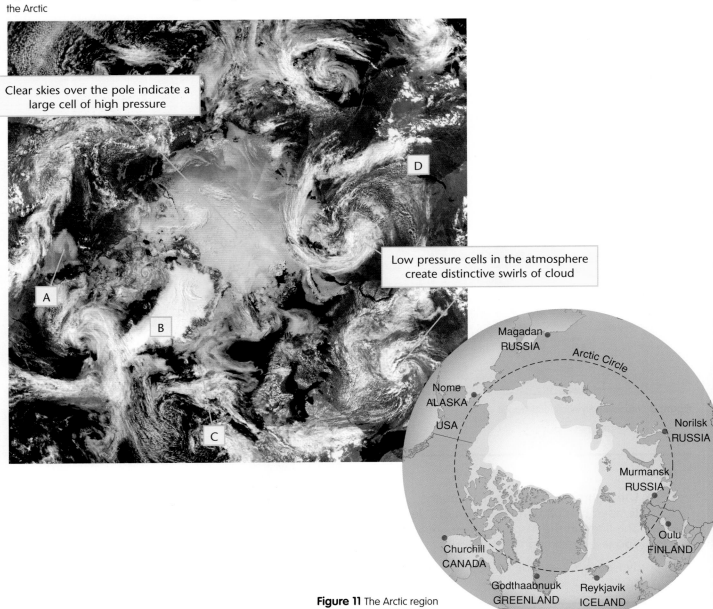

Clear skies over the pole indicate a large cell of high pressure

D

Low pressure cells in the atmosphere create distinctive swirls of cloud

A

B

C

Magadan
RUSSIA

Arctic Circle

Nome
ALASKA
USA

Norilsk
RUSSIA

Murmansk
RUSSIA

Oulu
FINLAND

Churchill
CANADA

Godthaabnuuk
GREENLAND

Reykjavik
ICELAND

Figure 11 The Arctic region

Station	Latitude/ Longitude	Min temp (°C)	Max temp (°C)	Temp range
Reykjavik, Iceland	64° 13'N 21° 90'W	–1	11	12
Oulu, Finland	64° 93'N 25° 36'E		16	26
Murmansk, Russia	68° 96'N 33° 5'E	–12		24
Norilsk, Russia	69° 33'N 88° 10'E	–32	15	
Magadan, Russia	59° 58'N 150° 78'E	–18	12	
Nome, Alaska	64° 30'N 165° 25'W	–16	11	
Churchill, Canada	58° 75'N 94° 6'W		12	38
Godthaabnuuk, Greenland	64° 16'N 51° 75'W	–10		16

Figure 12 Climate data for selected climate stations between 58°N and 70°N

Activity

1 Use Figure 11 to name five countries that have territory north of the Arctic Circle.

2 Use Figure 11 to name countries A, B, C and D on Figure 10.

3 Explain why the skies over the polar region of Figure 10 are cloudless.

4 Make a copy of Figure 12:
   a) Calculate the missing value for each climate station.
   b) Which station has the:
      i) coldest minimum temperature?
      ii) largest temperature range?
   c) Suggest reasons for the wide variation in temperature ranges at these climate stations.

5 **a)** Suggest a hypothesis you could investigate using climate data that links the following variables:

   minimum temperature
   latitude
   distance from the sea.

   b) Predict the likely outcome of your enquiry and explain why you expect this outcome.
   c) Compare the minimum temperatures in Iceland and Greenland. Do these temperatures follow your expected outcome?

Figure 13 House destroyed by permafrost, Canada

Permafrost

Permafrost is soil or rock that has remained frozen for at least two consecutive years. Approximately 26 per cent of the Earth's land area is affected by permafrost. The climate of permafrost regions reaches temperatures above 0°C during the summer, where a thin layer of soil at the surface thaws. This surface layer is known as the active layer. However, the ground beneath it stays permanently frozen. When water in the soil freezes, and when lenses of ice form in the soil, the ground surface is lifted: a process known as frost heave. In the late spring, when the active layer thaws, the ground surface subsides. This combination of heaving and collapsing can cause subsidence problems in roads and buildings. Scientists predict that global warming will increase the effect of subsidence problems on buildings and roads in Arctic regions.

6 Use the web link below to research the likely effects of global warming on permafrost. Prepare a three-minute presentation to give to the class.

www.acia.uaf.edu
Here you can access some excellent graphics, satellite images and maps describing the impact of climate change on the Arctic region.

Iceland

Investigating the effect of the sea: a case study of Iceland's maritime climate

We have seen how the land masses of Canada and Russia quickly lose their heat in the Arctic winter. By comparison, oceans cool down very slowly. So ocean currents are able to transfer heat from warm latitudes to cooler ones. Iceland's coastline is kept warm by one such current of warm water, the Gulf Stream. This brings warm water across the Atlantic from the tropics. This warm water heats the air above it and gives Iceland's coastal regions a maritime climate which is warmer and wetter than other places at similar latitudes.

How does Iceland's climate affect its people?

Iceland's climate has always been a challenge to the Icelandic people. Snow in the winter closes many roads and some are not passable until May. However, the Gulf Stream prevents ice forming in coastal waters so fishing boats can leave port throughout the year. Figure 18 summarises some of the impacts of Iceland's climate on the country's economy and its people.

Figure 14 Despite the Gulf Stream, Iceland has a cold and challenging winter climate. Europe's largest ice cap, Vatnajökull, and a number of smaller ice caps (like the one shown here) and glaciers cover around 11 per cent of the island

www.vedur.is/english/
The English homepage of the official website of the Icelandic Met Office. Use the link to find climate data or whether Iceland's roads are blocked with snow.

Month	Vestmannaeyjar Islands		Akureyri	
	°C	Precipitation (mm)	°C	Precipitation (mm)
Jan	1.3	158	−2.2	52
Feb	2.0	139	−1.5	43
Mar	1.7	141	−1.3	43
Apr	3.4	117	1.6	29
May	5.8	105	5.5	19
Jun	8.0	102	9.1	28
Jul	9.6	95	10.5	33
Aug	9.6	140	10.0	34
Sep	7.4	131	6.3	39
Oct	5.0	161	3.0	58
Nov	2.4	154	−0.4	54
Dec	1.4	193	−1.9	53
	4.8 av.	1588.6 total	3.2 av.	489.5 total

Figure 15 Climate data for selected climate stations in Iceland

Activity

1 Use Figure 15 to draw climate graphs for each weather station.

2 Using the geographical skills box 'Describing a climate graph' on page 81 to help you, describe the features of each of the climate graphs.

3 Draw an outline map of Iceland and a cross-section diagram like Figure 17. Use the additional labels to add extra annotations to your map and cross-section.

4 Use Figures 16 and 17 to explain why:
   a) winters in Akureyri are colder than in Reykjavik
   b) rainfall totals are relatively low in Akureyri but high in southern Iceland.

5 Look at Figure 18. Write a paragraph explaining how Iceland's climate affects its people.

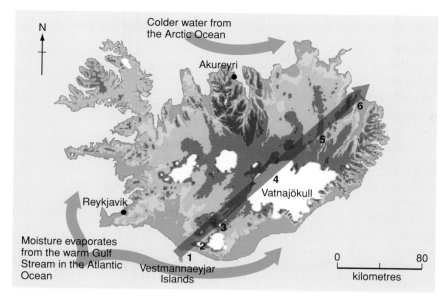

Additional labels for Figures 16 and 17

Air rises over the highlands of south Iceland.

An area of rain shadow where it seldom rains.

The wind often blows in from the south-west. This is the **prevailing wind** direction.

Some precipitation falls as snow on Vatnajökull, adding to the ice cap.

After crossing the highlands and ice cap, the air sinks and warms.

As the air rises it cools and water vapour condenses forming cloud and precipitation.

Figure 16 The factors that influence Iceland's regional patterns of climate

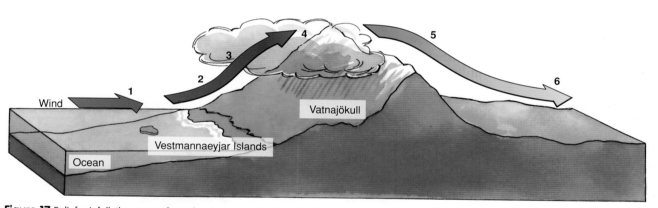

Figure 17 Relief rainfall: the reason for Iceland's regional pattern of rain

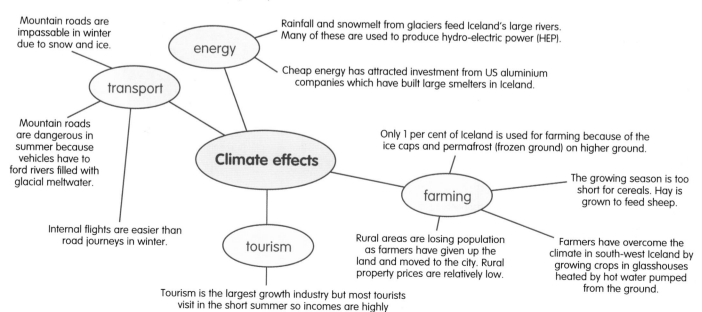

Mountain roads are impassable in winter due to snow and ice.

Rainfall and snowmelt from glaciers feed Iceland's large rivers. Many of these are used to produce hydro-electric power (HEP).

energy

Cheap energy has attracted investment from US aluminium companies which have built large smelters in Iceland.

transport

Mountain roads are dangerous in summer because vehicles have to ford rivers filled with glacial meltwater.

Climate effects

Only 1 per cent of Iceland is used for farming because of the ice caps and permafrost (frozen ground) on higher ground.

farming

The growing season is too short for cereals. Hay is grown to feed sheep.

Internal flights are easier than road journeys in winter.

tourism

Rural areas are losing population as farmers have given up the land and moved to the city. Rural property prices are relatively low.

Farmers have overcome the climate in south-west Iceland by growing crops in glasshouses heated by hot water pumped from the ground.

Tourism is the largest growth industry but most tourists visit in the short summer so incomes are highly seasonal.

Figure 18 How Iceland's climate affects people

Features of the tropical climate

Tropical climates are found within 15° of latitude either side of the equator. The climate close to the equator (within 5° of latitude) is hot throughout the year. No matter what time of year, the sun at midday is always high overhead and there are no seasonal variations like the winter and summer that we experience in the UK.

The climate of tropical regions is dominated by the **tropical rain belt** (or **ITCZ**). For example, in the Amazon region (which is within 5° of the equator) there is between 1500 mm and 2000 mm of rainfall a year. London, by comparison, has an average of 593 mm of rainfall each year. Regions between 5° and 15° of latitude either side of the equator have a seasonal pattern of rainfall with distinct wet and dry seasons.

Why does it rain so much in the tropics? In the heat of the tropics, large air masses are constantly warmed by the hot ground below. This creates massive zones of low pressure. These air masses are **unstable**, meaning that warm air is rising within them.

Warm air rises within the unstable air mass

Tiny water droplets join together

Atmospheric molecules get further apart

Water vapour in the air condenses

The atmosphere is heated by the ground

Rainclouds form

The ground is heated strongly at the equator by the sun

Air pressure falls

Figure 19 Atmospheric processes within the tropical rain belt

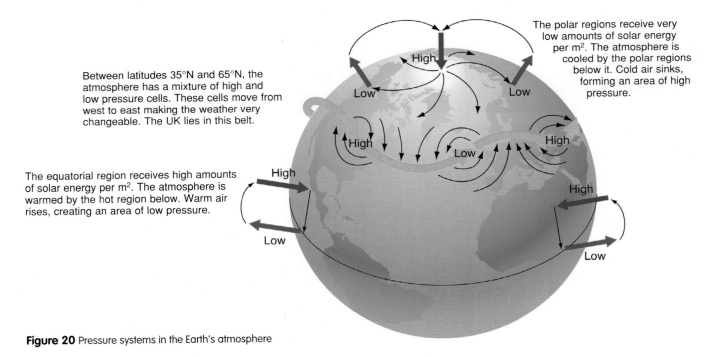

Between latitudes 35°N and 65°N, the atmosphere has a mixture of high and low pressure cells. These cells move from west to east making the weather very changeable. The UK lies in this belt.

The polar regions receive very low amounts of solar energy per m². The atmosphere is cooled by the polar regions below it. Cold air sinks, forming an area of high pressure.

The equatorial region receives high amounts of solar energy per m². The atmosphere is warmed by the hot region below. Warm air rises, creating an area of low pressure.

Figure 20 Pressure systems in the Earth's atmosphere

Figure 21 A satellite image of the tropical rain belt over the Pacific, Caribbean and Central America

		Jan	Feb	Mar	Apr	May	Jun	Jul	Aug	Sep	Oct	Nov	Dec
Belem, Brazil	Average temp °C	26	26	27	27	27	26	26	26	27	27	27	27
	Average rainfall mm	318	358	358	320	259	170	150	112	89	84	66	155
Trinidad	Average temp °C	26	26.5	26	26.5	27	27	26.5	26.5	27	27	27	26
	Average rainfall mm	69	41	46	53	94	193	218	246	193	170	183	125
Mexico City, Mexico	Average temp °C	12	13	16	18	19	18.5	17.5	17.5	17.5	17.5	14	11.5
	Average rainfall mm	13	5	10	20	53	119	170	152	130	51	18	8

Figure 22 Three contrasting tropical climates

Activity

1 Study Figures 20 and 21 and, using an atlas:
   a) Name the countries A, B, C, D and E.
   b) Working in pairs, match the following labels to letters F and G:
   - The atmosphere is warmed by the hot region below. Warm air rises, creating clouds and an area of low pressure.
   - Sinking air creates high pressure and cloudless skies.
   c) Explain why the clouds on Figure 21 indicate areas of low pressure.

2 Study Figure 20 and the phrases in Figure 19. Make a flow diagram that shows how large areas of low pressure are formed and how these create the tropical rain belt.

3 a) Use the data in Figure 22 to create three tropical climate graphs.
   b) Use Figure 21 and an atlas to describe the location of each place.
   c) Compare the rainfall patterns in Belem to Trinidad. How does their location help to explain the differences you have noted?
   d) Mexico City is 2000 metres above sea level. How does this fact help to explain the different climate here?

Why does the UK have such changeable weather conditions?

Study Figure 20 on page 88. It shows that the UK lies at a latitude that gets a mixture of air masses. Some are high pressure and others low pressure. These pressure systems come across the UK from the Atlantic or from Europe and bring with them very changeable patterns of weather.

Areas of high pressure are also known as anticyclones. Anticyclones bring dry, settled periods of weather. If an anticyclone becomes fixed over the UK in winter the weather is sunny and dry but cold, and especially cold at night. During the summer an anticyclone brings hot dry weather and can cause problems such as heatwaves or drought, for example in July and August 2003 when an anticyclone stayed over Europe for several weeks.

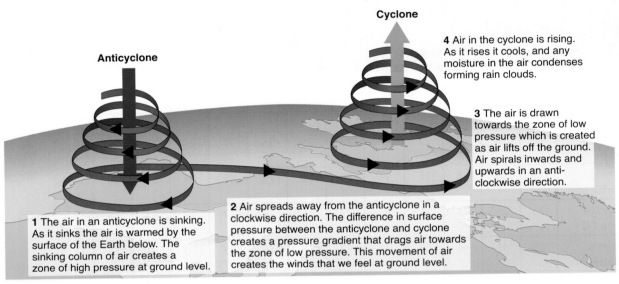

Anticyclone

Cyclone

4 Air in the cyclone is rising. As it rises it cools, and any moisture in the air condenses forming rain clouds.

3 The air is drawn towards the zone of low pressure which is created as air lifts off the ground. Air spirals inwards and upwards in an anti-clockwise direction.

1 The air in an anticyclone is sinking. As it sinks the air is warmed by the surface of the Earth below. The sinking column of air creates a zone of high pressure at ground level.

2 Air spreads away from the anticyclone in a clockwise direction. The difference in surface pressure between the anticyclone and cyclone creates a pressure gradient that drags air towards the zone of low pressure. This movement of air creates the winds that we feel at ground level.

Figure 23 The movement of air from areas of high pressure to areas of low pressure

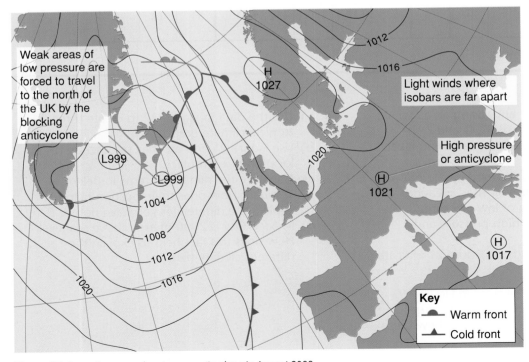

Weak areas of low pressure are forced to travel to the north of the UK by the blocking anticyclone

Light winds where isobars are far apart

High pressure or anticyclone

H 1027

L999

L999

H 1021

H 1017

1012
1016
1020
1004
1008
1012
1016
1020

Key
- ⌒ Warm front
- ▲ Cold front

Figure 24 A weather map showing an anticyclone in August 2003

When extreme weather is a hazard

The extreme heat of August 2003 caused suffering and discomfort for millions of people across Europe. The heat caused heatstroke and dehydration, especially among elderly people. It is estimated that 30,000 people died in the extreme heat. France was the worst hit. French doctors estimate that the heatwave caused 14,000 deaths. On a normal August day about 50 people are admitted to hospital suffering from heat exhaustion. In August 2003 that number rose to 500 and the hospitals struggled to cope. In addition, the heatwave also caused several forest fires in southern Europe. All in all, the extreme heat is estimated to have caused €1 billion of damage.

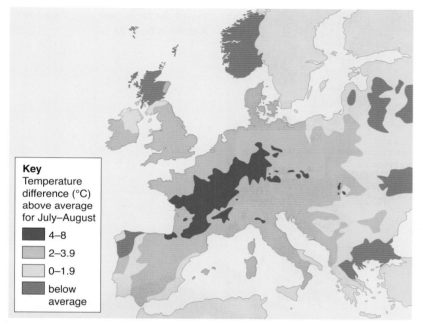

Figure 25 Temperature anomalies in Europe in August 2003

Key
Temperature difference (°C) above average for July–August

- 4–8
- 2–3.9
- 0–1.9
- below average

Activity

1 Use Figures 23 and 24 and the words below to complete the following sentences about pressure systems.

   stable/sinking/rising
   low/medium/high   light/gusty/strong

   The air in an anticyclone is ..... which creates a zone of ..... pressure at ground level.

   The air in a cyclone is ..... which creates a zone of ..... pressure at ground level.

   High pressure brings warm weather in summer with ..... winds.

2 Use Figure 24 and an atlas to describe:
   a) the location of the three zones of high pressure
   b) the cold front.

3 Use Figure 25 and an atlas to name five countries where temperatures were at least 4°C higher than average.

4 Suggest how the summer heatwave of 2003 might have affected:
   a) Owners of campsites in Cornwall.
   b) The sale of barbeques and charcoal in British supermarkets.
   c) Doctors and nurses in accident and emergency departments in France.
   d) The last-minute sale of holiday flights to Spain from the UK.
   e) Home owners in the parts of southern Europe affected by forest fires.

The effects of low pressure (or depressions)

Regions of low pressure in the atmosphere are formed when air lifts off the Earth's surface. It is common for several cells of low pressure, also known as **depressions**, to form in the North Atlantic at any one time. They then track eastwards towards Europe bringing changeable weather characterised by wind, cloud and rain. Depressions are more likely to be deeper (have lower pressure) in the winter months. These weather systems can bring damaging gusts of wind and large waves onto the coast as well as heavy rain. However, low pressure in the summer months is quite common: the floods of June, July 2007 and July 2012 were caused by depressions.

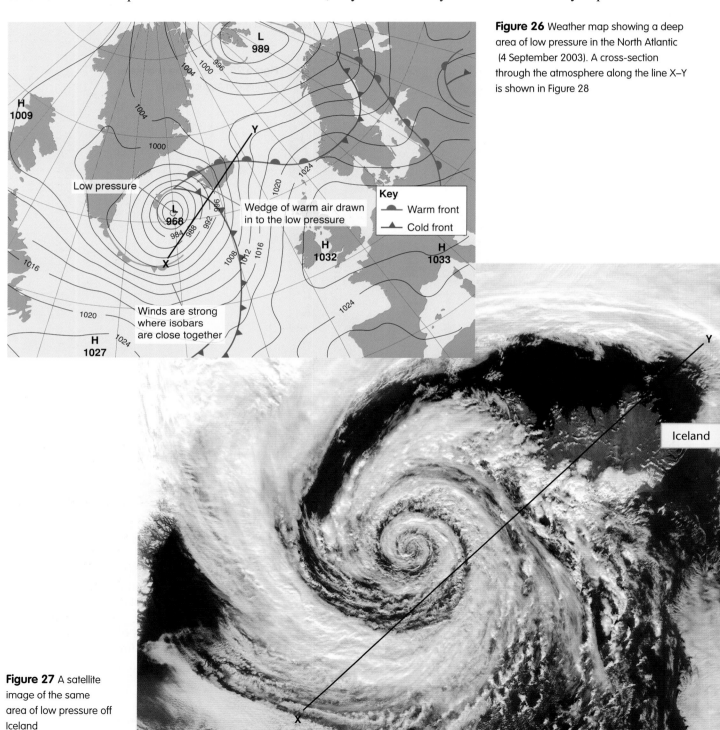

Figure 26 Weather map showing a deep area of low pressure in the North Atlantic (4 September 2003). A cross-section through the atmosphere along the line X–Y is shown in Figure 28

Figure 27 A satellite image of the same area of low pressure off Iceland (4 September 2003)

Inside the depression there is a battle between huge masses of warmer and colder air. These air masses revolve slowly around each other in an anti-clockwise direction (in the northern hemisphere) as the whole system tracks eastward. As the warmer air rises and rotates its moisture condenses, forming huge banks of cloud. Seen from above, these curving banks of cloud give the depression a characteristic shape.

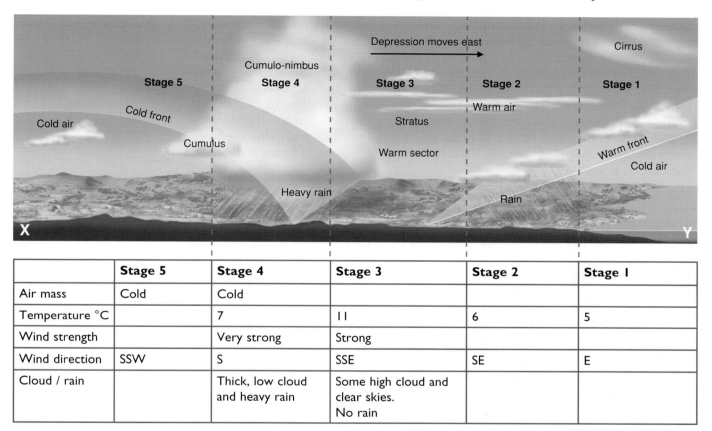

	Stage 5	Stage 4	Stage 3	Stage 2	Stage 1
Air mass	Cold	Cold			
Temperature °C		7	11	6	5
Wind strength		Very strong	Strong		
Wind direction	SSW	S	SSE	SE	E
Cloud / rain		Thick, low cloud and heavy rain	Some high cloud and clear skies. No rain		

Figure 28 Weather that would have been associated with the easterly progress of the depression shown in Figures 18 and 19

Feature	Cyclones or depressions	Anticyclones
Air pressure		High, usually above 1020 mb (millibars)
Air movement	Rising	
Wind strength	Strong	
Wind circulation		Clockwise
Typical winter weather		Cold and dry. Clear skies in the daytime. Frost at night.
Typical summer weather	Mild and wet. Cloudy with periods of heavy rain separated by showers.	

Figure 29 Comparing cyclones and anticyclones

Activity

1 Use an atlas and Figures 26 and 27. Describe the location of the areas of high and low pressure.

2 **a)** Make a copy of the table in Figure 28. Use the evidence in Figures 26 and 27 to complete the missing sections.
   b) Imagine you are a weather forecaster working in north-east Iceland. Prepare a local weather forecast for the next few hours.

3 Make a large copy of Figure 29 and use the information on pages 90–93 to complete the blank spaces.

Weather hazards caused by high pressure: a case study of drought in Barcelona 2008

Barcelona is the capital city of Catalonia, a prosperous region of Spain. A severe water shortage in 2007–2008 forced the city to take extraordinary steps to avoid running out of water. In February 2008 a drought order was imposed. This restricted the use of water by households, for example for watering the garden or washing the car. Water use was restricted in public places such as city parks and 10 per cent of public fountains were turned off. People who broke the rules faced fines: €30 for watering gardens and €3,000 for filling swimming pools. Similar restrictions were used in the south-east of England during the drought of 2006. By May 2008 the city was so desperate that a fleet of tankers, each carrying 28 million litres of water, started to bring water into the city's port. This so-called 'water bridge' transferred water to Barcelona from Tarragona in Spain and Marseille in France.

Figure 31 Rainfall and discharge data for R Llobregat, Barcelona (May 2007 – May 2008)

Figure 30 One of the tankers in the so-called 'water bridge' that brought water into Barcelona in spring 2008

		Discharge on the River Llobregat (m³/s)	Precipitation (mm)	
			2007–2008	Average
May	2007	6.66	21	54
Jun	2007	2.50	7	37
Jul	2007	2.21	0	27
Aug	2007	7.62	71	49
Sep	2007	2.30	18	76
Oct	2007	5.86	142	86
Nov	2007	2.00	0	52
Dec	2007	1.75	13	45
Jan	2008	2.47	18	31
Feb	2008	1.92	39	39
Mar	2008	1.42	26	48
Apr	2008	3.31	28	43
May	2008	11.26	78	54

Water conflict

The Catalonian government has suggested that its long-term water supply problem could be solved if water could be transferred into the city from other regions. They have suggested two plans, shown in Figure 32. However, water is a precious resource and both plans have been vigorously opposed. The River Segre runs for part of its course along the border with Aragon and the regional government objects to the use of what it regards as its water in Catalonia.

Meanwhile Catalonia has accused Aragon of wanting to use Barcelona's drinking water in the hotels and golf courses of Aragon. Aragon has appealed to the national government. For the moment the national government has backed Aragon and Catalonia cannot go ahead with the plan. In the meantime Barcelona is counting on the construction of a new desalination plant to turn sea water into fresh water. It opened in 2009.

Figure 32 Barcelona's water supply plans

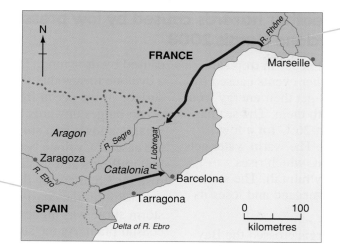

Water could be transferred from the River Rhône to Barcelona using a series of pipes and canals, but this plan is currently on hold.

Barcelona would like to transfer water from the River Segre, but this is opposed by the national government of Spain.

Figure 33 Points of view on the water shortage

The city authority is trying to make us look like criminals! Catalonia's swimming pool manufacturers are expected to lose €200m (approx £200 million) by the end of 2008. Who wants to buy a swimming pool if they can't fill it?

Building desalination plants is a big mistake. They use huge amounts of energy and therefore contribute to climate change. By building desalination plants Catalonia will actually be increasing the chance of drought. It's just not a sustainable option.

Swimming pool manufacturer

Householder

Climate expert

Protestor in France

I'm fed up with the water restrictions. I think our problem is that 70 per cent of Catalonia's water is used by farmers. A lot of them have really old irrigation systems that are leaking and they grow crops that aren't really suited to our dry climate. It's such a waste.

I belong to a protest group that opposes the plan to transfer water from France. The scheme would damage the ecosystem of the River Rhône. The people who stand to benefit most are the fat cats who own the water companies!

Activity

1 **a)** Use the data in Figure 31 to draw a series of graphs.
   b) Compare the rainfall for May 2007–2008 with the average pattern.
   c) Explain how this rainfall pattern has affected the discharge of the River Llobregat.

2 Suggest five ways that households in Barcelona could save water.

3 Use Figure 32.
   a) Describe the location of Barcelona.
   b) What is the approximate distance of each of the proposed water transfer schemes?

4 Discuss Figure 33.
   a) Suggest three other factors, apart from lack of rainfall, that have led to the water shortage.
   b) Make a list of short-term and long-term solutions to the shortage. You should find at least two of each.
   c) What do you think is the most sustainable solution to Barcelona's problem? Make sure that you justify your answer.

5 Is Aragon right to oppose Catalonia's plan? Write a letter to the Aragon government stating your point of view.

Burma

Weather hazards caused by low pressure: a case study of Cyclone Nargis 2008

Cyclones are severe storms that occur in tropical regions. They are extreme weather events caused by very low air pressure. Cyclones get their energy from the warm tropical waters beneath them. The sea has to be at a temperature of at least 26°C for a few weeks to generate such a storm. The warm water acts like fuel. It heats the air above it, which rises, creating storm clouds and heavy rainfall. The storm loses strength when it moves over land and loses its fuel supply.

In early May 2008 Cyclone Nargis crossed the Bay of Bengal and hit the coast of Burma (also known as Myanmar) killing an estimated 130,000 people. The winds peaked at 215 km/hr as the storm approached the coastline and these winds certainly caused damage as they would have flattened trees and torn the roofs off buildings. However, most deaths were caused by drowning. The very low air pressure during a cyclone means that there is less pressure on the surface of the ocean from above. Consequently the ocean bulges upwards beneath the storm creating what is known as a **storm surge** (or tidal surge). In the case of Cyclone Nargis the air pressure fell to 960 millibars and it is estimated that the sea level rose by 3.6 m during this storm surge. Unfortunately the storm hit the coast at high tide, meaning that the storm surge was higher than the level of the flat coastal plain. As the storm tracked along the densely populated southern coastline of Burma, the storm surge caused flooding for long distances inland. In addition to this the strong storm winds blowing over the ocean create huge waves. In the case of Nargis it is thought these waves reached a maximum height of 7.6 m on top of the storm surge.

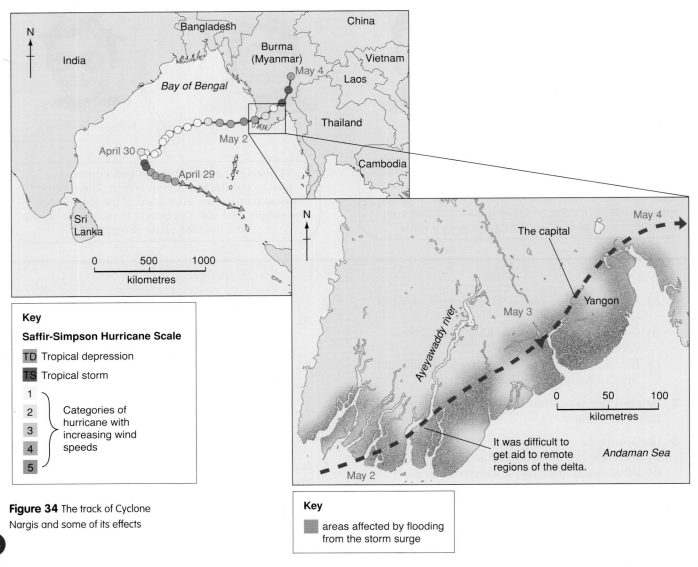

Figure 34 The track of Cyclone Nargis and some of its effects

Key

Saffir-Simpson Hurricane Scale

TD Tropical depression

TS Tropical storm

1
2   Categories of
    hurricane with
3   increasing wind
    speeds
4
5

Key

[■] areas affected by flooding from the storm surge

How were people affected by Nargis?

Nargis and its terrible floodwaters affected people in both the short term and long term. About 800,000 homes were damaged and many survivors were **displaced**. Most of these moved in with family members and 260,000 moved into refugee camps. Surprisingly, 80 per cent of the damaged homes were rebuilt by the end of June 2008. Land was flooded and rice crops destroyed. Over half of the survivors in the worst hit areas were short of food. Around 65 per cent of the population reported health problems in early June. These included 37 per cent of the population suffering from fever and 34 per cent from diarrhoea.

Only 8 per cent reported injuries but 23 per cent were suffering from mental health problems. Diseases such as diarrhoea are common after such events, because drinking water becomes polluted with sewage. After Nargis the number of people using pit latrines fell from 77 per cent to 60 per cent (because the latrines were damaged) which means that 40 per cent of people were not getting rid of sewage safely. Three-quarters of health centres in the region were damaged by the storm, so families had less access to immunisation and other types of care just when they needed it most. In the long term these facilities had to be rebuilt.

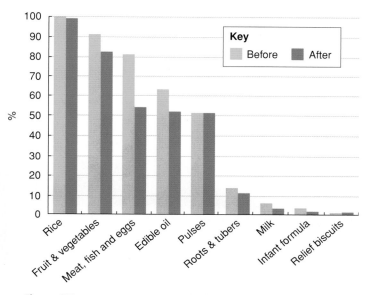

Figure 35 Diet in the delta before and after the cyclone

Figure 36 Percentage of deaths by age and gender

	Male	Female
Under 5	10	12
5–11	11	15
12–17	3	3
18–60	12	26
Over 60	3	5
Total	39	61

Activity

1 **a)** Describe the track of Cyclone Nargis.
   b) Describe the distribution of land affected by flooding.

2 Study Figure 35.
   a) Compare the quality of the diet before and after the cyclone.
   b) Suggest how this may have affected people.

3 **a)** Use the data in Figure 36 to draw a simple age–sex pyramid.
   b) Describe the shape of your pyramid. What does it tell you about the type of people who were worst affected?

4 Suggest how the activities of the following people might have been affected by the cyclone in both the short term (the first month) and longer term.
   a) A rice farmer who owned land that was flooded in one of the remote regions of the delta
   b) A family living in a shanty town in one of the affected cities.

Figure 2 Arctic tundra, Iceland

What are ecosystems?

An **ecosystem** is a community of plants and animals and the environment in which they live. Ecosystems contain both living and non-living parts. The living part includes such things as plants, insects and birds, which depend on each other for food. Plants may also depend on insects and birds for pollination and seed dispersal. The non-living part of an ecosystem includes such things as the climate, soils and rocks. This non-living environment provides nutrients, warmth, water and shelter for the living parts of the ecosystem.

Figure 3 Boreal (taiga) forest, Norway

Figure 4 Tropical rainforest, Gabon

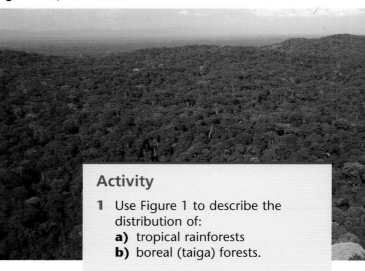

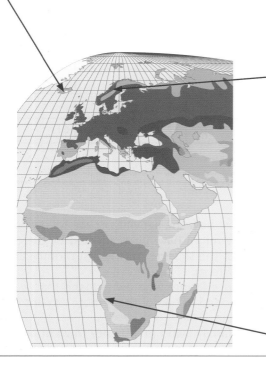

Key

- Tropical rainforests
- Savanna woodland
- Subtropical evergreen forest
- Deciduous forest
- Boreal (or taiga) forest
- Mediterranean forest or scrub
- Tall-grass prairie
- Short-grass prairie
- Semi-desert
- Desert shrub and desert
- Arctic and alpine tundra
- Ice sheet

Figure 1 Biomes of Africa and Europe

Activity

1 Use Figure 1 to describe the distribution of:
   a) tropical rainforests
   b) boreal (taiga) forests.

The global distribution pattern of biomes

Climate is such an important factor in influencing the natural vegetation and wildlife of a region that **biomes** (the largest-scale ecosystems) broadly match the world's climate zones.

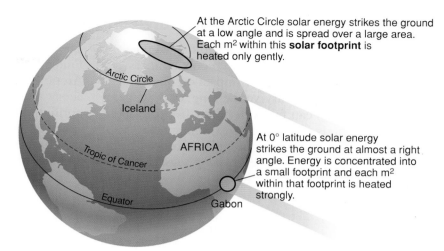

At the Arctic Circle solar energy strikes the ground at a low angle and is spread over a large area. Each m² within this **solar footprint** is heated only gently.

At 0° latitude solar energy strikes the ground at almost a right angle. Energy is concentrated into a small footprint and each m² within that footprint is heated strongly.

Figure 5 Solar heating of the Earth varies with latitude

Month	Tundra moorland 64°N, Iceland		Boreal (taiga) forest 65°N, Norway		Tropical rainforest 0°N, Gabon	
	Temperature (°C)	Precipitation (mm)	Temperature (°C)	Precipitation (mm)	Temperature (°C)	Precipitation (mm)
Jan	−0.5	145	−8.0	38	27.0	249
Feb	0.4	130	−7.5	30	26.5	236
Mar	0.5	115	−4.5	25	27.5	335
Apr	2.9	117	2.5	35	27.5	340
May	6.3	131	8.5	42	26.5	244
Jun	9.0	120	14.0	48	25.0	13
Jul	10.6	158	17.0	76	24.0	3
Aug	10.3	141	15.5	75	25.0	18
Sep	7.4	184	10.5	57	25.5	104
Oct	4.4	184	5.5	57	26.0	345
Nov	1.1	137	0	49	26.0	373
Dec	−0.2	133	−4.0	41	27.5	249

Figure 6 Climate data for three climate stations

Activity

2 Use the climate data in Figure 6 to complete a copy of the following table:

3 Suggest how the differences in climate might affect plant growth in the two forest systems.

	Tropical rainforest	Boreal forest	Tundra moorland
Temperature range			
Months above 10°C (length of growing season)			
Months below freezing			
Total annual rainfall			
Seasonal variation in rainfall			

Investigating the relationships between climate and ecosystems in the Arctic

The Arctic climate of Northern Scandinavia and Iceland has cold winters and short, cool summers. These conditions have a major impact on plant growth. Plants have to survive the long, dark winters when temperatures can fall well below freezing and when strong winds or snowfall can damage the branches of trees. In the summer, plants benefit from long hours of daylight but the growing season is very short. Plants therefore grow slowly.

The further north you go in Northern Norway and Finland, the smaller the plants become. South of the Arctic Circle, the ecosystem is taiga. This is a forest ecosystem of conifer trees and birches. As you travel north, the trees become shorter and grow further apart. Eventually, a little north of the Arctic Circle, the climate becomes too extreme for trees to grow and the treeless arctic **tundra** takes over.

1. Temperatures are only above 10° C (the temperature at which most plants grow) for two or three months ...		... plants grow close to the ground where they are less likely to be damaged.
2. Precipitation in the winter months falls as snow ...	**... so ...**	... plants have a short growing season.
3. Rocks weather (break down) slowly in the cold conditions which means soils have few nutrients ...		... plants are extremely slow growing.
4. With few trees around there is little shelter from wind ...		... plants have small leaves and so don't lose any moisture.

Figure 7 How the Arctic climate affects plant growth

Figure 9 Reindeer grazing on lichen in Arctic Norway

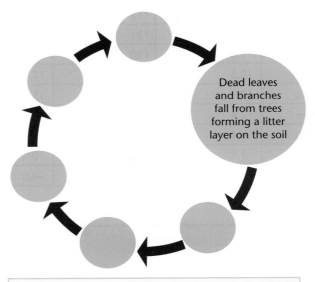

Dead leaves and branches fall from trees forming a litter layer on the soil

Leaf litter breaks down slowly in the cold conditions

Roots are shallow so they can take in nutrients near the surface

Decomposers such as beetles and fungi grow in the litter

Nutrients from leaf litter return to the soil

Plants use nutrients from the soil to help growth

Figure 10 Nutrient cycles in the taiga

Figure 8 Lichens growing on a rotting tree stump, Arctic Norway

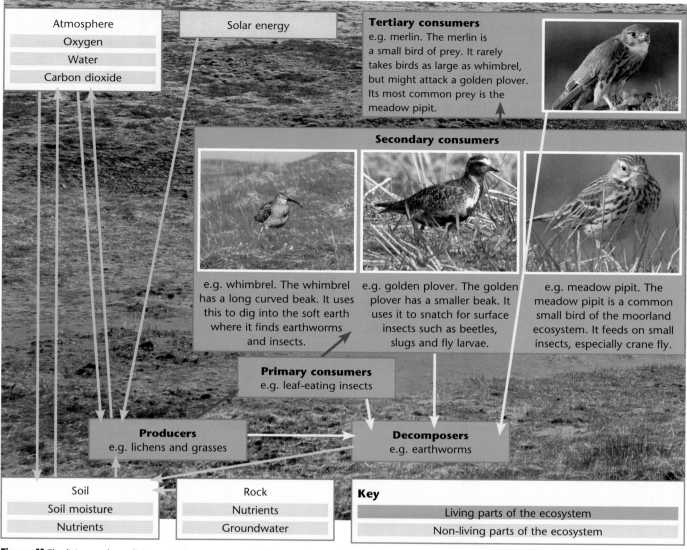

Figure 11 The living and non-living parts (or components) of the treeless tundra ecosystem in Iceland

Activity

1 Pair up the phrases in Figure 7 to make four sentences that explain the features of Arctic ecosystems.

2 Make a copy of Figure 10 and add the labels to the correct places to make a complete cycle.

3 Use Figure 11.
   a) Describe three non-living parts of the tundra ecosystem.

   b) Describe two ways that nutrients enter into the soil.
   c) Draw a food chain that includes meadow pipit.
   d) What would happen to the merlin if the population of meadow pipits fell for some reason (perhaps because a new predator was introduced to Iceland)?

Investigating the relationships between climate and ecosystems in the tropical rainforest

Biomes such as the **tropical rainforest** have climatic conditions that promote rapid plant growth. Tropical rainforest trees grow quickly and can reach a height of 40 m or more. Other biomes, like the tundra, have very slow-growing plants that never grow more than a few centimetres high. The differing growth rates of the plants in these biomes can be explained by factors such as the amount of sunlight, length of day, warmth, and amount of water. These factors all depend on either climate or latitude. Read the labels on Figure 12. Notice how the word 'so …' is used to explain how a feature of the climate has influenced plant growth in this ecosystem.

There is plenty of sunlight overhead so plants grow straight and tall

In equatorial regions the temperature is constantly above 25°C so plants can grow all year and grow quickly

Figure 12 Tropical rainforest in Reunion, Africa

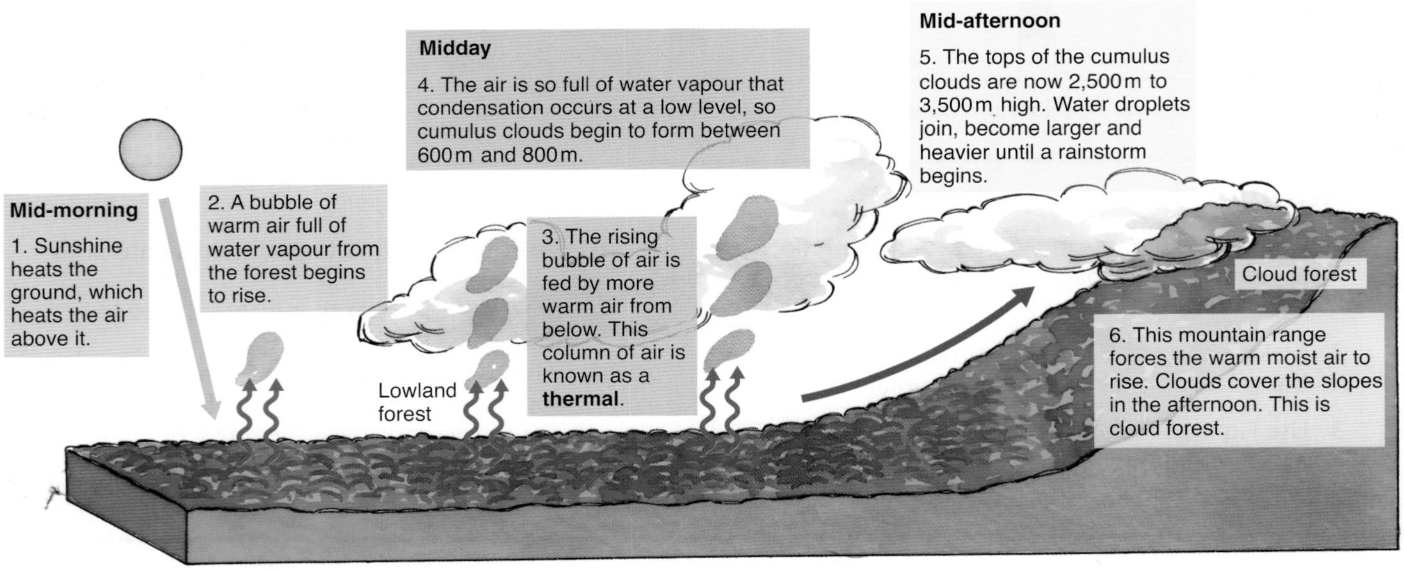

There is plenty of water, sunshine and nutrients so a wide variety of plants are able to grow. This allows a wide diversity of insects, birds and animals

Mid-morning

1. Sunshine heats the ground, which heats the air above it.

2. A bubble of warm air full of water vapour from the forest begins to rise.

3. The rising bubble of air is fed by more warm air from below. This column of air is known as a **thermal**.

Lowland forest

Midday

4. The air is so full of water vapour that condensation occurs at a low level, so cumulus clouds begin to form between 600 m and 800 m.

Mid-afternoon

5. The tops of the cumulus clouds are now 2,500 m to 3,500 m high. Water droplets join, become larger and heavier until a rainstorm begins.

Cloud forest

6. This mountain range forces the warm moist air to rise. Clouds cover the slopes in the afternoon. This is cloud forest.

Figure 13 Convectional rainfall over lowland rainforest and cloud forest

Nutrient cycles also depend on climate

Plants need minerals containing nitrogen and phosphates. These nutrients exist in rocks, water and the atmosphere. The plants take them from the soil, releasing them back into the soil when the plant dies. This process forms a continuous cycle.

Figure 14 represents nutrient stores and flows in the rainforest ecosystem. The circles represent **nutrient**

stores. The size of each circle is in proportion to the amount of nutrients kept in that part of the ecosystem. The arrows represent **nutrient flows** as minerals move from one store to another. The thickness of each arrow is in proportion to the size of the flow, so large flows of nutrients are shown with thick arrows whilst smaller flows are shown with narrow arrows.

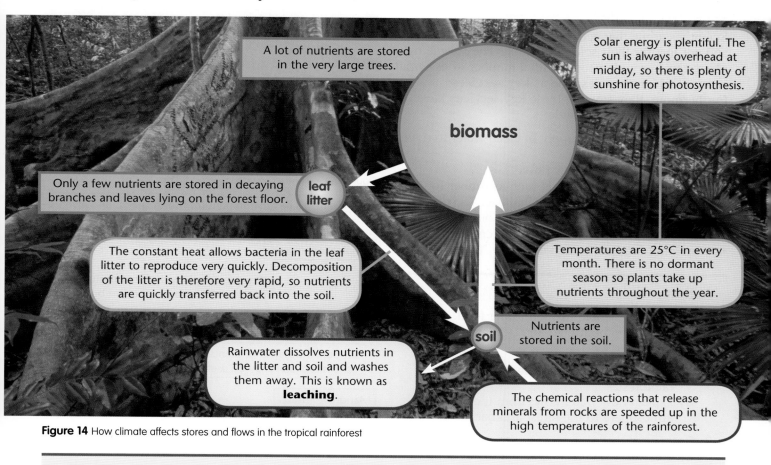

A lot of nutrients are stored in the very large trees.

Solar energy is plentiful. The sun is always overhead at midday, so there is plenty of sunshine for photosynthesis.

biomass

Only a few nutrients are stored in decaying branches and leaves lying on the forest floor.

leaf litter

The constant heat allows bacteria in the leaf litter to reproduce very quickly. Decomposition of the litter is therefore very rapid, so nutrients are quickly transferred back into the soil.

Temperatures are 25°C in every month. There is no dormant season so plants take up nutrients throughout the year.

soil

Nutrients are stored in the soil.

Rainwater dissolves nutrients in the litter and soil and washes them away. This is known as **leaching**.

The chemical reactions that release minerals from rocks are speeded up in the high temperatures of the rainforest.

Figure 14 How climate affects stores and flows in the tropical rainforest

Activity

1 Make a copy of Figure 13. Add the following labels to appropriate places on your diagram:

   evaporation   warm air rising
   condensation   precipitation

2 Explain why the climate of the cloud forest is cooler and wetter than in the lowland forest.

3 **a)** Define what is meant by *nutrient stores* and *nutrient flows*.
   b) Describe three places where nutrients are stored in an ecosystem.

4 Study Figure 14.
   a) Describe two ways that nutrients can enter the soil.

   b) Explain why these two nutrient flows are rapid in the rainforest.
   c) Explain why these nutrient flows are likely to be much slower in the boreal forest and tundra.

5 Study Figure 14. Explain why nutrient cycle diagrams for the tundra and boreal forest would have:
   a) a larger circle for leaf litter than in the rainforest
   b) a thinner arrow for leaching
   c) a thinner arrow showing nutrient flows into the biomass.

How do ecosystem processes benefit people?

Sadly logging, oil exploration, intensive farming and over-fishing are all damaging natural ecosystems. But does it really matter if there are fewer forests and less wildlife? After all, farming and fishing provide us with food, jobs and wealth.

Ecosystems provide key services

Scientists argue that ecosystems should be protected and not just for their scientific value. They argue that ecosystems provide people with a number of essential services which they describe as **key services**. Furthermore, they say that these key services have financial value. They include:

- maintaining a steady supply of clean water to rivers
- preventing soil erosion
- reducing the risk of river floods
- providing natural materials such as timber for building, or plants for medicinal use; 75 per cent of the world's population still rely on plant extracts to provide them with medication
- providing foodstuffs such as honey, fruit and nuts.

Figure 15 Bees provide a service to humans by pollinating our crops. Beetles also provide a key service. They digest waste materials such as leaf litter and dung

Figure 16 Key services provided by ecosystems

Provide a safe environment for fish to spawn and juvenile fish to mature, so helping to maintain fish stocks

Tropical rainforests

Provide people with the opportunity to develop recreation or tourism businesses

Coniferous (boreal or taiga) forests

Support thousands of plants and wild animals that contain chemicals that may be useful to agriculture or medicine

Mangrove forests

Inspire a sense of awe and wonder in human beings

Peat bogs/moors

Act as natural coastal defences against storm surges, strong winds and coastal floods

Tropical coral reefs

Soak up rainwater and release it slowly, therefore reducing the risk of flooding downstream

Sand dunes

Act as huge stores of carbon dioxide, so helping to regulate the greenhouse effect

Activity

1 Explain what would happen to our food production without bees and beetles.

2 Using Figure 17:
   a) List the places where water is stored in the rainforest.
   b) Explain how water flows from the atmosphere to the forest and back again.

3 Describe and explain why:
   a) areas of rainforest maintain a steady supply of water for local communities
   b) damaging the structure of the rainforest could affect local people, and people in the wider region.

4 Discuss the six ecosystems in Figure 16. For each ecosystem identify at least one key service (the yellow boxes) that it provides.

5 Write a letter campaigning for the conservation of Central America's cloud forest or mangrove forest. Use information from Figures 16 and 17 to provide evidence of the real value of these key services.

Tropical rainforests regulate water supply

Figure 17 shows how rainforests play an essential role in the regional **water cycle** of tropical areas. The forest acts as a **store** for water in between rainfall events. After a rainstorm it is thought that about 80 per cent of the rainfall is transferred back to the atmosphere by evaporation and transpiration. This moisture condenses forming rain clouds for the next rainstorm. So rainforests are a source of moisture for future rainfall events.

At least 200 million people live in the world's tropical rainforests. This includes the tribal groups, or **indigenous peoples**, of the rainforest. Many more people live downstream of the rivers that leave these forests. The forest maintains a constant and even supply of water to these rivers. If the rainforest water cycle were to be broken then the water supply of many millions of people could be put at risk. The total amount of water flowing in the rivers would be reduced and the supply would become more uneven with periods of low water supply punctuated by sudden flooding.

Conservationists argue that we need to place a greater value on these key services than on the value of the tropical timber alone. The benefit of a clean and regular water supply can be measured in financial terms. Rebuilding homes after a river flood can also be measured financially. The conservationists argue that these key services are more valuable in the long term than the short-term profits gained from logging.

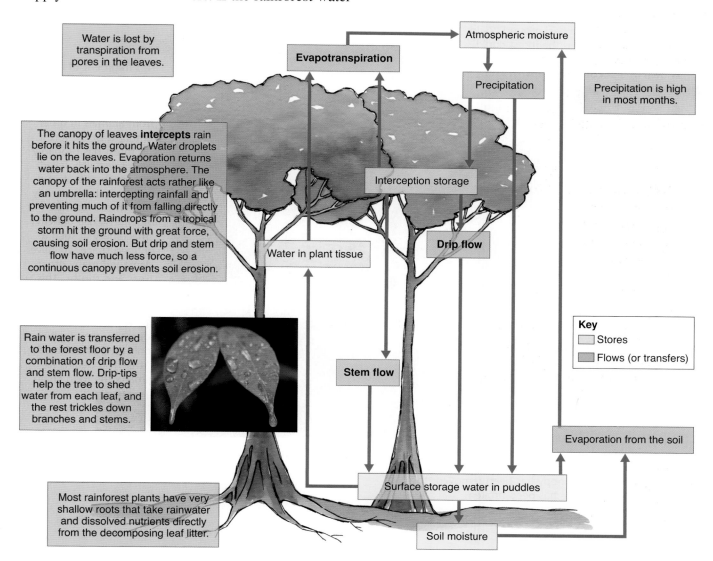

Figure 17 The water cycle in a tropical rainforest

How does the structure of the rainforest prevent soil erosion and flooding?

The canopy of the rainforest acts rather like an umbrella: intercepting rainfall and preventing much of it from falling directly to the ground. Raindrops from a tropical storm hit the ground with great force, causing soil erosion. But drip and stem flow have much less force, so a continuous canopy prevents soil erosion.

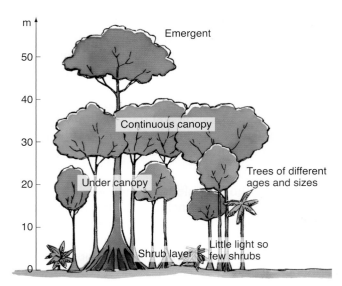

Figure 18 Typical structure of the tropical rainforest

The forest in the foreground was burnt a few months ago. The stumps and roots of larger trees have helped to retain soil. What was once the forest floor (and therefore starved of direct sunlight) is now open to sunlight and weeds have quickly colonised. Seeds from trees in the background could blow into this area and the forest could regrow in around 40 years (creating what is known as a **secondary rainforest**).

This fragment of forest is now an **ecological island**, and animals here are separated from animals in other remnants of the forest. This forest has probably been selectively felled: trees such as teak and mahogany have already been cut for their timber. The use of heavy machinery in such a confined space will have damaged many other trees and shrubs. This process opens up holes in the canopy. It also deprives insects of a food source (some of which only feed on selected trees) so begins to damage the food chain.

The forest here has been **clear felled** and recently burnt. The entire structure of canopy, under-canopy and shrub layer has been destroyed. The soils are vulnerable to erosion, especially on this slope. Obviously, since the canopy has been removed, the nutrient cycle has been broken.

Figure 19 Tropical rainforest cleared in Madagascar

Forest type	Location of study	Percentage intercepted and evaporated from canopy
Sitka spruce (conifer)	Scotland	28
Douglas fir (conifer)	Oregon (USA)	19
Beech (deciduous)	England	15
Tropical rainforest	Indonesia	21
Tropical rainforest	Dominica	27
Tropical rainforest	West Malaysia	27

Figure 20 Interception and evaporation of water from different forest canopies

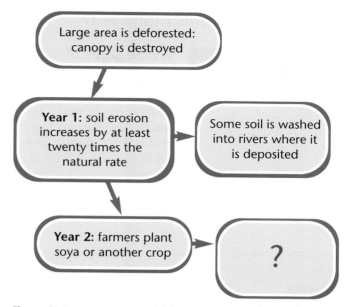

Figure 21 The consequences of deforestation

Figure 22 Logging next to a river in Borneo

Activity

1 Explain how the canopy of the rainforest reduces the risk of soil erosion.

2 **a)** Choose a suitable method to create a graph of the data in Figure 20.

   b) Calculate average interception rates for a coniferous forest, deciduous forest, and tropical rainforest.

   c) Suggest why the deciduous forest has significantly lower figures.

3 **a)** Using Figure 21 as a starting point, create a flowchart or spider diagram to explain the links between deforestation, soil erosion, silt deposition in rivers, and river floods.

   b) Write suitable annotations to fill the boxes on Figure 22.

How are ecosystems managed?

Solomon Islands

A case study of logging in the Solomon Islands

The Solomon Islands are a large group of islands in the Pacific Ocean. The natural ecosystem of these mountainous islands is tropical rainforest. The World Bank estimates GNI (per person) to be $730, making this the poorest country in the Pacific region. The country has one of the highest malaria rates in the world and infant mortality is high. Standards of education also need to be improved and adult literacy is relatively low compared with other Pacific countries. The country's economic and social development was crippled by fighting between different ethnic groups between 2000 and 2003. Since then the government has struggled to create economic growth.

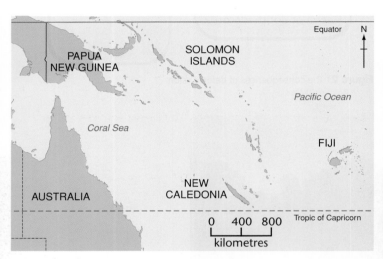

Figure 23 Location of the Solomon Islands

How has the tropical rainforest ecosystem traditionally been used?

More than 80 per cent of Solomon Islanders are subsistence farmers or fishermen. This means they only produce enough food to feed their own families and do not make much profit from their work. The islands are heavily forested and most communities are located around the coastline. The rainforest is still an important resource for villagers. They use it to gather foodstuffs such as fruit, nuts and honey. They also collect leaves, berries and bark to make traditional medicine. For many communities the forest is also an important source of timber not only for building and repairing their homes, but also to build their ocean-going fishing canoes.

Figure 24 Houses in coastal villages are still built using local materials and traditional methods. Houses are built on stilts using the trunks of young trees lashed together with rope made from vines. They have open windows to take advantage of sea breezes and are thatched using palm leaves from the sago tree

Activity

1 Use Figure 23 to copy and complete the following:

The Solomon Islands are located in the .... Ocean to the .... of Papua New Guinea. They are approximately .... km to the north of New Caledonia. They are between the Tropic of Capricorn and the ....

Logging and agri-business

Timber, oil palm and minerals are the main exports of the Solomon Islands. Logging is a fast-growing industry. Many **transnational companies (TNCs)** have recently bought logging rights to fell and export timber from the Solomons.

Most of the timber is exported as unprocessed logs. This means that jobs are not created in the Solomons to process the wood into planks, plywood or furniture – jobs which would help create wealth in this poor country.

China is one of the largest importers of timber from the Solomons. Global Timber, an NGO that monitors the logging trade, estimates that as much as 90 per cent of the tropical hardwood that China **imports** from the Solomon Islands has been felled illegally. Many ecologists are very worried about the damaging impact that this industry is having on the Solomon Islands' fragile environment. They believe that if felling continues at this rate, most of the country's rainforest will have been destroyed by 2020.

Where land has been cleared of forest it has often been converted to oil palm plantations. Huge areas of land that once had a vast diversity of plants and animals now have just oil palms. These plantations are run by internationally owned agricultural businesses (or **agri-business**). These trees produce an oil that can be used in the making of many products, including vegetable oil for cooking, soap, washing powder and bio-fuel (such as bio-diesel for cars).

	Solomon Islands	New Zealand	Fiji
GNI US$	730	28,780	3,800
Under 5 mortality (deaths per 1,000 live births)	73	6	18
Life expectancy	63	80	69
% infants with a low birth weight	13	6	10
% population using improved (safe) drinking water	70	100	47
Maternal mortality: Annual number of women who die from pregnancy-related causes per every 100,000 live births	220	9	210
Adult literacy (% who can read and write)	76	100	96

Figure 25 Development data for selected Pacific region countries. Source: Unicef

Figure 26 Logs felled by a Malaysian TNC are tagged before being exported to Malaysia

Activity

2 **a)** List the ways in which rural communities use the tropical rainforest as a resource.
  b) Explain why this type of use is unlikely to do lasting damage to the ecosystem.

3 **a)** Choose suitable graphical techniques to illustrate the development data in Figure 25. Use your graphs to make comparisons between the Solomon Islands and the other countries.
  b) Explain why the government of the Solomon Islands needs to create jobs and wealth.

4 Explain why converting the rainforest to oil palm plantations concerns many environmentalists.

Is logging sustainable?

The second largest island in the Solomons is Santa Isabel. The communities in North Isabel sold logging rights to a Malaysian TNC. This meant that the land was still owned by the community, but the logging company paid the community for the right to log timber for a fixed period of time. They made various promises to protect the environment during logging. Figures 27 and 28 provide evidence that the TNC operating in Santa Isabel broke these promises. Their poor logging practices have resulted in severe soil erosion, silting-up of rivers, and flooding.

Commercial logging firms such as this TNC make more profit if they work quickly. They use bulldozers to reach the valuable trees. For every tree cut for its timber, it is estimated that 40 or more are destroyed by the heavy machinery. This process destroys trees that have fruit, nuts or medicinal value to the villagers. The villagers have received payments from the TNC, but this amounts to only about 1 per cent of the value of the timber.

Deforestation damages wildlife habitats and often leads to problems of soil erosion. In many cases the logging companies are acting illegally. **Illegal logging** practices include:

- cutting trees without permission
- cutting trees close to rivers where soil erosion can then lead to flooding
- ignoring the rights of local land owners
- paying bribes to local officials
- non-payment of taxes.

Figure 27 A skid-track to remove felled logs has been created on a slope that is far too steep. This has caused soil erosion. The loggers had promised that they would not create this kind of problem

Figure 28 Waste timber from the logging process blocking the Kahigi river. The TNC agreed not to fell trees within 50 m of any major river or 25 m of any minor stream

	Jan	Feb	Mar	Apr	May	Jun	Jul	Aug	Sep	Oct	Nov	Dec
2009	85	111	138	52	109	88	108	86	108	81	73	87
2010	160	79	132	138	76	111	152	146	134	91	119	116
2011	182	40	263	39	219	92	157	184	127	159	169	143
2012	198	162	118	199	153	178	136	182				

Figure 29 Exports of timber (thousand m³) from Solomon Islands to China. Source: www.globaltimber.org.uk/solomonislands.htm

Could logging be sustainable?

Logging can provide a better income for local people and not cause long-term damage to the environment. This can be achieved in various ways:

- Only a few trees are felled. If only two trees per hectare are felled every ten years, a rainforest will naturally recover.
- Saplings are planted to replace cut trees.
- Local people fell the tree and process the timber on site using small portable tools.

The Isabel Sustainable Forestry Management Project is one small example. It was funded by aid (450,000 euros) given by the European Union in the mid-1990s.

The scheme created skilled labour for local people. Trees are carefully felled to avoid damage to trees of fruit or medicinal value. The timber is then cut into planks in the forest using a portable sawmill. This means that large machines are not needed. It also means that local people add value to the timber, so more profit is retained by the village. This method of processing the timber means that the community keeps about 40 per cent of the finished value of the timber.

The project was successful in protecting 17,000 hectares of forest. But the amount of timber produced has been very small.

Figure 30 Members of the Lobi Community in Morovo Lagoon use a portable sawmill to process a freshly felled log into planks. This tree was felled as part of a sustainable eco-forestry programme

Activity

1 a) Choose a suitable graph to represent the data in Figure 29.
   b) Describe the trend shown by your graph.

2 Use the text on this page to complete a table like this:

Effects on ...	Unsustainable logging practices	Sustainable logging practices
Soils		
Rivers		
Fruit, nut and medicinal trees		

3 Imagine you could visit the communities affected by commercial logging in Isabel. Discuss what they might tell you about the impact of the TNC on their lives.

4 Explain how the Isabel Sustainable Forestry Management Project is able to:
   a) improve standards of living today
   b) ensure decent standards of living for future generations.

Are mangrove ecosystems being used unsustainably?

Mangrove forests grow on tropical coastlines. The trees of the mangrove tolerate flooding by both fresh and salt water, so this is both a forest and a wetland, and it supports a very wide range of fish, insects and animals.

Big business regards mangrove forest as useless wasteland. Mangroves are cut down and the swampy land redeveloped. Over 25 million hectares of mangrove forest are estimated to have been destroyed in the last 100 years. The fastest rates of destruction are in Asia. For example, in the Philippines the amount of mangrove declined from 1 million hectares in 1960 to only 100,000 hectares in 1998. Mangrove forests in Central America currently have the second fastest rates of destruction.

One of the most common reasons for the destruction of mangroves is to convert the land for tourist developments. With their coastal location, mangroves provide a prime location for such things as yachting marinas and hotel complexes. The rapid growth of shrimp (or prawn) farming businesses is another threat to the remaining mangroves. Shrimp farming has grown rapidly over the last 20 years. It is estimated that 1 million hectares of coastal wetlands, including mangroves, has been destroyed in recent years to make the ponds needed by new shrimp farms.

Figure 31 Mangroves and cloud forests are two types of tropical forest. Mangroves grow in coastal regions whereas cloud forests grow in mountainous areas

The forest acts as a natural coastal defence. The roots hold the mud together, protecting the land from erosion and reducing the force of large storm waves.

The forest ecosystem supports a range of animals including howler monkeys, deer and armadillo. The canopy provides safe nesting sites for birds.

The wetlands support crocodiles, snakes and crabs. Tropical fish use these sheltered waters as a breeding ground and nursery.

Large prop roots support the tree above high tide. They trap fine sediment carried in the water, causing it to be deposited.

Figure 32 Why mangroves are important to Central American countries

A local fisherman

Local people lose out because they can no longer use the timber or other resources available in the mangrove forest. Local fishermen have noticed a fall in the number of fish they catch. This may be because the mangroves are a nursery ground for young fish. Shrimp farming releases a lot of fertilisers and other chemicals into the environment. Local people sometimes find that their fresh-water wells have become polluted by these chemicals. These are problems that are likely to affect coastal communities for many years after the farms have been abandoned.

Economics expert

The gains from shrimp farming are often short term. People make quick profits. However, after a few years ponds are abandoned because of disease and pollution. In Asia there are approximately 250,000 hectares of abandoned, polluted ponds where healthy forests once grew. This boom–bust cycle is about to be repeated in Latin America, Africa and the Pacific where shrimp farming is growing in popularity.

Consumer in the UK

The biggest consumers of shrimp (also known as prawns) are the USA, Canada, Japan and Europe. Perhaps consumers will be able to influence what happens to mangroves in Latin America if we demand to know more about how our food is produced. Then we might decide to only buy shrimps or other fish that have been farmed sustainably.

Figure 34 Views on whether the use of mangroves for shrimp farming is sustainable

Activity

1 Describe how mangrove forests provide benefits for wildlife and people.

2 Describe the location of the mangrove forests in Central America.

3 Working in groups, use Figure 33 to investigate the rate of destruction of mangroves in Central America.
   a) Draw a map or series of graphs to represent the data.
   b) Consider each of the following enquiry questions. The data you have may help you to suggest an answer. Discuss what other data you would need to find in order to answer each enquiry fully.
      i)   Which countries have the best record for conservation?
      ii) Are countries with larger tourist industries losing mangroves more rapidly than others?
      iii) Are the Caribbean coastlines losing mangroves faster than Pacific coastlines?

4 Study the points of view in Figure 34.
   a) What are the long-term benefits of shrimp farming and who gets these benefits?
   b) What problems does shrimp farming create for people and wildlife?
   c) Do you think shrimp farming is a sustainable use of this ecosystem? Explain your point of view.
   d) Discuss what consumers in the UK can do to help ensure that ecosystems (either mangroves or other ecosystems) are used sustainably.

	Amount of mangrove forest (hectares)			
Country	**1980**	**1990**	**2000**	**2005**
Antigua and Barbuda	1,570	1,200	850	700
Belize	78,500	78,500	76,500	76,000
Costa Rica	63,400	53,400	41,800	41,000
Cuba	537,400	541,400	545,500	547,500
Dominican Republic	34,400	25,800	19,400	16,800
El Salvador	46,700	35,300	28,500	28,000
Guatamala	18,600	17,400	17,500	17,500
Mexico	1,124,000	985,600	885,000	820,000
Nicaragua	103,400	79,300	65,000	65,000
Panama	250,000	190,000	174,400	170,000

Figure 33 Mangrove destruction in selected Central American and Caribbean countries

Sustainable rainforest management in Central America

Deforestation creates a major problem for wildlife: the forest becomes fragmented. As clearings get bigger the wildlife is restricted to isolated fragments of forest that are separated by farm land. The animals become trapped in islands of forest surrounded by an ocean of farmland.

The governments of Central America (also known as Mesoamerica) are co-operating with each other in an ambitious conservation project. They want to create a continuous **wildlife corridor** through the length of Central America. The corridors will be created by planting strips of forest to connect the remaining fragments of forest together. The project is called the Mesoamerican Biological Corridor (known by its Spanish initials, CBM) and involves all seven governments of Central America, plus Mexico.

Debt-for-nature swap

Mesoamerica is a **biodiversity hotspot**. It only amounts to 1 per cent of the world's land surface, but it is estimated to contain 7 per cent of the world's terrestrial (land-based) species. Western governments are encouraging conservation in this region by offering **debt-for-nature swaps**. Under these arrangements, the Central American governments agree to spend money conserving ecosystems and wildlife. In return, the Western governments agree to reduce the amount of money that is owed to them. One debt-for-nature swap was made between Costa Rica and the USA. In 2007 Costa Rica agreed to spend $26 million on conservation projects. In exchange, the US government and two non-governmental organisations (NGOs) agreed to buy back a similar amount of Costa Rica's debt.

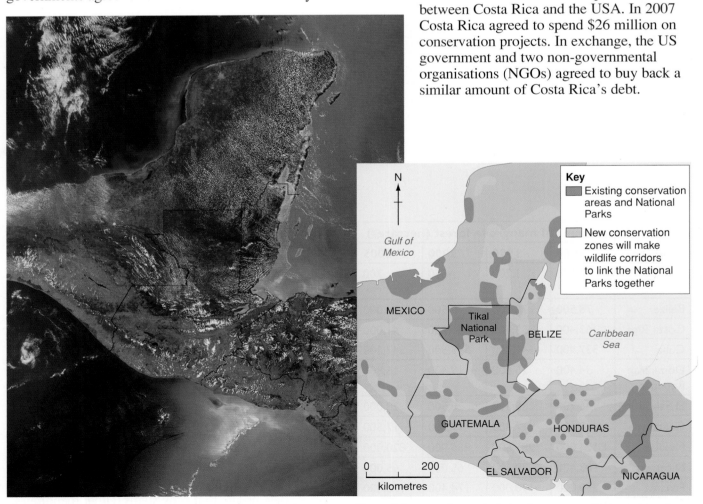

Figure 35 Satellite image of the Mesoamerican Biological Corridor (CBM) project. The red dots show where forest fires are burning

Figure 36 Protected areas (including forest reserves) in Central America and Mexico and the proposed wildlife corridors

Key
- Existing conservation areas and National Parks
- New conservation zones will make wildlife corridors to link the National Parks together

Costa Rica

Ecotourism in Costa Rica

The government and businesses in Costa Rica have also encouraged the growth of **ecotourism**. These are small-scale tourist projects that create money for conservation as well as creating local jobs. It is estimated that 70 per cent of Costa Rica's tourists visit the protected environments. In 2000 Costa Rica earned $1.25 billion from ecotourism. One successful example is the creation of a canopy walkway through a small, privately owned part of the Monteverde reserve. Tourists are charged $45 to climb up into the canopy and walk along rope bridges, the longest of which is 300 m long.

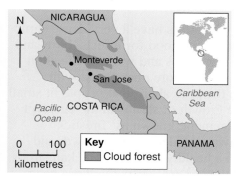

Figure 37
The location of Monteverde reserve

Figure 38 The canopy walkway allows visitors to see the birds and other wildlife that live in the canopy of the cloud forest

Country	Protected land as % of total area
Belize	47.5
Costa Rica	23.4
El Salvador	2.0
Guatemala	25.3
Honduras	20.8
Mexico	5.0
Nicaragua	21.3
Panama	19.5

Figure 39 Protected areas (including forest reserves) in Central America and Mexico. Source: Earthlands

Activity

1 Study Figures 35 and 36.
   a) Describe the location of Tikal National Park.
   b) Describe the distribution of forest fires. Do many appear to be burning in conservation areas?

2 Working in pairs, draw a spider diagram to show how fragmentation of the rainforest affects wildlife. Consider the likely impacts of fragmentation on:
   • food chains
   • success of mating
   • predator/prey relationships
   • pollination and seed dispersal.

3 Explain how the new wildlife corridors will help wildlife.

4 Describe the location of the Monteverde reserve.

5 Study Figure 39.
   a) Calculate the average amount of land that is protected in Central America and Mexico.
   b) Present the data in graphical form – include a bar for the average.
   c) How good is Costa Rica's record on conservation compared with that of its neighbours?

6 Suggest how Western governments benefit from debt-for-nature swaps.

Australia

How should the eucalypt forests of south-east Australia be managed?

Many species of trees and shrubs that are native to Australia contain flammable oil and resins. These oils ignite at temperatures as low as 60°C. The eucalypt forests that grow in south-eastern Australia have particularly high oil content.

Unmanaged eucalypt forests have a very dense shrub layer. This dense forest is good for insects, birds and lizards. However, kangaroos and wallabies feed on grasslands and so need a more open forest with plenty of grass. In the past, aboriginal people lit small fires to control the growth of shrubs in the eucalypt forests. This management, known as 'firestick' farming, cleared away the dense undergrowth and helped to maintain a healthy population of kangaroos for hunting. Over the last 100 years there has been less fire management of the eucalypt forests. This means the amount of shrubby vegetation has increased, and so has the risk of a big fire breaking out and spreading uncontrollably through the forest.

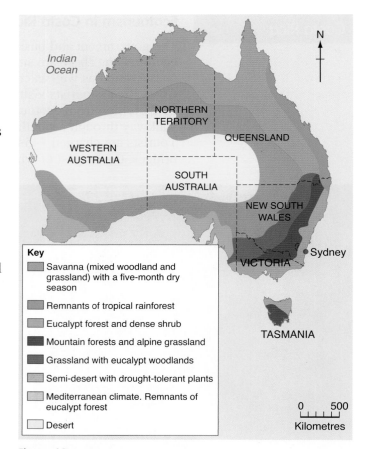

Figure 40 Ecosystems in Australia

Activity

1 Use Figure 41 to outline the main impacts of the forest fires. Use the following headings to organise your notes:
   • Environmental
   • Economic
   • Social

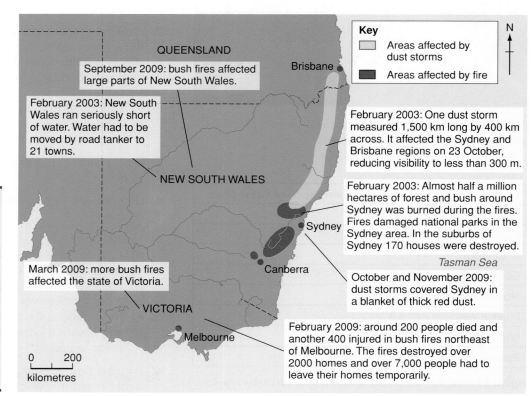

Figure 41 Forest fires in south-east Australia

Reducing the risk of future forest fires

The forest fires of 2003–9 have encouraged a debate about the management of Australia's forests. Managing the eucalypt forests by controlled burning is one possible way to reduce the risk of fire. Controlled fires clear away the fallen branches and scrub vegetation. This technique reduces the risk of big fires breaking out and spreading out of control. However, the different groups who use the eucalypt forests have different points of view about this issue.

Tourism is an essential part of the New South Wales economy. Tourists want to visit natural, undisturbed, unburned forests. They don't want to see smoke or evidence of fire damage. They also want access to all our forests. Controlled fires would restrict access for tourists.

Hotel owner

We are proud of our culture and tradition of 'firestick' farming (controlled fires). These small fires clear away areas of scrub and encourage the growth of grasses. This management creates a range of habitats ideal for different native animals such as kangaroos.

Aboriginal representative

Controlled burning causes smoke pollution. Smoke is a terrible nuisance and a health hazard. If they are going to manage the forests by burning them, then they can only do it when the weather conditions are just right. It can only be done when the ground is wet, or the fire could spread. Also, there must be no wind or the smoke blows into the suburbs.

Home owner in suburbs of Sydney

Privately owned forests are run as a business. They should be cleared of all shrubs and leaf litter. This reduces the risk of uncontrolled forest fires. It also makes it easier for our cattle to graze in the forest, and allows logging lorries to get in and out of the forest easily.

Private landowner of a forest

We are not opposed to the use of controlled burning to reduce shrubs and leaf litter. However, we believe that our national parks should be wild places and that these management techniques should be avoided wherever possible. I don't think that the national parks can be blamed for the fires. Most of the 2003 fires started in privately owned forests and spread into the national parks, not the other way around!

National Park ranger

Figure 42 Opinions about managing the eucalypt forests

Activity

1 Use the opinions in Figure 42. Copy and complete the following table.

	Arguments for controlled burning	**Arguments against controlled burning**
Economic		Burning is hazardous and expensive
Environmental		
Social (how different groups might be affected)		Smoke pollution will cause health problems for residents in the suburbs

2 In groups discuss the other possible options that could be used in south-east Australia.

Why is it difficult to manage ecosystems sustainably?

The Millennium Ecosystem Assessment (MA) is a scientific report into the state of the environment. Published in 2005, it took five years to write and involved the work of more than 1,360 experts from all parts of the world. The MA concludes that the world's resources have been used to create a better standard of living for billions of people. Ecosystems have been used to supply people with a range of resources including food, clothing, energy and fresh water. However, it also warns that economic activity has done a great deal of damage to the environment.

	Millennium Ecosystem Assessment
1	Modern fishing techniques do not allow fish stocks to recover. The amount of fish in the seas is decreasing rapidly.
2	The 2 billion people who live in the world's driest areas are increasingly at risk from drought and poverty.
3	We are using up fresh water supplies at a rate that is faster than they can be replaced.
4	Climate change will cause massive problems for many ecosystems.
5	The increasing use of artificial fertilisers and burning of fossil fuels has doubled the amount of nitrogen pollution. This is causing problems in river and marine ecosystems.
6	The destruction of ecosystems (for example, forests, coral reefs and wetlands) is causing the extinction of many species at a scale that is greater than anything seen in the past.

Figure 43 The six main problems identified by the Millennium Ecosystem Assessment

What is the evidence that marine ecosystems are used unsustainably?

One of the key findings of the Millennium Ecosystem Assessment is that the amount of fish in the seas is decreasing rapidly. If fish are caught faster than the population of fish can reproduce then the fishing industry is unsustainable.

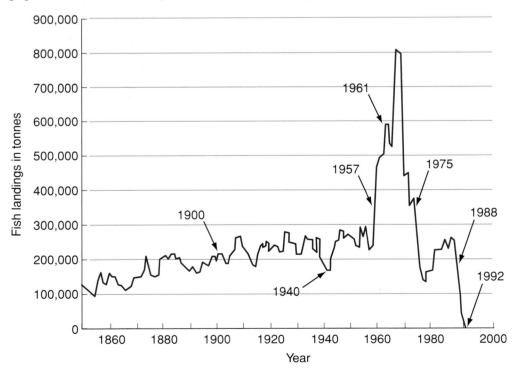

Figure 44 Overfishing caused the collapse of the Atlantic cod stocks off Newfoundland

Year	Fish (tonnes)
1986	23
1987	0
1988	0
1989	542
1990	99
1991	158
1992	301
1993	602
1994	656
1995	950
1996	1,004
1997	1,397
1998	1,642
1999	3,163
2000	3,630
2001	4,460
2002	4,400
2003	10,160
2004	11,428
2005	10,858
2006	7,624
2007	7,700

Figure 45 Amount of fish caught (tonnes) in Belize (see Figure 36 for the location of this Central American country)

Activity

1 Study each of the problems listed in Figure 43. Suggest how each of the following economic activities could have contributed to these problems.
- Agriculture
- Fishing
- Mining
- Timber extraction
- Manufacturing
- Tourism

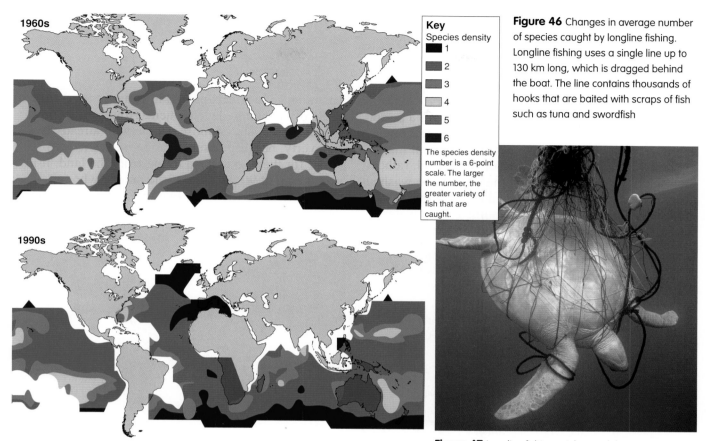

Key

Species density

- ■ 1
- ▨ 2
- ▧ 3
- ▨ 4
- ▨ 5
- ■ 6

The species density number is a 6-point scale. The larger the number, the greater variety of fish that are caught.

1960s

1990s

Figure 46 Changes in average number of species caught by longline fishing. Longline fishing uses a single line up to 130 km long, which is dragged behind the boat. The line contains thousands of hooks that are baited with scraps of fish such as tuna and swordfish

Figure 47 Longline fishing catches and drowns many sea birds and mammals such as turtles. This is known as bycatch

Activity

2 a) Make a sketch of Figure 44.
   b) Describe the trend of the cod catch:
   i) up to 1950   ii) after 1950.
   c) Working in pairs, discuss the labels below. Add these to your copy of the graph in Figure 44 as annotations that explain the trends on the graph.
   A John invests in expensive sonar equipment to find shoals of fish.
   B Tom notices that there are fewer larger (older) fish in the nets.
   C All families use small traditional fishing boats.
   D The Murphy family have to sell their house to repay their debts.
   E The price of locally caught fish rises sharply in the fish market.
   F Some fishing families join up and fight during the Second World War.
   G William finds that his small, traditional boat can no longer compete with the modern trawlers.
   d) Suggest how these changes affected people working in the local fishing industry.

3 a) Choose a suitable graphical method to represent Figure 45.
   b) What conclusions do you draw from the data in Figures 44 and 45?
   c) Is there an alternative explanation for the recent decline in the number of fish caught in Belize?

4 Conservationists are concerned that fish stocks in the North Sea could crash due to overfishing, just like the Atlantic cod crash off Newfoundland. Suggest:
   a) two alternative strategies to protect fish stocks in the North Sea from overfishing
   b) how fishermen, boat repair yards and fishmongers would be affected by your suggestions.

5 Use Figure 46 and an atlas to describe the changing distribution of fish species caught between the 1960s and 1990s.

Chapter 3
The issue of desertification

What is desertification?

Desertification is the process by which dry environments become more like desert. Over a period of years, the amount of natural vegetation decreases and the soil is exposed to the hot sun. When it rains, the rainwater runs over the surface of the soil, rather than soaking down into it, and the soil can be washed away. The soil becomes degraded or worn out. It's harder to grow crops and food shortages and water shortages may both become more common.

Desertification is a serious issue that affects over 1 billion people around the world. It affects large parts of North America, Africa, Central Asia and

Australia, so it affects people in countries at different levels of economic development. However, its most serious effects are on those people who already live in poverty, because desertification makes it even harder for them to make a living from the land. It is estimated that 90 per cent of the people who are affected by desertification live in the world's poorer countries and that US $42 billion worth of income is lost due to desertification every year.

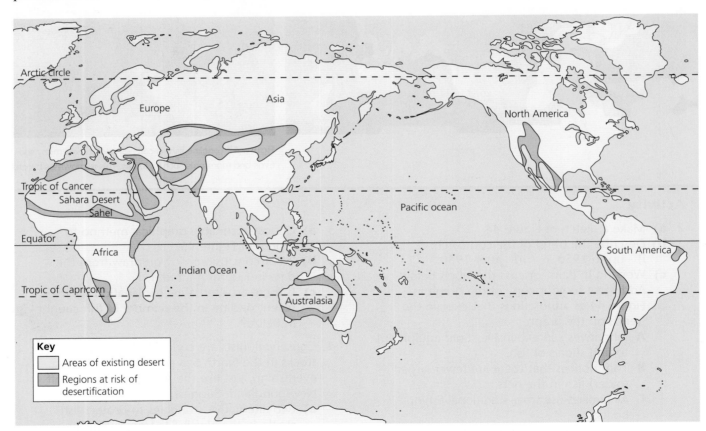

Figure 1 Regions at risk of desertification

Activity

1 Study Figure 1.
   a) Describe the location of the Sahel.
   b) Describe the distribution of other regions at risk of desertification.
   c) Name two wealthy countries at risk of desertification.

Unpredictable patterns of rainfall

Regions that have low rainfall totals each year are at most risk from desertification. The **Sahel** region of Africa is one such region. The Sahel has a long dry season of nine months, followed by a wet season of rainfall for three months. The total amount of rainfall over these three months is similar to the total amount of rainfall in Cambridge in a year. However, these wet seasons have become unpredictable, with short periods of heavy rainfall running off the land and failing to soak down into the soil where it is needed to recharge the soil moisture and rock **aquifers**.

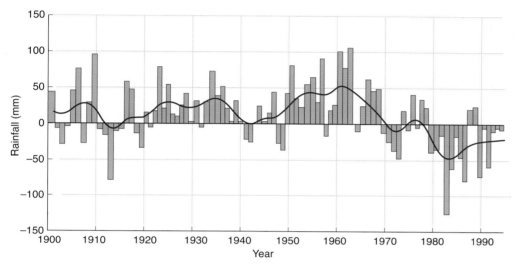

www.wateraid. org.uk

A number of Non-Governmental Organisations (NGOs), such as WaterAid, work in Mali to try to improve the amount of fresh water available.

Figure 2 Annual rainfall anomalies in Sahel countries 1900–95. Each bar represents whether the total rainfall in each year was above or below average. The line shows the trend.

Activity

2 Use Figure 2.
  a) How many years between 1900 and 1965 had:
    i) above-average rainfall of 50 mm or more?
    ii) below-average rainfall of –50 mm or less?
  b) How many years between 1965 and 1995 had:
    i) above-average rainfall of 50 mm or more?
    ii) below-average rainfall of –50 mm or less?
  c) Using evidence from Figure 2, compare rainfall patterns in the Sahel before 1965 with the period from 1965 to 1995.

3 Use the internet link to WaterAid, above, to research how this charity is helping to solve problems of water shortages in Africa. From the home page click on the drop-down menu under the heading 'Where we work'. Select Mali and then Ethiopia.
  a) Prepare a short report that focuses on:
    • a comparison of the water problems facing the two countries
    • how WaterAid and other NGOs are tackling problems in urban or rural areas in the two countries.
  b) Use the website to:
    • suggest how water and sanitation are linked to disease and poverty
    • explain why WaterAid thinks it is essential to involve women in their projects.

Seasonal rainfall patterns in the savanna

The regions that suffer from desertification are regions which have a tropical climate with a long dry season followed by a short rainy season. During the rainy season, rainfall is due to a combination of frontal rainfall and convectional rainfall. These regions naturally have a savanna ecosystem of grasses, shrubs and trees. The trees are scattered. They do not form a continuous canopy like that of a tropical rainforest. However, the trees, shrubs and grasses all protect the soil from erosion. In regions where the trees and shrubs have been cut down or burnt, the process of desertification has been rapid. Therefore, it seems that the process of desertification is caused, at least in part, by poor management of the land.

Figure 5 What farmers in Ghana had noticed about the changing environment in a 20-year period

Signs of desertification	% of people in survey
Poor rainfall	27
Less trees in the landscape	22
Less shade from trees and shrubs for animals	20
Poor harvest	16
Streams and ponds drying up	2

Figure 3 The seasonal movement of the tropical rain band (ITCZ) across Africa

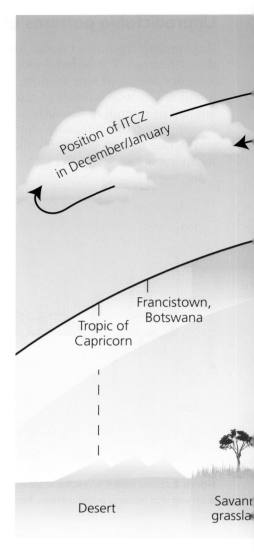

Figure 4 Annual rainfall totals in selected cities

	latitude	Jan	Feb	Mar	Apr	May	Jun	Jul	Aug	Sep	Oct	Nov	Dec
Bamako, Mali	12°N	0	0	3	15	74	137	279	348	206	43	15	0
Tamale, Ghana	9°N	3	3	53	69	104	142	125	196	226	99	10	5
Kumasi, Ghana	6°N	61	291	479	560	546	598	302	311	390	361	89	42
Francistown, Botswana	21°S	107	79	71	18	5	3	0	0	0	23	56	86

Activity

1 a) Draw a series of rainfall graphs for the four cities in Figure 4.
   b) For each graph, describe:
      i)   the total amount of annual rainfall
      ii) the length of the rainy season.
   c) Use Figure 2 on page 80 and Figure 3 above to explain why the tropical rain belt moves during the year.
   d) Use Figure 3 to predict the seasonal rainfall pattern of Lilongwe, Malawi (location is at latitude 14°S).

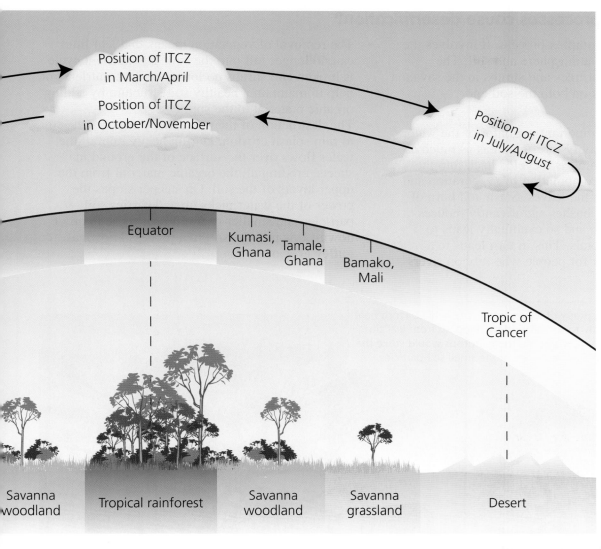

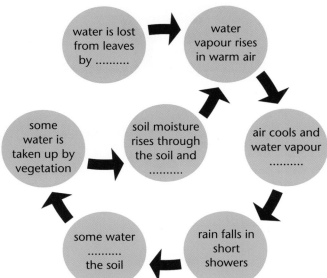

Figure 6 Convectional rainfall during the wet season

Activity

2 **a)** Make a copy of Figure 6. Complete the diagram by adding the correct words below:

evaporates condenses transpiration infiltrates

b) Predict what would happen to the amount of rainfall if lots of trees were cut down.

3 **a)** Produce a graph or graphs to represent the data in Figure 5.
b) Suggest how each of these 'signs of desertification' could have affected people, their health, their livestock **or** the natural environment.

What physical processes cause desertification?

Desertification is a complex process. It involves the interaction of plants, atmosphere and soil. The burning and felling of trees and shrubs in the savanna has a massive impact on both the soil and atmosphere:

- Vegetation is an important regulator of the water cycle. In more heavily forested areas as much as 80 per cent of rainfall is recycled back into the atmosphere by a combination of evaporation and transpiration from the leaves. Slash and burn of savanna trees and bushes significantly reduces evapotranspiration and so eventually leads to reduced rainfall totals. This in turn leads to a reduction in water for people who rely on rivers for water supply.

- The removal of vegetation means that leaf litter can no longer fall into the soil. The nutrient cycle is broken and shrubs no longer replace nutrients or help to maintain a healthy soil structure by adding organic material to the soil.

- The destruction of the tree canopy exposes the soil to rain splash erosion. During heavy rainfall the water flows over the surface of the ground in sheets, eroding all the organic material from the upper layers of the soil. On steeper slopes the power of the water picks up and carries soil particles and smaller rocks. It uses these to erode downwards into the soil in a process known as **gulley erosion**.

The dense canopy of leaves intercepts rainfall. From here it falls gently to the ground by dripping from leaf tips. Without this interception, the raindrops would strike the soil and their force can erode small soil particles.

The surface of the soil becomes baked in the heat. Moisture in the soil is drawn upwards and evaporates from the surface.

The canopy of leaves provides shade. Air temperatures in the shade can be 20°C cooler than in the open, so the soil stays cooler.

Roots help to bind the soil together and prevent gulley erosion.

Figure 7 Interactions between vegetation, soils and climate

Figure 8 Gulley erosion is a common problem in areas suffering from desertification. This farmer is placing large stones across the width of the gulley.

Farmers allow their goats to overgraze shrubs, and vegetation is killed

Annual rainfall totals are gradually falling

Trees and shrubs are burnt to clear land for farming or urbanisation

Trees are cut down for firewood for cooking

The rain in the wet season is unpredictable and can be very heavy, causing soil erosion

Commercial farms use the land so intensively that the soil is quickly worn out

Less vegetation means less water is returned to the atmosphere by evapotranspiration

Figure 9 Physical and human factors that may cause desertification

Activity

1   Sort the causes of desertification listed in Figure 9 into physical and human factors.

2   Study Figures 7 and 8. Use the information to write an explanation of what will happen if…

Farmers allow goats to overgraze	Effect on vegetation	
	Effect on soils	
	Effect on climate	

3   Explain why the farmer is placing rocks across the gulley in Figure 8.

4   **a)** Use pages 124–125, and the glossary, to make sure you understand the following key terms:

   infiltration   interception   overland flow evaporation of soil moisture   transpiration gulley erosion

   b) Predict whether each of the processes in question **4a** will increase or decrease during desertification.

   c) Write a short news report about the issue of desertification. Make sure you use each of the key terms from question **4a** in your report.

Ghana

A case study of desertification and poverty

Ghana is a tropical country in West Africa. Ghana covers an area of 238,000 square kilometres, making it very similar in size to the UK (244,000 square kilometres). While all parts of Ghana have a hot tropical climate, the amount of rainfall varies significantly from north to south. Northern Ghana is the driest part of the country, with a dry season that can last up to eight months of the year. The natural vegetation in this dry zone is grassland and savanna woodland. In recent years, huge numbers of trees from these environments have been felled to increase the size of farms or to use as firewood. Most rural people cook using wood or charcoal on open stoves. People in the cities buy wood from the countryside for cooking too. As a consequence of this damage to the vegetation, soil erosion has become a serious issue. Deforestation may even be contributing to local climate change by reducing the amount of water that can return back into the atmosphere through evapotranspiration.

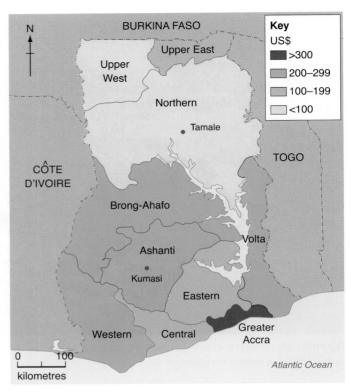

Figure 10 Regional differences in income in Ghana

Activity

1   Use Figure 10 to describe distribution of regions in Ghana where average incomes were below US $200 in 2000.

2   **a)** Use Figure 11 to describe how intensively arable crops are grown in Ashanti compared to the Northern region.

   b) Discuss the evidence on this page carefully. Is there any evidence linking poverty and desertification? If so, which do you think is the cause and which is the effect? Discuss what you think could be done to solve the problem.

Natural vegetation is savanna grassland. The risk of soil erosion in the Northern and Upper West regions is classified as Moderate to Very Severe.

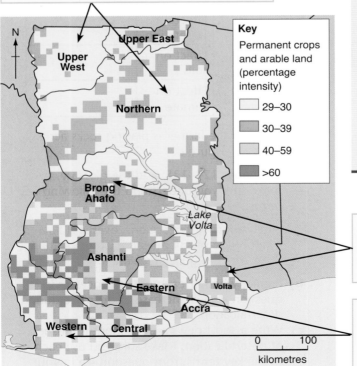

Natural vegetation is savannah woodland. The risk of soil erosion in Brong Ahafo and Volta is classified as Slight to Moderate.

Natural vegetation is tropical rainforest. The risk of soil erosion in Ashanti and Western regions is classified as Moderate to Severe.

Figure 11 Arable farming and the risk of soil erosion

How do differences in quality of life affect people in Ghana?

The northern regions of Ghana face severe problems such as poverty, lack of job opportunities (especially for women), and lack of safe drinking water. The region has a harsh climate and farming is an unreliable way of making a living. The lack of decent roads and public transport makes it difficult for rural families to get to local towns to visit friends, go to the shops, or get medical attention. There is a severe shortage of teachers in the northern regions of Ghana. In rural northern Ghana, the **infant mortality rate (IMR)** is twice as high as in urban areas in the south. Malaria, acute respiratory infections, diarrhoea, malnutrition and measles are still the five main causes of death in young children.

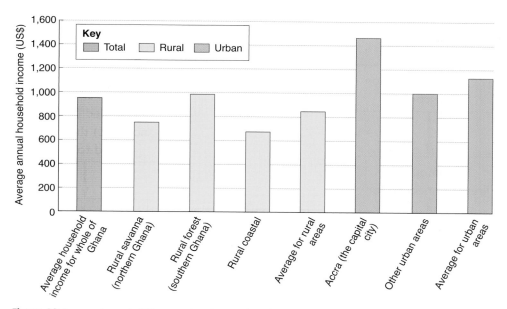

Figure 12 Average household incomes in urban and rural parts of Ghana (last survey 2000)

	Immunisation coverage (%)		
	1998	2003	Difference
National	62	69.4	7.4
Western	67.4	60.4	−7
Central	49.1	82.1	
Greater Accra	73.7	69.1	
Volta	59.8	82.3	
Eastern	52.1	65.6	
Ashanti	67.8	71.6	
Brong-Ahafo	66.6	79	
Northern	47.4	48	
Upper East	68	77	
Upper West	65.8	60.3	

Figure 13 Percentage of children immunised by region, Ghana

Activity

3 Use Figure 12 to compare the average household income in rural savanna regions to the urban areas of Ghana.

4 Suggest how each of the following factors contributes to the high infant mortality rates in the north of Ghana:
   a) poor transport networks.
   b) low family incomes.

5 a) Copy Figure 13 into your book and complete the final column (two rows have been done for you).
   b) Choose a suitable technique to map or graph the data in this column.
   c) Comment on the progress being made in Ghana to improve quality of life in rural areas.

Is poor land management the cause of desertification in Ghana?

Farming in the savanna region of Ghana is a mixture of crop growing and animal grazing. Farmers keep goats and cattle for both their milk and meat. Crops are grown using a traditional bush fallow system. Scrub vegetation is removed by slashing and burning. Crops such as maize, root crops and vegetables are grown for between one and three years. The land is then abandoned for between eight and fifteen years. This is known as the fallow period. During this fallow period, the natural shrubs grow back.

Leaves from the shrubs decompose in the soil, replacing organic fibre and nutrients that have been taken out by farming. This system is sustainable as long as the fallow period remains long enough. However, in some villages the fallow period is now only two to three years. This does not give the soil enough time to recover. It loses its organic content and its structure becomes dusty. This means that the soil is at risk of erosion from both wind and rainfall.

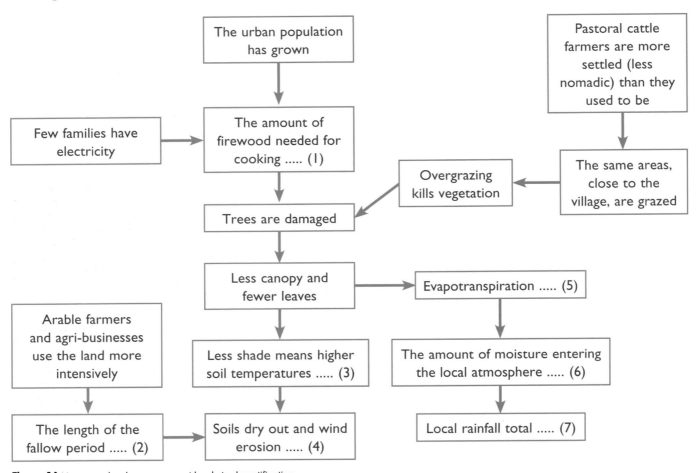

Figure 14 How poor land management leads to desertification

Activity

1 Copy and complete the following description of the bush fallow system:

   Natural vegetation is cleared using slash and ….. techniques. Crops are grown for one to ….. years. The land is then allowed to rest for at least ….. years in between crops. This is known as the ….. period. During this time ….. are returned to the soil.

2 Explain why:
   a) the traditional bush fallow system is sustainable
   b) reducing the length of the fallow period has degraded the soil.

3 Make a copy of Figure 14. Complete the boxes numbered 1–7 by adding the word *decreases* or *increases*.

Is commercial farming to blame for desertification and food shortages?

In recent years, many European Trans National Companies (TNCs) have either bought or leased land in Africa to grow crops. This means that land is converted from the traditional bush fallow system by large agricultural businesses (known as agri-businesses) that usually grow a single crop in very large fields. Some agri-businesses grow biofuel crops (crops that are then processed for their natural oils). These oils are then used in biofuels that replace diesel in European cars. One such crop is jatropha. A large number of foreign TNCs, including Agroils (Italy) and ScanFuel (Norway) have been buying or leasing land in Ghana over the last ten years. It is estimated that 5 million hectares (an area the size of Denmark) is now used for commercial farming by foreign agri-businesses in this way and that as much as 37 per cent of all of Ghana's cropland is now used to grow jatropha.

Figure 15 Jatropha is a crop grown for its oil content.

Some see this as an important way for Ghana to earn foreign income. In the past, Ghana earned most of its income from the export of tropical timbers. This led to a rapid loss of tropical rainforest during the period 1950–1980. Growing commercial crops such as jatropha should be more sustainable.

Figure 16 Stakeholder views on the growth of Jatropha in Ghana

> The European Union needs to tackle climate change. One way to achieve this is to reduce our use of petrol and diesel in Europe. We have therefore set a target of 10 per cent of transport fuels to come from renewable sources by 2020. There isn't enough space in Europe to grow all of the biofuels we need, so some has to be grown in Africa.

An EU spokesperson

> Small farmers like me, especially women farmers, are being pushed from our communal land by large commercial farms who are growing jatropha. I used to sell the fruit and nuts from my shea nut and dawadawa trees in the local market. But all of these different trees have been cleared away to make space for fields of jatropha. What will local people eat if we stop growing our own food?

A Ghanaian farmer

> Too much land is being grabbed by foreign companies to supply Europe with biofuels. The situation is out of control. Jatropha is not a wonder crop. It uses valuable water resources and needs expensive pesticides. In some regions food crops have been cleared to plant jatropha so local farmers have no source of food.

A spokesperson for Friends of the Earth

> I think that growing large fields of crops like jatropha puts too much strain on land that is at risk of desertification. The bush fallow system allows the soil to recover between crops. Commercial farms use the land more intensively. Some scientists believe that, without careful management, the soils will become worn out by commercial farming and then be at risk of erosion.

Soil scientist

Activity

4 Discuss the stakeholder views in Figure 16:
   a) Who benefits from planting crops such as jatropha?
   b) What are the main arguments for allowing agri-businesses to grow biofuel crops in Africa?
   c) What are the main arguments against this development?
   d) Create a newspaper article which describes this issue and provide an editorial comment either for or against the further development of biofuels in Africa.

Mali

Managing the problems of desertification in Mali and Niger

The twin problems of lack of water and soil erosion can be managed and the future of Sahel countries can be sustainable. What is needed is a combination of low-technology **rainwater harvesting** and soil conservation strategies, similar to those used in the drier regions of South Africa (see pages 252–53). These include:

- tree-planting schemes
- building small rock dams
- collecting rainwater from the roofs of buildings
- building terraces on steeper slopes
- building stone lines on gentle slopes
- planting grass strips along the contours of gentle slopes.

How do bunds help?

One strategy that has been used successfully in crop-growing regions of Burkina Faso and Mali is the construction of low stone lines known as bunds. Stones are placed along the contours on gentle slopes. Sometimes the bunds are reinforced by planting tough grasses along the lines. The stones and grass encourage rainwater to infiltrate the soil and reduce the amount of rainwater that is lost by run-off. They also prevent soil erosion.

Activity

1 Explain how stone lines are able to:
  a) reduce soil erosion
  b) increase soil moisture
  c) increase the amount of grain grown.

Run-off is slowed by the bund, giving more time for infiltration.

Rainwater infiltrates and recharges soil moisture.

Bunds are placed 10 to 25 m apart.

Any soil that has been eroded by run-off is trapped by the bund. Topsoil and organic matter (e.g. leaf litter) is deposited here.

Figure 17 How bunds work

130

Could better wood burning stoves be the answer?

Most cooking in both the rural and urban areas of the Sahel is done on traditional open fires or simple wood burning stoves. These stoves are very inefficient. They use a lot of fuel and produce a lot of smoke that, when breathed in over many years, can cause very serious health issues.

Practical Action is a charity that works with local communities in developing countries to produce appropriate technologies that are efficient and affordable for poorer families. One of their initiatives has been the design of the Upesi stove in Kenya. Women potters make the stoves using clay collected from local riverbanks. The clay is moulded into shape and then fired in a kiln. The stoves are affordable, costing about the same as a chicken.

 http://practicalaction.org/ is the website of Practical Action. They use technology to challenge poverty.

Figure 18 Women in Kenya making Upesi stoves which are much more efficient than traditional cooking stoves

GEOGRAPHICAL SKILLS

Diamond ranking

Diamond ranking, or diamond nine, is a useful technique to use when you have been asked to make a decision. Sometimes it's not easy to try to rank or prioritise ideas when there is no obvious answer. Use this technique to group your ideas, putting your favourite ideas near the top, and the ones you think are less convincing at the bottom of the diamond.

Activity

1 **a)** Discuss the nine benefits of the Upesi stove in Figure 19.
   b) Place each of the benefits into a copy of the diamond nine diagram.
   c) Explain why you have chosen your top three benefits.

2 'The Upesi stove is a sustainable solution to the problem of desertification'. How far do you agree with this statement? Consider the arguments for and against.

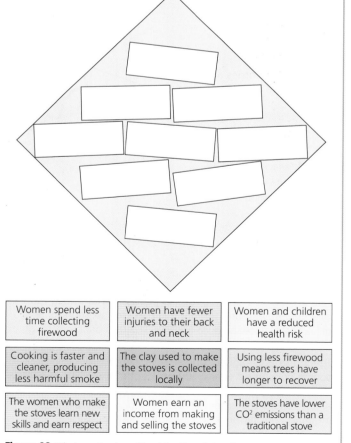

Women spend less time collecting firewood	Women have fewer injuries to their back and neck	Women and children have a reduced health risk
Cooking is faster and cleaner, producing less harmful smoke	The clay used to make the stoves is collected locally	Using less firewood means trees have longer to recover
The women who make the stoves learn new skills and earn respect	Women earn an income from making and selling the stoves	The stoves have lower CO_2 emissions than a traditional stove

Figure 19 What are the benefits of the Upesi stove?

Mali

How can the international community help?

The United Nations leads the international effort to tackle the issue of desertification through the UN Convention to Combat Desertification (UNCCD). Their aim is to encourage each country affected by desertification to set up a National Action Programme (NAP). They have been successful in getting 193 countries to sign up. In 2007 the UNCCD announced a 10-year strategy (2008–2018) to make drylands sustainable. It relies on each country raising funds and creating their own NAP. Critics say that the UNCCD strategy is flawed since the most badly affected countries are also the poorest and more should be done to help these countries work in partnership with each other.

Desertification, drought and food shortages

The international community is helping countries in the Sahel region of Africa to tackle some of the problems caused by desertification through a combination of emergency and long-term development aid projects. In 2004, the subsistence farmers of Mali and Niger were hit by a severe drought and a plague of locusts that almost destroyed their crops. By 2005 it was clear that 3.3 million people (including 800,000 children) were at risk from a serious food shortage.

Figure 20 Location of the 2005 food crisis in Africa and percentage of population in the region who are usually undernourished

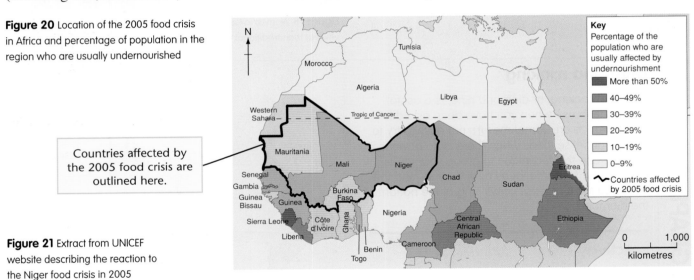

Countries affected by the 2005 food crisis are outlined here.

Key
Percentage of the population who are usually affected by undernourishment
- More than 50%
- 40–49%
- 30–39%
- 20–29%
- 10–19%
- 0–9%
- Countries affected by 2005 food crisis

Figure 21 Extract from UNICEF website describing the reaction to the Niger food crisis in 2005

In light of this emergency, UNICEF Niger has routed an additional US$270,000 to treat 14,000 malnourished children for six months.

However, the children's agency urgently needs US$1.03 million to treat another 17,000 severely malnourished children with therapeutic food (a peanut butter based food called plumpynut and therapeutic milk) for six months, and make cereal accessible to another 163,000 people through the purchase of 641 tonnes to restock 65 cereal banks.

During the 2004 agricultural season, swarms of desert locusts consumed nearly 100 per cent of the crops in some areas. In addition, parts of the country received insufficient rainfall resulting in poor harvests and dry pasturelands, affecting both farmers and livestock breeders.

On a regular basis, UNICEF implements strategies to prevent malnutrition at the community level. Here are some examples:

- 245 cereal banks were opened in UNICEF's intervention zones to make staple grains (millet and sorghum) available. Before the harvest, when food supplies are low and hunger increases, cereal banks loan food to mothers. After harvest, the women repay their loans in cash or grain.

- UNICEF also supports 300 women's groups that promote exclusive breastfeeding and monitor children's growth in the villages. Women with malnourished children receive loans of goats to enrich their families' diets with milk and cheese.

- Twice a year, vitamin A supplements are provided to all children under the age of five. Supplementary feeding centres receive therapeutic food for severely malnourished children. This food is high in protein and fat.

Long-term development aid projects in Niger and Mali

In 2005 the UK Government gave £3 million to the World Food Programme's emergency operation to help relieve the crisis in Niger. Each £1 million was enough to feed 200,000 people for one month. In 2006 the UK Government gave a further £2 million of emergency aid to support the diet of families in Niger before the next harvest was available.

The UK Government also funds a number of long-term development projects in this region. Between 2006 and 2009 the Government spent £500,000 each year in Niger, Mali and Burkina Faso, helping to improve diet and nutrition. It is also working with the French Government in a long-term project to improve girls' education in Niger.

Oxfam is one of many Non-Governmental Organisations that provide long-term development aid to Niger and Mali. In one of its projects it is working with the Association for the Indigenous Development of the Sahel (ADESAH), a local NGO, to support primary schools for the children of **pastoral farmers** who live in the border area between western Niger and northern Mali. This nomadic community of cattle and goat herders is very poor. Many families do not feel they can afford to send their children to school, especially girls. The project supports 48 primary schools. Its successes include the following:

Figure 22 Class in Taboye school, Mali, which has received support from Oxfam and the local NGO ADESAH. It's a Millennium Development Goal to ensure that all boys and girls in the world complete their primary education

- In 2004, 4,053 pupils were enrolled in school, including 1,818 girls (44.85 per cent).
- Women are deeply involved in the management of the schools and participate physically and financially in the payment of children's school fees and in the canteen.
- The ratio of books to pupils has improved from one book for five pupils to two books for three pupils.

Activity

1 Use Figure 20 to describe the distribution of countries that have:
   a) between 0 and 9 per cent of the population who are undernourished
   b) more than 30 per cent of the population who are undernourished.

2 Suggest reasons why some countries in Africa are more vulnerable to food shortages than others.

3 Read the web extract in Figure 21.
   a) Give two reasons for the food crisis.
   b) Use Figure 21 to give examples of both UNICEF's emergency aid and long-term aid programmes.

4 Explain the difference between the aims of UNICEF's emergency aid and long-term strategies to prevent malnutrition.

5 Give three details that describe the group who benefit from Oxfam's project.

6 Give two facts that can be used as measures of success of this project.

7 Try to explain why Oxfam may have chosen to fund a project that gives aid to girls and women.

8 Use the internet links below to prepare a brief report on a long-term aid programme to either Mali or Niger. Include in your report:
   - how different groups of people (for example children, women, farmers) benefit from the aid
   - facts you could use to evaluate the success of the project.

www.oxfam.org.uk
www.trickleup.org
www.wateraid.org.uk
The NGOs whose websites are listed above have long-term aid projects in Mali and Niger.

What are the possible effects of climate change on LEDCs?

Climate change is likely to have a serious impact on people and environments in Africa. More frequent extreme weather events, increased temperatures and more irregular patterns of rainfall will have effects on crop production, which in turn could damage some economies and cause food shortages. It is also likely that the mosquitoes that carry malaria will move into new regions so that the number of people at risk of infection will increase. Perhaps the largest concern is that the number of people who suffer from **water stress** (i.e. do not have access to enough fresh water) will increase. There are currently 1.7 billion people worldwide who suffer from water stress. Most of these are in Africa. As the population grows and the climate changes it is expected that this number will rise to 5 billion by 2025.

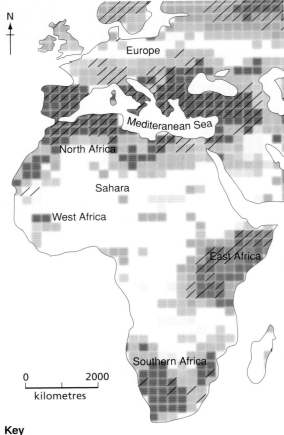

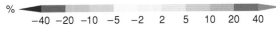

Key
percentage decrease (red) or increase (blue) in run-off as a result of changes to precipitation

% −40 −20 −10 −5 −2 2 5 10 20 40

White areas are where different computer simulations are contradictory so no firm predictions can be made. Hatched areas are where different computer simulations are all in agreement.

Figure 23 Future patterns of run-off in Europe and Africa in 2090–99 (compared with 1990–99)

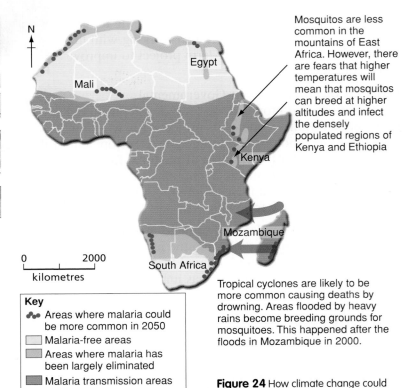

Mosquitos are less common in the mountains of East Africa. However, there are fears that higher temperatures will mean that mosquitos can breed at higher altitudes and infect the densely populated regions of Kenya and Ethiopia

Key
🦟 Areas where malaria could be more common in 2050
▢ Malaria-free areas
▢ Areas where malaria has been largely eliminated
▢ Malaria transmission areas
← The path of tropical cyclones

Tropical cyclones are likely to be more common causing deaths by drowning. Areas flooded by heavy rains become breeding grounds for mosquitoes. This happened after the floods in Mozambique in 2000.

Figure 24 How climate change could affect malaria by 2050

Activity

1 Use Figure 23 to describe the distribution of countries which are expected in the future to have:
   a) much less run-off
   b) much more run-off.
2 a) Explain how increased run-off might have positive and negative effects for people.
   b) Suggest why African countries might find it harder to cope with changes to run-off than European countries.
3 a) Use Figure 24 to describe the zone of Africa which is currently at risk from malaria.
   b) Describe how and why this zone is likely to change by 2050.

Chapter 4
River processes and landforms

What are river processes and what landforms do they create?

Figure 1 What landform processes created this landscape?

Activity

1 Work in pairs. Discuss the landscape in Figure 1 before answering the following questions.
   a) Describe how the river and its valley change as it flows towards you. Use the following table to compare the river and its valley at A and B.

	River at A	River at B
Gradient of channel (steepness of the river)		
Width of valley floor		
Shape of river channel (plan view)		
Words that describe the landforms you can see		
The processes that might occur in this section of river		

   b) How might climate affect the development of a landscape? Think particularly about the upland area across the top of the photo. Using evidence from this part of the photo explain how the climate might affect the river and the vegetation.

2 This photo was taken at 65° North and the mountains are 600 metres above sea level.
   The photo was taken in May.
   a) Suggest how this landscape would be different in winter.
   b) Suggest how this location could affect the river processes throughout the year.

River processes

Figure 2 A number of different river processes are evident in this Icelandic river

From the moment water begins to flow over the surface of the land, gravity gives it the power to erode the landscape. The gravitational energy of the flowing water enables the river to **transport** its **load** of boulders, gravel, sand and silt downstream. Where energy levels are high the main river process is erosion. At other times of the year, or in other parts of the river where energy levels are lower, the main process is **deposition**.

Erosion occurs where the river has plenty of energy so, for example, where the river is flowing quickly or when the river is full of water after heavy rain. Rivers that are flowing across gentle slopes (such as the river in Figure 2) tend to flow with greatest force on the outer bend of each curve (or **meander**). Water is thrown sideways into the river bank, which is eroded by both hydraulic action and abrasion. The bank gradually becomes undercut. The overhanging soil slumps into the river channel where this new load of material can be picked up and transported downstream by the flowing water.

Transportation process	Sediment size or type	Typical flow conditions	Description of the process
Solution	Soluble minerals such as calcium carbonate	Any	Minerals are dissolved from soil or rocks and carried along in the flow
Suspension	Small particles e.g. clay and silt	Suspension occurs in all but the slowest flowing rivers	Tiny particles are carried long distances in the flowing water
Saltation	Sand and small gravels	More energetic rivers with higher velocities	The sediment bounces and skips along
Traction	Larger gravels, cobbles and boulders	Only common in high energy river channels or during flood events	The bed load rolls along in contact with the river bed

Figure 3 The transportation of sediment

Erosional processes

Hydraulic action – water crashes into gaps in the soil and rock, compressing the air and forcing particles apart

Abrasion – the flowing water picks up rocks from the bed that smash against the river banks

Attrition – rocks carried by the river smash against one another, so they wear down into smaller and more rounded particles

Corrosion – minerals such as calcium carbonate (the main part of chalk and limestone rocks) are dissolved in the river water

Figure 4 Four processes of river channel erosion

The process of deposition occurs where the river loses its energy. For example, where a river enters a lake and its flow is slowed by the body of still water. Deposition also occurs in very shallow sections of a river channel where friction between the river bed and the water causes the river to lose its energy and deposit its load. The process of deposition creates layers of sand and gravel that are often sorted by sediment size because the coarsest sediment is deposited first.

Activity

1 Study Figure 2. Use evidence from the photograph to suggest what river processes are occurring at A, B and C.

2 Draw four diagrams or cartoons to illustrate the ways in which a river transports material.

3 Study Figure 5 and explain how erosion, transportation and deposition have created this landform.

4 Study Figures 1, 2 and 5. Use evidence in these photos to explain the difference between abrasion, hydraulic action and attrition.

Figure 5 This river channel has split into a number of smaller distributaries as it flows into this much larger body of water

Investigating river processes and landforms

The river at A in Figure 1 (on page 135) and the river in Figure 6 show typical features of a river flowing over steeper gradients. These rivers are eroding vertically more than from side to side. As the river erodes downwards it cuts into its channel and produces a narrow valley with steep V-shaped sides. The rocks of the river bed may show evidence of abrasion in the form of smoothly cut potholes (also known as scour holes).

Rivers flowing over steep gradients have enough energy to erode and transport a large quantity of material. The load on the river bed here is large and angular. As a river flows downstream the process of attrition gradually reduces the overall size of the load.

Figure 6 Ashes Valley, Shropshire is a typical V-shaped valley. The National Trust owns the site and encourages students to visit. As many as 40,000 geography students visit every year

Rivers flowing over gentle gradients tend to swing from side to side. The water flows fastest on the outside bend of each meander. This causes erosion of the banks rather than the bed, a process known as **lateral erosion**. Meanwhile, the slow flowing water on the inside of each bend loses energy and deposits its load. The material is sorted with the larger gravel being deposited first, then the sand and finally the silt.

Meandering rivers such as the River Severn shown in Figure 8 tend to flow across a wide **floodplain**. This feature has been created over many thousands of years by the processes of lateral erosion and deposition.

Figure 7 Sediment size (cm) from two sites in Ashes Valley, Shropshire

Site 1 Upstream			Site 2 Downstream		
Left bank	Middle	Right bank	Left bank	Middle	Right bank
16.1	22.0	10.1	7.8	11.1	2.4
10.4	10.5	10.4	7.6	2.1	6.1
22.0	9.0	3.0	3.6	7.0	1.8
6.5	3.6	1.5	1.5	1.3	10.6
12.0	7.9	6.4	1.4	2.7	6.0
7.4	2.1	6.0	2.2	5.1	2.0
7.4	3.5	1.6	9.0	1.1	6.7
6.5	8.9	3.8	0.9	1.3	2.1
11.0	8.4	5.4	4.3	2.0	4.7

Activity

1 Study Figure 6. Explain how each of the following features was formed:
    a) V-shaped valley sides
    b) large angular boulders in the stream bed
    c) interlocking spurs.

2 A student has collected sediment data from two sites in Ashes Valley and put it in a table (Figure 7).
    a) Draw a graph to compare the sediment size for the two sites.
    b) Describe how the size of the sediment changes:
       i) across the width of the river
       ii) as the river moves downstream.
    c) Explain the processes that cause the sediment size to change.

3 Study Figures 8 and 9. Describe each of the following features and explain how it was formed:
    a) point bar
    b) floodplain.

4 a) Use the information in Figures 10 and 11 to draw a cross section of the River Onny.
    b) Describe and explain the shape of this channel.

Figure 8 Features of river meanders and floodplain of the River Severn at Ironbridge

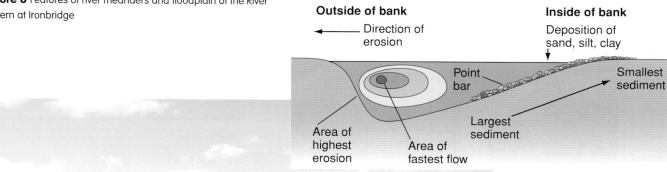

Figure 9 Processes at work on a river meander

Figure 10 Collecting data in order to draw a cross section of a river channel, the River Onny, Shropshire

Width across river (m)	0	0.5	1.0	1.5	2.0	2.5	3.0	3.5	4.0	4.5	5.0	5.5	6.0	6.5	7.0
Depth to bed from line (cm)	20	115	112	102	87	82	78	80	72	68	60	55	48	42	36

Figure 11 Depth measurements taken by students in the River Onny. The depth of water at 4 m across the stream was 22 cm

Investigating river landforms: waterfalls and gorges

Iceland has a large number of waterfalls including Gullfoss and Dettifoss, which are Europe's largest waterfalls. In this case study we will investigate some of the different ways in which waterfalls are made.

Figure 12 Gullfoss waterfall. The upper step of the falls can be clearly seen in the upper part of the photo. The top of the second step can be seen at the bottom of the photo

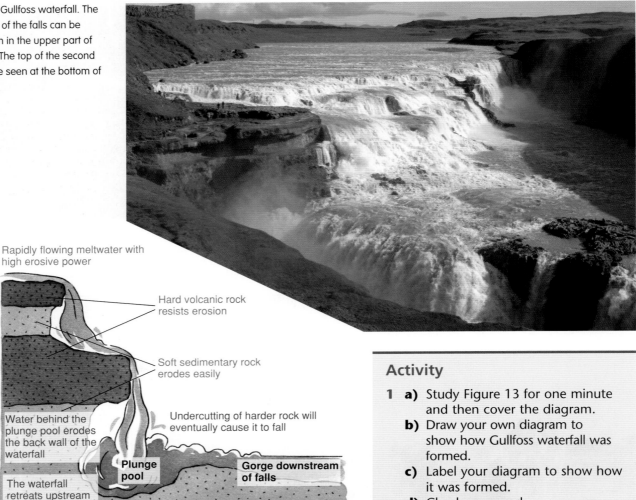

Figure 13 Features and processes that produce the waterfall at Gullfoss

Activity

1 a) Study Figure 13 for one minute and then cover the diagram.
   b) Draw your own diagram to show how Gullfoss waterfall was formed.
   c) Label your diagram to show how it was formed.
   d) Check your work.

Gullfoss waterfall is located in central southern Iceland, 100 km east of the capital city Reykjavik. It is where the River Hvitá drops a total of 31 m over two vertical steps. Below the waterfall is a narrow valley with almost vertical sides. This feature is known as a **gorge**. Gullfoss and its gorge were formed by the processes of river erosion. The landscape here is made of alternating layers of lava and sedimentary rocks. The lava is very resistant to erosion whereas the sedimentary rocks are eroded more easily. As the river plunges over the first thin layer of lava it pours on to the softer rock below. A combination of hydraulic action and abrasion erodes this rock relatively easily creating a plunge pool. Abrasion at the back of the plunge pool undercuts the layers of volcanic rock. Eventually this overhang will fracture and the rocks will fall into the plunge pool where they are broken up by attrition. So each step is gradually cut back and the waterfall retreats backwards along the river's course. It is this process of retreat that has cut the gorge.

How else are waterfalls formed?

Many waterfalls in Iceland (and in other parts of northern Europe including the UK) are formed due to landform processes that occurred at the end of the ice age around 10,000 years ago. During the ice age, ice sheets expanded over large parts of central Iceland and valley glaciers flowed from these ice sheets towards the sea. The glaciers carved deep, steep sided or **U-shaped valleys** into the landscape. Figure 14 shows how this glacial landscape created the waterfalls we see today.

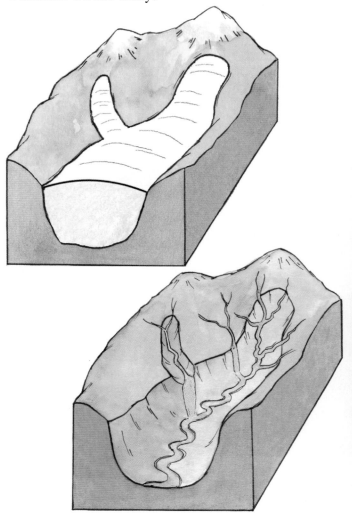

Figure 14 Glacial landscape and today's landscape

years before present		
12,000	glacial period	Huge amounts of water were trapped in ice sheets and glaciers. Sea levels were much lower than today.
10,000	gradually warming	As the ice melted the glaciers retreated and meltwater ran into the sea. Sea levels began to rise.
8,000		
6,000	warmest period	Sea levels reached a peak. Waves cut cliffs 40–60 metres high along the southern coastline.
4,000		The weight of ice during the glacial period had forced the crust to sink slightly. Now that the weight of ice had gone the crust began to slowly rise back up again. The effect of this is that the sea level slowly fell. The sea cliffs on the south coast were raised above sea level and the coastline retreated several kilometres creating new flat land along Iceland's south coast.
2,000		
today		

Figure 15 Timeline explaining the impact of the ice age on sea levels around Iceland

Figure 16 Seljalandsfoss waterfall, south Iceland, plunges over a raised sea cliff formed by sea level changes explained in Figure 15

Activity

2 Study the pair of diagrams in Figure 14. Use as many geographical terms as you can to explain how today's landscape has been formed.

3 Use Figure 15 to draw a series of simple diagrams or cartoons to show how the height of the sea level has changed. Use these diagrams to explain why there are so many waterfalls in south Iceland.

GEOGRAPHICAL SKILLS

Labelling and annotation

Labelling a photograph, map or fieldsketch is a simple but effective way of showing what you know. There is an important difference between the two skills of labelling and annotation:

- Labels are simple descriptive statements. For example, in Figure 17, the word 'distributary' is a label. It is the name given to a small channel that has split away from the main river channel.
- Annotations are more complex statements and are best used to explain a feature. For example, if you were asked to annotate a photo of a river landform you should begin by thinking about the processes of erosion, transport and deposition that might be responsible for creating the different features of that landform. By numbering your annotations you can encourage the reader to read them in sequence and thereby understand a chain of events.

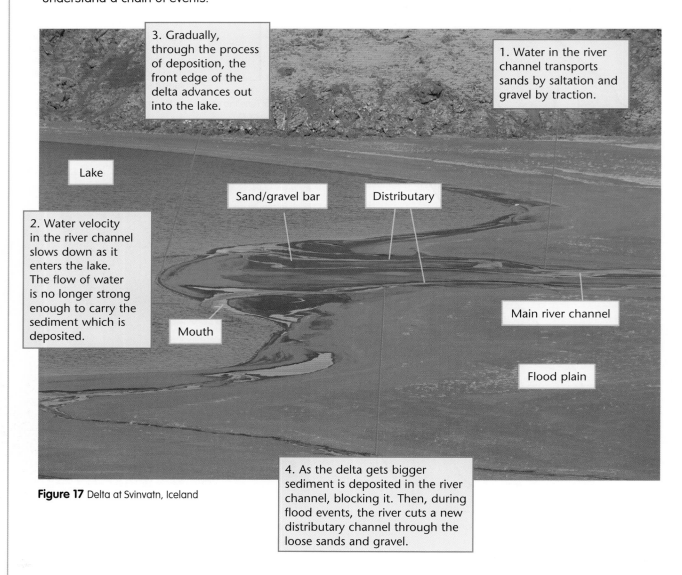

3. Gradually, through the process of deposition, the front edge of the delta advances out into the lake.

1. Water in the river channel transports sands by saltation and gravel by traction.

Lake

Sand/gravel bar

Distributary

2. Water velocity in the river channel slows down as it enters the lake. The flow of water is no longer strong enough to carry the sediment which is deposited.

Mouth

Main river channel

Flood plain

4. As the delta gets bigger sediment is deposited in the river channel, blocking it. Then, during flood events, the river cuts a new distributary channel through the loose sands and gravel.

Figure 17 Delta at Svinvatn, Iceland

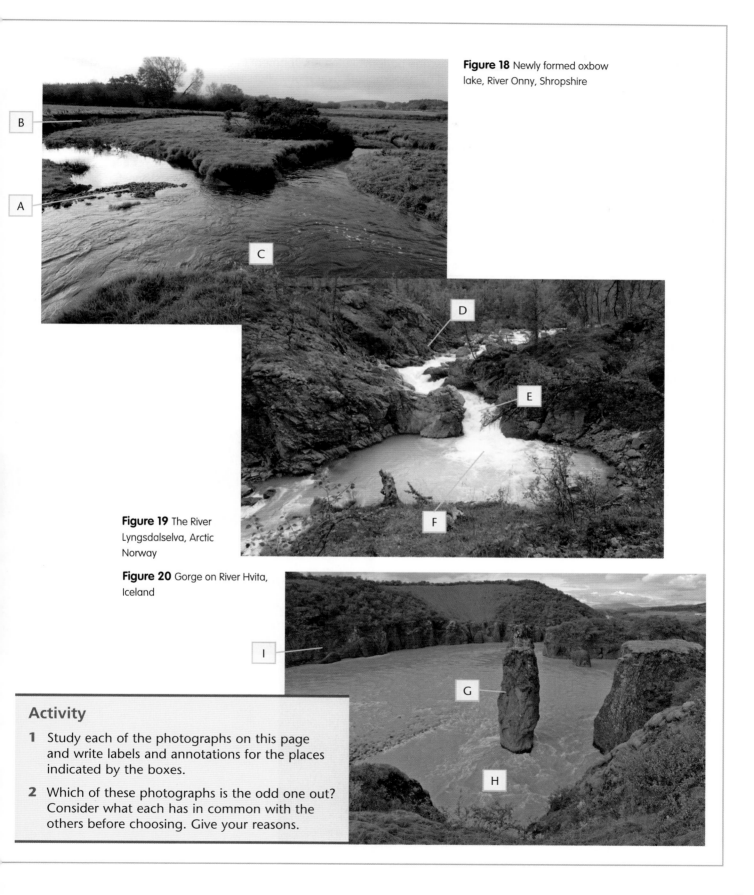

Figure 18 Newly formed oxbow lake, River Onny, Shropshire

Figure 19 The River Lyngsdalselva, Arctic Norway

Figure 20 Gorge on River Hvita, Iceland

Activity

1 Study each of the photographs on this page and write labels and annotations for the places indicated by the boxes.

2 Which of these photographs is the odd one out? Consider what each has in common with the others before choosing. Give your reasons.

Recognising patterns

Like other scientists, geographers like to describe patterns in the environment in an attempt to understand it better. One pattern that has been described by geographers over many years relates to rivers and it is described in Figure 21.

Figure 21 The 'typical' pattern of a river's course

Upper course	The river flows down steep gradients. The channel is usually shallow and there is a lot of friction between the water and the river bed. Sediment in the river has not yet been eroded by attrition so it is common to find large stones and boulders in the river channel.
Middle course	The river now flows over gentle gradients. The channel is wider and deeper and flows smoothly with less friction. Discharge is higher than in the upper course. The river usually meanders from side to side. Sediment on the river bed is smaller and rounded by attrition.
Lower course	The river flows across very gentle gradients. The channel is wide and deep and flows with little friction. Discharge reaches its highest values. Meanders form wide loops.

The general patterns described in Figure 21 may well apply to many rivers. If we assume that they are generally true, then one important geographical skill is to apply this general understanding of rivers to the study of an actual river. The best way to do this, of course, is to visit a real river and take measurements of features such as gradient, cross-sectional profile, discharge and sediment size. You can then compare your observations of the actual river to the general pattern and decide whether your river follows this pattern or not. This is known as the application of your knowledge and understanding.

Figure 22b Location A looking downstream

Figure 22a The River Lyngsdalselva in Arctic Norway. Location A looking upstream

Activity

1 Study each photo of this Norwegian river carefully and describe the features you can see, such as gradient, width, depth of channel and sediment size. What processes appear to be happening in each photo?

2 Discuss the sequence of the photographs. Which photo do you think was taken nearest the source and which nearest the mouth? Give reasons for your answers.

Figure 23 The River Lyngsdalselva in Arctic Norway. Location B looking upstream

Figure 24 The River Lyngsdalselva. Location C looking downstream

Location A is the upper course. It was taken approximately 2 km from the source of the river. The river is fed by meltwater from a glacier. The river flows along a U-shaped valley cut by the glacier which has retreated over the last 200 years. The river has a gentle gradient and deposits lots of gravel to create a braided channel.

Location B is in the middle course, about 2 km downstream of photo A.

Location C is in the lower course. It is about 3 km downstream of photo B. The river here is only 1 km from the sea. Large boulders lie in the stream bed. They have probably fallen here from the steep slopes on either side of the river or been left by the retreating glacier.

The river here has cut a narrow, deep channel over a resistant band of rock. The river plunges over a series of small waterfalls and rapids.

Why did this river flood?

What can be done to manage the river in the future?

Figure 25 The floods in Boscastle, Cornwall, in August 2004

Activity

1 Imagine you were rescued from a rooftop in Boscastle. Use Figure 25 to describe what you could see and describe how you would have felt during the flood.

2 Explain why a river in flood is able to:
   a) carry out much more erosion than usual
   b) deposit large amounts of sediment.

Investigating water movement through the drainage basin

The River Valency is a short river that flows in a steep V-shaped valley into the sea at Boscastle, Cornwall. Normally, the hills that form the catchment area for the River Valency get 100–120 mm of rainfall during August. But on the afternoon of 16 August 2004, the hills above Boscastle were hit by a freak rain storm. In just four hours 200 mm of rainfall fell causing the river to burst its banks. The river flooded the town's car park and carried 80 cars out into the sea. The force of the water rushing through the town caused the collapse of five buildings and another 37 were damaged. Thankfully nobody was killed during this flood. Emergency helicopters arrived quickly and were able to rescue people from the rooftops of flooded buildings.

During the flood of 2004 it is estimated that the River Valency had the same amount of water flowing in it as the River Thames where it flows past the Houses of Parliament in London. Every litre of water weighs one kilogram so you can imagine how much force the river had to perform hydraulic action. Rivers that are in flood are also able to transport much more load. During this flood the River Valency had enough energy to pick up and carry large boulders. This caused abrasion of the bed and banks. As flood water leaves the channel and flows over the floodplain it loses its energy and large quantities of sediment are deposited.

To understand flood events like the one in Boscastle we need to understand the way in which the drainage basin of a river works. Very little precipitation falls directly into rivers. Most falls on hillsides, fields and forests and takes time to enter a river. Precipitation falling in the drainage basin shown in Figure 26 may take one of a number of different routes before it enters the river. On hitting the ground, surface water will either flow over the surface as **overland flow** or it will infiltrate into the soil store. Once in the soil, water moves slowly downhill as **throughflow**. Eventually soil water percolates deeper into the ground and enters the bedrock where it continues to travel as **groundwater flow**. Rates of infiltration, throughflow and groundwater flow will depend on the type of soil and rock.

Figure 26 Stores and flows of water in a natural drainage basin

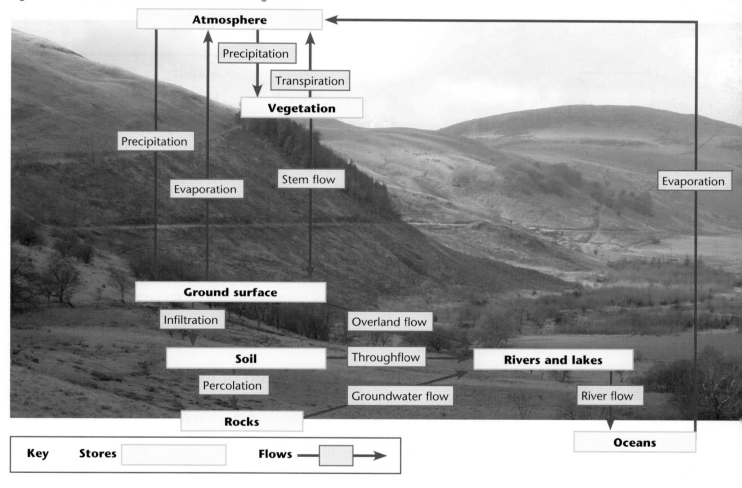

Activity

3 Use Figure 26 to name:
   a) three surface stores of water
   b) two places water is stored below the surface.

4 Suggest why precipitation falling into a drainage basin of impermeable rocks is likely to reach the river much more quickly than rainwater falling in an area of porous rocks.

Why do floods occur?

Flooding occurs when conditions cause water to flow overland rather than by infiltrating into the soil. A flood can occur when:

- the ground is already saturated with water after a long period of rain
- the ground is frozen
- the rainfall is so intense that all of it cannot soak into the ground.

Paving over the soil creates an **impermeable** surface, so the growth of urban areas increases the risk of flooding. A flood hydrograph shows the discharge of a river over the period of a flood. The example in

Figure 27 shows how a small river might respond to a flood event. The blue bar represents a sudden downpour of rain, like the one at Boscastle. In this example it takes two hours for overland flow from the drainage basin to reach the river channel. At this point the amount of water in the channel rises rapidly. The time between the peak rainfall and the **peak discharge** is known as **lag time**. The lag time and height of the peak discharge depend on the features of the drainage basin. In drainage basins where infiltration is reduced, the lag time will be shorter and the peak discharge larger. Some of these factors are illustrated in Figures 28 and 29.

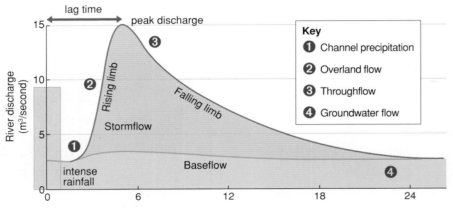

Figure 27 A simple flood hydrograph

Activity

1 Study Figure 27.
   a) Use times and discharge figures from the hydrograph to describe:
      i)   the shape of the rising limb and the lag time
      ii) the shape of the falling limb and baseflow.
   b) Use your understanding of Figure 26 on page 147 to explain how overland flow, throughflow and groundwater flow all contribute to a flood at different times.

Case study of the drainage basin of the River Valency

River Valency

The River Valency in Cornwall is a very short river as it flows less than 10 km from its **source** to its **mouth**. The source of the river is at 280 metres above sea level. The high source and short length make the river's gradient rather steep. The total size of the drainage basin is around 26 km². The rocks of the drainage basin are mainly slates, which are impermeable. The river has a number of small tributaries. These streams have cut deep V-shaped valleys into this landscape.

There are no large towns in the drainage basin. Boscastle itself covers less than 1 km². The upland part of the drainage basin is used for grazing. Some of the valleys are wooded. Trees help to remove some water from the soil before it reaches the river. However, during flood events, tree branches that are overhanging the river can be broken off. These branches then restrict the flow of water in the river, especially if they get caught against the piers of bridges. In these conditions a narrow stone bridge begins to act more like a dam than a bridge causing the river channel to become blocked.

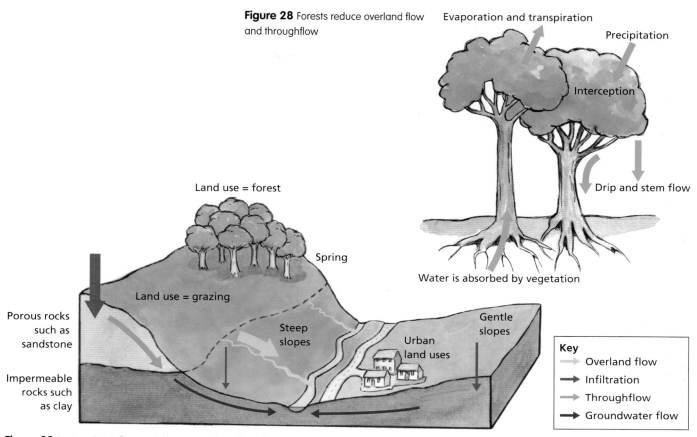

Figure 28 Forests reduce overland flow and throughflow

Evaporation and transpiration

Precipitation

Interception

Drip and stem flow

Water is absorbed by vegetation

Land use = forest

Spring

Land use = grazing

Porous rocks such as sandstone

Impermeable rocks such as clay

Steep slopes

Urban land uses

Gentle slopes

Key
→ Overland flow
→ Infiltration
→ Throughflow
→ Groundwater flow

Figure 29 Factors that influence infiltration and overland flow in the drainage basin. The arrows are in proportion to the amount of flow.

Activity

2 Use Figure 28 to explain how cutting down a large forest could affect lag time and peak discharge in a nearby river.

3 Use Figures 26, 27, 28 and 29 to help you copy and complete the following table.

Drainage basin factor	Impact on infiltration	Impact on overland flow and throughflow	Impact on lag time
Steep slopes			
Gentle slopes			
Porous rocks			
Impermeable rocks			
Urban land uses			
Planting more trees			

4 Draw a pair of flood hydrographs to show the difference between similar sized drainage basins that have:
   a) porous rocks compared with impermeable rocks
   b) urban land uses compared with lots of forests.

5 Suggest how the features of the drainage basin of the River Valency affected the river's lag time during the 2004 flood.

River Valency drainage basin

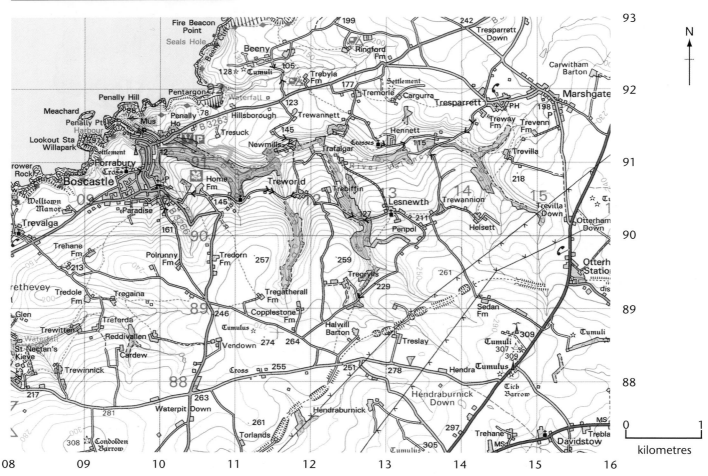

Figure 30 An Ordnance Survey extract of the catchment area of the River Valency. Scale 1:50,000 Sheet 190. © Crown Copyright and/or database right. All rights reserved. Licence number 100036470

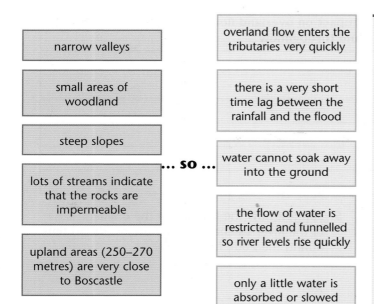

narrow valleys		overland flow enters the tributaries very quickly
small areas of woodland		there is a very short time lag between the rainfall and the flood
steep slopes	**... so ...**	water cannot soak away into the ground
lots of streams indicate that the rocks are impermeable		the flow of water is restricted and funnelled so river levels rise quickly
upland areas (250–270 metres) are very close to Boscastle		only a little water is absorbed or slowed

Figure 31 Reasons for the sudden rise of the River Valency during the flood in 2004

Activity

1 **a)** Match the pairs of statements shown in Figure 31 to make five sentences that help to explain how the character of this drainage basin led to the flooding in 2004.

   b) Use the OS map (Figure 30) to find five different grid squares, which provide evidence, for your five sentences. For example, you could choose 0989 to match with 'upland areas are very close to Boscastle ... so ...'

   c) Using Figure 32 as a simple outline, draw your own sketch map of the drainage basin of the River Valency. Add your five statements to appropriate places on the map as annotations.

2 Summarise how woodland areas close to the river could have affected the flood.

GEOGRAPHICAL SKILLS

Using geographical terms

You should always try to use the correct geographical terms in your extended writing. Using the correct terms will improve your communication skills. This chapter contains lots of new terms and some are listed here. Can you match the term to its correct meaning?

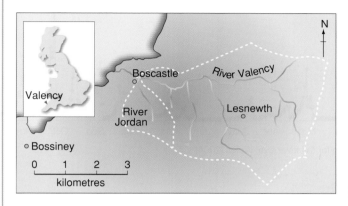

Figure 32 The drainage basin of the River Valency

Names of drainage basin features
Catchment area/drainage basin
Confluence
Source
Tributary
Watershed
Water table

Flows/stores of water within the drainage basin
Evaporation
Groundwater
Groundwater flow
Infiltration
Interception
Overland flow
Percolation
Throughflow
Transpiration

Definitions
The place where a river starts to flow
A smaller river which flows into a larger river channel
The boundary of a drainage basin
The movement of water from the ground surface into the soil
Where water changes state from liquid into vapour
Water in the ground below the water table
Soil or rock which does not allow water to pass through it, such as clay
The flow of water across the ground either in a channel or as sheet wash across the soil
The area a river collects its water from
The flow of water through rocks
Water transferred from plants, through pores in the leaves, to the atmosphere
The downhill flow of water through the soil
The transfer of water out of the soil and into the rocks below
When water is prevented from falling directly to the ground by vegetation
The point at which one river flows into another
The level in the ground below which the soil and rock pores are full of water

How does geology affect flows and stores of water?

So far we have seen that a number of factors affect the flow of water through a drainage basin. These include:

- the size and shape of the drainage basin
- the steepness of its slopes
- the amount of forest in the drainage basin
- whether towns and cities have covered the soil in impermeable tarmac and concrete.

There is one other important factor that has a major influence on how quickly water flows through a drainage basin and, therefore, whether flooding is likely: the rock type or geology. Study Figures 33 and 34. They are annual hydrographs (graphs showing the pattern of discharge through a whole year) for two rivers that have similar sized catchment areas. However, the geology of the two drainage basins is quite different and this affects the flow of water through each basin.

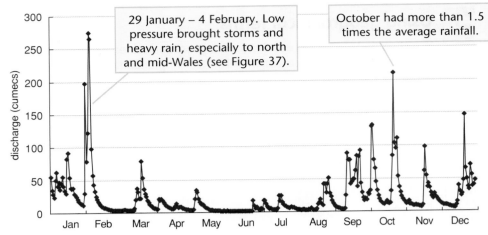

29 January – 4 February. Low pressure brought storms and heavy rain, especially to north and mid-Wales (see Figure 37).

October had more than 1.5 times the average rainfall.

Figure 33 Hydrograph for the River Dyfi, Wales (2004)

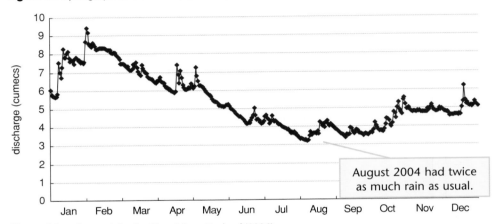

August 2004 had twice as much rain as usual.

Figure 34 Hydrograph for the River Itchen, England (2004)

River	River Dyfi	River Itchen
Location	West Wales	South-east England
Total average rainfall	1834 mm	838 mm
Geology	100% impermeable rocks	90% chalk
Size of catchment area (above the gauging station)	471 km²	360 km²
Landscape	Steeply sloping hills and mountains reaching a maximum of 907 m above sea level	Rolling hills. Maximum height 208 m above sea level
Land use	60% grassland (sheep pasture); 30% forest; 10% moorland	Mainly arable (cereal) farmland with some grassland
Human factors affecting run-off	There are virtually no human influences on run-off	Run-off is reduced by some abstraction for water supply. Some water is used to recharge groundwater in the chalk aquifer

Figure 35 Fact file on the River Dyfi and River Itchen

Activity

1 Compare Figures 33 and 34. Describe:
   a) one similarity
   b) three differences.

2 Use Figure 35 to suggest how each of the following factors may have affected the flow:

   rainfall total   geology
   landscape   land use

3 Imagine you work for a water company. Suggest how each river could be used for water supply.

Figure 36 Recent floods on the River Severn

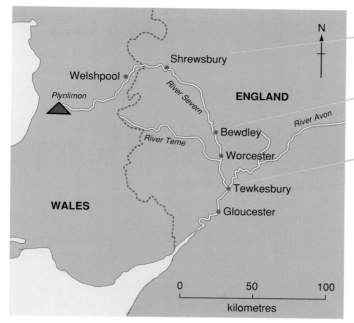

Shrewsbury. Flood damage in 1998, 2000, 2002 and 2004. The severe floods of 2000 led to the construction of flood defences completed in spring 2007.

Bewdley. Flood damage in 1998, 2000 and 2002. Flood defences (including demountable barriers) were completed before the February 2004 flood.

Tewkesbury is on the confluence of the River Avon and River Severn. Both Tewkesbury and **Gloucester** were badly affected by the floods in 2000 and 2007.

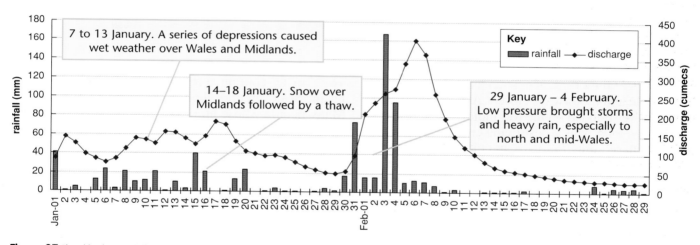

7 to 13 January. A series of depressions caused wet weather over Wales and Midlands.

14–18 January. Snow over Midlands followed by a thaw.

29 January – 4 February. Low pressure brought storms and heavy rain, especially to north and mid-Wales.

Key
rainfall ◆ discharge

Figure 37 Flood hydrograph for the River Severn at Bewdley (January–February 2004). Rainfall data is for Capel Curig, North Wales

Activity

4 Describe the course of the River Severn.

5 Explain why rivers continue to flow even during times of low rainfall.

6 Study Figure 37.
   a) Describe how each of the weather events described in the labels affected the flow of the river.

   b) Carefully describe the shape of the flood hydrograph between 29 January and 29 February.
   c) Use Figures 36 and 37 to suggest how the Environment Agency uses rainfall data from Wales to predict flood events in Bewdley.

What effect does flooding have?

In June, July and August 2007 the UK suffered its worst floods in living memory. Heavy rainfall in June caused flooding in the East Midlands and Yorkshire. More heavy rain in July caused flooding along the rivers Severn, Thames and Ouse. The floods caused loss of life, widespread damage to property and disruption to transport.

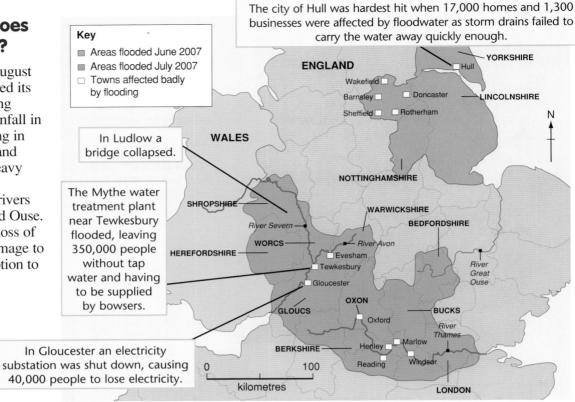

Key
- Areas flooded June 2007
- Areas flooded July 2007
- Towns affected badly by flooding

The city of Hull was hardest hit when 17,000 homes and 1,300 businesses were affected by floodwater as storm drains failed to carry the water away quickly enough.

In Ludlow a bridge collapsed.

The Mythe water treatment plant near Tewkesbury flooded, leaving 350,000 people without tap water and having to be supplied by bowsers.

In Gloucester an electricity substation was shut down, causing 40,000 people to lose electricity.

Figure 38 The areas affected by the summer floods of 2007

Thousands of motorists were stranded as roads became impassable and motorways closed. As many as 10,000 people were stranded on the M5 motorway. Rivers overflowed their banks, destroying crops that were ready for harvesting. In towns and cities the sewage and drainage systems could not cope with the huge quantities of water causing flooding of streets, homes and businesses.

The disaster continued to affect people and businesses even after the floodwaters had gone down. Many people whose homes had been flooded had to stay with relatives or in caravans and hotels. Businesses had to be cleared out and many lost orders whilst they repaired the damage. Some children had to be taught in temporary classrooms without books, which had been lost in the floods. Farmers lost crops worth over £11 million.

Activity

1 Use pages 154–155 to help you complete the following sentences about the effect of flooding.
   a) Roads are blocked by floodwater so …
   b) Floodwater carries silt into people's homes so …
   c) Floodwater damages plasterwork and carpets so …
   d) Wiring in flooded homes is unsafe so …

2 One effect of flooding is that roads become impassable and homes may become cut off while flood waters are at a peak. Consider how these conditions would affect each of the following groups of people:

   a) elderly people living alone who rely on regular visits from friends or family
   b) the emergency services
   c) supermarkets which need regular deliveries to restock their shelves.

3 Use Figure 38 to compare the distribution of the areas affected by the floods in June and July 2007.

4 In small groups discuss the difference between short-term and long-term effects, using pages 154–155.

5 Plot the places listed in Figure 41 onto an outline map of England and Wales.

Effects of flooding in June 2012

April to June 2012 were the wettest three months in England and Wales since 1910. The torrential rain caused widespread problems and many rivers flooded. In Aberystwyth, West Wales, a month's rainfall fell in 24 hours. This localised downpour caused severe flash flooding. Roads were blocked, homes and shops flooded and caravans on a holiday park were damaged by water when the nearby River Rheidol flooded. Over 1000 people had to leave their homes temporarily, either because of flood damage or because of the high risk of flooding. Essential repairs to roads and bridges alone cost £300,000. In the long term, local businesses are worried that the floods will damage the reputation of the area for holiday-makers.

Some other effects of the rain and flooding across England and Wales are summarised in Figure 41.

Figure 39 Andrea Jones, of Capel Bangor near Aberystwyth, cleans up the mess made of her property following the flash floods that hit the Aberystwyth area on Saturday 9 June, 2012

- Ludlow, Shropshire. A man drowned in a stream when his car was caught in floodwater.
- Tyne and Wear, Northumberland. More than 40 schools were closed, either because of damage to their buildings or because it was unsafe to travel by road.
- Coventry. A music festival which should have attracted 100,000 people was cancelled.
- Harrogate, Yorkshire. The county's agricultural show was cancelled because the showground was saturated and was unsafe for vehicles.
- Todmorden, Yorkshire. Firefighters responded to a large number of flood calls from anxious residents.
- Croston, Lancashire. More than 70 homes were flooded when the River Yarrow burst its banks.
- Yorkshire Dales. Nine people were rescued when their cars got stuck in flood water.
- Train services between Glasgow, Edinburgh and Carlisle were suspended due to landslips and flooding on the rail line.

Figure 41 Some effects of the floods of June 2012

Figure 40 Emergency firefighter crews from all over Mid and South Wales worked hard to pump floodwater out of properties on the outskirts of Aberystwyth

How should rivers be managed?

In the UK it is the responsibility of the Environment Agency to warn people about flood hazards and to reduce the risk of both river and coastal floods. They estimate that in England and Wales around 5 million people live in areas that are at risk of flooding.

Boscastle's flood defences

Boscastle

After the flood of 2004, the Environment Agency was responsible for designing a flood defence scheme for Boscastle. The defences cost £4.6 million and took two years to complete (2006–8). Many of the important features of this scheme are shown in Figure 43. One of the main features has been to widen and deepen the river channel so that it can carry more water. This type of river management is known as **hard engineering** as it involves artificially controlling the course of the river. Engineers were aware that during the flood the road and foot bridges in the town became blocked by large branches that had been washed downstream. They decided to deepen the river bed under the main bridge and to replace the other two bridges with new structures. These new bridges have much wider spans so it is more difficult for them to become blocked with debris.

The National Trust owns a large part of the lower section of the valley of the Valency. In the past the river was straightened and dredged so that its water could be used to power water mills. The National Trust and Environment Agency are now restoring parts of the river to take on a more natural form. For example, just before it enters the town the river has been given a wider, shallow channel. This should slow the flow of water and encourage deposition of gravel in a natural **braided** pattern. During another large flood this 'natural' section of river would help trap boulders and other load before it entered the town where it could cause damage. Using the natural features of a river in this way is known as **soft engineering**.

Figure 42 The section of river between the main bridge and the harbour has been lowered by 75 cm. The river has also been widened

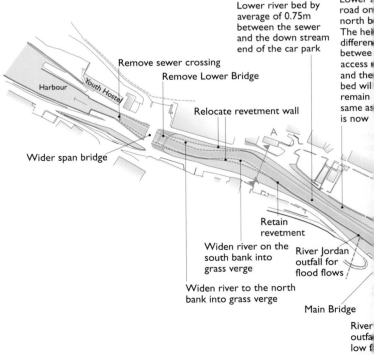

Figure 43 A plan of the Boscastle flood defences designed by the Environment Agency and built 2006–8

Figure 44 Workmen using a JCB to dig out the rocky bed of the river under the main bridge during 2007. This is the same bridge as in Figure 25 on page 146

Figure 45 One of the new footbridges and a view east along the widened river. The car park is behind the building in the left of the photo

Activity

1 Use Figure 43 to describe the flow of the River Valency through Boscastle.

2 Use Figure 43 to explain why the Bridge Walk shops were at risk during the 2004 flood.

3 Explain how each of the following features shown in Figure 43 will reduce the risk of future floods:
   a) lowering the river bed
   b) widening the river channel
   c) removal of trees next to the river
   d) replacing two of the bridges with wider spans.

4 Use Figures 42–45 to give examples of different types of:
   a) hard engineering
   b) soft engineering.

Widen river channel adjacent to the car park and create riverside walkway

...den river channel adjacent to the ...erside Hotel; set back patio; and ...lace and extend footbridge

Raise car park areas so that cars are above a design flood level

Extend car park upstream, away from the river

Remove trees

New flood defence wall

Form wide, braided river channel upstream of the car park to create an area of slower flow, where larger sediment will deposit

...ge Walk Shops

Riverside Walkway

River Valency

Realign existing channel

Remove trees

...ood defence wall

Tree and debris catching facility

Catchment management work upstream

0   10   50m
N

Are attitudes changing to flood defence?

Up until quite recently, councils in the UK have tried to prevent river floods by using hard engineering. For example, by building earth embankments alongside river channels, like the one in Figure 46, the water is kept in the channel and moved quickly downstream and away from any local housing or businesses that might be flooded. But building these structures is both expensive and controversial. Some scientists argue that straightening rivers and building flood embankments just moves water quickly downstream and increases the risk of flooding elsewhere.

The Environment Agency, which is responsible for giving flood warnings in the UK, estimates that around 5 million people live in areas that are at risk of flooding in England and Wales. Building flood defences for them all may not be economically desirable or sustainable. They recommend that people who are at risk of flooding should have a flood plan (Figure 47).

Figure 46 Flood embankments are a form of hard engineering

your flood plan

Know how to turn off your gas, electricity and water mains supplies

Start preparing today before a flood happens. Use this checklist as your flood plan.

1. **Check your insurance cover**
   - Check your buildings and contents insurance policy.
   - Confirm you are covered for flooding.
   - Find out if the policy replaces new for old, and if it has a limit on repairs.
   - Don't underestimate the value of your contents.

2. **Know how to turn off your gas, electricity and water mains supplies**
   - Ask your supplier how to do this.
   - Mark taps or switches with stickers to help you remember.

3. **Prepare a flood kit of essential items** (please tick)
   - ☐ Copies of your home insurance documents.
   - ☐ A torch with spare batteries.
   - ☐ A wind-up or battery radio.
   - ☐ Warm, waterproof clothing and blankets.
   - ☐ A first aid kit and prescription medication.
   - ☐ Bottled water and non-perishable foods.
   - ☐ Baby food and baby care items.
   - ☐ This leaflet including your list of important contact numbers.
   - ☐ Keep your flood kit handy.

4. **Know who to contact and how**
   - Agree where you will go and how to contact each other.
   - Check with your council if pets are allowed at evacuation centres.
   - Keep a list with all your important contacts to hand.

5. **Think about what you can move now**
   - Don't wait for a flood. Move items of personal value such as photo albums, family videos and treasured mementos to a safe place.

6. **Think about what you would want to move to safety during a flood**
   - Outdoor pets
   - Cars
   - Furniture
   - Electrical equipment
   - Garden pot plants and furniture
   - What else? ....
   ....

Figure 47

Screenshot from the Environment Agency website showing 'Your flood plan'

Activity

1. Suggest why the embankment in Figure 46 is lined with concrete blocks.

2. For each of the six points in the flood action plan (Figure 47), explain how each might reduce the losses suffered during a flood.

3. Suggest why planners might prevent the building of new homes on the flood plain of the River Severn.

4. Suggest why local residents might prefer demountable barriers to walls and embankments.

5. The defences in Shrewsbury do not prevent flooding of car parks and playing fields that are close to the river. Explain why it makes sense both economically and environmentally to not defend these areas with hard engineering structures.

River Severn

Flood management

The River Severn is Britain's longest river. Shrewsbury, Tewkesbury, Bewdley, Worcester and Gloucester are all on its course and many homes are at risk of flooding. A series of floods in the last 10 years (shown in Figure 36, page 153) have prompted flood defences to be built in Shrewsbury and Bewdley. These include a mixture of earth embankments, flood walls and demountable flood barriers (shown in Figure 48). The demountable barriers are made of aluminium panels. They can be slotted together before the flood arrives to protect properties. The flood defences in Shrewsbury were completed in 2004 at a cost of £4.6 million. But not everywhere is protected. The car park in Figure 48 is not protected. It provides a safe area for water to be 'stored' during a flood event.

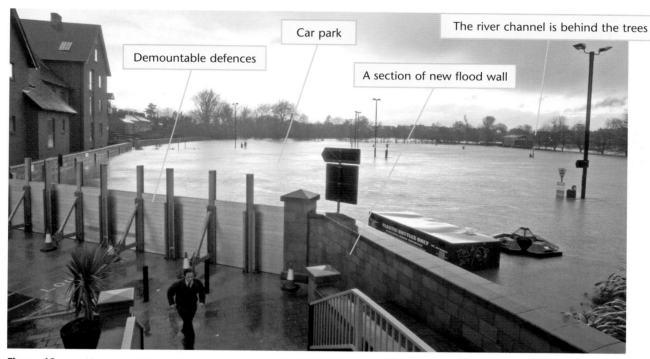

Figure 48 A total length of 700 m of flood embankments and walls has been built where the river enters the town to prevent floods in Shrewsbury. A further 155 m of river bank is protected using demountable defences

Figure 49 Guildhall and Frankwell car park, SY3 8HQ, the same location as shown in Figure 48.

GIS Activity: Using the Environment Agency website

www.environment-agency.gov.uk

The Environment Agency operates a simple GIS that shows flood hazards. Follow the weblink above and click on 'Flood map and how to use it' within the 'Prepare for Flooding' section. You can now search the atlas using postcodes. Figure 50 shows that central Tewkesbury is at risk of being surrounded by water from the rivers Avon and Severn during a flood.

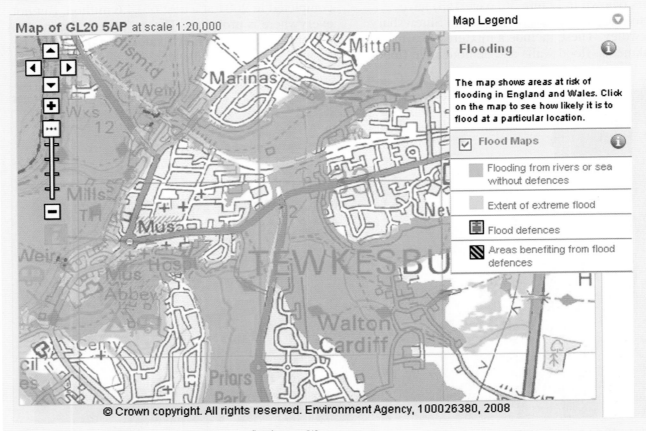

Figure 50 A screenshot for the Environment Agency flood maps GIS

Activity

1 Use the following postcodes to examine the flood risk to towns along the River Severn (the postcodes are in order going from source to mouth)

   SY16 2LN   SY21 7DG   SY3 8HQ   DY12 2AE   GL20 5AP

   a) For each town identify:
   i)   the extent (area) that is at risk
   ii) which main roads are at risk of flooding
   iii) whether residential areas are at risk or not
   iv) whether the town has any flood defences.
   b) Based on your findings, suggest which of these towns most needs new flood defences.

Geography Futures

Should we change our approach to river and floodplain management in the future?

In 2004 the UK government commissioned a scientific report on the future of river and coastal floods in the UK. The scientists considered how climate change and growing populations might affect the risk of flooding by the year 2080. The main findings of the 'Foresight Report' are:

- The number of people at high risk of flooding could rise from 1.5 million to 3.5 million.
- The economic cost of flood damage will rise. At the moment flooding costs the UK £1 billion a year. By 2080 it could cost as much as £27 billion.
- One of the main causes of the extra flood risk is climate change. The UK's climate is likely to become stormier with more frequent heavy rain. Sea level rise will increase the risk of coastal floods.
- About 10 per cent of the UK's housing is already built on the floodplains of rivers and these homes are at risk of river floods. Hundreds of thousands of new houses will be built in the next 20 years and many of these could also be at risk.
- River floods could cause massive health risks if the flood water contains untreated sewage or chemicals that have been washed off farm land.
- Towns and cities will be at risk of flash floods even if they are not built near a river. Drains that are supposed to carry away rainwater will not be able to cope with sudden downpours of rain. This kind of flooding could affect as many as 710,000 people.

Activity

1 Use Figure 51 to describe the distribution of areas where there are high numbers of people at risk of flooding.
2 Describe how future floods are likely to affect people living:
   a) in coastal areas
   b) close to rivers
   c) in towns and cities.
3 What are the main reasons for extra flood hazards in the future?

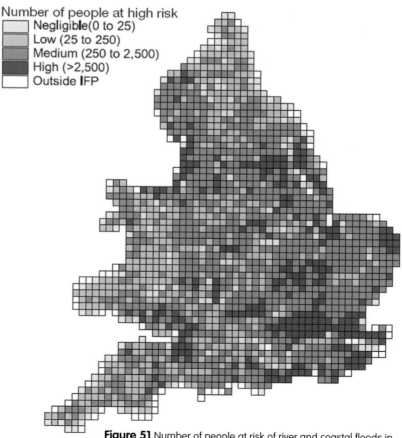

Number of people at high risk
- Negligible (0 to 25)
- Low (25 to 250)
- Medium (250 to 2,500)
- High (>2,500)
- Outside IFP

Figure 51 Number of people at risk of river and coastal floods in 2080 assuming that carbon dioxide emissions remain high

Geography Futures

What should be done to reduce the risk of future floods?

Planner

Householders should be encouraged not to pave over their gardens. Paving and tarmac are impermeable. Rainwater goes straight down into storm drains and into the river rather than soaking slowly into the soil. Advice needs to be given so that gravel and permeable surfaces are used instead of tarmac. We also need to replace old storm drains which are too old and small to cope with heavy rain storms. However, motorists won't like that because it will mean digging up urban roads!

The scientists who wrote the 'Futures Report' into flooding identified that poor land management had increased the risk of river floods. For example, over the last 50 years farmers in upland areas of England and Wales have added drains to their fields to improve the amount of grass that can be grown. However, these field drains have had an effect on the flow of rivers further downstream. We are involved in a scheme to restore the old peat bogs in upland Wales. Between 2006 and 2011 we are going to block a total of 90 km of old land drains on the hills close to Lake Vyrnwy. We are using bales made from heather to block the drains. This will slow down the overland flow and force water to soak back into the soil. Not only will this help reduce the risk of floods but it will also improve the moorland ecosystem and will help to protect rare birds of prey like the merlin and hen harrier.

Spokesperson for RSPB

River scientist

Hard engineering schemes, like the flood walls and embankments in Shrewsbury, speed up the flow of water. These schemes may funnel water along to the next community living further downstream and actually increase their risk of flooding. What we need to do is to return river valleys to a more natural state. We should use floodplains as temporary water stores so that flooding can occur away from built-up areas.

Homes can be made more flood proof with measures such as putting plug sockets higher up the walls and replacing wooden floors and carpets with tiles.

House builder

Resident in Shrewsbury

I'm really pleased with the new flood defences. My property has flooded in the past but was protected during 2007. The Shrewsbury flood defence scheme cost £4.6 million but I think it was worth it.

We need to build an extra 3 million homes in the UK by 2020. Almost half of them are in the Midlands and the south of England which are the same areas hit by flooding in 2007. Some of these houses will have to be built on greenfield sites. However, we should restrict building on floodplains in the future.

Government housing minister

Figure 52 Alternative points of view on solving the flood problem

a) The natural system

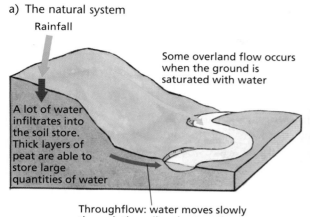

Rainfall

Some overland flow occurs when the ground is saturated with water

A lot of water infiltrates into the soil store. Thick layers of peat are able to store large quantities of water

Throughflow: water moves slowly through the soil and enters the river several hours or days after the rainfall

b) Field drains were added to improve grazing

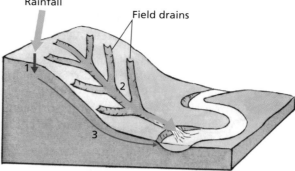

Rainfall

Field drains

Figure 53 The movement of water through upland drainage basins in mid-Wales was altered when field drains were added. The size of the arrows is in proportion to the amount of each flow

Activity

1 Study Figure 53.
   a) Make a copy of diagram b. Add labels that explain water flows at 1, 2 and 3.
   b) Explain how the differences in the two diagrams would affect the flow of water in the river downstream.
2 You have been asked to advise Tewksbury Council on flood prevention. What do you think should be done to prevent future floods in the town?
   a) Use what you have learned in this chapter, and the points of view in Figure 52 to complete a copy of the table.

Possible solution	Short-term benefits and problems	Long-term benefits and problems	Who might agree and disagree with this solution
Building flood defences like those in Shrewsbury			
Restoring bogs and moorland in mid-Wales by blocking drains			
Tighter controls on building on floodplains and paving over gardens			
Allowing rivers to flow naturally and spill over on to the floodplain			

   b) Now you need to recommend your plan. What do you think should be done and why do you think your plan will work? Use the following table to plan your answer.

Key questions to ask yourself	My answers
Is my plan realistic, affordable and achievable?	
Which groups of people will benefit from my plan?	
How will the environment be affected?	
Why is this plan better than the alternatives?	

Chapter 5
Coastal processes and coastal management

What processes are associated with the sea?

Waves provide the force that shapes our coastline. Waves are created by friction between wind and the surface of the sea. Stronger winds make bigger waves. Large waves also need time and space in which to develop. So larger waves need the wind to blow for a long time over a large surface area of water. The distance over which a wave has developed is known as **fetch**, so the largest waves need strong winds and a long fetch.

The water in a wave moves in a circular motion. A lot of energy is spent moving the water up and down. So waves in deep water have little energy to erode a coastline. However, as a wave enters shallow water near the shore its motion changes. The water below the surface is slowed by friction with the sea bed while the water at the surface surges forward freely. It is this forward motion of the breaking wave that causes erosion.

<table>
<tr><td>

Activity

1 Make a copy of Figure 1 and add the following labels in appropriate places.
- Waves in deeper water
- Circular motion
- Breaking wave
- Water thrown forward
- Friction with the sea bed

</td></tr>
</table>

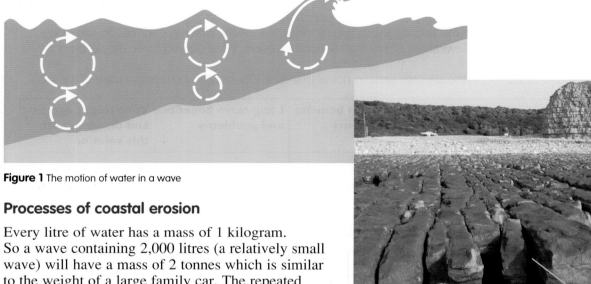

Figure 1 The motion of water in a wave

Processes of coastal erosion

Every litre of water has a mass of 1 kilogram. So a wave containing 2,000 litres (a relatively small wave) will have a mass of 2 tonnes which is similar to the weight of a large family car. The repeated pounding of large waves at the foot of a cliff can cause enormous damage through the process of **hydraulic action**. The repeated hammering effect of the waves on this narrow zone creates a **wave-cut notch**. Cliffs that are already weakened by joints or cracks can collapse and the top of the cliff **retreats** inland. Coastal retreat is particularly rapid on sections of the North Sea coast of England. On some sections of coastline here cliffs are retreating at an average of 2 m a year. The **wave-cut platform** in Figure 2 has been formed by the gradual retreat of the cliffs.

vertical joints in the wave-cut platform

pothole

Figure 2 The rocky shore of the Glamorgan Heritage Coast

Erosional processes

Hydraulic action – waves crash against the cliff, compressing the water and air into cracks and forcing the rocks apart.

Abrasion – waves pick up rocks from the sea bed or beach and smash them against the cliffs.

Corrosion – minerals such as calcium carbonate (the main part of chalk and limestone rocks) are slowly dissolved in sea water.

Attrition – sand and pebbles are picked up by the sea and smash against one another, wearing them down into smaller and more rounded particles.

Figure 3 Four processes of coastal erosion

A huge mass of rocks overhang the notch. This will be the next section of cliff to collapse.

Horizontal bedding planes and vertical joints in the rock are lines of weakness that can be eroded rapidly by hydraulic action.

A recent rock fall. This debris will break the force of the waves so, for a while at least, the cliff behind will be protected from the battering of the waves.

Waves use pebbles from the beach to erode a notch at the foot of the cliff through the process of abrasion.

Figure 4 Evidence of erosion in cliffs on the Glamorgan Heritage Coast

On a map, the blue line showing the coastline of the UK looks like a fixed and permanent feature. In reality, the coastline is a constantly changing environment. Sometimes, battered by storms, it can change overnight with the erosion of tonnes of beach material or the collapse of a massive section of cliff.

Activity

2 Study Figures 2 and 3.
   a) Use the correct erosion terms to complete the annotations below.
      Joints in the rock are widened in the process of … which is when …
      Boulders on the beach are rounded because …
      This pothole has been scoured into the rock by …
   b) Make a simple sketch of Figure 2 and add your annotations.

3 Discuss Figure 4 and its annotations.
   a) Write a list (or draw a timeline) that puts the events acting on this cliff in the correct sequence.
   b) Make another list (or timeline) suggesting what will happen to this cliff in the next few years.
   c) Over the next 100 years this coastline will retreat by about 20–40 m. Draw a series of simple diagrams to show how this process of retreat creates the rocky wave-cut platform in front of the cliff.

How are coastal processes affected by geology?

The rate of coastal erosion depends on a number of factors including rock type and rock structure. The cliffs at Happisburgh in Norfolk are between 6 and 10 m high. They are made of loosely compacted layers of sand, silt and clay deposited at the end of the ice age. These sedimentary rocks are not very resistant. Erosion by waves at the toe of the cliff causes large sections of the cliff to slump and collapse onto the beach where it is easily washed away. Slumping is speeded up when rain water flows over the upper slope, eroding gulleys.

Wooden barriers known as revetments that should break the force of the waves before they reach the toe of the cliff

D

C

B

A

The remains of a concrete slipway that have collapsed during a landslide

Figure 5 The coastline at Happisburgh 2011

Activity

1 Imagine you live near the cliff edge in Happisburgh. How might coastal erosion affect:
   a) your quality of life
   b) the chances of being able to sell your home?

2 Historical records show that the cliffs here retreated by 250 m between 1600 and 1850. What is the average rate of erosion per year?

3 Read the following annotations and decide where they fit best on Figure 5.
   • Waves have eroded the toe of the cliff here
   • The vegetation on this slope proves that it hasn't slumped for several months
   • Concrete blocks on the beach may protect the cliff from wave erosion
   • Evidence of gulley erosion by rain water on these slopes

4 Write suitable labels and annotations for the boxes on Figure 7.

Headlands and bays on the Jurassic Coast

The Jurassic coastline of Dorset is made up of alternating bands of sandstone, limestone and clay. The sandstones and limestones are quite resistant to erosion and make tall, almost vertical cliffs. The clays are much more easily eroded. Like all sedimentary rocks, these have been formed by deposition of sediment in horizontal beds. Over millions of years the beds have been lifted and tilted. In some places, like at Lulworth, the beds of limestone dip almost vertically.

Cliffs made of softer rocks and clays have been easily eroded

What remains of a narrow band of very resistant limestone

Waves have eroded the narrow band of limestone and are now quickly eroding a semi-circular bay in the softer clays

Figure 6 A cove on the Jurassic coast near Lulworth

A

B

C

E

D

Figure 7 Durdle Door, a natural arch, on the Jurassic coastline

Beach and sand dune processes

Beaches are dynamic environments. In other words, the energy of the wind and waves is constantly moving sediment around and changing the shape of the beach. Where the waves approach the beach at an angle, some of the sediment is transported along the coastline in a process known as **longshore drift**. However, most sediment is simply moved up and down the beach. Each wave transports sediment up the beach in the **swash** and back down again in the **backwash**. All of this movement uses a lot of the wave's energy, so a wide, thick beach is a good natural defence against coastal erosion.

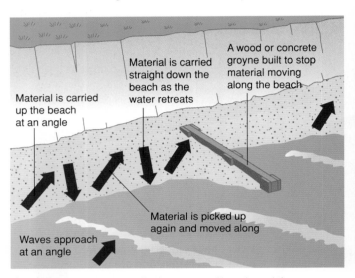

Material is carried up the beach at an angle

Material is carried straight down the beach as the water retreats

A wood or concrete groyne built to stop material moving along the beach

Material is picked up again and moved along

Waves approach at an angle

Figure 8 Sediment transport by the process of longshore drift

Figure 9 The beach at Borth seen from the cliffs to the south of the pebble ridge

Borth, Ceredigion

Case study of sediment movement at Borth on the Ceredigion coast

The sand and pebbles on a beach usually come from the local environment. Neighbouring cliffs may supply some sediment if they are being actively eroded by wave action. A lot of finer silts and sands are brought down to the coast by rivers. This sediment is then deposited in the estuary or on an **offshore bar** at the mouth of the river. It will be washed onshore by the swash of the waves and deposited on the beach.

At Borth, on the Ceredigion coast, there is a pebble ridge making a **spit** on the southern side of the estuary. These pebbles came from cliffs to the south. Figure 11 shows the processes that are supplying and transporting material on this coastline.

Figure 10 The sand dunes at Ynyslas seen from Aberdyfi on the north side of the Dyfi estuary

Activity

1. Describe the landforms seen at A, B and C on Figures 9 and 10.

2. Study Figures 8, 9 and 11. Use an annotated diagram to explain the formation of the pebble ridge on which the village of Borth is built.

3. Study Figures 10 and 11. Make a sketch of Figure 10. Annotate it to explain the processes that have formed the sand dunes at C.

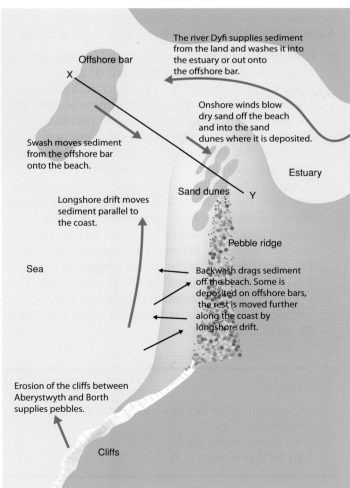

Figure 11 The transport of beach sediment at Borth and Ynyslas on the Ceredigion coast

Why are sea levels changing and how will these changes affect people?

Sea levels are rising. Scientists in Amsterdam in the Netherlands, began taking measurements of sea level in 1700 and similar readings were started in Liverpool in 1768. Readings taken in Europe and the USA over the last 100 years prove that sea levels have risen by around 180 mm (an average of 1.8 mm per year). This rise is largely due to climate change. Higher temperatures mean two things:

• Warm water expands slightly in volume, so as the oceans get warmer they also get slightly higher.
• The ice sheets that cover large parts of Antarctica and Greenland are melting. As the ice melts, water that has been trapped as ice for tens of thousands of years flows into the oceans.

Why are some coastlines more at risk than others?

As well as the general rise in sea levels of 1.8 mm per year, there are local factors that mean that some coastlines are more at risk than others. This is because some coasts are sinking or subsiding. **Subsidence** can be caused by more than one factor.

• River estuaries and deltas sink under their own weight. A river delta, such as that of the Mississippi in the USA, is made of millions of tonnes of loosely compacted sediment and water. As more sediment is deposited, the particles become more compressed and the water is squeezed out. Parts of the city of New Orleans, USA, are subsiding by 28 mm a year.
• In some parts of England the crust has been sinking ever since the ice melted 10,000 years ago at the end of the Ice Age. Northern parts of the UK were covered by thick layers of heavy ice and the crust was pressed down. When the ice melted, the crust in this part of the UK began to rise slowly. At the same time, the southern part of the UK began to sink. This process is called **postglacial rebound**. The subsidence due to rebound is about 2 mm per year in the south-east of England.

Figure 12 These icebergs have broken away from the huge Vatnajokull ice sheet in Iceland. As they melt their water flows out into the North Atlantic, adding to the amount of water in that ocean

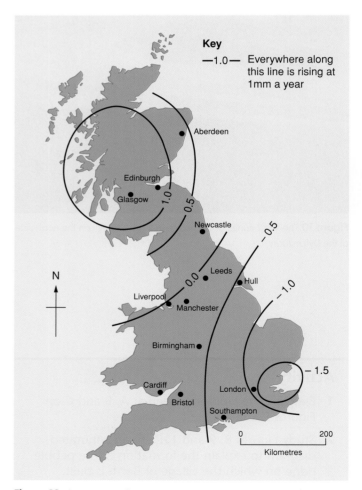

Figure 13 The amount of postglacial rebound (mm per year). Positive numbers mean the land is rising relative to sea level and negative numbers mean the land is sinking

Activity

1 Use Figure 13 to describe the parts of the UK where:
   a) land is rising fastest
   b) land is sinking fastest.

Geography Futures

How much will sea level rise in the future?

Predictions of future sea-level rise vary quite a lot. Scientists make their predictions using computer models. They feed data that has already been observed, about such things as carbon dioxide emissions, sea levels and temperatures, into the computer model and the model makes a prediction. The problem is that the processes that take place in our atmosphere, oceans and ice sheets are very complex and it is difficult to model them accurately in a computer program. Some of these different predictions are shown in the purple area of Figure 15. Scientists agree that the complete melting of the Greenland ice sheet would cause a global sea-level rise of between 6 and 7 m. This would probably take many hundreds or thousands of years, although recent evidence suggests that Greenland's ice is melting faster than we originally expected.

Vertical land movement due to postglacial rebound (mm per year)	Sea level rise (mm per year)			
	1990–2025	2025–2055	2055–2085	2085–2115
–0.5	3.5	8.0	11.5	14.5

Figure 14 Predicted change in sea level in south-west England and Wales. Source: Defra

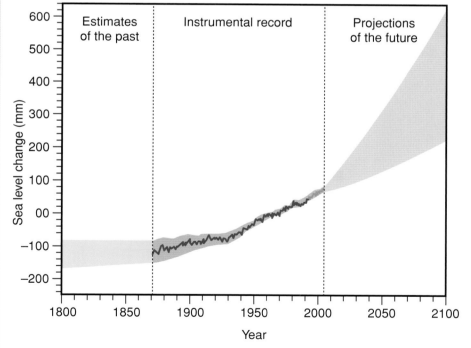

Figure 15 Sea-level rise

Activity

1 a) Choose a suitable technique to graph the data in Figure 14.
   b) Calculate the number of years in each of the four time periods. Multiply this by the amount of sea-level rise per year in each period. By how much will average sea level have increased by 2115 in Wales?
2 Study Figure 15.
   a) Describe the shape of the graph between 1870 and 2000.
   b) Use figures from the graph to describe the range of estimates of sea-level rise by 2100.

How will these changes to our coastline affect people?

Rising sea levels will increase the rate of coastal erosion. More farmland will be lost and more expensive sea defences will be needed to 'hold the line' against erosion of our towns and cities. Climate change also means a warmer atmosphere which means more storms like the devastating storm surge that flooded Jaywick in 1953.

In tropical regions the warmer atmosphere will mean more frequent and larger hurricanes flooding coastal regions. The tourist economy of the Caribbean region could be badly affected as beaches are eroded. Small island nations such as the Maldives in the Indian Ocean and the Marshall Islands in the Pacific are very low-lying. A 1 m rise in sea level by 2100 would flood up to 75 per cent of the land of these nations.

The worst-affected coastal communities would be those living on the world's major river deltas. People living here are affected by subsidence of the soft land as well as by sea-level rise. Millions of people live on deltas in Bangladesh, Egypt, Nigeria, Thailand and Cambodia. People will be forced to flee. They would become **environmental refugees**.

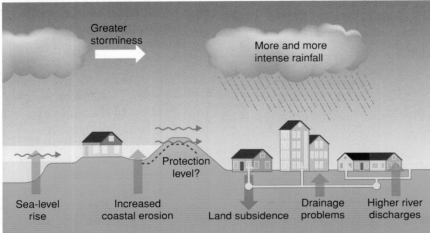

Figure 16 Some of the impacts of climate change on our coastline by 2050

Activity

1 Use Figure 16 to describe five different impacts of sea-level rise on coastal communities in the UK.

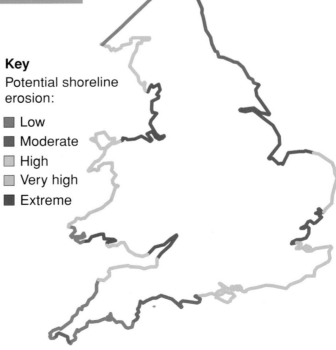

Key
Potential shoreline erosion:

- Low
- Moderate
- High
- Very high
- Extreme

Figure 17 Coastal erosion if carbon dioxide emissions continue to increase and sea levels rise

Activity

2 Use Figure 17 and an atlas to name:
   a) five counties in England facing problems of extreme coastal erosion
   b) three counties in Wales facing very high rates of erosion.

3 Suggest how sea-level rise might affect:
   a) poor people living in low-lying coastal areas of Bangladesh
   b) the tourist industry in the Caribbean.

How are coasts managed?

The usual way to manage coastlines has been through a combination of hard and soft engineering strategies. Hard engineering means building structures that prevent erosion and fix the coastline in place. The concrete sea wall and boulders in Figure 18 are a typical example. Wide beaches soak up a lot of wave energy and are a natural defence against coastal erosion. Soft engineering strategies mimic this by encouraging natural deposition to take place along the coastline. In Figure 19 you can see that an artificial rock reef has been built parallel to the coastline. This encourages deposition on the beach behind.

Figure 18 The sea wall at Sea Palling, Norfolk is an example of hard engineering

Figure 19 There are a total of nine artificial reefs at Sea Palling. Notice how sand has been deposited behind the reef, joining it to the beach

Ceredigion

Shoreline Management Plans

Coastal communities expect the government to help protect them from erosion and coastal floods. However, managing the coastline is very expensive. Furthermore, there is no legal duty for the government to build coastal defences to protect people or their property. It is the responsibility of the local councils of England and Wales to prepare a **Shoreline Management Plan (SMP)** for their section of coast. In deciding whether or not to build new coastal defences (or repair old ones) the local council needs to weigh up the benefits of building the defences against the costs. They may consider factors such as:

- How many people are threatened by erosion and what is their property worth?
- How much would it cost to replace infrastructure such as roads or railway lines if they were washed away?
- Are there historic or natural features that should be conserved? Do these features have an economic value, for example by attracting tourists to the area?

Option	Description	Comment
Do nothing	Do nothing and allow gradual erosion.	This is an option if the land has a lower value than the cost of building sea defences, which can be very expensive.
Hold the line	Use hard engineering such as timber or rock groynes and concrete sea walls to protect the coastline, or add extra sand to a beach to make it more effective at absorbing wave energy.	Sea walls cost about £6,000 per metre to build. Sea-level rise means that such defences need to be constantly maintained, and will eventually need to be replaced with larger structures. For this reason hard engineering is usually only used where the land that is being protected is particularly valuable.
Retreat the line	Punch a hole in an existing coastal defence to allow land to flood naturally between low and high tide (the intertidal zone).	Sand dunes and salt marshes provide a natural barrier to flooding and help to absorb wave energy. They adapt naturally to changing sea levels through a process of erosion at the seaward side and deposition further inland.
Advance the line	Build new coastal defences further out to sea.	This requires a huge engineering project and would be the most expensive option. The advantage would be that new, flat land would be available that could be used as a port or airport facility.

Figure 20 The options available to local councils when they prepare a Shoreline Management Plan

Activity

1 Use Figures 21 and 22.
   a) Describe these structures.
   b) Explain how they have helped to protect Borth from erosion and flooding.

Figure 21 Wooden groynes on Borth beach

Management at Borth, Ceredigion

The village of Borth is built on the southern end of a pebble ridge, or spit, that sticks out into the Dyfi estuary. Sand is trapped on the beach by wooden groynes. The sand absorbs wave energy and prevents waves from eroding the pebble ridge. However, the groynes are in poor condition and are at the end of their working lives. What should be done?

The Ceredigion SMP divides the coast up into small Management Units (MU). Figure 23 shows the extent of five of these MUs.

Figure 22 The wooden sea wall at the top of the pebble ridge

Activity

2 Work in pairs.
   Use Figure 23 to provide map evidence which suggests that this coast is worth protecting. Copy and complete the table below and add at least five more pieces of evidence.

MU	
16.2	Railway station at 609901 would be expensive to replace
16.3	
16.4	The campsite in 6192 provides local jobs
17.1	

3 Read Figure 20 carefully. Decide which option you would choose for MU16.2.

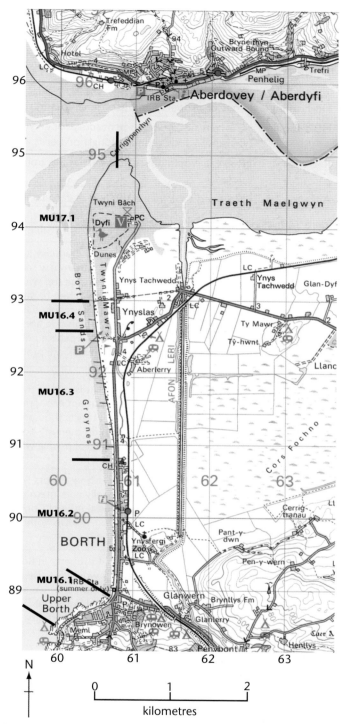

Figure 23 An Ordnance Survey extract of Borth. Scale 1:50,000 Sheet 135.

What coastal management is appropriate for Borth?

Ceredigion council decided that there were two possible options for MU16.2 that needed further consideration. Read the points of view in Figure 25 before deciding what you would do.

Do nothing	Loss of property and economic loss in the short term. Change to Borth Bog.	Consider further
Hold the line	Current policy which protects property and businesses. Coastal processes disrupted with reduced longshore drift.	Consider further
Retreat	Retreat would affect homes that are immediately behind the existing line of defence.	Not considered further
Advance	No need to advance the line except to improve the tourist facilities.	Not considered further

Figure 24 The initial decision of the Ceredigion Council for MU16.2

Sand from the southern end of the beach is gradually being eroded by longshore drift, moving it northwards. This process is happening faster than new sand is being deposited. The beach is getting thinner and is less able to protect the pebble ridge (on which Borth is built) from erosion. If the council does nothing then the pebble ridge will be breached by storm waves and the town of Borth, and Borth Bog (Cors Fochno) will be flooded by the sea. This could happen in the next 10 to 15 years. The peat bog at Cors Fochno will be covered in sea water at high tide and its existing ecosystem lost. Over the next few years erosion will punch more holes through the pebble ridge. A new spit of pebbles will eventually form further to the east. The sand dunes at Ynyslas will probably be cut off and form a small island.

Scientist

The beach and landscape of the spit, including the sand dunes at Ynyslas, are an important economic asset to the village. It's this natural environment that attracts thousands of holidaymakers each year. If the council does nothing then my home and many others will be flooded and local people will lose their livelihoods.

The peat bog at Cors Fochno should be protected from flooding. It is a nationally and internationally important ecosystem. It has protection as a Special Area of Conservation and is also recognised by UNESCO. 'Do nothing' is an unacceptable option.

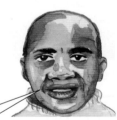

Scientist

B&B owner

We calculate that property in Borth village is worth £10.75 million. On top of this there are many local businesses which would lose their income from tourism if we do nothing. The cost of holding the line is around £7 million. However, we are concerned that building new groynes will prevent longshore drift. We need to consider the impact of that. Currently the sediment moves to Ynyslas where it provides a natural defence to the whole estuary (including the larger village of Aberdyfi) from south-westerly storms.

Local councillor

Figure 25 Views on the future management of MU16.2

Activity

1 Working in pairs, read Figure 25 before completing a copy of this table.

	Do nothing	**Hold the line**
Economic impacts		
Social impacts		
Environmental impacts		

2 State which option you would recommend. Explain why you think your option is best for this stretch of coast.

3 Would you have made a different decision for MU16.3 or 17.1? Explain which management option might be worth considering for each of these stretches of coastline.

Essex

Managing the coastal flood risk: a case study in Essex

Jaywick is a seaside town in Essex. The flat land here has been flooded by the sea several times. The worst occasion was in January 1953 when 37 people were drowned during a storm surge. Low pressure in the atmosphere has a dramatic affect at sea. As air pressure drops during a storm, sea levels rise in a huge bulge known as a storm surge.

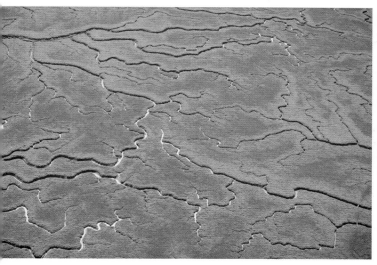

Area of low pressure moving in this direction

Area of lowest pressure

Wind-driven surge

Pressure surge

Figure 27 Storm surge due to low pressure

Figure 26 Salt marshes seen from the air. This is the type of environment that is found in grid square 0913 in Figure 31.

A great deal of the land edging the parish is composed of salt marsh and mudflats, which have been a natural flood plain for centuries. As development has taken place so properties have been built in these flood plains without much thought to what might happen if the sea rose abnormally. Such an event occurred January 31st–February 1st 1953, the worst weather event of the last century.
A combination of a predicted high tide with a deep low pressure area moving south east from Iceland into the North Sea and a storm surge hit the coast, first Scotland then of eastern England. Over 1,000 miles of coastline was flooded, over 30,000 people had to be evacuated from their homes and 307 people lost their lives. In Essex alone nearly 50,000 acres of land were flooded and 113 people died.

Jaywick, which had over 1,700 chalet bungalows, of which over 200 were thought to be occupied, was worst hit. The sea wall was broken in 22 places along our bank of the Colne Estuary and water swept around across St Osyth marshes to the back of Jaywick, a direction from which water was not expected, only to be made worse by yet more breaks in the bank along St Osyth Beach. 35 people were drowned in Jaywick. In Point Clear the two people who ran the grocery store in the Bay were also tragically drowned.

Figure 28 An extract from the St Osyth local government website describing the flood of 1953

Figure 29 Predicted sea-level rise at Jaywick

Year	2007	2032	2057	2082	2107
Rise in sea level (cm)	0	13	35	65	102

Activity

4 Use Figure 27 to give two explanations for the rise in sea level during a storm surge.

5 Use Figure 29 to draw a graph of the predicted sea-level rise at Jaywick.

6 Imagine that you live in Jaywick. Read Figure 28. Given that a lot of land is salt marsh and mudflats, is it sensible for people to continue to live here? Summarise the arguments for each of the following coastal management strategies:
a) Holding the line
b) Retreating the line.

Coastal management at Jaywick

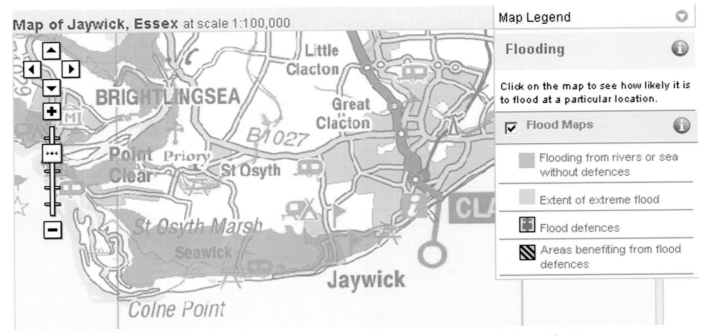

Figure 30 A screenshot from the Environment Agency website showing areas close to Jaywick that are at risk of coastal flooding

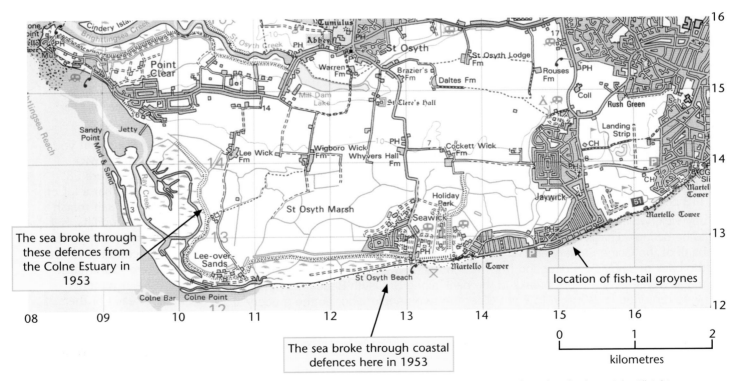

Figure 31 An Ordnance Survey extract of Colne Point and Jaywick. Scale 1:50,000 Sheet 169. © Crown Copyright and/or database right. All rights reserved. Licence number 100036470

Fish-tail groynes

Artificial reef

Figure 32 An aerial photograph of Jaywick and two breakwaters

Since 1953 the sea defences at Jaywick have had to be strengthened several times. Continual erosion of sand from the beach leaves the sea wall with little protection and it is attacked by pebbles that are thrown against it in the waves (the process of abrasion). In recent years coastal erosion has been managed using both hard and soft engineering techniques. Hard engineering is the use of artificial structures such as sea walls and breakwaters to slow erosion or prevent flooding. Soft engineering is the use of natural materials such as sand which replace sediment eroded from the beach.

Two differently shaped breakwaters can be seen in Figure 32. Another breakwater was added in 2009. The breakwaters are built using blocks of granite from Sweden. Each rock weighs 6–8 tonnes so is too heavy to be eroded by wave action. They are designed to slow down the waves and encourage deposition of sand between the breakwater and the beach. They also slow down the rate of longshore drift, but do not prevent it. In the latest scheme, 250,000 tonnes of sand were sucked up from an offshore sand bar, pumped through pipes and onto the beach. The whole scheme cost £10 million and protects 2,600 properties. It should prevent a flood of 4.1 m above normal sea level. This is the kind of flood that is caused by low air pressure and massive waves. A flood of this size could occur, on average, once in every 200 years.

Activity

1 Describe the relief shown on Figure 31.

2 Most of the deaths in 1953 were in the Broadlands housing estate at B (Figure 32). Use the OS map extract to give a grid reference for this area.

3 Compare the width of the beach at C on the map and photo. What does this suggest about the success or otherwise of the hard engineering?

4 Use Figures 30 and 31 to identify settlements that are at risk of coastal floods.

5 Use evidence from Figures 28, 30, 31 and 32 to draw a sketch map of Jaywick and the area flooded in 1953. Annotate it to show where the flood came from, the areas it covered and why it spread so quickly.

6 a) Use evidence from the OS map and Figure 32 to state the direction of longshore drift.
   b) Suggest how the breakwaters at Jaywick might affect coastal processes at Colne Point.

7 Make a sketch of Figure 32. Annotate it to show how the coastal management scheme protects this stretch of coastline.

Australia

Why does coastal management create controversy?

It is natural that people who live near to the coast expect to be protected from erosion and flooding. However, the usual strategies of hard and soft engineering are expensive and, in the face of rising sea levels, may not be sustainable. Planners now believe that a mixture of engineering strategies and coastal land-use zoning is needed to manage coastlines in the future. These zones will include some urban areas where future building will be prevented and others where homes will be rebuilt further inland and coastal retreat will be managed.

The idea of moving urban areas further inland is now being considered by scientists and some politicians in Australia but many residents of coastal towns, such as Byron Bay in New South Wales, are unhappy.

Sand has been eroded during a tropical storm

The remaining beach is now very narrow and offers little natural defence against further storm waves

Figure 33 Erosion of the beach on the Gold Coast, Australia

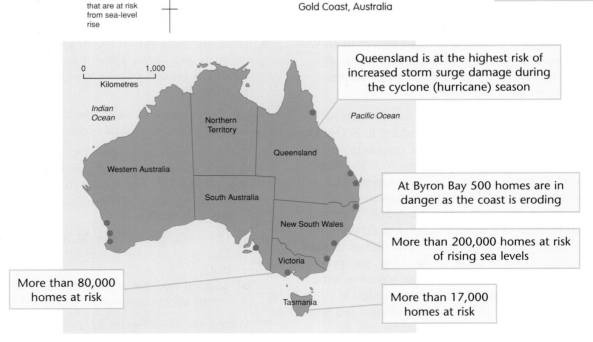

Key

● Communities that are at risk from sea-level rise

N

0 — 1,000
Kilometres

Indian Ocean

Northern Territory

Pacific Ocean

Western Australia

Queensland

South Australia

New South Wales

Victoria

Tasmania

Queensland is at the highest risk of increased storm surge damage during the cyclone (hurricane) season

At Byron Bay 500 homes are in danger as the coast is eroding

More than 200,000 homes at risk of rising sea levels

More than 80,000 homes at risk

More than 17,000 homes at risk

Figure 34 Areas which the Australian government believes are under threat from rising sea levels

> We cannot afford to 'hold the line' by repairing sea defences. That strategy just isn't sustainable in the face of climate change and rising sea levels. We believe that 'retreating the line' is the best strategy for Byron Bay.

Local councillor in Byron Bay and Green Party member

> This is our home and we don't want to leave it. The local council should protect us from coastal erosion by repairing the sea defences.

Local resident in Byron Bay, New South Wales

> If the local council is not prepared to pay for repairs to the coastal defences then they should allow local residents to pay for the repairs themselves.

Spokesperson for the State Government of New South Wales

> Sea levels are rising and it's not possible to continue to defend our entire coastline. The government will have to identify coastal areas where new residential developments will not be permitted. They must also consider forced retreats, where people are moved from their homes and the sea is allowed to flood low-lying coastlines.

Spokesperson for an environmental committee that reported to the Australian government

> When it comes to rising sea levels, I am alert, but I can't say that I'm particularly alarmed. The fact is that sea levels have risen along the New South Wales coast by more than 20 cm over the last century. Has anyone noticed it? No, they haven't. Obviously an 80 cm rise in sea levels would be more serious but I'm confident that we have the resources to cope.

Tony Abbott, Liberal MP in the national government

Figure 35 Stakeholder views on coastal erosion at Byron Bay, New South Wales

Climate change threatens Australia's coastal lifestyle, report warns

An Australian government environmental committee report warns that thousands of miles of coastline are under threat from rising sea levels and suggests banning people from living in vulnerable areas.

Beach culture is as much part of the Australian identity as the bush and barbecues, but that could have to change according to a government report that raises the unsettling prospect of banning its citizens from coastal regions at risk of rising seas. The report, from a parliamentary climate change committee, said that AUS$150bn (£84bn) worth of property was at risk from rising sea levels and more frequent storms. With 80 per cent of Australians living along the coastline, the report warns that 'the time to act is now'.

Australia has no national coastal plan despite the prospect of losing large swaths of coastal land as each centimetre rise in sea levels is expected to carve a metre or more off the shoreline. If sea levels rise 80 cm by 2100, some 711,000 homes, businesses and properties, which sit less than 6 m above sea level and lie within 3 km of the coast, will be vulnerable to flooding, erosion, high tides and surging storms. It argues that Australia needs a national policy to respond to sea level rise brought on by global warming, which could see people forced to abandon homes and banned from building at the beachside, according to the committee on climate change, water, environment and the arts.

Figure 36 News extract from the *Guardian*, 27 October 2009

Activity

1 Work in pairs and study Figures 34, 35 and 36. On a poster or in a PowerPoint presentation, summarise the main impacts that sea-level rise will have on the Australian coast. Your poster/presentation should include:
   - graphical techniques to represent the data
   - a summary of the economic impacts and social impacts
   - an explanation of the viewpoints of Byron Bay Council and the opposing view of the residents of Byron Bay.

Mexico

Managing the beach at Cancun, Mexico causes controversy

The Mexican resort of Cancun is built on a long, thin barrier of sand in the north-east of the Yucatan peninsula. Like other long spits and **tombolos**, the Cancun–Nizuc barrier was formed by the process of longshore drift which transports sediment parallel to the coast. The white sandy beach is a major tourist attraction. It also helps to absorb wave energy and protect the resort from storm surges. It therefore needs careful management.

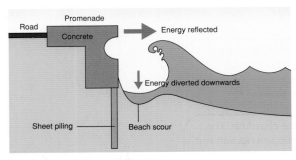

Figure 37 Badly designed sea walls can cause erosion of the beach

Cancun's beach was severely eroded by Hurricane Gilbert in 1988 and again by Wilma, which blasted the resort in 2005. However, scientists believe that people are also to blame for the loss of sand from the barrier. Sand was taken from the beach during the 1970s and 80s to be used in the construction of the hotels. Some hotels built vertical sea walls to protect their property. These divert the energy of the wave downwards and cause scouring of sand from the beach. Scientists fear that these changes have left the resort more vulnerable to coastal erosion and to flooding during tropical storms.

Artificial reefs

In 1998 engineers pumped a mixture of sea water and sand into several fabric tubes known as 'sandtainers'. These tubes were positioned in two lines to make a pair of artificial reefs parallel to the shore. The finished reef was 800 m long. It encouraged the deposition of sediment behind the reef and also on the beach.

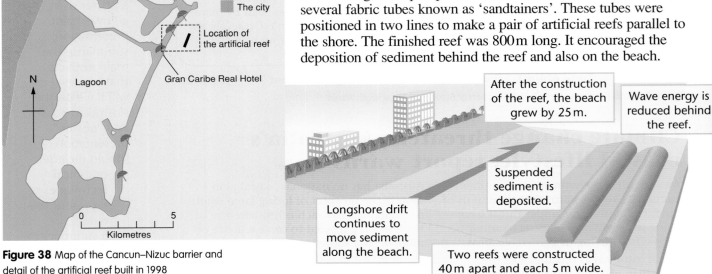

Figure 38 Map of the Cancun–Nizuc barrier and detail of the artificial reef built in 1998

Activity

1 Describe how the coastline at Cancun has affected the local economy.

2 Make a copy of Figure 38. Mark on it the direction of longshore drift. Use your diagram to explain how this landform was made.

3 Read Figure 39. Use your map of the Cancun–Nizuc barrier to explain how building a breakwater or groyne outside the Gran Caribe Real Hotel would:
   a) improve business for this hotel
   b) affect the hotels further along the beach (state whether it would have affected hotels to the north or south).

Beach replenishment

On 21 October 2005 Cancun was hit by Hurricane Wilma which caused widespread damage to the resort's hotels and its beaches. It cost $1.5 billion to repair the damage done by Wilma. One of the biggest challenges was to repair the damage to the beach. The storm surge eroded millions of tonnes of sand from Cancun's beach. The original beach had been 20 m wide and covered in fine white sand. The storm waves eroded all of the sand, exposing the rocky wave-cut platform underneath.

The beach was repaired using a technique known as **beach replenishment**. The work was carried out by a Belgian engineering firm, Jan de Nul, which used a boat to dredge sand from the sea bed and pump it back onto the beach. About 2.7 million m³ of sand were sucked up from two offshore sand banks. The new beach was 45 m wide and 12 km long. It took six months to complete the task, which was finished in June 2006. Beach replenishment is an example of soft engineering where natural materials, in this case sand, are used rather than artificial materials such as concrete.

'Beach war' hotels probed over sand theft

Surprised tourists found their little piece of Cancun beach paradise ringed by crime-scene tape on Thursday. Environmental enforcement officers backed by Mexican navy personnel closed off dozens of metres of powder-white coastline in front of a hotel accused of illegally accumulating sand on its beach.

Mexico spent US$19 million to replace Cancun beaches washed away by Hurricane Wilma in 2005. But much of the sand pumped from the sea floor has since washed away, leading some property owners to build breakwaters in a bid to retain sand. The practice often merely shifts sand loss to beaches below the breakwaters.

'Today we made the decision to close this stretch of ill-gotten, illegally accumulated sand,' said Patricio Patron, Mexico's attorney general for environmental protection. 'This hotel was telling its tourists: "Come here, I have sand ... the other hotels don't, because I stole it."'

Patron said five people were detained in a raid for allegedly using pumps to move sand from the sea floor onto the beach in front of the Gran Caribe Real Hotel. The hotel is also suspected of illegally building a breakwater that impeded the natural flow of sand onto other hotels' beaches.

Figure 39 A news report of conflict over management of the beach at Cancun, Mexico, 31 July 2009

Activity

4   Use this case study to explain why the local council should decide how the coast is managed rather than individual land owners.

5   Use evidence from pages 173–83 to complete the following table. Make sure you describe and explain each advantage and disadvantage.

Type of management	Examples	Advantages	Disadvantages
Hard engineering	Breakwaters at Jaywick	Homes are protected so …	
	Groynes at Borth		
	Sea walls at Cancun		
Soft engineering	Beach replenishment		The process has to be repeated in a few years because …
	Artificial sandtainer reef at Cancun		

Essex

Is managed realignment the most sustainable option?

The Essex coastline contains many creeks, salt marshes and mud banks (as you can see in grid square 0913 in Figure 31 on page 178. These features are a natural water store and help to soak up water during a storm surge. However, as sea levels rise, they are rapidly being eroded, as you can see in Figure 41. The erosion of these salt marshes leaves Essex even more vulnerable to coastal floods in the future.

Activity

1 Use Figure 40 to describe the location of Tollesbury.

2 Make a copy of Figure 41.
  a) Calculate the amount of salt marsh that will be left in each estuary by 2050.
  b) Make a simple sketch of Figure 40. Add bars to your map to represent the amount of land eroded in each estuary by 2050. Locate your bars in the correct locations.

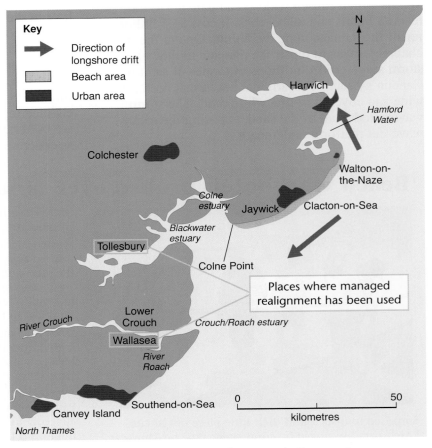

Figure 40 Location of different management techniques on the Essex coast

Estuary	Area in 1998 (hectares)	Area (hectares) eroded by 2050 at present rates	Area (hectares) left by 2050
North Thames	181	−175	
Crouch/Roach	308	−198	
Blackwater	684	−274	
Colne	695	−247	
Hamford Water	621	−722	

Figure 41 Predicted future erosion of salt marsh in Essex estuaries

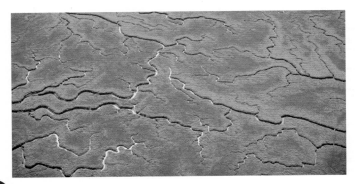

Activity

3 Use Figure 43 to describe:
  a) the distribution of breaches
  b) the amount and value of flooded land.

4 Suggest why the cost of flood damage in Essex would be lower than that in London.

5 Explain how managed realignment in Essex could protect people who live in London in the future.

Figure 42 Salt marshes seen from the air

Figure 43 The cost of flood damage in 2050 after a flood similar to the 1953 storm surge. Red spots show where coastal defences would be breached

Managed realignment is being tested near Tollesbury in the Blackwater estuary, and at also at Wallasea in the Crouch estuary. Old earth embankments have kept the sea off these low-lying fields for centuries. Holes have now been punched through the embankments. This is an example of 'retreating the line' which is an option available in all Shoreline Management Plans.

The invading sea water moves slowly across the land at high tide and as it does it deposits mud. This process recreates natural mudflats and salt marshes. The deposits of mud will absorb wave energy and act as a natural buffer against erosion. The marshes will also help to store water during a storm surge. During a massive flood storm surge, like the one of 1953 that flooded Jaywick, these salt marshes would be flooded. They would store floodwater, meaning that less floodwater would enter the Thames estuary. This should help prevent flooding of many homes and businesses in the Thames estuary and London.

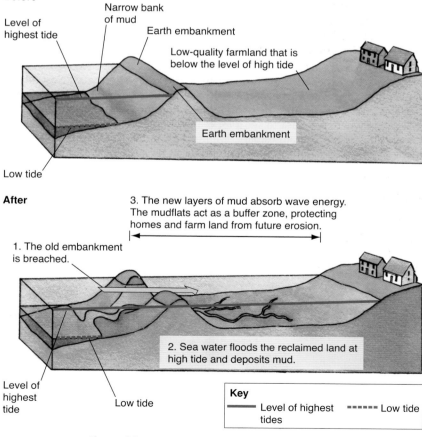

Figure 44 How managed realignment protects the coast

Is everyone in favour of managed realignment?

Managed realignment is much cheaper than hard engineering. Some scientists say it is more sustainable too. Sea walls need constant repair and as sea levels rise will need to be made bigger and stronger. Managed realignment creates a natural buffer zone between coastal communities and the sea. As we have seen, it could even help prevent a disastrous flood in London.

Activity

1 Work in pairs.
   a) Suggest why so many new homes are needed.
   b) List five groups who might oppose plans for new housing and five who might benefit from it.

2 How would you manage the Essex coastline? Produce a report. Include:
   a) a description of the advantages and disadvantages of managed realignment
   b) an explanation of the different points of view about how this coast should be managed
   c) the reason you think that your decision is sustainable.

Figure 45 Opinions about coastal management in Essex

Farmer

The cost of maintaining the sea defences along many parts of the Essex coast is greater than the benefits of those defences. The land is poor-quality farmland. It doesn't make sense to keep paying for the maintenance of structures like groynes.

The council should be strengthening sea defences all along the Essex coast like they have at Jaywick. My family has lived here and farmed this land for generations. The old embankment has kept the sea out for many years. I don't believe that a rise in sea level of a few centimetres will make any difference.

Government (Defra) spokesperson

The UK is experiencing a housing crisis. It is estimated that at least an extra 223,000 new houses or flats are needed every year. That's an extra 3 million homes between 2007 and 2020. The greatest demand for new housing is in the south-east of England. One location where we want to see a lot of new homes is in the Thames Gateway which is on both sides of the Thames estuary. We need a coastal management plan that will protect all of this new housing for at least the next 100 years.

Government housing minister

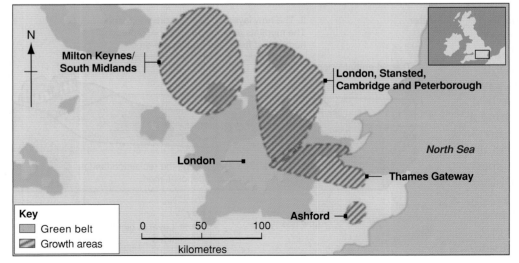

Figure 46 Key areas for new homes in south-east England

Theme 3: Uneven Development and Sustainable Environments

An airbus A321 tanked up with biofuel. Lufthansa has been testing the use of biofuels since July 2011 on a daily flight between Frankfurt and Hamburg. One turbine is powered with 50 per cent bio-synthetic kerosene called Pure Sky – a mixture of jatropha, camelina oil and animal grease

Chapter 1
Employment structures and opportunities

How do we classify and record employment?

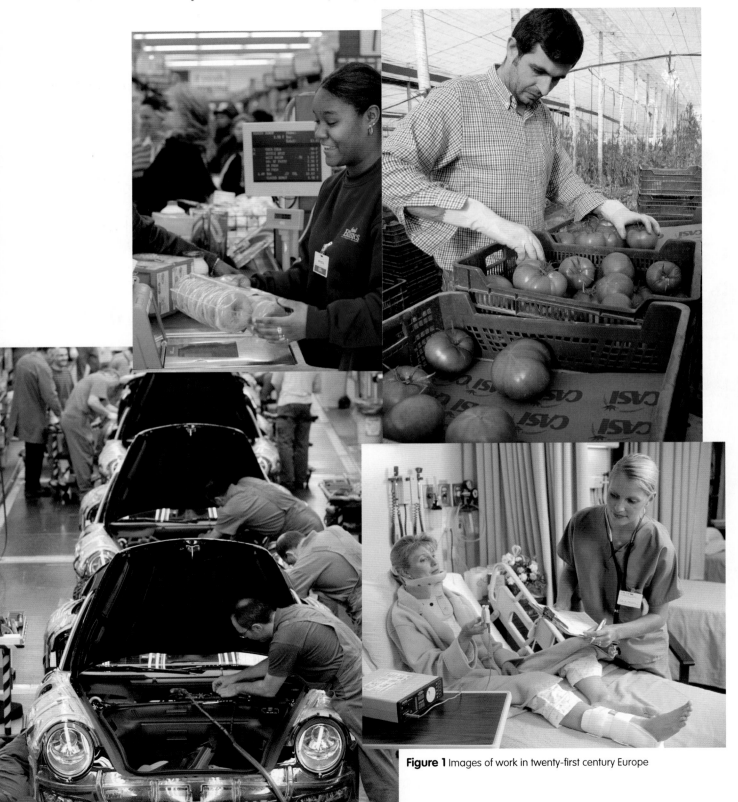

Figure 1 Images of work in twenty-first century Europe

Primary, secondary and tertiary sectors

The usual way to classify employment is to sort all economic activities into one of three sectors of the economy. The three sectors are:

- **Primary sector.** This sector of the economy produces raw materials such as a food crop, timber or mineral. Occupations in fishing, farming, forestry and mining are all examples of primary economic activities.
- **Secondary sector.** The secondary sector is involved in processing and manufacturing. Food processing, the textile and clothing industry and the manufacture of microchips are all examples of secondary occupations.
- **Tertiary sector.** This sector provides services to other industries or to individual consumers like you and me. Employment in a school, shop, office or hospital are all examples of tertiary occupations.

The number of people working in the primary, secondary and tertiary sectors of the economy is known as the **employment structure** of that region or country. The primary sector is the world's largest employer. On a global scale, 43 per cent of the world's 3 billion workers have occupations in agriculture.

Employment structure varies considerably from one country to another. In the poorest countries, such as Mali, most jobs are in the primary sector and are **labour intensive**. This means that work is still done by hand rather than using labour-saving machines. Wealthier developing countries, such as Malaysia, have smaller primary sectors and much larger secondary sectors. MEDCs have even fewer people employed in the primary sector.

In Europe less than 5 per cent of people are employed in primary economic activities, and in the UK this figure is less than 2 per cent.

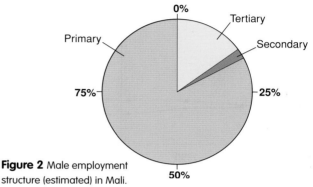

Figure 2 Male employment structure (estimated) in Mali. Source: World Bank

	UK		Malaysia		Romania	
Male employment	1980	2010	1980	2010	1980	2010
Primary	3	2	34	17	22	29
Secondary	48	29	26	32	52	36
Tertiary	49	69	40	51	26	35
Female employment	1980	2010	1980	2010	1980	2010
Primary	1	1	44	9	39	31
Secondary	23	7	20	23	34	20
Tertiary	76	92	36	68	27	49

Figure 3 Changing employment structure (figures show percentage employed in each sector). Source: World Bank

Activity

1 Study the jobs shown in Figure 1.
   a) Sort these jobs into the primary, secondary or tertiary sectors.
   b) Sort each of the jobs into the private or public sectors.

2 Study Figure 2. What percentage of Mali's population works in each sector of the economy?

3 Use Figure 3.
   a) Choose a suitable graphical technique to illustrate all the data.
   b) Describe the main similarities and differences you see between:
      i) how employment has changed between 1980 and 2010
      ii) patterns of employment in UK and Malaysia
      iii) male and female employment.

Public and private sectors of the economy

Employment can be recorded as being in either the public sector or private sector.

• People working in the **public sector** are employed by the national, regional or local government. A wide range of jobs that provide a service is available including doctors, nurses, teachers, planners, social workers, soldiers, refuse collectors.

• People working in the **private sector** are either **self-employed** or they work for a larger company or organisation that is not owned by the government. The private sector provides a wide range of jobs on the land (such as farming and forestry), in construction (design, engineering and building), in **manufacturing** and in services (offices, shops, and leisure and tourism).

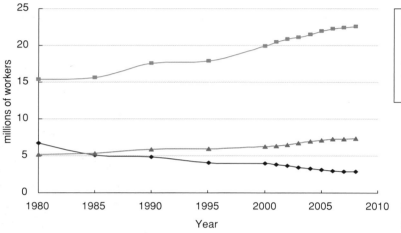
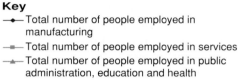

Key
— Total number of people employed in manufacturing
— Total number of people employed in services
— Total number of people employed in public administration, education and health

Figure 4 Changing UK employment in manufacturing and services (millions of workers). Source: Office of National Statistics

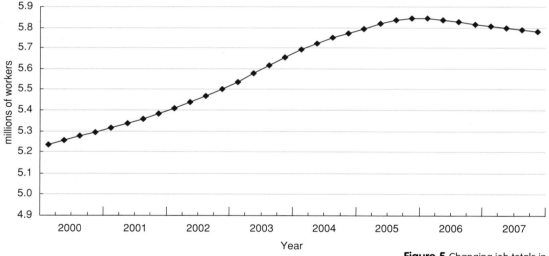

Figure 5 Changing job totals in UK public sector jobs (millions)

Activity

1 Use Figure 4.
  a) Describe the trend in manufacturing and identify the five-year period in which most jobs were lost.
  b) Compare the trends in service jobs and administration, education and health. Comment on the similarities and any differences.

  c) Suggest three reasons for the changes you have identified.

2 Use Figure 5 to describe the trend in public service employment.

How is technology changing the way we work?

The world of work is changing fast. The government believes that as many as seven out of ten children who are starting primary school today will eventually work in jobs that haven't been invented yet! Find that hard to believe? Just consider some of the jobs that we take for granted today. For example, when you surf the web you are viewing pages designed by web designers: a job that didn't exist in the 1980s. Figure 6 shows another example of how technology is changing the workplace.

Figure 6 A computer-generated image (CGI) from King Kong. An example of one of thousands of new jobs created by computing

Technological change is having a massive impact on all sectors of the economy. **Mechanisation**, which is the increased use of machines to replace human labour, has been a major cause of job losses on many European farms and factories. At the same time, new computer and communication technology is creating new jobs in some service industries. For example, the growth of some of the world's fastest-growing businesses is connected directly to growth in the internet. Google™, the search engine, and eBay, the online auction site, have grown rapidly since the mid-1990s as a direct result of the increased internet access of consumers like you and me.

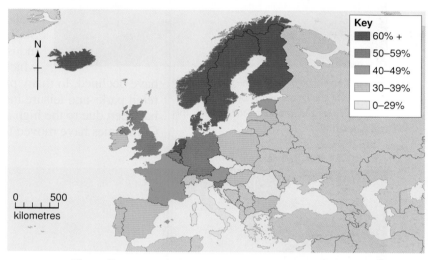

Key
- 60% +
- 50–59%
- 40–49%
- 30–39%
- 0–29%

0   500
kilometres

Figure 7 Percentage of the population of Europe with internet access (2007).

Figure 8 The growth of retail sales over the internet in the UK

Year	% UK households with broadband connection	% of all UK retail sales made online	£ billions spent on online purchases
2003	11	1.5	9.2
2004	16	2.3	18.1
2005	32	4.1	21.4
2011	80	9.5	546.4
2012	86	12.2	787.9

Activity

3 **a)** Study Figure 8 and suggest an enquiry question or hypothesis linking the three sets of data.
   b) Choose a suitable technique to graph the data.
   c) Comment on the pattern shown on your graph. Explain what it shows.

4 **a)** Working with a partner, suggest a list of jobs that you think might be associated with each of the following industries:
   i)   fashion
   ii) the film industry
   iii) travel and tourism.
   b) Now imagine you could go back in time to 1990, a time before most people had mobile phones, powerful graphics on their computers, or access to the internet. Suggest how some of the jobs you have identified would have been different without this modern technology.

5 Look at Figure 7.
   a) Describe the distribution of internet access in Europe.
   b) Suggest reasons for the pattern that you see.

West Midlands, UK

Investigating the changing employment structure of the West Midlands

Figure 9 An image of work in the mid-twentieth century. C.W. Brown painted scenes of coal mines and iron works in North Staffordshire. This one is dated 1947

From the 1950s through to the 1980s, the West Midlands was regarded as the home of UK manufacturing. However, since then, the West Midlands has seen a massive decline in the number of manufacturing jobs. At the same time, the number of people working in jobs that provide a service, such as the health service, retailing, banking, and leisure and tourism, has increased. This shift in employment is known as **de-industrialisation**.

The most obvious effect of this change is in the industrial landscape: just compare the images of North Staffordshire in Figures 9 and 10. The so-called 'heavy industries' of steel making, engineering and mining, which employed tens of thousands of (mainly) men, have declined. In many places they have been replaced by out-of-town retail parks and leisure industries. The decline of manufacturing since 1980 has been due to the high costs of both labour and production in the UK. Companies have moved to other regions of the world where costs are lower.

Figure 10 An image of work in the twenty-first century. This retail park occupies the same space as C.W. Brown's painting (Figure 9)

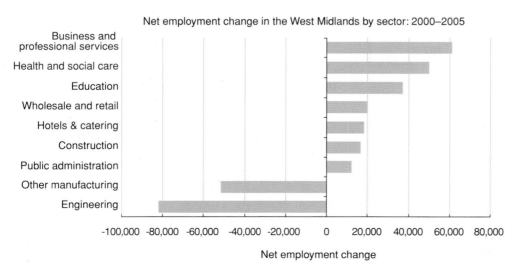

Figure 11 Jobs gained or lost in the West Midlands, 2000–05. Source: West Midlands Regional Observatory

Activity

1 **a)** State whether the industries shown in Figures 9 and 10 belong to the primary, secondary or tertiary sectors.
   b) What does this tell you about how jobs changed between 1947 and 2006 in North Staffordshire?

2 Study Figures 9 and 10. Compare the two images using these headings:

   Landscape Pollution
   Job opportunities.

What is the knowledge economy?

A recent development in the way we record employment is to identify jobs in the **knowledge economy**. These jobs require high levels of education or training. This sector of the economy includes:

- Manufacturing jobs:
  a) **High-tech industries** such as defence systems and medical equipment.
  b) Medium/high-tech jobs such as electronics.
- **Knowledge Intensive Service (KIS)** industries such as finance and education.

Approximately half of all workers in the UK work in the knowledge sector of the economy. The West Midlands has fewer workers in the knowledge sector of the economy than most other regions of the UK. Figure 12 compares employment in the knowledge sector in Staffordshire, in the North of the region, with the rest of the West Midlands and the UK.

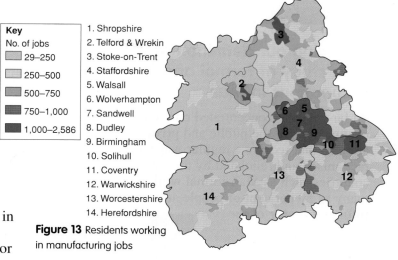

Key
No. of jobs
- 29–250
- 250–500
- 500–750
- 750–1,000
- 1,000–2,586

1. Shropshire
2. Telford & Wrekin
3. Stoke-on-Trent
4. Staffordshire
5. Walsall
6. Wolverhampton
7. Sandwell
8. Dudley
9. Birmingham
10. Solihull
11. Coventry
12. Warwickshire
13. Worcestershire
14. Herefordshire

Figure 13 Residents working in manufacturing jobs

		Staffs	**West Midlands**	**UK**
Jobs in high-tech and medium-technology manufacturing	as a % of all jobs	6.6	6.4	4.4
	% gain or loss	–39.0	–32.5	–25.0
Jobs in Knowledge Intensive Services (KIS)	as a % of all jobs	39.0	42.3	45.9
	% gain or loss	18.8	18.2	19.0

Figure 12 Percentage of jobs in the knowledge economy in Staffordshire

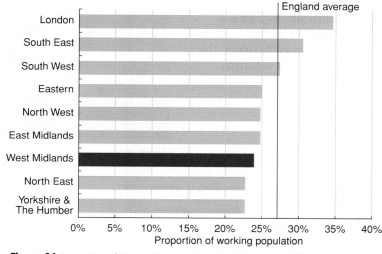

Proportion of the working age population with Level 4+ qualifications in 2006

Figure 14 Proportion of the working population with level 4 qualifications (2006). Level 4 qualifications require specialist knowledge of jobs/skills

Activity

3 Use Figure 11.

   a) How many jobs were gained or lost in each of the following sectors?

   i) engineering ii) construction iii) education.

   b) Identify the service jobs that are mainly public sector jobs. How many gains or losses were there in the public sector?

4 Use Figure 13 to describe the distribution of people working in manufacturing jobs in the West Midlands region.

5 Use Figure 14 to compare the skill levels of people working in the West Midlands with other regions of the UK.

6 Choose a suitable graphical technique to show the data in Figure 12.

7 Give two reasons why the employment structure in the West Midlands is changing.

8 **a)** Discuss the changing pattern of work and employment in the West Midlands. Consider how education and technology could change employment in the future using evidence from pages 190–3.

   b) Write two contrasting predictions for the future of this region.

Mali

Widening our definition of work: a case study of formal and informal occupations in Mali

So far we have concentrated on the **formal occupations** of the public and private sector. These are jobs that receive a regular wage and that are recognised and regulated by the state. In the poorest countries such as Mali formal work is scarce, so as many as 50 per cent of people are occupied in the

Figure 15 Work in Mali: collecting water

informal sector of the economy. This sector includes many types of irregular jobs as well as types of work such as household chores and childcare. Figure 18 summarises the differences between the formal and informal sectors of the economy.

Figure 16 Work in Mali: scaring birds from the millet crop on a smallholding

Figure 17 Work in Mali: musicians

	Informal economy		Formal economy
	Reproduction and subsistence	**Petty commodity production**	
Examples of occupations	Daily household chores like: • fetching water • collecting firewood • childcare • preparing meals. Subsistence means that a farmer with a small parcel of land produces only enough food to feed the family with no surplus to sell for cash.	Work in this sector involves the production of low-value goods or services. Examples in Mali include: 1. Growing cotton to sell to foreign buyers 2. Selling surplus fruit or vegetables on a street market, 3. Recycling scrap metal into a useful object such as a hoe or plough.	Since there are very few jobs in manufacturing, most formal economy jobs in Mali are in a service industry such as: • a shop • school • hospital or health clinic • a Non-Governmental Organisation (NGO) providing aid or advice. These occupations may be either full time or part time.
Earnings	No earnings	Low earnings and irregular payments	Regular wage
Rights	No contract. No holidays or sickness benefit. No rules to protect your health and safety at work.		Most formal occupations benefit from a contract, entitlement to holidays and sick pay, etc.
Responsibilities	It is unusual for workers to pay tax.		Workers pay tax.

Figure 18 The formal and informal sectors of the economy in Mali

Figure 19 Work in Mali: a blacksmith recycling scrap metal

Waste recycling: an example of informal work

Bamako is the capital of Mali. It has a population of at least 1.2 million and has grown quickly in recent years. The number of formal jobs available in the city has not grown as quickly as the city has, so many people find it hard to get a job with a regular salary. Consequently, many people work in the informal sector of the economy.

Typical informal jobs include working on street markets, running bars and recycling waste. Some workers collect waste, sort it and wash it. Others recycle it into useful tools and these are sold on market stalls. Organic waste is composted and sold to farmers on the outskirts of the city.

The city authorities recognise the value of the informal sector. The collection and disposal of solid waste had become a problem but has been solved by the informal sector.

There is a large market area in Bamako. All sorts of scrap metal is collected from all over the city and brought here where it is sorted and sold to specialist dealers. Everything from car parts to railways is brought here.

Some of the smaller scrap is sold simply as scrap, but a lot of it goes directly for recycling. There are workshops everywhere in this area, all making different items out of recycled metal: trunks, wheelbarrows, braziers and farming implements are just a few of the things they make.

The recycling market has been here for more than 20 years. Recycling began in the rural areas but now it has become more commercial.

Ploughs and hoes, as well as other farming implements, are made from scrap metal. Through this recycling market a car from Europe, say a Renault or a Peugeot, could end up being used to make ploughs for a poor rural farmer in the smallest, most distant village in Mali. When a car is imported it is used for as long as possible and when it can no longer be driven it's dismantled and every last piece of it is used to make something else.

Daouda Ballo, Bamako Market

Figure 20 Extract from the Cool Planet section of Oxfam's website 2007

Activity

1 Study the photographs on these two pages.
   a) Describe whether the work shown belongs to the primary, secondary or tertiary sector of the economy.
   b) Study Figure 18 and use it to describe whether the work in each photo belongs to the informal or formal sector. You could use a table like the one to the right for your answer.

2 Use Figure 20 to explain the benefits of the informal sector.

3 Produce a chart that summarises the main differences between the formal and informal sectors.

Figure	Formal or informal?	If informal, is this an example of reproduction, subsistence or petty commodity production?	Reason
15			
16			
17			
19			

What are the costs and benefits of informal work for people and government?

Workers in the formal sector usually have a contract, which gives them some rights. They earn a regular wage, which means they can save and plan ahead. Regular wage earners find it easier to borrow money and pay rent for housing. This sector is regulated by the state, so most employees will pay some tax. The government can then use this money to improve quality of life by investing in health and education.

But many people in Mali work in the informal sector of the economy. Earnings in this sector are low and irregular. This means that informal workers find it very hard to save, borrow money, or pay rent. That's why many people in African cities live in shanty towns (or informal settlements). Furthermore, the informal sector is not regulated by the state, so the government does not earn any tax from it. In this respect the informal sector can be seen as a problem for developing countries like Mali, one of the world's ten poorest countries that need to invest heavily in better health and education.

However, governments of poor countries like Mali would find it hard to create enough formal-sector jobs for the number of children leaving education each year (see Figure 21). During the 1990s, the informal sector created 90 per cent of all new jobs in African countries. If people didn't take up informal work they would be unemployed.

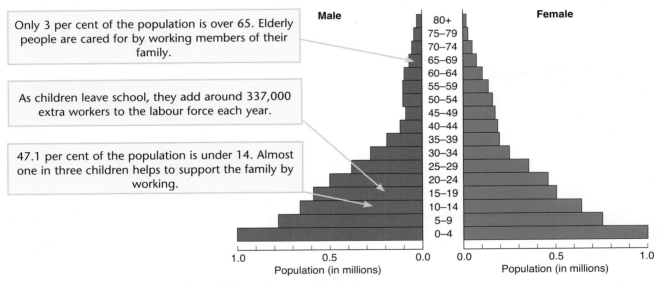

Only 3 per cent of the population is over 65. Elderly people are cared for by working members of their family.

As children leave school, they add around 337,000 extra workers to the labour force each year.

47.1 per cent of the population is under 14. Almost one in three children helps to support the family by working.

Figure 21 Population pyramid for Mali

Activity

1 Study Figure 21.
   a) Compare the percentage of under 15s to the percentage of over 65s.
   b) Explain how this population structure creates both benefits and challenges for the government of Mali.

- BUT WHAT WILL WOMEN DO
IF THEY DON'T HAVE TO
CARRY WATER FOUR HOURS
A DAY?

Figure 22 African women spend a lot of time doing work that does not contribute directly to family or state income

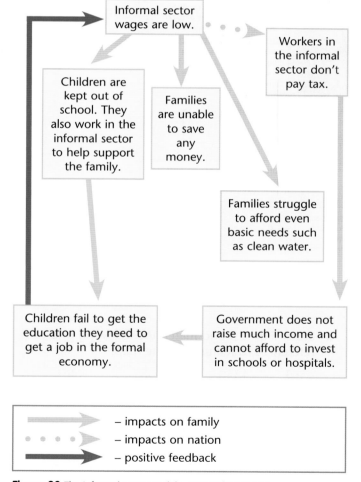

– impacts on family
– impacts on nation
– positive feedback

Figure 23 The informal sector and the national economy

Long working days are the norm for women in the **Sahel.** Women work up to a total of 16 hours per day in the growing season, of which about half is spent on agricultural work. Time allocation studies from Burkina Faso and Mali show women working one to three hours a day more than men. In rural areas, the lack of basic services such as reliable water supplies, health centres, stores (shops) and transport adds considerably to the time women must also spend on household chores. Shortage of time constrains women's attendance at activities to benefit them, the time and attention they can pay to productive activities, and visits to health facilities.

Figure 24 Extract from a World Bank report

Activity

2 Study Figures 22 and 24.
   a) Give three reasons why women in Sahel countries such as Mali have such long working days.
   b) Suggest a number of ways in which the lives of rural African women and children would be improved if they had access to a clean and safe water supply close to their home.
   c) Suggest how women in Mali might use four extra hours a day.

3 Study Figure 23. Explain carefully how a large informal sector in the economy may prevent:
   a) the country from developing greater wealth in its economy
   b) the development of improved education, training and healthcare facilities.

4 Using all of the information on pages 194–97, summarise the costs and benefits of the informal economy by completing a large table like this:

	Costs	Benefits
For the government of Mali		
For individuals working in the informal sector		

Chapter 2
The location of economic activities

What factors influence the location of industry?

In this chapter we will investigate case studies of a number of different industries including tourism, creative industries and manufacturing. What factors influence their location? Is it to do with their labour needs, physical environments/raw materials, communication networks, the forces of globalisation or government policy and incentives? All play a part. But which factors are most important?

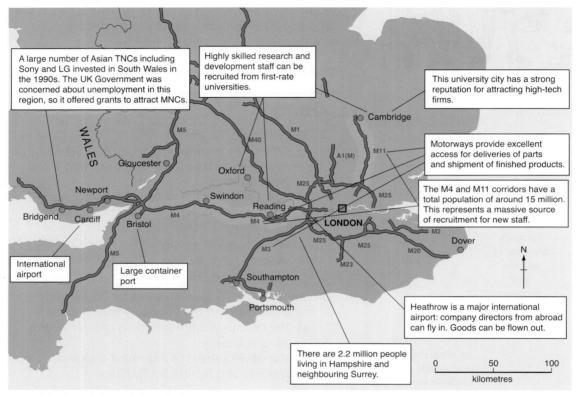

A large number of Asian TNCs including Sony and LG invested in South Wales in the 1990s. The UK Government was concerned about unemployment in this region, so it offered grants to attract MNCs.

Highly skilled research and development staff can be recruited from first-rate universities.

This university city has a strong reputation for attracting high-tech firms.

Motorways provide excellent access for deliveries of parts and shipment of finished products.

The M4 and M11 corridors have a total population of around 15 million. This represents a massive source of recruitment for new staff.

International airport

Large container port

Heathrow is a major international airport: company directors from abroad can fly in. Goods can be flown out.

There are 2.2 million people living in Hampshire and neighbouring Surrey.

Figure 1 The location of the M4/M11 corridor

Activity

1 Use Figure 1 to identify five specific reasons why multinational companies (MNCs) might wish to locate in the M4 or M11 corridors. Make sure you include:

   recruiting new workers
   selling their products in European markets
   possible government incentives

2 a) Describe the location of Cambridge on Figure 1.
   b) Describe the location of the Science Park on Figure 3 (in 4661) using words.
   c) Suggest three reasons why this is a great location for high tech footloose industries.

3 Study Figure 3 and match the following grid references to features on the map:

   4561   4858   4458   4461

   Intersection of the A14 and B1049
   Cambridge Airport
   College next to the A14
   Colleges near the city centre

4 a) Choose a suitable technique to graph the data in Figure 2.
   b) Suggest what benefits these businesses bring to the local economy of Cambridge.

What attracts businesses to Cambridge Science Park?

A wide variety of manufacturing and service industries are located in a zone stretching along the M4 from South Wales to London and up the M11 to Cambridge. These businesses are located close to a skilled workforce and with great transport links to their market. This makes them **footloose industries**.

One example is ANT Software, which provides software for TV devices and broadcasters. This is a **multi-national company (MNC)** with its headquarters in Cambridge and branches in America, Europe and Asia. Like other high tech firms located at the Cambridge Science Park they chose to locate here because they benefit from being close to other businesses that conduct similar research or can supply specialist components, advice or expertise. These businesses employ staff who are highly skilled with expertise in science, engineering or ICT. Many staff are recruited directly from the neighbouring university.

Type of business	Number	Foreign MNCs
Biomedical	18	4
Computers and telecommunications	25	8
Technical consultants	7	2
Energy	1	0
Environmental	1	1
Financial	4	0
Industrial technologies	4	1
Other	13	4
Total	73	20

Figure 2 Types of business, and number owned by foreign MNCs, on Cambridge Science Park

GEOGRAPHICAL SKILLS

Locating places on an OS map

The vertical grid lines on an OS map are eastings. The horizontal ones are northings. Each grid square is known by the intersection in its lower left corner. When you want to locate a place on an OS map you must give the easting first, then the northing. The church in Chesterton, located about 3 km to the north-east of Cambridge city centre, is in grid square 4660.

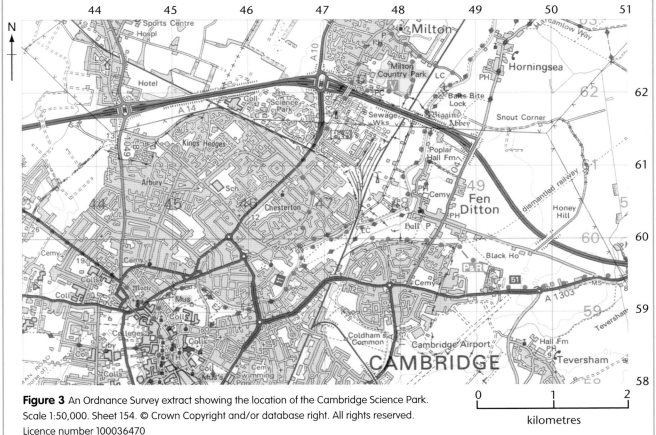

Figure 3 An Ordnance Survey extract showing the location of the Cambridge Science Park. Scale 1:50,000. Sheet 154. © Crown Copyright and/or database right. All rights reserved. Licence number 100036470

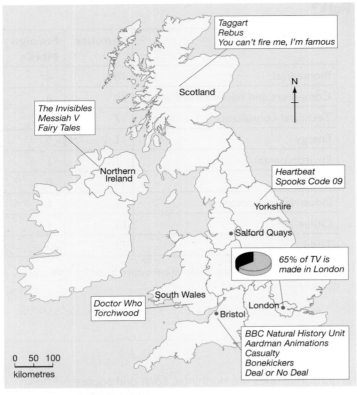

Figure 4 The location of the TV industry in the UK

Salford Quays

Where is UK TV and film made?

The creative industries in the UK are an important part of the service (or tertiary) sector of the economy. This sector includes jobs in TV, film, publishing, design and video game programming. It is estimated that these kinds of industries add over £100 billion to the national economy each year and employ 2 million people. There are jobs all over the country. Yorkshire, for example, is home to four of the world's top video game programming companies. However, two-thirds of the UK's TV and film is made in London. Figure 4 shows the location of some of the programmes made outside the capital.

In 2012, the BBC moved the production of some of its TV and radio programmes from London to Salford Quays, Manchester. A new development, MediaCityUK, has been purpose built. It includes seven high definition TV studios and is thought to be the largest of its kind in Europe.

About 7.5 million people live in London. So over 50 million people live in other parts of the UK

In other words, TV made by the big broadcasters such as the BBC or ITV

Companies who are based in London but who make television programmes that they then sell to the broadcasters like BBC or ITV

Who do you think the author means here?

The motorway that surrounds London

A national issue

Does British TV reflect life in Britain today? London represents 12.5 per cent of the population, yet around 65 per cent of television is made in-house in London or by London-based independent production companies.

The capital is obviously the media centre of the UK, where much of the TV money is and where much of the talent gathers, but there are those who argue it would be healthier if more networked programmes were made beyond the M25. They say it would enrich our viewing, educate and entertain more, and fulfil the much-trumpeted public-service broadcasting remits of the broadcasters.

According to its charter, the BBC is supposed 'to represent the UK, its nations, regions and communities', but does it? And what about the other broadcasters?

Certainly if you poll people who live outside London they want more regional programming and more national networked programmes made regionally.

The success of the likes of *Heartbeat*, made in Yorkshire, *Doctor Who* (Cardiff), *Hollyoaks* (Liverpool) and *Casualty* (Bristol) proves that the talent and infrastructure are there outside London.

Figure 5 A newspaper extract. Source: The Guardian 23 June 2008

Some rural communities complain that too much TV (especially the news) is about urban areas. Do you think they have a point?

Why do you think the author chose these particular programmes?

Who decides where your TV programmes are made?

Why did the BBC decide to relocate? One reason may have been that their facilities in London were old and needed replacing. Property values are cheaper in Salford than in London so the BBC believe the move will eventually save them some money. However, one of the strongest reasons was pressure from Ofcom to make more programmes outside London. Ofcom is the body that keeps an eye on the TV, radio and telecoms businesses. It has to report its findings annually to the government. Ofcom believes that more of your TV programmes should be made regionally. This reflects a government aim to create jobs in the regions outside of the South East of England. Ofcom also believes that more regional TV is wanted by the consumers. They have, therefore, introduced quotas for each broadcaster. ITV should make 50 per cent of its programmes outside London. For BBC the quota is 30 per cent, Channel 4's is also 30 per cent, and Five's is 10 per cent.

Figure 6 MediaCityUK is a 200-acre (81 ha) mixed-use property development site at Salford Quays on the banks of the Manchester Ship Canal in Salford

Figure 7 Factors affecting the location of the TV and film industry

Regional universities are producing creative graduates with the right skills for the industry.

Ashley Pharoah (*Life on Mars* and *Bonekickers*) chose to shoot *Bonekickers* in Bath. The city has not been used as a location for much TV before, so he thinks it makes the programme seem fresh and new.

The actor's union, Equity, claims that 40 per cent of all the UK's actors live in London.

TV producers often work to tight deadlines. They don't have time to look for talented actors or technicians outside London.

Some writers like to work from home. Russell T. Davies (*Doctor Who*) was born in Swansea and had moved back to Wales before *Doctor Who* was made in Cardiff.

One-third of TV script writers live and work in London.

People want to watch TV programmes made in their own regions featuring local people with local accents.

There is a lot of creative talent in the regions. Yorkshire, for example, is home to 100 new media companies.

The big film studios, like Pinewood (where 007 films are shot), are all on the outskirts of London, so there is a concentration of specialised film jobs there.

Ofcom is setting challenging quotas to create programmes in the regions.

Activity

1 Describe the distribution of TV production in the UK.

2 Working in pairs, discuss Figures 4 and 5.
   a) Outline the arguments for making more TV outside London.
   b) Do you think TV represents your local area or your (urban or rural) community? Explain how increased regional TV production could help your community. If you have access to ICT or a video camera, use it to make your case.

3 Identify three different groups of people who influence the decision about where TV is made.

4 Use Figure 7. Fully explain the reasons:
   a) for continuing to make TV in London
   b) for moving more production to the regions.

What is the future of UK TV and film?

The TV and film industry is changing rapidly. Changing technology has allowed the number of channels to expand rapidly. Up until 1980 there were only three (terrestrial) channels in the UK. Channel 4 was added in 1982 and Five was added in 1996. Since 1994 there has been a massive increase in channels available to UK viewers via satellite or cable TV. By 2002 it was estimated that UK viewers could watch 320 different channels. Now that many more homes have broadband connections the option of watching TV on your computer means that many households can watch hundreds of different channels. This has meant a lot of extra competition for the main terrestrial channels such as BBC1 and ITV. As we have seen, these channels are expected to produce some of their programmes in the UK's regions. However, ITV has struggled in recent years to meet its Ofcom target of 50 per cent of production to be made outside London. In 2006–2007 it managed 42 per cent and in 2007–2008 it produced 44 per cent in the regions. In 2008 Ofcom announced it would reduce its target to 35 per cent. This has allowed ITV to make cuts in its regional production. In autumn 2008 ITV announced that it would be reducing the number of regional news programmes it makes from 17 down to 9. This would cause job losses and would save the company £40 million.

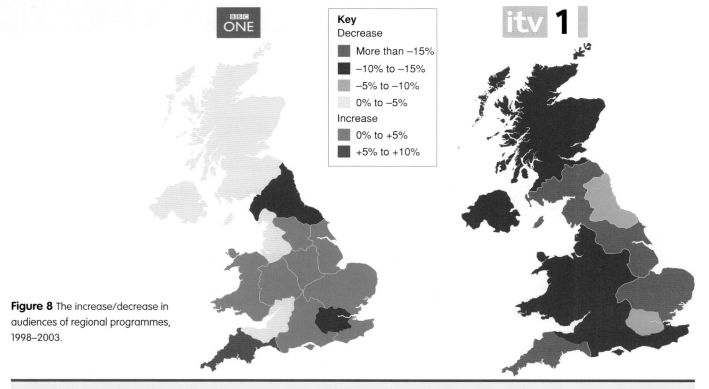

Key
Decrease
- More than −15%
- −10% to −15%
- −5% to −10%
- 0% to −5%

Increase
- 0% to +5%
- +5% to +10%

Figure 8 The increase/decrease in audiences of regional programmes, 1998–2003.

Activity

1 **a)** Describe and explain how TV is changing.
   b) Suggest how the growth of satellite or internet TV will affect TV production in the UK regions.

2 Use Figure 8 to describe the distribution of TV regions where viewing has:
   a) declined
   b) increased.

3 Use Figure 9 to outline the arguments for and against:
   a) moving more TV production to London
   b) moving all TV production to London.
   c) Suggest how these changes will affect the economy of places like Plymouth where a TV studio is likely to close.

4 **a)** Use Figure 10 to identify the main threats to the UK's creative industries.
   b) Explain what would happen in the UK if some of our creative industries decided to relocate to other parts of the globe.

Figure 9 Different points of view: should ITV move some of its production from the regions to London?

ITV manager

We have to win the battle for TV ratings. We rely on advertising to fund our TV production. Advertisers want their adverts to be seen by millions of viewers. Unfortunately, regional programmes do not get huge numbers of viewers. Nearly all of our most successful programmes, including the soaps, are made in London. In London there is a concentration of skilled people working in the TV industry so we can make more popular programmes more cheaply here. So we want to make more TV programmes in London and we believe by closing some regional studios we can save £40 million.

Regional TV producer

Our viewers want to see TV dramas and documentaries that reflect their community and culture. I believe that we can make really popular regional television, but it's almost impossible to persuade the ITV bosses to give us the peak slots in the evening. So our programmes are only shown when there are fewer viewers watching and the advertisers don't want to invest money in those programmes.

Member of National Union of Journalists

These cuts in regional TV will mean 430 people will lose their jobs. For example, ITV are planning to cut 90 jobs in the South West when the Plymouth TV studio is closed. Unless the bosses at ITV discuss their plans for the future of regional news with the union there will be industrial action.

Viewer

I would like to see more television programmes made locally. It seems to me that a lot of TV is made in London. It doesn't represent the issues or interests of people living in my part of the country. Besides, if more TV were made here it would help boost the local economy.

Figure 10 Extract from a speech by James Purnell, Parliamentary Under-Secretary of State for Creative Industries and Tourism

Making Britain the World's Creative Hub

Look at the way the creative industries have helped to transform Manchester, Gateshead or Glasgow. Over the last decade, your sectors have grown twice as fast as the overall economy. Today, they employ 2 million people – and account for a twelfth of our economy, more than in any other country.

Once we were known as the workshop of the world; but many of those industries have shrunk or disappeared. It would be a terrible day if in twenty or thirty years' time, people were saying the same about our creative industries. If they were saying, remember when we used to have the world's best advertising agencies. Or remember when Britain's television or design were the envy of the world?

That is a genuine threat. In terms of sheer volume, Bollywood is the biggest film industry in the world. China turned out over 2 million graduates last year. South Korea has one of the best online content industries in the world and a digital infrastructure of which most Western countries can only dream.

But the UK's current strength in creative industries is also a real opportunity. The UN estimates that creative industries account for 7 per cent of global GDP and are growing at 10 per cent a year. As people grow richer and become better educated, they spend more of their income on leisure activities.

So, the opportunity is clear – these markets will continue to grow, and Britain is good at them.

Mexico

What factors make the ideal location for a tourism resort?

The Yucatan is a large peninsula of land that juts out of Central America into the Caribbean Sea. It is mostly occupied by the Mexican state of Quintana Roo with the small tropical country of Belize in the south-eastern part of the region. The Yucatan has a lot more to offer than just the traditional attractions of sun, sea and sand. The eastern coastline has the second longest **barrier reef** in the world, providing excellent opportunities for diving and other water sports. Wildlife enthusiasts can explore rainforests, watch turtles and go bird-watching. The Yucatan is also famous for the archaeological remains of the Mayan civilisation which collapsed mysteriously in 1441, leaving behind stunning temples and pyramids in the Yucatan's rainforest.

Figure 11 The factors that affect the nature of tourism

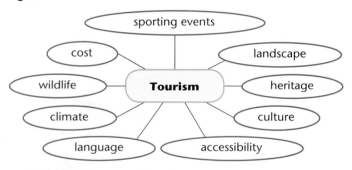

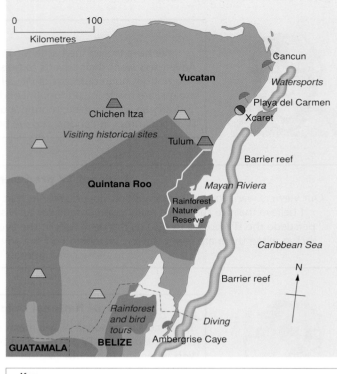

Figure 12 Tourist attractions of the Yucatan

Figure 13 Remains of the Mayan civilisation are scattered throughout the Yucatan

Figure 14 Tourists swimming with dolphins at Xcaret

The resort of Cancun was the brainchild of FUNATOR, the Mexican National Tourism Development Agency, which believed that a new mass tourist resort would create massive **positive multiplier effects** in the regional and national economies. The agency examined both the Pacific and Caribbean coastlines carefully before choosing this site as the best place to build the brand new resort. It chose a long spit of sand in the Yucatan. There was nothing but a tiny fishing village here until the 1970s. The first hotel opened in 1974, and the resort has grown rapidly ever since.

The tropical location means hot temperatures all year – lots of sunshine and blue skies, especially in the dry season from November to March.

Big hotels owned by transnational companies.

Sea temperatures are above 25 °C all year round, making it ideal for watersports.

Long, white sandy beaches.

Figure 15 Factors influencing visitor numbers to Cancun

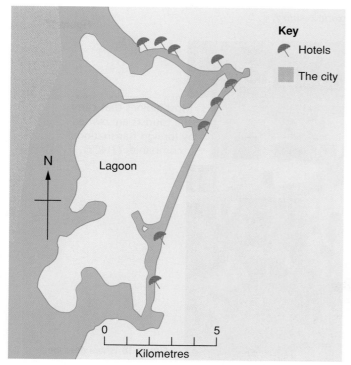

Key

🏖 Hotels

⬛ The city

N

Lagoon

0   5

Kilometres

Figure 16 Map of Cancun

Activity

1 Use Figure 12 to describe the location of Cancun.

2 **a)** Explain why FUNATOR wanted to develop Cancun.
   b) Make a copy of Figure 11. Use Figure 10 to add labels explaining why FUNATOR chose Cancun as the site for its new resort.

3 A student has annotated Figure 15. Two of these labels explain the factors that affect the nature of tourism better than the other two.
   a) Identify which are the better annotations and explain your choice.
   b) Suggest how the other two labels could be improved.

4 Study Figures 11 to 16. Create a piece of promotional material (a poster, podcast or leaflet) advertising holidays in the Yucatan to a specific group of people (e.g. young families or backpackers).

Mexico

The social costs of tourism in Cancun

Tourism certainly has created many jobs in the Yucatan, but what are its wider effects for local people? In Cancun the hotel zone is separate from the local community: a design known as a **tourist enclave**. Whilst the tourists stay in air-conditioned comfort in their hotels, the workers travel home to **shanty housing** in Puerto Juarez which is one hour away by bus. Local people aren't even allowed on the beaches. The beaches are owned by the state, but controlled by the hotels. They keep local people away to prevent tourists from being hassled by vendors who try to sell food, drinks or their services as guides.

Activity

1 Study Figure 17.
   a) Suggest a suitable caption for this cartoon.
   b) Justify the view that enclaves are bad for both tourists and local people.
   c) Suggest why Cancun was developed as an enclave.

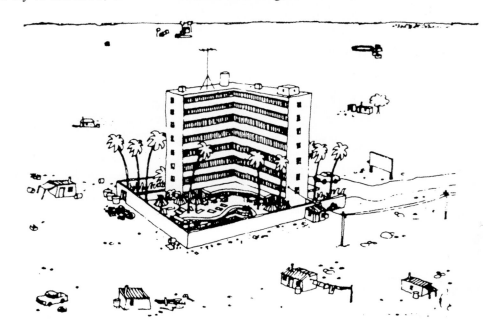

"Dear George, here we are in the middle of things having a great time. We feel we're really getting to know this exotic country..."

Figure 17

Most airlines that carry the tourists are owned by foreign transnational companies (TNCs).

The buses have been imported. They take tourists to foreign-owned hotels which serve a lot of imported food and drink.

Figure 18 Where does the money go?

A report by Tourism Concern concludes that working conditions for workers in the tourism industry in Cancun are poor. Many earn only US$5 for working a 12- to 14-hour day. Many workers in the large hotels are only offered short, temporary contracts. This means that workers can be laid off at the end of a one- or three-month contract if the seasonal pattern of visitors means there is insufficient work.

The contrast in wealth between tourists and the local community can create conflict and frustration. Local teenagers grow up expecting to enjoy similar consumer goods to those they see being enjoyed by the tourists, but they can't always afford them. Shops sell imported foods, soft drinks and clothing but these are often more expensive than local products and are too expensive for local people to buy.

Figure 19 Views on the development of tourism in Cancun

> I can't afford a decent home. I live in a rented shack. It costs $80 a month. I share the outside toilet with neighbours and the tin roof leaks when it rains heavily. The tourists have everything they need, but we have no space or leisure facilities. We're not even allowed on the beach!

Hotel worker

> In resorts like Cancun and the Maya Riviera, the cost of living is very high and is not matched by wages. Average salaries are rarely above $4 a day, while a flat of one or two rooms in Playa can cost $150 a month.

Campaign worker for Tourism Concern
(who campaigns on tourism and human rights issues)

Figure 20 In a shanty town close to Cancun, the bar advertises a TNC soft drink

> We use security guards to keep locals off the beach. The problem is that some 'beach boys' hassle the tourists. They try to sell fast food or souvenirs. Sometimes there have been problems with drug dealers and even muggings.

Hotel manager

> Many people who work in the hotels of Cancun are migrants from other parts of Mexico. They suffer because they are separated from their families and original communities. Most of them are badly paid and rely on tips to make up their wages. Many work long hours and have stressful working conditions. Some suffer from alcohol or drug abuse.

Social worker

Figure 21 The conflicting demands of sustainable tourism

> Local people need to benefit. This may take the form of new jobs and better pay. Where poverty is widespread it should also provide better basic services such as clean water, sewage treatment systems and schools for local people.

> The environment (including wildlife/ ecosystems) should not be damaged so much by the growth of tourism that it cannot recover.

> The growth of tourism should not create problems for future generations of local people. For example, if the development of tourism uses more clean water than can be replaced by natural processes then tourism is unsustainable.

> The growth of tourism should not create so many problems that tourists soon stop coming (because the environment has been spoilt).

Activity

2 Discuss the points of view in Figure 19.
   a) Sort the issues raised (for example, one heading you could use would be income).
   b) What are the main causes of these issues?
   c) Suggest possible solutions to one of these issues.

Can tourism be developed sustainably in the Yucatan?

Ideally, tourism should be sustainable, meaning that it should have long lasting benefits. However, for tourism to be developed in a sustainable fashion it needs to satisfy several conflicting needs. These are summarised in Figure 21 on page 207.

There is evidence that the development of **mass tourism** in Cancun during the 1970s and 80s caused problems for local people and the environment. During the building of the resort, thousands of mangrove trees were cleared from the lagoon to make room for yacht marinas and water sports. By the late 1990s it was obvious that the lagoon was badly polluted by sewage and with oil spilled from the boats. The barrier reef along the coastline was also getting damaged. Coral reefs are very fragile and slow-growing. They are vulnerable to diseases caused by sewage in the sea. They are also easily broken when divers stand on the reef, or when the anchors of dive boats are dragged across the corals.

Fearful that tourists would stop coming if the environment was spoilt, the governor of Quintana Roo has insisted that more effort must be made to protect the environment. New hotels have to meet higher standards of energy and water conservation. The most popular snorkelling and diving area off Cancun was designated as a National Marine Park. Despite this there are still so many divers that damage to the reef's ecosystem is inevitable. Biologists now refer to this area as a 'sacrificial reef'. They think it's better to concentrate the divers here rather than let them spread out onto other sections of the reef which are currently visited less and are in better condition.

Figure 22 Very strict laws prevent tourists from taking coral souvenirs out of Mexico. This street vendor is selling coral and sharks' teeth to visitors to Cancun

Activity

1   Outline at least two different ways in which tourism in Cancun has failed to be sustainable.

2   Discuss:
   a) what you consider to be the advantages and disadvantages of mass tourism for the local people and economy of Yucatan
   b) the reasons for the governor of Quintana Roo trying to change the image of the resort of Cancun
   c) the advantages and disadvantages of allowing part of the Yucatan barrier reef to become a 'sacrificial reef'.

3   Suggest how the governor of Quintana Roo should plan tourist developments in the Yucatan over the next ten to twenty years. Give reasons for your choices.

Nokia

A case study of a multinational company

Nokia is the world's largest manufacturer of mobile phones and other mobile devices. It also provides network and communication services to other businesses, improving communications. Nokia is a Finnish MNC. Its head office is in Helsinki, Finland, but it has offices and factories all around the globe. Nokia and Nokia Siemens Networks employ more than 112,000 people worldwide. Nokia has **plants** (offices, factories and laboratories) in many different countries:

- research and development laboratories (R&D) in ten countries employing 30,415 people
- factories in ten countries
- sales offices in more than 150 countries.

Why does Nokia have plants located in so many different countries?

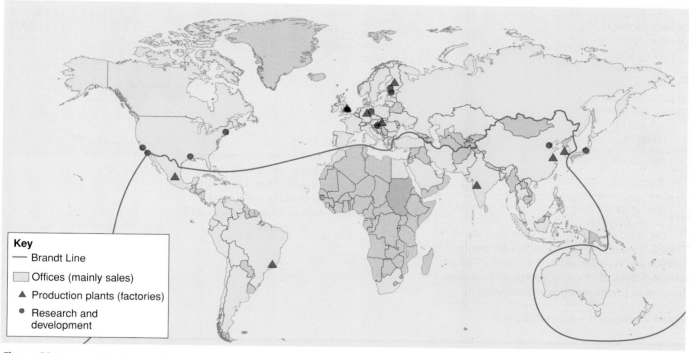

Key
— Brandt Line
▢ Offices (mainly sales)
▲ Production plants (factories)
● Research and development

Figure 23 The global distribution of Nokia's factories, laboratories and offices

Activity

4 Study Figure 23.
   a) Describe the distribution of countries in which Nokia has production plants.
   b) Describe the distribution of countries in which Nokia has R&D laboratories.

Figure 24 Adverts for Nokia and Pepsi (another MNC) in Moscow, Russia

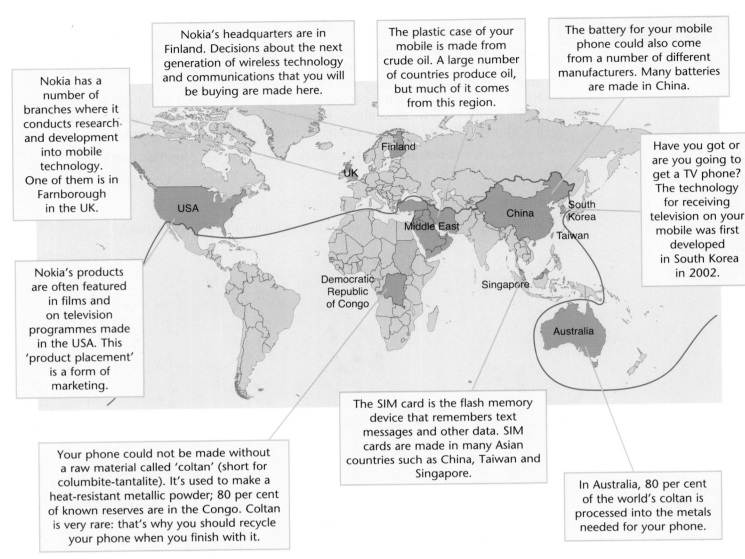

Nokia has a number of branches where it conducts research and development into mobile technology. One of them is in Farnborough in the UK.

Nokia's headquarters are in Finland. Decisions about the next generation of wireless technology and communications that you will be buying are made here.

The plastic case of your mobile is made from crude oil. A large number of countries produce oil, but much of it comes from this region.

The battery for your mobile phone could also come from a number of different manufacturers. Many batteries are made in China.

Have you got or are you going to get a TV phone? The technology for receiving television on your mobile was first developed in South Korea in 2002.

Nokia's products are often featured in films and on television programmes made in the USA. This 'product placement' is a form of marketing.

Your phone could not be made without a raw material called 'coltan' (short for columbite-tantalite). It's used to make a heat-resistant metallic powder; 80 per cent of known reserves are in the Congo. Coltan is very rare: that's why you should recycle your phone when you finish with it.

The SIM card is the flash memory device that remembers text messages and other data. SIM cards are made in many Asian countries such as China, Taiwan and Singapore.

In Australia, 80 per cent of the world's coltan is processed into the metals needed for your phone.

Figure 25 The world in your mobile phone

Activity

1 Study Figure 25 and use it to complete a table like the one below:

Type of employment	Example	Place	MEDC or LEDC
Primary	1 Drilling for oil 2		
Secondary	1 Processing coltan 2	China	LEDC
Tertiary	1 2		

2 Work in pairs to structure a globalisation enquiry.
   a) Choose one of these titles: 'World in your living room' or 'World in your wardrobe'.
   b) Discuss all the different places you might find 'Made in…' information.
   c) Design a data collection sheet that you could use to record results from your classmates.
   d) Collect the data from at least five classmates and plot the data on a world outline map or make a large poster with photos you have collected from magazines or the internet.

3 Suggest why Nokia equips its phones with SIM cards and batteries made by a number of different manufacturers in Asia.

Locating business to minimise costs

MNCs such as Nokia have branches in many countries because they want to reduce costs. With lower costs, their profits are higher. MNCs such as Nokia keep costs low by opening factories and offices in regions of the world that have:

- low labour costs
- cheap land or building costs
- low business rates (the tax paid by a company).

Locating business to be close to the customer

Another reason why Nokia is constantly expanding its range of factories and offices is to be close to its customers, who are spread right across the globe. Nokia's products have massive appeal. Nokia estimated that the mobile phone market had around 2.2 billion people in 2005 and this was expected to rise to 4 billion in 2009. Growth in mobile phone ownership and subscription has been particularly strong in **Newly Industrialised Countries (NICs)**. As consumers in LEDCs have become wealthier, Nokia has expanded its business into Asia, Africa and South America. It has, therefore, opened new sales offices in many NICs, located closer to these new customers.

Different jobs in different locations

Nokia employs a wide range of staff. Some are highly qualified or skilled, such as business managers or R&D staff. Other staff, such as some assembly workers or sales staff, do not require high-level qualifications or as much training. So, like many other MNCs, Nokia has chosen to locate the assembly of basic products in their range in NICs where wages are lower.

However, the more highly trained R&D staff tend to work in Europe. Here, Nokia develops new products, such as hand-held devices capable of filming video, playing games and surfing the web. These devices use the latest technology and therefore need more highly trained staff to develop and produce them. These high-tech products are also aimed at wealthier consumers, so it makes sense to make them in Europe.

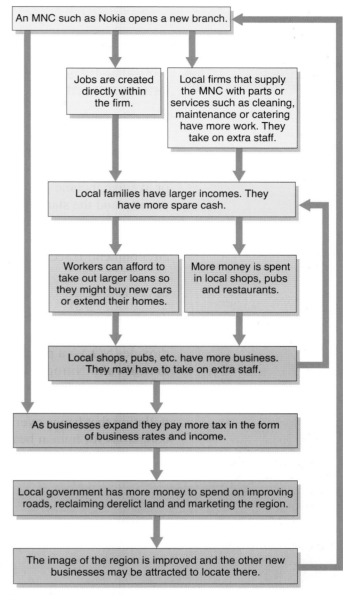

Figure 26 The positive multiplier

Activity

4 Explain the difference between direct and indirect benefits of MNC investment in a new factory or office.

5 Summarise the benefits of the positive multiplier under these headings:
   a) Jobs
   b) Earnings
   c) Spending
   d) Image of the region.

6 Explain why Nokia continues to expand in Africa.

7 Summarise the benefits that Nokia gets from opening new branches in NICs.

Chapter 3
Economic activity and the environment

Investigating economic growth in China and its impact on the environment

Since the early 1990s China's economy has been growing rapidly. Chinese businesses and foreign multinational companies (MNCs) have invested in new service industries and factories making everything from shoes to high-tech electronics. As China's economy has grown, the **Gross National Income (GNI)** or average income per person has also grown. Fewer people in China live in poverty and the standard of living for ordinary Chinese people is improving. By 2020, it is expected that the Chinese GNI per person will be similar to the GNI in the USA today. However, this development is causing a massive impact on the environment. It seems that this type of growth is unsustainable.

Local impacts

The factories and power plants that have created China's economic success are also creating a pollution problem. The burning of fossil fuels releases nitrogen dioxide (NO_2) – a pollutant that combines with moisture in the air and results in **acid rain**. Nitrogen dioxide also causes breathing and other health problems. As the Chinese have become wealthier, car ownership has increased rapidly. Cars also emit nitrogen dioxide from their exhausts. The result is a thick smog of pollution that hangs over eastern China. This smog often reaches levels that are dangerous for human health in cities such as Beijing. Research by the European Space Agency shows that **emissions** of nitrogen dioxide in China increased by 50 per cent in the period from 1995 to 2005. Chinese official figures admit that 400,000 Chinese people die every year from diseases caused by air pollution. The World Bank says that 16 of the 20 most polluted cities in the world are in China.

Figure 1 Smog in Beijing reduces visibility and causes breathing problems and eye irritations

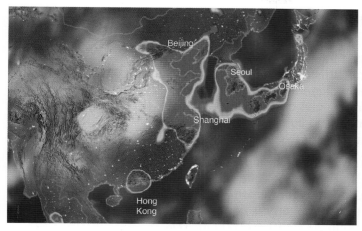

Figure 2 A false-colour satellite image of East Asia showing levels of nitrogen dioxide pollution. The brightest red colours show the highest concentrations of NO_2. Yellows and greens show lower concentrations of NO_2

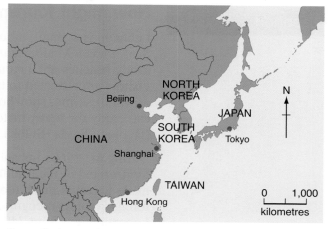

Figure 3 China and east Asia

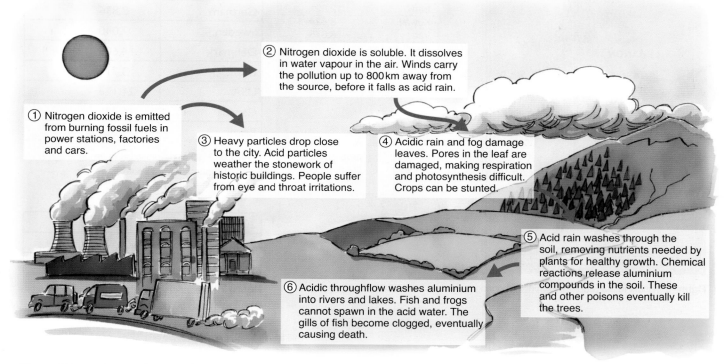

Figure 4 How emissions of nitrogen dioxide lead to acid rain

Activity

1 List three sources of nitrogen dioxide pollution.

2 Use Figures 2 and 3 to describe the distribution of the highest concentrations of nitrogen dioxide.

3 Use Figure 4 to help explain the pollution pattern on Figure 2.

4 List the effects of acid pollution under the headings:
Human health
The environment
The economy.

Lebanon

How might tourism affect the environment?

Lebanon is a small, mountainous country at the eastern end of the Mediterranean Sea. It has a Mediterranean climate with hot, dry summers and mild winters. The sandy beaches are a natural attraction for visitors in the summer. In the winter visitors are attracted to the mountains where there is plenty of powder snow for downhill skiing, snowboarding and cross-country skiing. All year round visitors can enjoy the many historical and cultural sites such as the ancient cities of Jbail (Byblos), Saida (Sidon) and Sour (Tyre).

During the 1960s Lebanon was a popular tourist destination. It was known as 'The Switzerland of the Middle East'. But violence and conflict during the 1970s and 80s made Lebanon much too dangerous for tourism. Tourism has grown steadily as foreign visitors recognise that the country is now stable and safe to visit. Arrivals in Lebanon grew from 740,000 in 2000 to 1,400,000 in 2008.

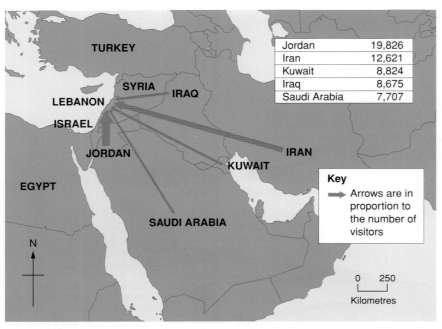

Jordan	19,826
Iran	12,621
Kuwait	8,824
Iraq	8,675
Saudi Arabia	7,707

Key
→ Arrows are in proportion to the number of visitors

0   250
Kilometres

Figure 5 Visitors to the Lebanon from neighbouring countries, June 2009

Country	Number of visitors
France	10,107
Germany	8,836
Sweden	7,040
Denmark	4,605
UK	3,714
USA	21,126
Canada	16,735
Brazil	2,656

Figure 6 Origin of visitors to Lebanon, June 2009.
Source: Lebanese Tourist Board

2007	41,2041
2008	47,3574
2009	76,1415

Figure 7 Number of visitors to Lebanon (six-month totals from January to June).
Source: Lebanese Tourist Board

Activity

1 Describe three features that attract tourists to Lebanon.

2 **a)** Using Lebanon as an example, explain why jobs in the tourist industry depend on good security.
  b) Suggest two different strategies that the Lebanese government could use to increase the number of tourist visitors.

3 Use Figures 5, 6 and 7:
  a) Use suitable techniques to represent the data in Figures 6 and 7.
  b) Describe and explain the patterns shown in this data.

Keeping tourists in their zone: a strategy in Tyre, Lebanon

The Tyre coast in southern Lebanon is Lebanon's largest and best preserved sandy beach. The Lebanese government would like to encourage tourism, but recognises that mass tourism would conflict with the needs of local people and would damage a fragile environment. One potential conflict here is over water. It is estimated that tourists to the Mediterranean use between 300 and 850 litres of water per person per day: tourist uses of water include cleaning processes such as laundry in hotels, and washing-up in restaurants. By contrast, water use in Lebanon is estimated to be 200 litres of water per person per day. The Tyre region relies on natural supplies of groundwater. This supply is **recharged** from water that seeps slowly down into the rocks from melting snow in the mountains (see Figure 9). There is very little recharge from rainfall in the long dry summers when demand from both tourism and local farmers is high.

The Tyre coast also includes a number of fragile ecosystems that would be easily damaged by the development of tourism. These include beaches that are nesting sites for endangered loggerhead and green sea turtles. The sand dunes and wetlands behind the beach are also home to frogs, insects, several rare plants and animals such as the Arabian spiny mouse. The area has been protected since 1998 when a Nature Reserve covering 380 hectares was created. Tyre Coast Reserve is cut into two segments by the Rashidiyeh refugee camp. The reserve itself has been zoned into different land uses with the highest levels of protection being placed on the conservation zone.

Activity

4 Explain why water resources need to be considered when deciding whether a planned tourist development is likely to be sustainable.

5 Use Figure 8.
   a) Describe the location of the tourist zone.
   b) Explain why this zone has been separated from each of the other zones.

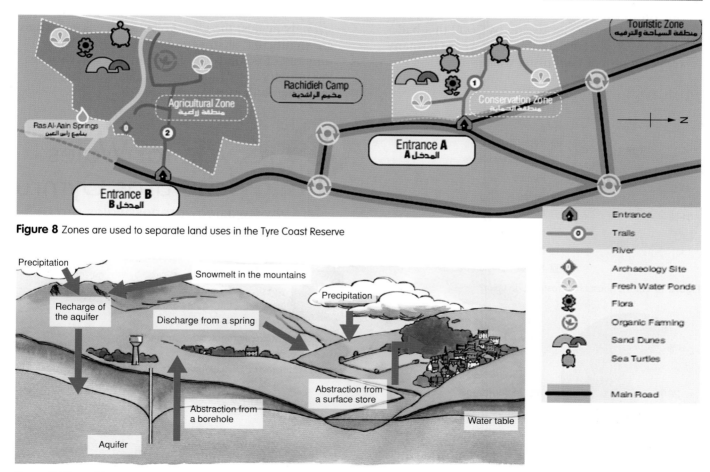

Figure 8 Zones are used to separate land uses in the Tyre Coast Reserve

Figure 9 What will happen to the level of the water table if groundwater is abstracted faster than it is recharged?

Merthyr Tydfil

What is the impact of our consumer society on the environment?

The disposal of household waste is a messy and controversial issue. There are wide-ranging views and heated arguments taking place all over the UK, not least when news breaks that a named area is the favoured location for a new landfill or incinerator site. In this case study we look at the background to the issue and then focus on the hugely controversial debate surrounding an incinerator for Merthyr Tydfil, Wales.

Did you know …?

- Every year each UK household produces over 1 tonne of rubbish.
- Every person in the UK throws away their own body weight in rubbish every seven weeks.
- In recent years, local and national governments have spent millions of pounds persuading consumers and producers to reduce packaging and recycle waste. The many initiatives that exist have had some effect but the UK still lags behind our European neighbours. In 1997 we recycled just 7 per cent of our waste, by 2009 this had risen to 38 per cent. In the same year Germany recycled 48 per cent of its waste.

- Landfills have been the most common way to dispose of waste in the UK. There are many advantages of using this method: it is relatively cheap; lots of different waste can be disposed of without the cost of sorting; the gasses given off can be used for heating; the waste remains in the UK and doesn't become a burden for less developed countries. However there are increasingly few new sites available as old sites become full.
- As available landfill sites are used up and recycling continues to gather pace, but only slowly, local authorities are increasingly turning to incinerators to dispose of waste. There are advantages such as: electricity can be generated in the process; the bulk of waste is reduced by as much as 95 per cent; they are increasingly cost effective compared with landfill; they are a good business opportunity for international companies. However, the use of incinerators attracts significant opposition: voters who live near proposed sites will probably be strongly against the idea; greenhouse gas emissions are significant; at some sites, there have been rumours of noxious gas emissions such as dioxins; the introduction of incinerators detracts from local recycling initiatives.

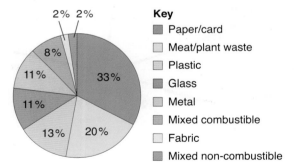

Key
- Paper/card
- Meat/plant waste
- Plastic
- Glass
- Metal
- Mixed combustible
- Fabric
- Mixed non-combustible

2% 2%
8%
11%
11%
13% 20% 33%

Figure 10 What is household waste made up of?

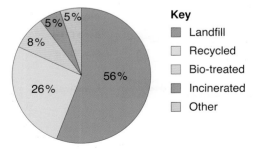

Key
- Landfill
- Recycled
- Bio-treated
- Incinerated
- Other

5% 5%
5%
8%
26% 56%

Figure 11 Where does UK waste go?

recycle for Wales
ailgylchu dros Gymru
www.wasteawarenesswales.org.uk

Figure 12 Recycle for Wales logo

Find out more about recycling by visiting these websites.
www.recycling-guide.org.uk
www.recycle-more.co.uk
www.defra.gov.uk/environment/waste/index.htm
www.wasteawarenesswales.org.uk
www.craffamwastraff.org.uk/index.html (Welsh language version)

Incinerator planned for Merthyr?

In 2009 Covanta Energy announced it was applying to build a waste incinerator close to Merthyr Tydfil. Figure 13 presents the mixed views of the stakeholders to this proposal.

£400m giant waste incinerator bid for Ffos-y-fran

5 February 2009 by Jackie Bow, Merthyr Express

PLANS for a massive £400m energy-producing waste incinerator next to the controversial Ffos-y-fran opencast site have been revealed. The new facility, known as Brig-y-Cwm, would create up to 600 jobs, 500 during construction and 100 full-time jobs when operating.

The incinerator's backers American owners Covanta Energy, the Welsh Assembly Government and International Business Wales, expect the plant to generate about 70 megawatts of electricity – enough to supply power to up to 180,000 homes from around 750,000 tonnes of waste.

The proposed site on land at Cwmbargoed, borders Merthyr Tydfil and Caerphilly. Environmentalists and residents living near the proposed site greeted the news with dismay.

Malcolm Chilton, Covanta Energy's UK managing director, said: 'We supply millions of homes with clean energy from non-recyclable waste, and we pledge to consult with local people in the months ahead to seek views and suggestions on our proposal for Merthyr Tydfil.'

If it gets the go-ahead the plant, financed and operated by Covanta, will be operational by 2013–14. The waste would arrive by rail in sealed containers from various locations across Wales. There would be less need for local authorities to use landfill sites, cutting costs, and it could mean cheaper electricity for people in neighbouring communities.

Council leader Jeff Edwards said he had not been involved in any negotiations. He believes it is: 'A very positive project and a huge opportunity for Merthyr Tydfil' with job creation, reduced electricity charges, and savings for the Council on landfill. 'I know one of the concerns raised was the emission from the plant. It will not include dioxins and will meet American emission standards, which are far higher than European and UK standards.'

Haf Elgar, a Friends of the Earth campaigner, warned that the proposed plant would probably take all the waste from Wales and parts of England and bring it to South Wales. She said: 'A plant of that size would probably take more residual waste than is produced in Wales. It completely goes against the principle of dealing with waste locally and would mean even more pollution for residents of the Merthyr area.'

Figure 13 A newspaper article on a proposed incinerator in Merthyr Tydfil

Activity

1 Read Figure 13. Name three stakeholders and explain each of their points of view.

2 Suggest two different ways the proposed incinerator plant would have affected the environment of Wales.

3 In October 2011 Covanta withdrew their application to build this incinerator because of local oppposition to their plan.

   Do you think the company should have gone ahead with the scheme? Justify your decision.

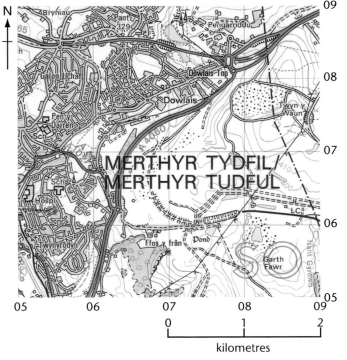

Figure 14 An Ordance Survey extract of the location of the proposed incinerator south-east of Merthyr. Scale 1:50,000 Sheet 160. © Crown Copyright and/or database right. All rights reserved. Licence number 100036470

Can environments damaged by economic activity be restored?

The London Wetlands Centre in Barnes, south London, has been created on the site of four disused Victorian water storage reservoirs. The reservoirs were designated as a Site of Special Scientific Interest (SSSI) in 1975 because of the large numbers of ducks using the site. The reservoirs were no longer needed, so in 1995 a huge reclamation project began to convert the reservoirs into a 40 hectare wetland ecosystem that would benefit a wide biodiversity.

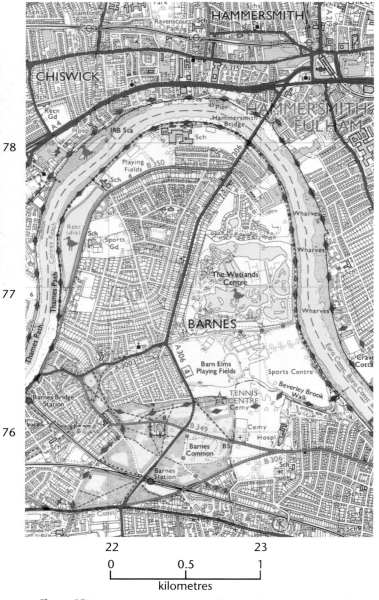

Figure 15 An Ordnance Survey extract featuring the London Wetlands Centre. Scale 1:25,000 Sheet 161. © Crown Copyright and/or database right. All rights reserved. Licence number 100036470

Activity

1 Use Figure 15.
   a) Describe the location of the Wetlands Centre.
   b) Give six-figure grid references for:
      i) Hammersmith Bridge   ii) Barnes Station.
   c) Give directions, including distances, for a visitor approaching the Wetlands Visitor Centre (at 226767) on foot from:
      i) Hammersmith Bridge   ii) Barnes Station.
   d) What is the approximate area of the Wetlands Centre?
      i)   A little less than 1 km²
      ii) A little more than 1 km²
      iii) 2 km²

2 a) Make a sketch of Figure 16.
   b) Pair up the phrases below to make three labels for Figure 16.
      Deeper water with submerged vegetation provides …
      Shallow water with emerging vegetation provides …
      Wetland margin with moisture loving vegetation provides …
      … safe places for wading birds to create their nests.
      … food for diving ducks.
      … sites for dragonflies to lay eggs.
   c) Use Figure 17 to help you decide where each of your three labels should be placed on your sketch.
   d) Explain how the structure of this ecosystem provides a variety of habitats for insects such as dragonflies.

3 Suggest how each of the following non-living features of a pond might influence a plant, insect or fish living in the pond:
   a) water depth
   b) water temperature
   c) amount of light reaching the bottom of the pond
   d) amount of oxygen dissolved in the water
   e) quantity of fertiliser washed into the pond.

London Wetlands Centre facts and figures
- The site contains over 30 different wetlands.
- There are 600 m of boardwalk and 3.4 km of pathway.
- Over 130 species of wild bird.
- 24 species of butterfly and 260 moths.
- 18 dragonfly and damselfly species.
- 4 species of amphibian.

How the restoration of Barn Elms reservoir created a variety of habitats

The Victorian reservoirs at Barn Elms covered 40 hectares, were several metres deep and lined with concrete. When the Wildfowl and Wetland Trust (WWT) redeveloped the site, they wanted to create as many different habitats as possible to encourage a variety of wildlife into the area. The concrete linings were broken up and recycled as paths around the site and some was used to create an artificial reef in the deepest pool for fish to use as a nursery. The finished reserve has 30 different wetlands of different sizes and depths, each surrounded by shingle beaches or boggy grassland habitats. WWT planted 300,000 aquatic plants, as well as 27,000 trees.

Figure 17 shows that within this ecosystem there is a horizontal structure which is determined by water depth. Variation in water depth (just one non-living part of this ecosystem) provides conditions for different groups of plants. These in turn provide different habitats for various damselflies or dragonflies that are the predators of the insect world in this ecosystem. They in turn may be eaten by birds such as yellow wagtail or hobby (which is a small bird of prey). The dragonfly larvae live underwater and are eaten by fish, frogs, toads or newts. The fish and frogs may be eaten by larger birds such as heron.

Figure 16 A variety of habitats at the London Wetlands Centre is provided by the horizontal structure of the wetland ecosystem

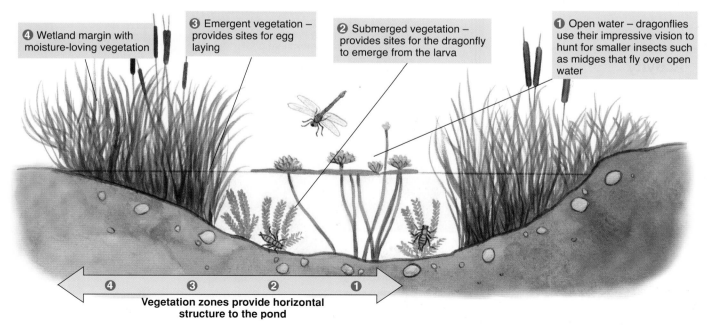

❹ Wetland margin with moisture-loving vegetation

❸ Emergent vegetation – provides sites for egg laying

❷ Submerged vegetation – provides sites for the dragonfly to emerge from the larva

❶ Open water – dragonflies use their impressive vision to hunt for smaller insects such as midges that fly over open water

Vegetation zones provide horizontal structure to the pond

Figure 17 Structure of a pond, and the life cycle of a dragonfly

What are the causes and evidence for climate change?

The drought in Australia between 2002 and 2008 has been described as the worst drought to affect the country for 1000 years.

Are extreme weather events like this evidence of climate change?

How might climate change in the future?

What can we do to reduce the effects of climate change?

Figure 18 Forest fires burning close to Sydney, Australia, January 2003. Widespread forest fires in February 2009 in the state of Victoria killed over 200 people

What is the greenhouse effect?

The greenhouse effect is a natural process of our atmosphere. Without it, the average surface temperature of the Earth would be –17 Celsius rather than the 15 Celsius we currently experience. At these temperatures life would not have evolved on Earth in its present form and we probably wouldn't exist!

The greenhouse effect, shown in Figure 19, means that Earth's atmosphere acts like an insulating blanket. Light (short wave) and heat (long wave) energy from the sun pass through the atmosphere quite easily. The sun's energy heats the Earth and it radiates its own energy back into the atmosphere. The long-wave heat energy coming from the Earth is quite easily absorbed by naturally occurring gases in the atmosphere. These are known as **greenhouse gases.** They include carbon dioxide (CO_2), methane (CH_4) and water vapour (H_2O). Carbon dioxide is the fourth most common gas in the atmosphere. It occurs naturally in the atmosphere as a product of respiration from all living things. So carbon dioxide has existed in the atmosphere for as long as there has been life on Earth. Methane and water vapour have been in the atmosphere for even longer, so the greenhouse effect has been affecting our climate for thousands of millions of years.

Activity

1 Use Figure 19 to explain the greenhouse effect.

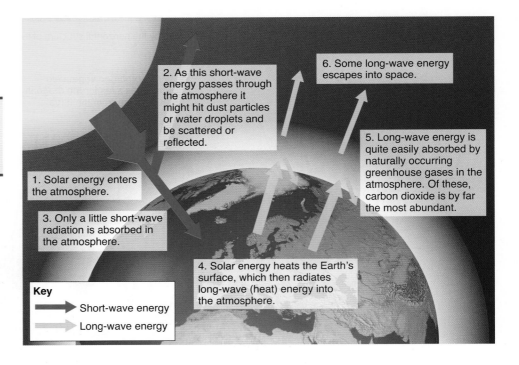

2. As this short-wave energy passes through the atmosphere it might hit dust particles or water droplets and be scattered or reflected.

6. Some long-wave energy escapes into space.

5. Long-wave energy is quite easily absorbed by naturally occurring greenhouse gases in the atmosphere. Of these, carbon dioxide is by far the most abundant.

1. Solar energy enters the atmosphere.

3. Only a little short-wave radiation is absorbed in the atmosphere.

4. Solar energy heats the Earth's surface, which then radiates long-wave (heat) energy into the atmosphere.

Key

→ Short-wave energy

→ Long-wave energy

Figure 19 The greenhouse effect

How have people's actions affected the greenhouse effect?

Carbon is one of the most common elements in the environment. It is present in:

- all organic substances, i.e. all living things
- simple compounds such as CO_2, which exists as a gas in the atmosphere and is dissolved in the oceans
- complex compounds, for example hydrocarbons found in fossil fuels such as oil, coal and gas.

Carbon is able to transfer from one part of the environment to another through a series of biological processes, such as respiration, and chemical processes such as solution. These transfers take place between parts of the environment that release carbon, known as sources, and parts of the environment that absorb the carbon over long periods of time, known as carbon sinks. The transfer between sources and sinks is shown in the carbon cycle diagrams, Figures 20 and 21.

Figure 20 A simplified carbon cycle

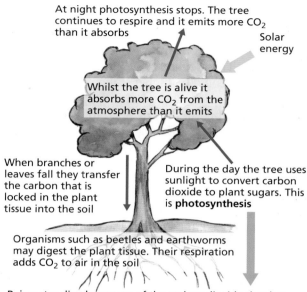

At night photosynthesis stops. The tree continues to respire and it emits more CO_2 than it absorbs

Solar energy

Whilst the tree is alive it absorbs more CO_2 from the atmosphere than it emits

When branches or leaves fall they transfer the carbon that is locked in the plant tissue into the soil

During the day the tree uses sunlight to convert carbon dioxide to plant sugars. This is **photosynthesis**

Organisms such as beetles and earthworms may digest the plant tissue. Their respiration adds CO_2 to air in the soil

Rainwater dissolves some of the carbon dioxide that has come from soil organisms. This water may carry the dissolved CO_2 into a river and eventually to the sea.

Figure 21 The carbon cycle, showing fast and slow transfers

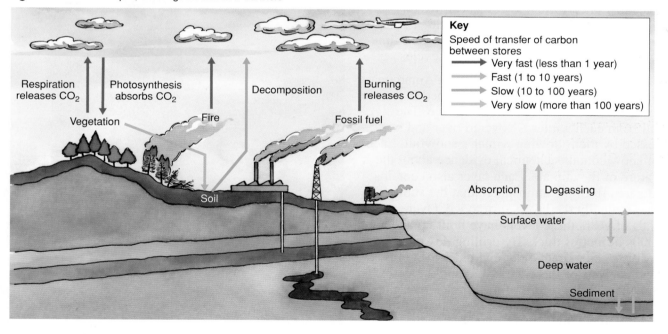

Respiration releases CO_2

Photosynthesis absorbs CO_2

Decomposition

Burning releases CO_2

Vegetation

Fire

Fossil fuel

Soil

Key
Speed of transfer of carbon between stores
→ Very fast (less than 1 year)
→ Fast (1 to 10 years)
→ Slow (10 to 100 years)
→ Very slow (more than 100 years)

Absorption   Degassing

Surface water

Deep water

Sediment

Activity

2 Study Figures 20 and 21.
  a) Describe the human actions that release CO_2 into the atmosphere.
  b) Explain the processes that allow forests to act as a carbon sink.
  c) Give two reasons why the burning of tropical rainforests will increase the amount of CO_2 in the atmosphere.

3 Use Figure 21.
  a) Describe the difference in the speed of transfer of carbon in the natural part of the cycle compared with the part of the cycle affected by human action.
  b) Explain what difference this makes to the amount of carbon stored in the atmosphere compared with the long-lasting carbon sinks. Explain why this is alarming.

How conclusive is the evidence for climate change?

In 1958 a team of scientists began to take regular measurements of carbon dioxide concentrations from the atmosphere. They realised that local levels of CO_2 could be higher if the sampling took place close to industry or traffic congestion. So they decided to conduct their tests on Mauna Loa, Hawaii. They thought that this would give them readings that would represent average CO_2 levels in the atmosphere. The sampling has been conducted regularly ever since and the graph, known as the Keeling Curve, is shown in Figure 22.

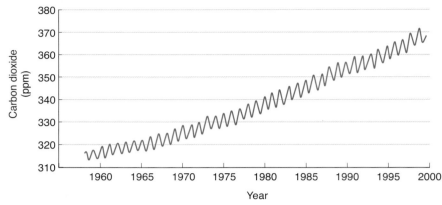

Figure 22 The Keeling Curve shows the rise of carbon dioxide in the atmosphere since monitoring began in 1958 (ppm = parts per million)

Evidence from the ice cores

We have already seen that scientific evidence from Hawaii proves that carbon dioxide levels have been rising steadily since 1958. However, can we be certain that this isn't part of a natural cycle? Perhaps carbon dioxide levels vary over long periods of time and the recent rise is part of one of those cycles.

Scientists working in both Greenland and Antarctica have been investigating information trapped in the ice to uncover evidence of past climate change. The snowfall from each winter is covered over and compressed by the following winter's snowfall. Each layer of snow contains chemical evidence about the temperature of the climate. Each layer also contains trapped gases from the atmosphere that the snow fell through. Gradually the layers turn to ice. Over thousands of years these layers have built up and are now 1000s of metres thick. By drilling down into the ice, scientists can extract older and older ice cores. Chemical analysis of these ice layers and the gases they contain reveal a record of the climate over the last 420,000 years. This evidence suggests that the climate has indeed gone through natural cycles of colder (**glacials**) and warmer periods (**interglacials**). They also show that levels of carbon dioxide in the atmosphere have also gone up and down as part of a natural cycle.

Activity

1 **a)** Describe and explain the trend of the Keeling Curve.
   b) Explain why the scientists chose Hawaii as a good place to collect their samples.

Figure 23 Scientists taking ice core samples from the ice sheet in Greenland

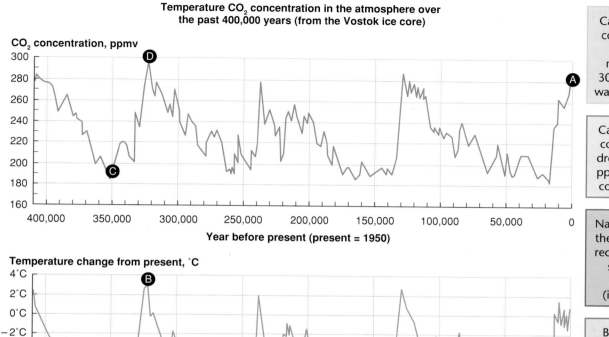

Carbon dioxide concentrations reached a maximum of 300 ppm in the warmest periods.

Carbon dioxide concentrations dropped to 180 ppm during the coldest periods

Narrow peaks in the temperature record represent short warm episodes (interglacials)

Broad dips in temperature represent glacial periods

Carbon dioxide concentrations were at about 280 ppm in 1950

Figure 24 Temperature and CO_2 concentration (ppm) in the atmosphere over the past 420,000 years

Activity

2 Use Figure 24.
a) Match the five statements to the correct place on the graph shown by the letters A, B, C, D and E.
b) Use the graph to copy and complete the following statement:
The graph shows natural cycles of .... periods and .... periods. Average temperatures were higher than present on *three / four / five* occasions. These are known as .... periods. The current interglacial period appears to have lasted *much longer than/shorter than* previous periods.

3 Use your understanding of the greenhouse effect to explain why reduced levels of carbon dioxide in the atmosphere might be linked to cooler periods of climate.

4 Compare Figure 24 with Figure 22.
a) How many times in the last 420,000 years have CO_2 levels been as high as in 2000?
b) Based on the ice core data, do you think that the Keeling Curve fits into a similar natural cycle of carbon dioxide concentrations? Explain your answer fully.

5 How conclusive do you find the evidence for:
a) natural cycles of climate change over the last 420,000 years?
b) an unusual rise in carbon dioxide levels since 1958?

What are the possible consequences of climate change for countries at different levels of development?

Global changes in the climate due to greenhouse gas emissions are likely to have a wide variety of impacts and some places could be worse hit than others.

In 2005, New Orleans was flooded by a storm surge of water created by Hurricane Katrina. A total of 1,836 people were killed by Katrina. Much of the city is built below sea level. The city is built on the soft sands of a river delta and as these dry out the city gradually sinks. This subsidence, combined with rising sea levels, means that New Orleans is at increasing risk of more floods.

About 3.6 billion people (or 60 per cent of the world's population) live within 60 km of the coast. This is likely to rise to 6.4 billion (75 per cent of the world's population) by 2030.

Between 1900 and 2000 the world's sea levels rose on average by 2 mm per year. This is mainly due to the melting of ice on the world's continents, especially in Greenland and Antarctica.

Of the world's 23 mega-cities, sixteen are in coastal regions and are at risk from further sea-level rise. Many of these cities are in Less Economically Developed Countries (LEDCs) and are continuing to grow rapidly. This photograph was taken in Mumbai, the world's second largest city, during the floods in August 2005.

If greenhouse emissions continue at their present rate it is likely that sea levels will continue to rise by, on average, 4mm a year over the next 100 years.

The Thames flood barrier was completed in 1982 to protect London from tidal surges of water coming up the river from the North Sea. Tide levels are rising in the Thames estuary by about 6 mm per year (60 cm in 100 years). A major flood would perhaps cause damage to the value of £30,000 million and would certainly cause many deaths.

What will be the impact on the billions of people living in coastal regions?

Figure 25 The impact of climate change on coastal populations

Category 5: Over 250 kph. Complete failure of some smaller buildings. Failure of the roofs of large industrial buildings. Extensive coastal flooding damages the ground floor of many buildings.

Category 4: 211–250 kph. Complete destruction of the roofs of smaller buildings and more extensive damage to the walls. All signs and trees are blown down. Flooding of coastal areas 3 to 5 hours before the arrival of the storm may cut off escape routes.

Category 3: 178–210 kph. Severe damage to the roofs of small buildings. Some structural damage to walls. Mobile homes destroyed. Poorly constructed road signs destroyed. Large trees blown down.

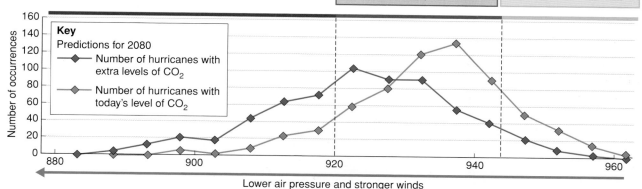

Key
Predictions for 2080
— Number of hurricanes with extra levels of CO_2
— Number of hurricanes with today's level of CO_2

Lower air pressure and stronger winds

The strongest hurricanes in the present climate may be upstaged by even more intense hurricanes over the next century as the Earth's climate is warmed by increasing levels of greenhouse gases in the atmosphere. Although we cannot say at present whether more or fewer hurricanes will occur in the future with global warming, the hurricanes that do occur near the end of the 21st century are expected to be stronger and have significantly more intense rainfall than under present-day climate conditions.

Figure 26 The National Oceanic and Atmosphere Administration (NOAA) has used computer models to predict frequency and intensity of hurricanes in 2080

Activity

1 Outline how climate change could affect people living in coastal areas.

2 Study Figure 26. Describe how the frequency and violence of hurricanes are expected to change.

3 a) Use the data in Figure 28 to produce a graph of closures.
   b) Describe the trend of your graph.
   c) Explain how this graph could be seen to be more evidence for climate change.

4 Use evidence from pages 224–225 to explain why global warming is an 'issue of international concern'.

5 Suggest why people living in cities in developed countries may be able to cope with climate change and extreme weather better than people living in cities in the world's poorest countries.

'The potential for fairly significant rises in temperature in Arctic regions seems to be quite high. And should that happen, especially over a time scale of decades, the possibility of marine mammals being able to adapt rapidly enough is very low.'

Figure 27 The opinion of Dr Malcolm Ramsay, Professor of Biology at the University of Saskatchewan, Canada

Figure 28 Closures of the Thames barrier to protect against storm (tidal) surges (1983–2007)

Year	Number of closures
1983	1
1984	0
1985	0
1986	0
1987	1
1988	1
1989	0
1990	3
1991	0
1992	1
1993	5
1994	1
1995	3
1996	4
1997	0
1998	3
1999	3
2000	6
2001	11
2002	2
2003	8
2004	2
2005	5
2006	1
2007	11

Iceland

How will climate change affect Iceland?

The Arctic is one region where climate change is predicted to have huge impacts. Iceland's landscape will certainly change as its ice caps and glaciers melt. However, in the short term the economy could benefit as melting glaciers feed Iceland's rivers and these provide **hydro-electric power (HEP)** for Iceland's industry. Run-off from glaciers will peak sometime in the next 100 years and, according to computer models, Iceland's glaciers will have disappeared by 2200.

How will climate change affect this landscape?

What will happen to the ice and to this river?

Will people still want to visit this wilderness region?

Figure 29 Fording the rivers of central Iceland can only be attempted during July and August

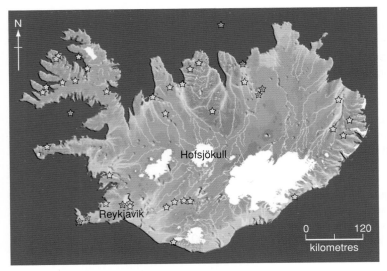

Key

Power plants

☆ Diesel   ☆ Hydro-electric power   ☆ Geothermal heat

Figure 30 Iceland's power stations

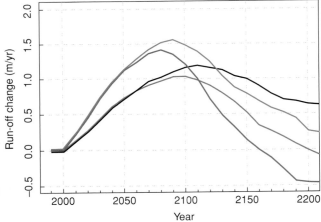

The four lines show predicted run-off using four different computer models

Figure 31 Predicted changes in run-off (river discharge) from Hofsjökull ice cap in central Iceland. The lines show predicted run-off compared with averages in the year 2000

Between 1570 and 1890 Iceland's climate was at least 1°C cooler than today. Sea ice came down from the Arctic and surrounded Iceland, making it difficult to bring fishing boats onshore. Glaciers expanded and covered some farms. Grain and hay crops failed and there was famine. If the temperature rises 1°C above today's temperature then farmers will be able to start growing wheat. They will also greatly increase the number of cattle and sheep they keep because they will be able to grow 20 per cent more hay.

We are obviously concerned about the negative impacts of climate change. Most of the 300,000 people in Iceland live close to the coast. Sea-level rise will threaten Reykjavik and many other smaller towns. Extreme weather events caused by low pressure will become more common. Storm surges will cause coastal erosion and flooding. Of greatest concern is the future of the fishing industry which is so important to our economy. Even small changes in the ocean currents could affect fish stocks in the seas around Iceland but the scientific predictions on this are still unclear.

A climate expert

Spokesperson for a power company

A government spokesperson

A tour rep

Around 87 per cent of Iceland's electricity is generated by HEP stations (and most of the rest comes from other renewables, particularly geothermal power). The construction of a new dam at Kárahnjúkar in East Iceland recently has been criticised by environmentalists. They don't like the loss of wilderness, but I say that Iceland is creating clean energy because we do not rely on fossil fuels. Climate change will gradually cause the glaciers and ice caps to melt. This means that rivers will have even greater discharges during the spring and summer months. We will be able to create even more electricity. That will make Iceland an even bigger attraction to energy-hungry industries such as aluminium smelting and web servers.

Iceland's tourist industry has grown rapidly in the last 20 years. Most tourists arrive by air but environmental campaigners criticise air travel, saying that it causes carbon dioxide emissions. They say flying should cost more. Will people still come here if the cost of flying becomes more expensive? Something else worries me: most tourists come here to see our beautiful landscape and wilderness areas. Will people still visit Iceland if there is no ice?

Figure 32 Differing viewpoints on climate change in Iceland

Activity

1 Discuss Figure 29. List the changes you might expect to see in this landscape in 30 years' time and in 200 years' time.

2 Look at Figure 30.
   a) Describe the location of the Hofsjökull ice cap.
   b) Describe the distribution of:
      i) geothermal power stations
      ii) HEP stations.

3 Use Figure 31 to predict what might happen to Iceland's production of HEP by 2050, 2100 and 2200. Explain why Iceland's energy companies need to find alternative sources of power.

4 **a)** Use the views in Figure 32 to complete a copy of the following table:

	Short-term changes	Longer-term changes
Views that are generally positive		
Views that are generally negative		

   b) Use your completed table to explain what you would do if you were in government in Iceland to try to create a sustainable future for your country.

How can we create an alternative, low carbon future?

World leaders met in Kyoto, Japan to try to agree on how to tackle climate change. Many developed nations agreed to reduce their emission of greenhouse gases by five per cent below the levels they were emitting in 1990. This agreement is called the Kyoto Protocol.

However, the Kyoto Protocol is only a small step towards a low carbon future. While countries like the UK try to cut emissions, the growing economies of India and China are increasing their emissions. They argue that they need to increase electrical production to create wealth and get rid of poverty. So carbon dioxide levels (currently at around 380 ppm) are likely to increase for some years, even if European and other countries reduce their emissions. In 2008 the members of the EU agreed two new targets:

- to reduce overall CO_2 emissions by 20 per cent of their 1990 levels by the year 2020. This would be achieved by investment in renewable energy production using wind, solar and hydro-electricity.
- for each state to source at least 10 per cent of its transport fuel from biofuel. Biofuel is the kind of fuel that is made from natural plant oils. It is considered to be carbon neutral because these quick growing crops absorb as much carbon from the atmosphere while they are growing as they give off when they are burnt as fuel.

Activity

1   Create an advert or poster for biofuels that explains why they are carbon neutral.

2   a) Use Figure 33 to suggest why the EU is keen to set much higher targets for carbon emission reductions than the Kyoto Protocol.

   b) At what point do you think India and China should start reducing their emissions?

Model	Peak CO_2 level (ppm)	Year peak CO_2 is reached (year)	Change in CO_2 emissions in 2050 compared with 2000 (per cent)	Global average temperature increase compared with pre-industrial age (Celsius)	Global average sea level rise due to expansion of sea water but not taking ice melting into account (metres)
I	350–400	2000–2015	−85 to −50	2.0–2.4	0.4–1.4
2	400–440	2000–2020	−60 to −30	2.4–2.8	0.5–1.7
3	440–485	2010–2030	−30 to +5	2.8–3.2	0.6–1.9
4	485–570	2020–2060	+10 to +60	3.2–4.0	0.6–2.4
5	570–660	2050–2080	+25 to +85	4.0–4.9	0.8–2.9
6	660–790	2060–2090	+90 to +140	4.9–6.1	1.0–3.7

Figure 33 Computer models from the Intergovernmental Panel on Climate Change (IPCC) , a highly respected group of climate scientists. Their computer models show that temperatures will rise even if we are able to control CO_2 concentrations below 400 ppm in the next five or so years. Model 1 would require the biggest and quickest cuts in CO_2 emissions, while model 6 allows countries to make smaller, slower cuts

Can new renewable technologies help us achieve a low carbon future?

Figure 34 may be a glimpse of a future, low carbon Europe. A field of 600 steel mirrors reflects solar energy. They direct a beam of light and heat to the top of a 40 m tower where the energy is focused on to water pipes. The heat turns the water to steam which then turns a turbine to generate electricity. The whole system is computer controlled so that each mirror tilts at exactly the right angle. At the moment this **solar furnace** produces enough energy for 6,000 homes, but the plant is being extended and will eventually provide power for the whole of the city of Seville, Spain.

In the future it would be possible to build more solar furnaces in the Sahara desert and bring their electricity into Europe through a new 'super-grid' of cables. Scientists believe that all of Europe's electricity could be generated from just 0.3 per cent of the sunlight that falls on the Sahara. The cost of the super-grid alone would be around €45 billion. This would certainly reduce Europe's carbon emissions dramatically, but critics point out that Africa should also benefit from some of this clean energy.

Figure 34 The new solar furnace which provides electricity for the city of Seville, Spain

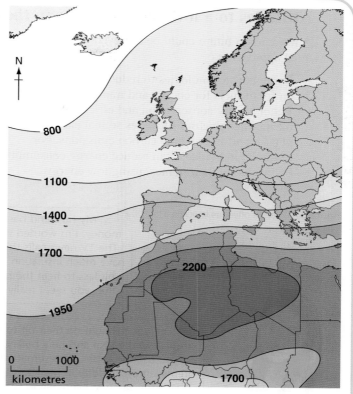

Figure 35 Patterns of solar energy across Europe and Africa. (kilowatts/m²/year)

Activity

3 Use Figure 35 to describe the distribution of countries that have:
   a) between 1,100 and 1,400 kilowatts/m²/year
   b) more than 2,200 kilowatts/m²/year.
4 Use Figure 36 to describe the distribution of:
   a) countries currently producing more than 2,000 megawatts of wind energy a year
   b) countries that could use their seas to make high levels of wave power.
5 Make a poster about renewable energy in Europe. Focus on wind, wave and solar. Include facts and figures about how much renewable energy is made in at least one European country.

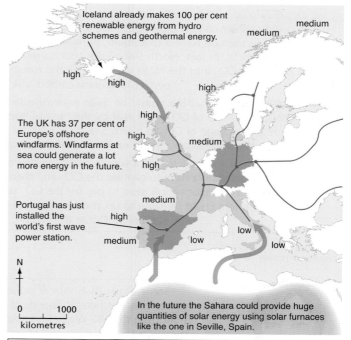

Figure 36 In the future an international grid of power cables could link the countries of Europe and North Africa so that renewable energy made in the Sahara could be fed into your home

Iceland already makes 100 per cent renewable energy from hydro schemes and geothermal energy.

The UK has 37 per cent of Europe's offshore windfarms. Windfarms at sea could generate a lot more energy in the future.

Portugal has just installed the world's first wave power station.

In the future the Sahara could provide huge quantities of solar energy using solar furnaces like the one in Seville, Spain.

Key

Countries already producing more than 10,000 mega watts of electricity from wind energy. One mega watt of wind energy is enough energy for around 300 homes.

Countries already producing 2,000–4,000 mega watts of electricity from wind energy.

high | Areas of sea where wave power could be used to generate electricity.

Geography Futures

Attitudes to a low carbon future in the UK

A low carbon future could be achieved by combining three approaches.

- Using new technologies to reduce our dependence on fossil fuels for energy and transport.
- Better energy conservation and efficiency. This means changing our lifestyles so that each of us plays a part in reducing carbon emissions. For example, individuals can reduce energy consumption by insulating their homes, using low energy appliances, using more public transport and taking fewer flights.
- Finding ways to remove carbon dioxide from the atmosphere and storing it in long-term sinks such as forests or in rocks underground.

Each of these approaches to the low carbon future has advantages and disadvantages, and some may prove more popular than others. Figure 37 examines some different points of view on these low carbon solutions.

Figure 37 Different attitudes towards a low carbon future

Energy conservation and efficiency

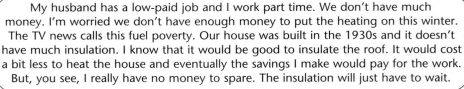

My husband has a low-paid job and I work part time. We don't have much money. I'm worried we don't have enough money to put the heating on this winter. The TV news calls this fuel poverty. Our house was built in the 1930s and it doesn't have much insulation. I know that it would be good to insulate the roof. It would cost a bit less to heat the house and eventually the savings I make would pay for the work. But, you see, I really have no money to spare. The insulation will just have to wait.

Liberal Democrat politician

Everyone should do their bit to help save energy. Simple things like insulating the roof and only boiling as much water as you need every time you use the kettle. We estimate that the CO_2 emissions from electrical items left on standby in the UK is the same as 1.4 million long-haul flights. That's the same as everyone in Glasgow flying to New York and back! And the number of TVs is growing fast. We think that by 2020 there will be 74 million TVs in the UK, that's more TVs than people!

Young family

Carbon capture and storage

We could capture carbon dioxide emissions from coal- and gas-fired power stations. The gas could then be turned to a liquid, pumped down into the ground and stored in sedimentary rocks. In fact, North Sea oil rigs that currently pump oil out of the ground could pump the CO_2 into the rocks when the oil has run out. Those rocks would make a perfect long-term carbon sink.

The process is not difficult but would be quite expensive to set up. Each person in the UK makes about 10 tonnes of CO_2 each year by their use of energy. We estimate that the cost for capture and storage of CO_2 in North Sea rocks is about £20 per tonne. So it will cost about £200 per person each year. Would people want to pay?

The government will have to find a way to make the power companies start to do this. The electricity generators have to capture the CO_2 and then transport it to a disposal site. The oil exploration companies will need to pay for the CO_2 to be stored deep underground. The government could threaten to tax these companies more unless they begin to capture and store the carbon.

Scientist

Nuclear power or renewables?

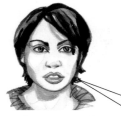

Spokesperson for Friends of the Earth

Some argue that nuclear power is a solution to climate change because it has no carbon emissions. But here at Friends of the Earth we oppose the building of any new nuclear power stations in the UK. We believe that nuclear power is dangerous for a number of reasons. Firstly, there is a security issue and power stations could be targets for terrorists. Secondly, there is the hazardous radioactive waste that will need careful management for generations. Finally, nuclear waste can be converted to be used in weapons.

We are in favour of green energy which is energy from renewables such as wind and solar. These technologies are a safer, cheaper and cleaner solution to the problem of climate change.

Biofuels

There are a number of crops that produce oil that can be processed to make fuel for either cars or aircraft. The growth of these biofuels could reduce poverty in developing countries by creating jobs and wealth for farmers. At the same time people in the developed nations can continue to use their cars and take flights without the fear of oil shortages.

Industry spokesperson

Biofuel crops are causing poverty and hunger in some developing countries. Farmers are being encouraged to grow biofuels instead of food so that we can drive our cars without feeling guilty about carbon emissions. But here at Oxfam we believe that in 2007 and 2008 this has been a factor in the rising cost of food. Using the World Bank's figures we reckon that rising food prices have pushed 100 million people worldwide below the poverty line.

Since April 2008, all petrol and diesel in Britain has had to include 2.5 per cent from biofuels. The European Union considered raising that target to 10 per cent by 2020. However it is now concerned that this could push food prices even higher.

Spokesperson for Oxfam

Forest sinks

Spokesperson for Greenpeace

Planting trees seems like a really a good solution to climate change. They soak up carbon from the atmosphere and store it. However, here at Greenpeace we don't think that planting trees is enough. People have got to actually reduce their carbon emissions in order to tackle climate change. So planting a tree to offset your emissions is just not good enough.

We have been raising awareness of some companies who plant trees to offset their carbon emissions. For example, there is a Japanese power company who wanted to offset their carbon emissions by planting trees. So they bought some land in Tasmania, Australia. They cut down the natural forest that was growing here so they could plant 3,000 hectares of fast growing eucalyptus trees to soak up the carbon. How crazy is that!

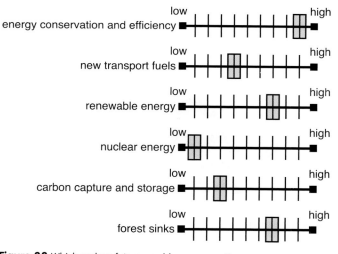

Figure 38 Which carbon future would you support?

Activity

1 Discuss the points of view shown in Figure 37. Outline some advantages and disadvantages of:
   a) energy efficiency and conservation
   b) biofuels
   c) nuclear power.
2 Explain why some environmentalists argue that planting forests is not a good enough option.
3 Working in pairs, study Figure 38.
   a) Imagine each slider represents the amount of effort and investment that could be made in the six possible solutions to climate change. Agree with your partner how each slider should be placed in your ideal low carbon future. Be prepared to justify your decision.
   b) Team up with another pair. Each pair must give a short presentation to describe and justify their low carbon future. Can you persuade the other pair to change their minds?

Chapter 4
Development

How are global patterns of development identified?

What do we mean by development?

One common view of development is that it can be measured economically: that increasing wealth or decreasing levels of poverty are indicators of development. This notion is examined in more detail on pages 234–235. However, development may also be measured in terms of social improvements to health, education or equality. This chapter looks at all of these measures and examines whether the development gap is closing.

Development is...
- reducing levels of poverty
- increasing levels of wealth
- reducing the gap between the richest and poorest members of society
- creating equal status for men and women
- creating justice, freedom of speech and political participation for everyone
- ensuring that everyone is safe from conflict and terrorism
- ensuring that everyone fulfils their basic needs: food, water and shelter
- ensuring that all children have good standards of education.

Figure 1 Different ways of seeing development

Figure 2 Development is ...

Figure 3 Development is ...

Activity

1 Study Figure 1. Work in pairs to discuss this list.
   a) What are the advantages and disadvantages of each of these statements as a definition of development?
   b) Choose the five statements that you think give the best definition of development. Join with another pair and justify your choice.

   c) Working in a team of four, produce a joint statement that defines development. Each member of the team must contribute and agree with the statement.

2 Working on your own, explain which aspects of human development are illustrated by Figures 2 and 3. Write a caption for each figure.

Changes to average life expectancy

Between 1960 and 2007, life expectancy increased in most countries of the world. Some of the biggest improvements were in poorer countries. For example, average life expectancy in South Asia leapt from 48 to 64 years. However, due to HIV/AIDS average life expectancy decreased in 21 countries during the 1990s. All but one of these countries is in Africa. In Zimbabwe, the average life expectancy fell by a staggering 22 years from 55 to 33.

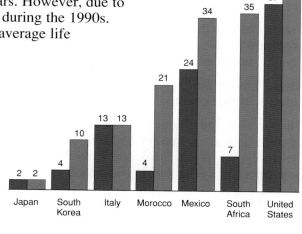

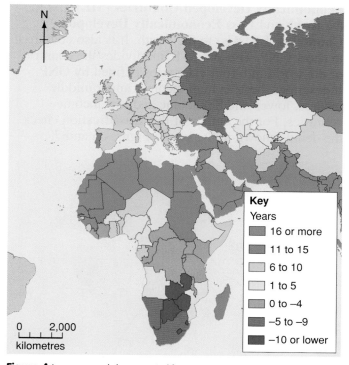

Figure 4 Increase and decrease in life expectancy, 1960 to 2003

Key
Percentage of adults who are obese (2005)
■ Males, ages 15+
■ Females, ages 15+

Figure 5 Percentage of adults who are obese in selected countries

How will the ageing population affect our health?

In wealthy countries primary health care is generally very good and people have long life expectancy. However, the cause of death is often influenced by people's choice of lifestyle. Over-eating, lack of exercise and alcohol/drug addiction often contribute to the cause of death. For example, poor diet and lack of exercise can lead to weight gain and then to obesity. Obesity increases the risk of a number of long-term (or chronic) health problems. It increases the risk of stroke, heart disease and can also lead to Type 2 diabetes. A recent report in the UK predicts that by 2050:

- 60 per cent of adult men in the UK will be obese
- 50 per cent of adult women will be obese
- 25 per cent of all children under 16 will be obese
- the current cost to the NHS of treating people who are ill because they are overweight will double from £5 billion to £10 billion a year
- the cost to society and business (through, for example, days lost from work due to ill health) will rise to £49.9 billion by 2050.

Activity

3 Study Figure 4. Describe the distribution of countries which have the most improved life expectancy.

4 Suggest why life expectancy has increased in some countries more than others.

5 a) Explain why people in wealthy countries do not always have healthy diets.
   b) Explain what effect these diets might have on health data.

6 a) Do some research into the main causes of death in MEDCs and LEDCs.
   b) Choose one major cause of death that is easily preventable in LEDCs and explain how this issue could be solved.

7 Produce a poster or PowerPoint presentation. Use your poster or presentation to show:
   a) how our lifestyle decisions can affect our health; or
   b) how the cause of death varies from one country to another; or
   c) how rising levels of obesity will have negative impacts on the UK's future.

Using national wealth as a measure of development

The wealth of a country is usually measured by its Gross National Product (GNP) per person. The GNP per person of a country is calculated by:

Step 1 Add up the total value of goods and services produced by people living in that country and by people abroad who are still citizens of that country.

Step 2 Divide this figure by the total number of citizens of that country.

This gives a figure which can be thought of as the average annual income for a citizen of that country. Helpfully, the World Bank and United Nations (UN) now refer to GNP as Gross National Income (GNI) per person. So for example, the average annual income (GNI or GNP) in Mali, Africa, is US$350 (or about US$1 a day). Remember, this is an average, so some people earn more than this and others earn less. In fact, 73 per cent of Mali's population earns less than US$1 a day.

Figure 6 shows the 1980 Brandt Line which divides countries into one of two categories: **More Economically Developed Countries (MEDCs)** to the North and **Less Economically Developed Countries (LEDCs)** to the South. It is also coloured to show GNP. The World Bank divides the countries of the world into four categories defined by GNP. It describes these as high income, upper middle income, lower middle income and low income countries. For the details of this classification check the details shown in the key to Figures 6 and 7.

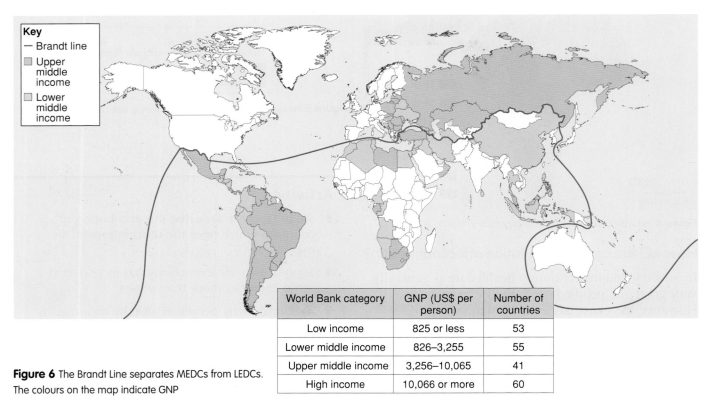

Key
— Brandt line
▓ Upper middle income
░ Lower middle income

World Bank category	GNP (US$ per person)	Number of countries
Low income	825 or less	53
Lower middle income	826–3,255	55
Upper middle income	3,256–10,065	41
High income	10,066 or more	60

Figure 6 The Brandt Line separates MEDCs from LEDCs. The colours on the map indicate GNP

The Brandt Line

Public awareness of the development gap is not new. It was first brought into the news headlines in the Brandt Report in 1980. This report, by Willy Brandt, a German politician, drew a line on the map that separated the richer countries from the poorer ones. This map was developed to separate the More Economically Developed Countries (MEDCs) from the Less Economically Developed Countries (LEDCs). As you can see on Figure 7, the MEDCs are situated mainly in the northern hemisphere. The LEDCs are mainly in the tropics and southern hemisphere. The line loops around Australia and New Zealand to include them in the richer half of the map. This famous map draws attention to the gap between the richer North and the poorer South and is still in use today. But is it still relevant and accurate?

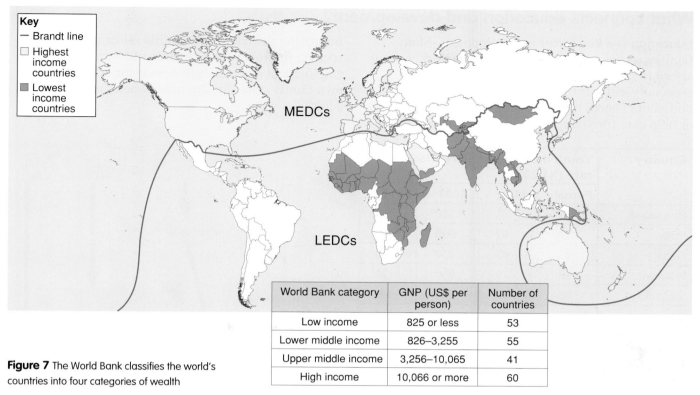

Key
— Brandt line
☐ Highest income countries
■ Lowest income countries

MEDCs

LEDCs

World Bank category	GNP (US$ per person)	Number of countries
Low income	825 or less	53
Lower middle income	826–3,255	55
Upper middle income	3,256–10,065	41
High income	10,066 or more	60

Figure 7 The World Bank classifies the world's countries into four categories of wealth

Figure 8 How do you see the world?

Activity

1 Discuss the cartoon in Figure 8.
   a) Describe each character. How are they dressed and what are they doing?
   b) Who do the two figures represent?
   c) Explain the actions of the larger figure.

2 Use Figure 7.
   a) Describe the distribution of highest income countries.
   b) Describe the distribution of lowest income countries.

3 Study Figure 6.
   a) Describe the distribution of :
      i) lower middle income countries
      ii) upper middle income countries.

   b) Identify countries that have:
      i) an upper middle income but are south of the Brandt Line
      ii) a lower middle income but are north of the Brandt Line.

4 Study Figures 6 and 7.
   Which do you find more helpful: the two categories of the Brandt Line or the four categories defined by the World Bank?
   a) Suggest the advantages and disadvantages of each system.
   b) Do you think there is an argument to redraw the Brandt Line? If so, where should it go?

What connects education and development?

Education is a key factor in development. Many families in the poorest countries of the world cannot afford to send their children to school. Children, especially girls, are expected to help their mothers do household chores like collecting firewood or water, or help care for younger brothers and sisters.

Improving the education of girls raises their status in society, improves their chances of formal employment and can even reduce the size of their own family (their fertility rate) when they are an adult.

Country	Youth literacy rate (%) 2007		GNI US$	
	Female	Male	2007	2011
Bangladesh	73	71	520	770
India	77	87	950	1410
Nepal	73	85	350	540
Pakistan	58	79	850	1120
Sri Lanka	98	97	1540	2580
Ghana	76	80	710	1410
Malawi	82	84	250	340
Mozambique	47	95	340	470
Nigeria	85	89	970	1200
Sierra Leone	44	64	280	340
Tanzania	76	79	410	540
Uganda	84	88	380	510
Zambia	68	82	750	1160

Youth literacy is the % of people aged 15–24 who can read and write. Source: World Bank and Unesco

Selected South Asian countries
Selected Sub Saharan Africa countries

Figure 9 The state of education in selected countries

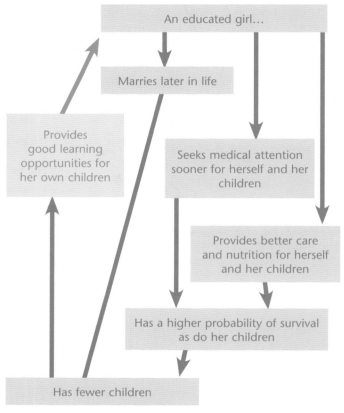

Figure 10 The advantages of better education for girls

Activity

1. Use Figure 9 to draw a graph showing the difference in female and male literacy. Where does female education need to make most progress?

2. **a)** Use Figure 9 to investigate the connection between female literacy and GNI (2007) by drawing a scattergraph.
   b) Describe what your graph is telling you about female education in South Asia compared to sub-Saharan Africa. Are there any countries that are doing particularly well, or particularly badly?

3. **a)** Study Figure 11 and describe the distribution of states which have a fertility:
   i) higher than 3
   ii) lower than 2.

   b) Explain how improving access to regular pay and improved education could reduce fertility.

4. Use the data in Figure 12 to investigate each of the following enquiries:
   a) Do states with higher levels of female literacy have lower fertility?
   b) Is fertility higher in those states with more poor households (indicated by lower percentages of houses with electricity)?
   c) Do the states with low status for women (indicated by low sex ratios) also have higher fertility?

India

Investigating patterns of fertility in India

Fertility within India varies considerably from state to state. This pattern may be explained by:

- variations in family income with some states having more opportunities for regularly paid jobs than others
- better education for girls in some states means that young women delay having their first child in order to take paid work and pursue a career.

In some parts of South Asia, including some Indian states, daughters have lower status than sons. In a poor household this may mean that girls have fewer educational opportunities than boys. Girls from poor households with little education often marry young. These young women then have large families because that is what their husbands want. Furthermore, poor families may prefer to have sons rather than daughters because a son will help support family income. In some cases this leads to women terminating their pregnancies if they discover they are carrying a daughter. In other cases, young girls suffer neglect and die. This explains why there are fewer women than men in most Indian states.

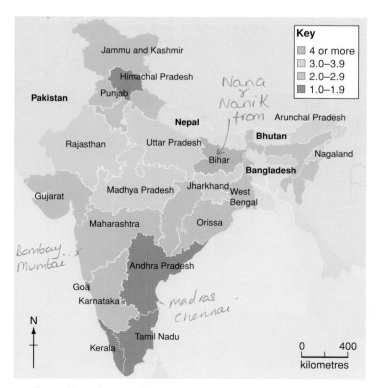

Figure 11 Fertility varies from state to state in India

State	Sex ratio	Female literacy	Fertility	Percentage homes with electricity
Andhra Pradesh	978	50.4	1.8	88.4
Arunachal Pradesh	893	43.5	3.0	76.9
Assam	935	54.6	2.4	38.1
Bihar	919	33.1	4.0	27.7
Chhattisgarh	989	51.9	2.6	71.4
Goa	961	75.4	1.8	96.4
Gujarat	920	57.8	2.4	89.3
Haryana	861	55.7	2.7	91.5
Himachal Pradesh	968	67.4	1.9	98.5
Jammu & Kashmir	892	43.0	2.4	93.2
Jharkhand	941	38.9	3.3	40.2
Karnataka	965	56.9	2.1	89.3
Kerala	1,058	87.7	1.9	91.0
Madhya Pradesh	919	50.3	3.1	71.4
Maharastra	922	67.0	2.1	83.5
Manipur	974	56.8	2.8	87.0
Meghalaya	972	59.6	3.8	70.4
Mizoram	935	86.7	2.9	92.3
Nagaland	900	61.5	3.7	82.9
Orissa	972	50.5	2.4	45.4
Punjab	876	63.4	2.0	96.3
Rajasthan	921	43.9	3.2	66.1
Sikkim	875	60.4	2.0	92.1
Tamil Nadu	987	64.4	1.8	88.6
Tripura	948	64.9	2.4	68.8
Uttar Pradesh	898	42.2	3.8	42.8
Uttaranchal	962	59.6	2.6	80.0
West Bengal	934	59.6	2.3	52.5

Figure 12 Selected data for Indian states. The sex ratio is the number of women for every 1,000 men. Female literacy is the percentage of women who can read and write

Development issues in sub-Saharan Africa

Sub-Saharan Africa is the world's poorest region. Within this region there are some countries that have made good progress at reducing poverty. Countries such as Mauritius and, to a lesser extent, South Africa, have seen improvements in incomes, health care and education. However, the region has the highest infant mortality rates in the world and, as Figure 13 shows, they are only coming down slowly. A key population issue for Africa is to reduce infant mortality and improve primary health care. How can this be done?

Investigating the impact of malaria

Malaria is spread by mosquitoes carrying a parasite that infects a person when bitten. It is an entirely preventable disease. However, every year 300 million people get malaria resulting in over 1 million deaths worldwide. Malaria is a health threat in tropical regions of the world. Around 40 per cent of the world's population live in areas where malaria is **endemic** (i.e. malaria is constantly present) but 90 per cent of deaths occur in sub-Saharan Africa.

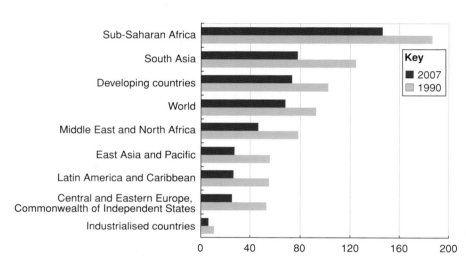

Figure 13 Infant mortality rates (deaths of children under 1 for every 1,000 births)

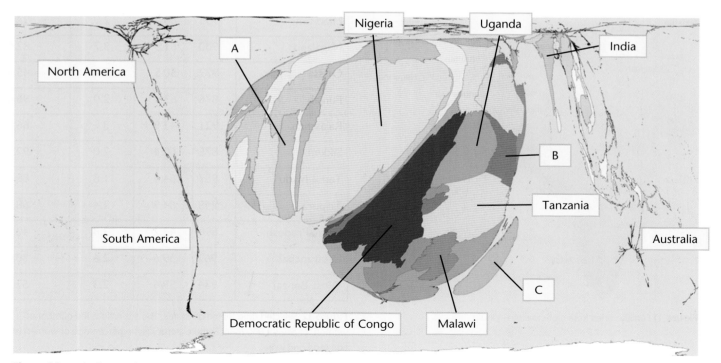

Figure 14 Deaths from malaria. Countries are shown in proportion to the number of deaths from malaria in one year (2002)

Malawi

Case study of malaria in Malawi

Malaria is one of Malawi's most serious heath problems. In Malawi, the risk from malaria varies across the country and also throughout the year. The shores of Lake Malawi provide ideal breeding conditions for mosquitoes, with warm temperatures and stagnant water. The highland areas are generally cooler and drier. Here, malaria is seasonal with cases reaching a peak during the rainy season when ditches and puddles quickly form and attract mosquitoes. Around 83 per cent of Malawi's population live in rural areas. Deaths from malaria are significantly higher in rural areas than they are in the cities of Blantyre and Lilongwe. Houses in rural areas are constructed of mud bricks with thatched roofs and offer little protection from mosquitoes.

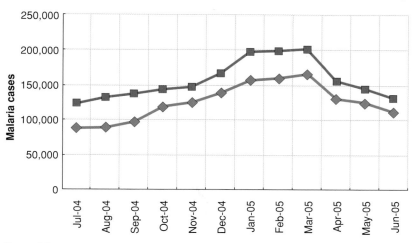

Key
- Malaria under 5 years - new
- Malaria 5 years and older - new

Figure 15 New malaria cases per month in Malawi (July 2004–June 2005)

	Mean minimum temp (Celsius)	Mean maximum temp (Celsius)	Average precipitation (mm)
Jan	17	27	208
Feb	17	27	218
March	16	27	125
April	14	27	43
May	11	25	3
June	8	23	0
July	7	23	0
Aug	8	25	0
Sept	12	27	0
Oct	15	30	0
Nov	17	29	53
Dec	18	28	125

Figure 16 Climate for Lilongwe, Malawi

Activity

1 Use Figure 14 and an atlas to find out:
   a) which tropical region has very few cases of malaria?
   b) the names of countries A, B and C
   c) which region of the world, after sub-Saharan Africa, has the next largest number of cases of malaria?

2 Use Figure 15. Describe the annual pattern of new malaria cases for children under five. Refer to figures in your answer.

3 Use Figure 16.
   a) Draw a climate chart for Malawi.
   b) Describe the annual pattern of rainfall.

4 Using evidence from Figures 15 and 16, explain why new cases of malaria are more common at certain times of the year.

Malawi

Are some people at more risk from malaria than others?

The health risks of malaria vary widely for different groups of people. Not everyone who catches malaria will die. In fact, over time, continued infection from mosquito bites will lead to a person becoming immune. Prevalence rates in Malawi show that 60 per cent of babies and children under three years old had malaria compared with only 12 per cent for adult men. As children and adults age, they develop resistance to the disease and the numbers of deaths go down.

Some people are at greater risk of death from malaria than others. The groups at highest risk are children and pregnant women, especially those in their first pregnancy. Around 40 per cent of child deaths (children under five) are from malaria. People with poor immune systems are at high risk. It is estimated that 12 per cent of Malawi's population is living with the HIV virus, which destroys a person's immune system. They are unable to fend off diseases and the death rate from malaria is higher than for people without HIV. Pregnancy also leads to a slight decline in immunity levels. This results in slightly more pregnant women dying from the disease than non-pregnant women.

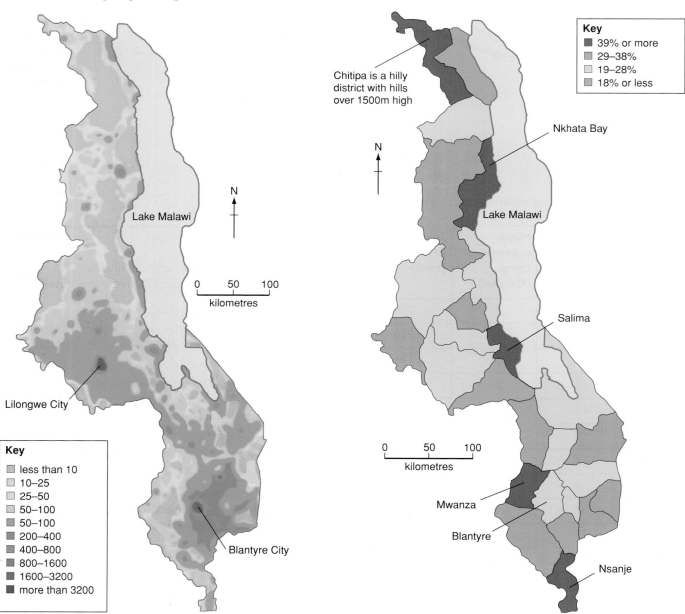

Chitipa is a hilly district with hills over 1500m high

Nkhata Bay

Lake Malawi

Salima

Mwanza

Blantyre

Nsanje

Key
- 39% or more
- 29–38%
- 19–28%
- 18% or less

Lake Malawi

Lilongwe City

Blantyre City

0   50   100
kilometres

Key
- less than 10
- 10–25
- 25–50
- 50–100
- 50–100
- 200–400
- 400–800
- 800–1600
- 1600–3200
- more than 3200

Figure 17 Population densities in Malawi. Rural areas generally have lower population densities than urban areas

Figure 18 Distribution of malaria in Malawi (on average 28% of the population have malaria)

Strategies to combat malaria

A number of strategies have been implemented in Malawi to combat the disease. In 2000, the **Millennium Development Goals (MDGs)** were adopted by governments around the world. One of the goals was to reduce the number of cases of malaria by 2015. One way this goal can be reached is by encouraging the use of Insecticide Treated Bed nets (ITNs). This is a very effective way of reducing incidents of malaria and is relatively cheap. Each bed net costs only £3. However, many people in rural Malawi are unable to afford this. In the last 15 years, the Ministry of Health, and charities such as Nothing but Nets, have distributed bed nets across Malawi. In 1997 only 8 per cent of homes in Malawi had bed nets. By 2004 the average was 50 per cent. To maintain effectiveness, nets need to be retreated every 6–12 months and this is something that is easily forgotten.

Insecticides are sprayed in areas where mosquitoes are likely to come into contact with humans. The problem is that mosquitoes have developed a resistance to insecticides and they aren't as effective as they could be. Similarly the malaria parasite has become resistant to drugs. New drugs need to be developed urgently. Once a person starts to show signs of malaria, they need to take anti-malarial drugs as soon as possible to stand a better chance of fighting the disease. Unfortunately, not everyone in Malawi is able to access drugs when they need them. This is often because people living in rural areas have to travel a long way to reach a doctor. Also, because the early symptoms of malaria are similar to many other conditions, people often don't realise until it's too late. Malaria has the biggest impact on poor people, as they cannot afford to buy nets and get the treatment they need. It can become a vicious circle where people are prevented from getting out of poverty because of the burden malaria has on their lives.

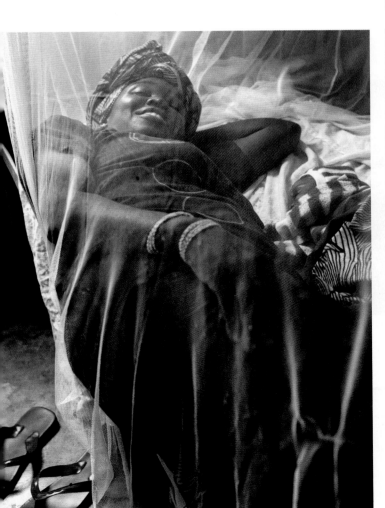

Figure 19 Deaths due to malaria can be prevented using Insecticide Treated Bed nets (ITNs)

Activity

1 **a)** Identify which three groups of people are most at risk from malaria.
   b) Explain why some people are more at risk than others.

2 **a)** Use Figure 18 to describe the distribution of malaria in Malawi.
   b) Use evidence from the text on pages 239–240 to suggest different reasons for the high rates of malaria in two of the named districts on Figure 18.
   c) Compare Figures 17 and 18. Use these maps to provide evidence that malaria is more common in rural areas.

3 Produce a short newspaper article. Use the following as a headline: 'Malaria, the forgotten killer'.

4 Work in pairs. Discuss each of the following and then summarise your conclusions in two spider diagrams.
   a) Does malaria cause poverty or is it a result of poverty?
   b) Which groups should be targeted for ITNs?

Chapter 5
Development issues and water

What are the main sources of fresh water?

More than 69 per cent of the surface of planet Earth is covered in water. But only about 4 per cent is fresh water. There are five main types of freshwater store, as you can see in Figure 1.

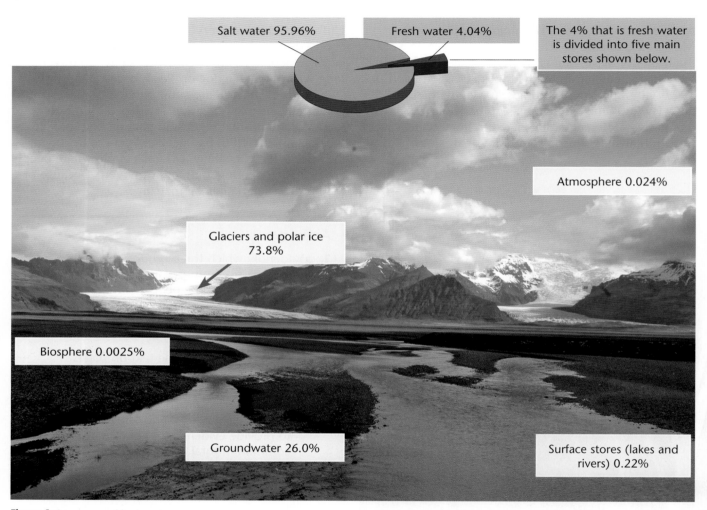

Salt water 95.96%

Fresh water 4.04%

The 4% that is fresh water is divided into five main stores shown below.

Atmosphere 0.024%

Glaciers and polar ice 73.8%

Biosphere 0.0025%

Groundwater 26.0%

Surface stores (lakes and rivers) 0.22%

Figure 1 The sources of fresh water

Activity

1 Using Figure 1, make a list of the five freshwater stores. Do this in rank order, starting with the largest.

2 Describe the water cycle in your own words using the terms stores and flows.

3 How would the different flows through the water cycle change due to climate and vegetation in Antarctica compared with the Amazon rainforest?

Geology is the main factor in determining where water is stored within the drainage basin. This fact is critical to the water companies who supply us with water to our homes and businesses. In regions where the geology is impermeable, water can be stored at the surface. In regions where the geology is porous, such as sandstone, water is stored naturally in the rocks underground. These natural stores of groundwater are called aquifers.

Surface stores include lakes and rivers. Rivers can be dammed to control flooding and create reservoirs for water supply. There are more than 47,000 large dams in the world and nearly half of these are in China. However, surface stores can also be very small. Take rainwater harvesting, for example. If you have a water-butt in your garden that collects rainwater from the gutters, you are creating a small surface store of fresh water.

Groundwater stores occur when water infiltrates into the ground and gets trapped in the fractures and the pore spaces of rocks and sediments. Water that enters an aquifer is called **recharge**; water that leaves an aquifer is discharge. When water is taken from either a surface or groundwater store by human action we say the water is abstracted. If water is taken from a store faster than it can be recharged we say that **over-abstraction** is taking place.

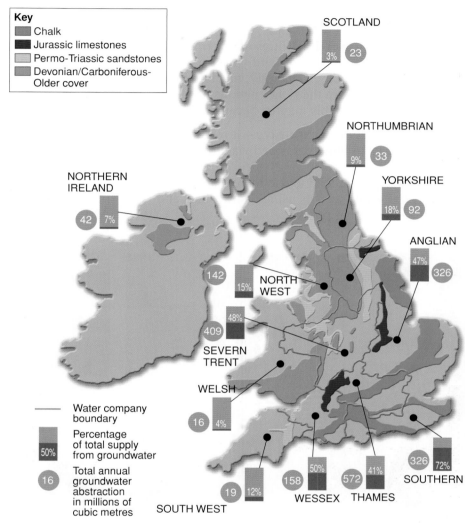

Key
- Chalk
- Jurassic limestones
- Permo-Triassic sandstones
- Devonian/Carboniferous-Older cover

— Water company boundary

50% Percentage of total supply from groundwater

16 Total annual groundwater abstraction in millions of cubic metres

Figure 2 Major aquifers in the UK. Located bar graphs indicate the percentage of water supply that comes from groundwater supply. The remainder will come from surface stores (rivers and reservoirs)

Activity

4 Define the following terms when applied to an aquifer:

discharge   abstraction   over-abstraction

5 Use Figure 2.
   a) Make a table of the 12 water companies and put them in rank order by the percentage of their water supply that comes from groundwater.
   b) For each company calculate the percentage of its supply that comes from surface stores.

6 Use Figure 2 and an atlas.
   a) Describe the distribution of water companies that abstract more than 300 million cubic metres of water a year from groundwater.
   b) Describe the distribution of water companies that take less than 10 per cent of their supply from groundwater.
   c) Find a population density map for the UK in your atlas. Predict what will happen to groundwater supplies in London and the South East if population continues to grow.

Why is water a development issue?

Everyone needs water. It is essential for healthy life. We also use vast quantities of water to grow food and in many industrial processes. However, the amount of water used by each person varies greatly from one country to another. For example, the average American family uses 1304 litres of water a day, whereas the average African family uses only 22 litres of water a day. Generally, much more water is used, per person, in the richer nations of the world than in the poorest. This may be because:

- water abstraction is expensive – it requires huge investments to build dams and water transfer schemes
- wealthier people tend to use more water in non-essential ways, such as using dishwashers and filling swimming pools.

Some groups of people have very poor access to water. Many people in rural regions of sub-Saharan Africa have to collect water and carry it some distance from their home. Collecting water is time-consuming and heavy work. A piped supply to the home would not only be safer, it would save time and provide dignity and privacy.

In Sub-Saharan Africa, people living in urban areas are twice as likely to have access to safe, piped water as people living in rural areas. However, in the informal settlements of Africa's cities, many people do not have access to piped water and cannot afford to drill a borehole. They are forced to buy water from private sellers off the back of carts. As a result, people who live in cities in shanty towns of some African cities can pay up to 50 times the amount for water as people living in European cities.

Figure 3 Children collecting water in Ghana (%)

Figure 4 An extravagant use of water? A desert golf course in USA

Type of water supply		In Accra	In savanna regions of N Ghana	All of Ghana
Pipe	Indoor	42.2	2.2	14.5
	Public standpipe	4.5	1.2	10.7
	Other	37.6	2.5	14.3
Pipe total		**84.3**	**5.9**	**39.5**
Well	Borehole or protected well	1.2	55.2	36.6
	Unprotected well	0	6.9	4.1
Well total		**1.2**	**62.1**	**40.7**
Natural e.g. streams and ponds		**0.2**	**31.9**	**15.7**
Other (includes water vendor)		**14.3**	**0.0**	**4.1**

Figure 5 Water supply in Ghana

Water, sanitation and health

It is estimated that almost one-tenth of all disease could be prevented if everyone had access to clean water and proper **sanitation** (the safe disposal of waste water). Diarrhoea accounts for around 17 per cent of all deaths of under-five-year-olds. A total of 1.4 million deaths a year could be saved from preventable diarrhoeal disease if water supply, hygiene and sanitation were improved. The other major child-killer, malaria, could also be reduced by 40 per cent if water supply, irrigation ditches and stagnant water bodies were managed better.

Poor diet or malnutrition is the underlying cause of just over half of all deaths of children under five. Water is needed to grow crops, so improving water supply could save many of these lives. However, around 50 per cent of malnutrition is actually related to repeated diarrhoea or infection by intestinal worms. Again, these problems can be tackled by improving water supply, hygiene and sanitation.

The United Nations set a Millennium Development Goal for access to water. The target is to halve the number of people that do not have access to clean water and sanitation between 1990 and 2015.

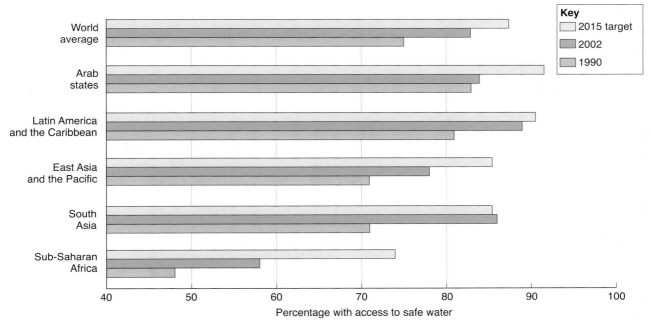

Figure 6 Will each region achieve its Millennium Development Goal for safe water?

Activity

1 **a)** Working with a partner, make a list of all the ways that you use water every day.
   b) How many of these uses are essential and how many could you live without?

2 Suggest five reasons why families in richer countries like the UK use more water than families in the world's poorest countries.

3 Using the data in Figure 5, draw a graph to highlight the difference in water supply between Accra (the capital city) and the rural savanna regions of northern Ghana. Suggest how this would affect quality of life for families in:

   a) Accra
   b) Rural regions

4 Study Figure 6.
   a) Which regions are:
      i) likely to reach their target?
      ii) unlikely to reach their target?
   b) Discuss why we need to set these targets.

5 Produce a 400-word newspaper article explaining:
   a) why we need to achieve the Millennium Development target for water and sanitation
   b) how we could achieve it.

South Africa

Investigating patterns of water supply in South Africa

On average, South Africa has about half as much rainfall as the UK. But rainfall is not distributed evenly over South Africa. The east coast receives a lot more rain than the west (see Figure 7). This is because moist air comes in from the Indian Ocean forming rain clouds over the highlands of eastern South Africa and Lesotho. Lesotho is a small mountainous country that is entirely surrounded by South Africa.

Geographical patterns of rainfall in this region don't match the distribution of population. For example, parts of Lesotho receive 1,200 mm of rain a year (similar to mid-Wales) but Lesotho has only a low population. This is good for Lesotho because it can sell its excess water to parts of South Africa where the population is higher but rainfall is lower.

The amount of precipitation also varies through the year. For some regions in South Africa this difference can be quite extreme, resulting in a dry season and a wet season. This seasonal variation in rainfall has an impact on the amount of water flowing in South Africa's rivers. Without careful management some parts of South Africa would suffer seasonal water shortages.

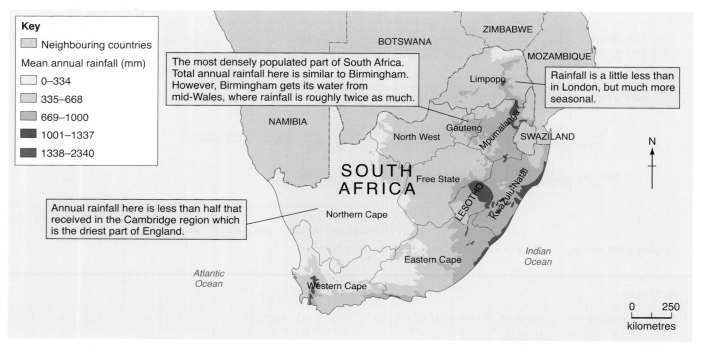

Figure 7 Average annual rainfall in South Africa

www.weathersa.co.za
is the meteorological office
for South Africa.

Figure 8 Rainfall (mm) for selected regions of South Africa

	Jan	Feb	Mar	Apr	May	Jun	Jul	Aug	Sep	Oct	Nov	Dec	Total
Western Cape	8	4	11	24	40	41	47	45	24	12	12	10	278
Gauteng	125	90	91	54	13	9	4	6	27	72	117	105	713

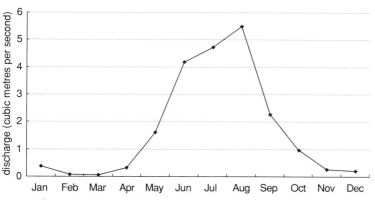

Figure 9 Hydrograph for the River Dorling, Western Cape Province, South Africa. The **catchment area** of the River Dorling before this station is 6,900 km²

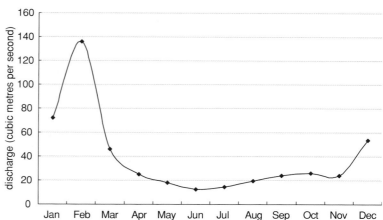

Figure 10 Hydrograph for the River Vaal, Gauteng Province, South Africa. The catchment area of the River Vaal before this station is 38,560 km²

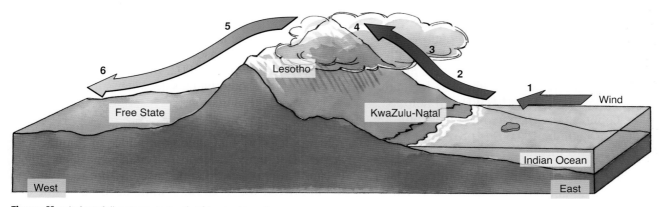

Figure 11 Relief rainfall patterns in South Africa and Lesotho

Activity

1 Use Figure 7 to describe the distribution of rainfall in South Africa.

2 Explain why Lesotho is able to sell water to South Africa and why South Africa wants to buy it.

3 **a)** Use Figure 8 to draw a pair of rainfall graphs.
   b) Compare your rainfall graphs with Figures 9 and 10.
   c) At which times of year do these two regions face possible water shortages?

4 Use Figure 11 to explain why Lesotho has so much more rainfall than Free State in South Africa. Describe what is happening at each point (1–6) on the diagram.

Lesotho

Investigating a major water management and transfer scheme

The Lesotho Highlands Water Project (LHWP) is an example of a large-scale water management scheme. There are four phases to the project, which involves the construction of six major dams in Lesotho and 200 km of tunnel systems to transfer water to areas with low water supply in the neighbouring country of South Africa. It is the largest water-transfer scheme in Africa, diverting 40 per cent of the water in the Senqu river basin in Lesotho to the Vaal river system in the Orange Free State of South Africa (see Figure 12). The River Vaal then carries the water into Gauteng Province. This is a very industrial and highly populated region of South Africa, which has a high demand for fresh water.

The project was agreed between South Africa and Lesotho in 1986. So far, only one of the four phases has been completed. The third major dam of the project, the Mohale dam, was finished in 2002.

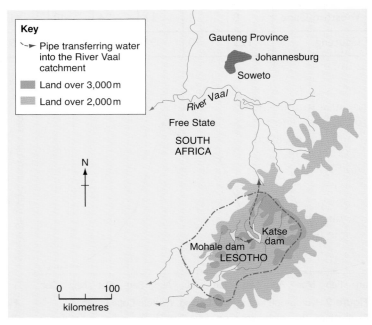

Figure 12 A map of the LHWP water management and transfer scheme

What are the advantages and disadvantages of the LHWP?

Lesotho is one of the world's poorest countries. Its Gross National Income per person is US$590, it has an unemployment rate of around 50 per cent and no natural resources to sell except water. The Lesotho government is hoping that the LHWP will help to develop the country. The income received from selling water through the LHWP is providing 75 per cent of the country's income.

The project is predicted to cost US$8 billion, which is being given on loan from the World Bank. The South African government will eventually have to pay this money back. The Lesotho government will receive income for the sale of its water. In the long term this could help Lesotho develop its own water management schemes.

In the short term Lesotho is still struggling with water shortages and poor sanitation. Local people have not had access to any of the water supplied by the dams since all of the water is being piped to South Africa.

But the percentage of people with a safe water supply in South Africa increased from 83 per cent to 87 per cent between 1990 and 2002. In 2002 only 76 per cent of people in Lesotho had a safe water supply and only 37 per cent had sanitation.

Most of the LHWP water is being transferred to Johannesburg in the Gauteng province of South Africa. But many residents of Johannesburg are angry because their water bills increased before receiving the improved water service. Some of these people did not even have access to basic water resources. Bills went up to fund the dam and to pay for repairs to leaking pipes.

Local people launched a campaign to halt the construction of the Mohale dam until the water pipes in Johannesburg improved. In 2000 up to 50 per cent of water was simply being wasted through leaking pipes. Despite this, construction of the Mohale dam continued ahead of schedule.

The dams will provide hydro-electric power (HEP) as well as water. The Muela dam is connected to a 72 megawatt hydro-electric power station that is providing a renewable source of cheap electricity for Lesotho. Lesotho is also benefiting from improved roads which were constructed to gain access to the dam sites.

However, many people have been displaced by the construction of the dams and the flooding of the reservoirs. The Katse dam, the first major dam of the project, completed in 1998, affected more than 20,000 people. Many of these people were relocated and given compensation but they claim the money they received was too late. They were also given training so that they could find new jobs, but the training has been criticised and most of the displaced people are still in low-income jobs.

New job opportunities have been created working on the construction of the project. About 20,000 people have moved into informal settlements to work on the dams. However, this has led to a massive increase in AIDS, prostitution and alcoholism.

The project has also destroyed thousands of hectares of grazing and arable land. Since only 9 per cent of Lesotho is considered arable, this could lead to huge problems in the nation's food supply.

The project will affect the flow of water downstream of the dams. As well as a decrease in the amount of water, it is thought that the dams will reduce the amount of sediment, oxygen levels, nutrients and even the temperature of the water. This will have negative impacts on people, wetland habitats and wildlife, including many endangered species.

Figure 13 The Mohale dam. You can see this dam on Google Earth: reference location: 29 27'29.97"S, 28 5'56.17"E

River	Senqunyane
Capacity	958 million m³
Height	145 m
Material	A concrete-faced embankment filled with 7.8 million m³ of rock
Interconnecting tunnel	To Katse (32 km long)
Water transfer capacity	10.1 m³ per second
Initial loan	US$45 million (funded to Lesotho and to be repaid to the World Bank by South Africa)
Number of affected people	7,400, many of whom lost their homes

Activity

1 Summarise the aims of the Lesotho Highlands Water Project.

2 Use the text on these pages to complete a copy of the following table. You should find more to write in some boxes than in others.

	Short-term advantages (+) and disadvantages (−) of LHWP	Long-term advantages (+) and disadvantages (−) of LHWP
Lesotho	+ −	+ −
South Africa	+ −	+ −

3 Summarise what each of the following groups of people might think about the LHWP:
   a) a farmer in the Lesotho Highlands
   b) a government minister in Lesotho
   c) residents in Johannesburg.

4 Do you think the LHWP is an example of a good, sustainable water management project? Explain your reasons.

Figure 14 Factfile on the Mohale dam (completed 2002)

Soweto

Improving quality of life in Soweto

In the 1980s water supply in Soweto was very poor. The iron pipes carrying water were rusted and between 50 and 60 per cent of water was wasted in leaks. Many districts were able to have water only at night. Obviously, this was a major health concern. Gradually the situation has improved. Many new water pipes have been laid, and township roads have been paved. The local authority employed local people to do the work, so Sowetans benefited from extra jobs as well as improved services.

Figure 15 The township of Soweto is home to 1 million people

Activity

1 Explain how each of the following would affect quality of life:
   a) High population density
   b) Irregular water supply
   c) Unpaved roads.

2 If you have access to a computer, use the internet to research and find definitions for the following terms:
   a) socio-economic group   c) apartheid
   b) housing tenure   d) township.

   Read the advice that follows on how to find definitions.

Using the internet to find definitions of geographical terms

Using the internet to research the meaning of a term is easy.

1 Use a search engine such as GoogleTM.
2 Type in 'define': in the dialog box, and the word you want to define (see example on the right).
3 View the sites that are returned in your web search (see below). Some sites are more reliable than others. For example, university and government sites tend to be factual and accurate, whereas weblogs often contain opinions that may not be factually correct.

Definitions of **quality of life** on the Web:

• The overall enjoyment of life. Many clinical trials measure aspects of a patient's sense of well-being and ability to perform various tasks to assess the effects that cancer and its treatment have on the patient.
nydailynews.healthology.com/nydailynews/15836.htm

• The level of enjoyment and fulfillment derived by humans from the life they live within their local economic, cultural, social, and environmental conditions. The Jacksonville Community Council defines quality of life as the "feeling of wellbeing, fulfillment, or satisfaction resulting from factors in the external environments." Quality of life, in this sense, is most directly measured using subjective indicators. ...
indicators.top10by2010.org/glossary.cfm

Will Johannesburg meet its target?

The South African government has the aim of replacing all informal housing with low-cost social housing by 2014. The United Nations (UN) estimates that, in 2001, 33 per cent of South Africans were living in slum housing. This is a term not usually used by geographers, but it obviously means that this housing is inadequate. The UN does not believe that South Africa can achieve its target. Despite building 200,000 low-cost houses every year, they estimate that another 2.4 million will still be needed in 2014.

The Johannesburg City Authority is much more positive about progress. They claim that residents of Johannesburg (or Jo'burg) already have the highest standard of living in South Africa. Their report on change in the city (see Figure 16) makes very positive reading.

Jo'burg advertises its successes

February 15, 2006 By Ndaba Dlamini

The City is drawing attention to successes attained over the past five years through a media campaign currently under way.

THE City of Johannesburg has made positive strides over the past five years in its efforts to deliver quality services to its citizens. To highlight some of these achievements, it is running an advertising campaign in various media.

It focuses on:

- The tarring of roads, in particular in Soweto, where 232 km of roads were tarred over the past three years at a cost of Rand 74 million. In addition, the city maintains 30,000 km of roads annually.

- The upgrading of the water supply, namely that through Operation Gcin'amanzi the City has delivered water to and upgraded water supplies to 98 per cent of its households.

- Increasing the number of street lights – in the past five years the City has installed and upgraded 16,427 street lights, making it a safer place for all its citizens.

- Job creation, namely that in the past eight years more than 316,000 jobs have been created in Jo'burg, which is more than in any other major city in South Africa. In addition, while South Africa's economy has grown by 2.9 per cent since 1996, Jo'burg's has grown by a exceptional 4.5 per cent. Jo'burg is booming!

- The building of new and upgrading of existing parks – in the last five years Jo'burg has spent Rand 31 million on its parks. With more than 6 million trees, it is now the biggest man-made forest in the world, and the City employs more than 2,000 people to maintain these trees and parks every day.

- Increased metro police presence, which has risen by 331 per cent in the past five years.

- Housing – in the past five years the City has facilitated housing for 8,000 families.

Figure 16 Extract from the official Johannesburg website (www.joburg.org.za)

Activity

3 Study Figure 16. Explain how each of the initiatives described in the article has affected quality of life.

4 Explain why the Johannesburg City Council has done much more than just provide low-cost housing.

5 Write a 250-word newspaper article about urban improvement in South Africa. The article must have a positive point of view.

South Africa

Activity

1 Choose five techniques shown in Figure 17. For each technique explain how it either collects rain water or recharges groundwater.

2 Explain why this type of management is sustainable.

Are there alternative ways to manage South Africa's water?

South Africa has 539 large dams, which is almost half of all the dams in Africa. But despite this, there are still a large number of South Africans without access to clean drinking water. Many of these people live in rural, remote parts of South Africa; they are too isolated to become part of the big projects such as the LHWP and they are too poor to drill boreholes to tap into groundwater supplies. Instead they have to rely on cheap, small-scale methods of rainwater harvesting.

A case study of sustainable water management on a small farm

Ma Tshepo Khumbane is a South African farmer who teaches rainwater harvesting techniques. Her management strategies are affordable and practical for families, no matter how small the farm is or how little money they have.

Rainwater harvesting can be carried out by individual households or involve whole communities. These methods of water management are not usually big enough to have negative impacts on the surrounding drainage basin so they are sustainable. They use ways that are cheap, practical and easy to maintain using appropriate technology. A number of these techniques are shown in Figure 17; they are designed to:

- collect and use rainwater, for example, by collecting water from the roof of the farm
- maintain soil moisture by encouraging as much infiltration as possible; in this way groundwater stores are recharged.

Figure 17 Rainwater harvesting techniques used by Ma Tshepo Khumbane

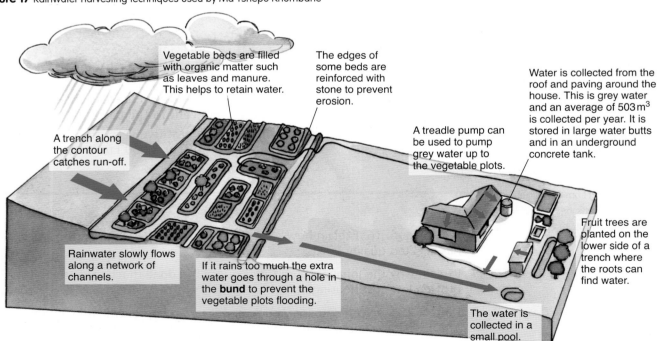

The village of Athol in Limpopo province is one community to have benefited from the teachings of Ma Tshepo Khumbane. In 1982 the community was struggling with drought and malnutrition. Despite having no regular access to water, the villagers of Athol have learned to manage their water sustainably by collecting rainwater and maintaining soil moisture. The villagers' next aim is to build a small stone dam to collect and store rainwater; this will provide a more secure water supply. They are appealing to the government to provide tractors to speed up the process.

Figure 18 Ma Tshepo Khumbane inspects vegetables growing in an earth basin. The good soil in the middle of each basin collects rainwater

Going further

Could South Africa harvest water from fog?

Fog has been 'harvested' to provide clean drinking water to isolated rural communities since 1987 when a scheme was set up in Chungungo, Chile. Since then, similar systems have been used successfully in Peru, Ecuador, Ethiopia and South Africa. It is another form of appropriate technology because it is relatively cheap to install and maintain. To collect water from fog, a simple system of fine-mesh nylon nets are suspended vertically between tall poles. The fog condenses on the net and drips into a gutter below. It then passes through sand before being piped to where it is needed.

Fog harvesting works best in in upland regions (at least 400m above sea level) that experience moist air being blown from the coast. As the air rises it condenses to form fog. So would fog harvesting work in Limpopo in South Africa? Most of Limpopo is over 1000m above sea level. Moist air from the Indian Ocean is blown inland by prevailing easterly winds. The first fog harvesting scheme was built at Tshanowa Primary School in Limpopo. All 130 school children used to bring bottled water to school every day. Now they drink pure water collected from fog. The nets cover an area of 72m² and produce, on average 180 litres of water a day.

It is not foggy every day.

The nets and poles are relatively cheap to buy.

Repairs are essential. Nets are easily torn in the wind.

Repairs are easy to make and require little training.

Ground water is contaminated.

Fog harvesting technology does not need any electrical energy.

Many rural areas do not have a piped supply from a reservoir.

Some of the foggiest sites are some distance from rural communities.

Figure 19 Advantages and disadvantages of fog harvesting in Limpopo

Activity

3 **a)** Use figure 19 to sort the advantages and disadvantages of fog harvesting.

   b) Based on the evidence in figure 19, explain why fog harvesting may be considered to be an appropriate technology for a poor rural community.

4 Research the fog harvesting systems in Chungungo and Tshanowa by typing the names into a search engine. To what extent has each scheme been a success?

http://www.weathersa.co.za/ is the website of the South African weather service. Click on the Limpopo link to find out how foggy it will be in the next 5 days. Or, scroll to the bottom of the home page to find recent rainfall maps.

River Mekong

A trans-boundary water issue

Many rivers cross from one country into another on their long journey to the sea. The River Mekong, for example, flows through six countries between its source in Yunan province in China and its mouth in the South China Sea. Each country relies on the river for water supply and for food. For example, fishermen in Cambodia catch about 2 million tonnes of fish a year from the river. It is thought that no other country on Earth relies so much on wild protein in its diet. But the fishermen in Cambodia are unhappy. They say that they catch fewer fish each year and that the fish that are caught are smaller. They blame a series of dams recently built in China.

Cambodia, in south-east Asia, has a tropical climate with a seasonal pattern of rainfall. Spring has low rainfall and drought and food shortages are possible. Then late summer is dominated by low pressure that usually brings heavy rainfall known as the monsoon. This can cause flooding on the River Mekong. The worst floods in recent years in Cambodia were in 2000 when 347 people were killed, 80 per cent of these were children. However, seasonal floods deposit fertile silt onto the flood plain and many farmers rely on these floods to water their rice crops. About 80 per cent of the rice production in the countries of the lower Mekong basin relies on these natural flood events.

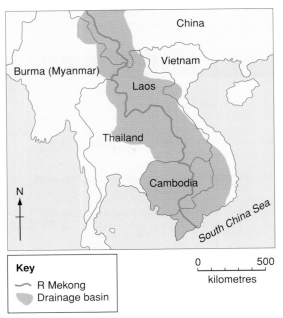

Figure 20 The location of the River Mekong and its river basin

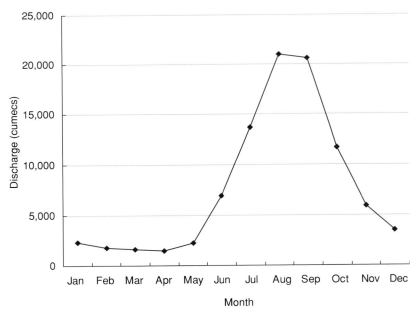

Figure 21 Hydrograph for the River Mekong, Cambodia (discharge in cubic metres per second)

Disaster	Date	Number affected (thousands)	People killed	Damage US$ (thousands)
Drought	June 1994	5,000		100,000
Flood	September 1996	1,310	59	3,542
Epidemic	April 1999	no data	56	
Flood	August 1999	536	7	500
Flood	October 1999	124		
Flood	July 2000	3,448	347	160,000
Flood	August 2001	1,669	56	15,000
Drought	January 2002	650		38,000
Flood	August 2002	1,470	29	100
Epidemic	February 2005	no data	7	
Drought	April 2005	600		
Flood	September 2005	no data	16	
Flood	August 2006	33	5	
Epidemic	July 2007	no data	182	

Figure 22 Disasters affecting Cambodia (1994–2007)

Figure 23 The River Mekong in this photo is brown because it is full of sediment. Many boatmen have noticed that sediment banks in the river are increasing in size. Some larger boats, such as ferries, are struggling to cross the river without running aground. Are dams in China responsible for this change?

Activity

1 Name the six countries that share the River Mekong.

2 Describe the pattern of river discharge on the River Mekong in Cambodia.

3 'Low to medium-sized floods are beneficial to living conditions in the region. Floods of higher magnitude cause devastation.' Explain the beginning of this government report.

4 Analyse the data in Figure 22.
   a) Total the number of people affected by each type of disaster. Which one has affected most people?
   b) How many people have been killed in floods since 1994 and what has been their economic cost?
   c) How does this compare with the numbers for other disasters?
   d) Plot a bar graph for the numbers affected by all disasters with time on the horizontal axis. Does your graph show any pattern?

Are dams the answer or the problem?

Dams certainly have benefits. The dams in China have been built to generate hydro-electric power (HEP) to feed power into China's fast-growing economy. Dams also reduce the risk of flooding. The dams built on the Mekong have evened out its flow and should reduce the size of the annual floods suffered in Cambodia and Vietnam. However, dams also have disadvantages. For example, the building of the Manwan dam (completed in 1993) displaced 25,000 people in China when their homes were flooded. So large dam projects create conflict between people who benefit and people who lose out when they are built. And dams on international rivers, like the Mekong, can create conflict between the different countries that are dependent on the water. Building a dam in one country alters the flow of water causing problems for people who live further downstream. So as more water is used in China, less

arrives in Cambodia and farmers are fearful that there will be insufficient water for a good rice harvest.

The Cambodian government feels that, as the country that is furthest downstream, it is most vulnerable to changes made to the river by other countries. It feels that river management upstream is affecting the frequency of floods, rates of sediment deposition and the fish population. The dams prevent migration and the number of fish making their annual journey downstream has been cut. The fishermen need the seasonal rise and fall in the river's flow because the fish spread out into the lakes and ponds of the flood plain during the flood season, where they are caught. The massive dams are evening out the seasonal ups and downs in the Mekong's pattern of discharge and reducing the overall size of the flood.

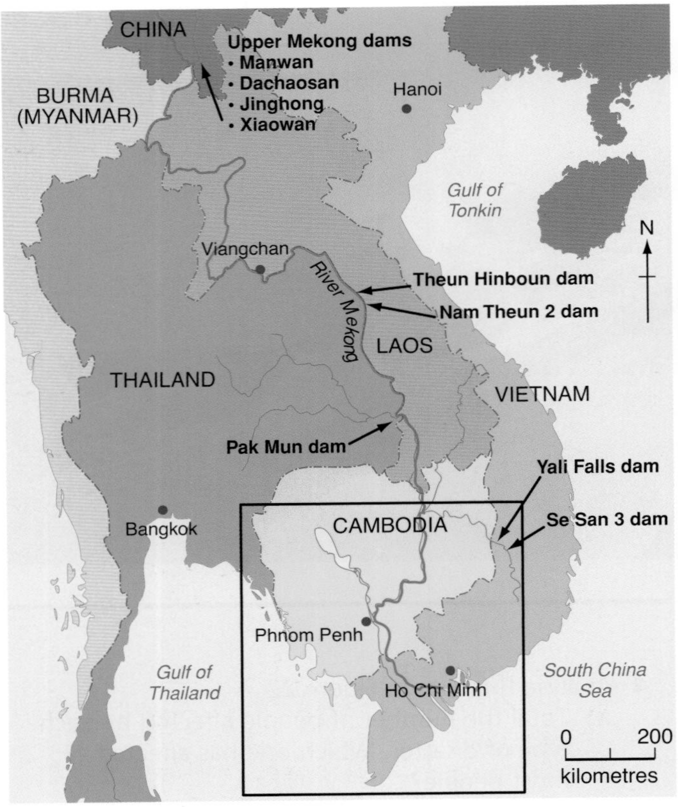

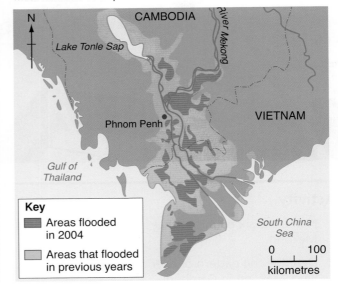

Figure 24 Major dam projects built or under construction on the River Mekong (the area of Figure 25 is shown by the box)

Figure 25 Flooding in Cambodia and Vietnam on the Mekong in 2004. 30,000 people had to leave their homes during the floods, which lasted for 59 days

How should the river be managed in the future?

Only Phnom Penh is protected by flood embankments. Most other towns are unprotected and rural families live in houses built on stilts. The government is having to consider a range of options in order to reduce the risk of both drought and flood.

a) Fund a flood control centre to collect data and issue forecasts

b) Assess flood risks in each community

c) Produce advice to householders on how to protect themselves

d) Build flood walls and embankments

e) Build small dams to hold back floodwater

f) Better land use planning so that homes are not built on flood plains

g) Start to talk to neighbouring governments about river management

h) Set up an annual flood conference where guests are invited from neighbouring countries

i) Assist neighbouring countries with aid during emergencies

Figure 26 Strategies used in Cambodia since 2005 to reduce flood and drought risk

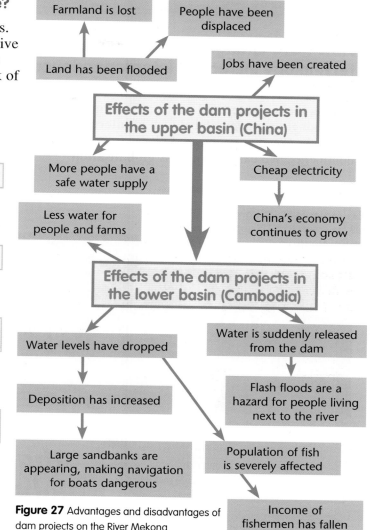

Figure 27 Advantages and disadvantages of dam projects on the River Mekong

---

Activity

1 Use Figures 24 and 25 to describe the location of the:
   a) Pak Mun dam
   b) mouth of the Mekong.

2 Describe the distribution of the dams on the Mekong River and its tributaries.

3 **a)** Describe the location of the floods in 2004.
   b) Suggest how building more dams in the future might reduce the risk of flooding.

4 Study Figures 24 and 27.
   a) What are the advantages of building more dams on the Mekong?
   b) Explain why some countries benefit from these dams more than others.

   c) Do you think Thailand should complete the Pak Mun dam? Explain the advantages and disadvantages that this dam is likely to create.

5 Discuss Figure 26.
   a) Sort the strategies into short-term and long-term responses.
   b) How many of these do you think will help Cambodia deal with the international dimension of its problem?
   c) Suggest how international co-operation between the six countries on the Mekong could reduce the risk of flooding:
      i) in the short term
      ii) in the long term.

How have changes in business and technology increased interdependence?

This theme is about the global economy. Flows of people, ideas, money and goods are making an increasingly complex global web of **interdependence** that links together people and places from distant continents. We call this process **globalisation**.

Figure 1 The factors that drive globalisation

Example: avocados grown in Mexico will be flown to a UK supermarket. This improves customer choice but food air miles have an impact on carbon emissions.

Example: local people demonstrating about the falling water levels in their wells after this soft-drinks company opened a bottling plant in Kerala, India.

Multinational companies: Large companies open branches in several different countries throughout the world.

Trade: Improved technology and cheap aviation fuel mean that fresh food can be flown from distant places to our supermarkets.

The factors that drive globalisation

Ideas and communication: The growth of communication technology such as the internet, mobile phones and satellite television has vastly improved global interdependence.

Culture: Certain styles of music, television and film are now shown around the world.

Example: films made in Hollywood, USA, advertised in an Asian street. But will local styles of music and entertainment survive?

Activity

1 Outline how India benefits from greater interdependence.

2 Use Figure 2.
   a) Compare the rise in mobile phone ownership in India and China.
   b) Compare mobile phone ownership in India and Japan.
   c) The population in China is only slightly larger than India. Japan has a population of only 127 million. Predict how the mobile phone market might change in the future in these three countries?

3 Using Figure 2 for ideas, create a display for your classroom that shows how India is connected to the rest of the world. You should include at least one map or graph. You could also use a search engine to find images of Indian products and brand names.

India

How have newly industrialised countries such as India and China benefited from globalisation?

Newly industrialised countries (NICs) such as India and China have benefited from globalisation with economic growth, due to the interdependence in the global economy. Their economies have benefited from recent technological changes and from the interdependence created by flows of people, ideas and investment.

Rank	Forbes 2000 list (2008)	Number of companies
1	USA	598
2	Japan	259
3	United Kingdom	123
4	China (inc. Hong Kong)	109
5	France	67
6	Canada	59
7	Germany	59
8	South Korea	52
9	Australia	51
10	India	48

Rank	Country of birth of resident UK population	Population in thousands
1	India	613
2	Republic of Ireland	420
3	Poland	405
4	Pakistan	377
5	Germany	266
6	Bangladesh	205
7	South Africa	201
8	United States of America	188
9	Jamaica	166
10	Nigeria	140

Foreign investments Indian-owned multinational companies, like Tata, are very successful in the world economy. In 2008 India was ranked 10th country in the world by Forbes 2000, which lists the location of the world's biggest 2000 companies.

Flows of people Indian migrants work in many other parts of the world, earning money and learning new skills that can be re-invested in the Indian economy. For example, 613,000 people who were born in India currently live and work in the UK.

Improved communication technologies India has excellent universities and good communication networks. It produces thousands of IT and software graduates each year. One example of India's growing demand for consumer items is the rapid growth of mobile phone ownership.

Examples of India's interdependence with the world economy

Flows of ideas and culture The Hindi movie industry based in Mumbai (known as Bollywood) produced 267 films in 2007. These films are extremely popular in South Asia and, with the growth of satellite TV, are now easily accessible in other parts of the world. Their growing popularity led to a stage show, *The Merchants of Bollywood*, which toured successfully in Europe and Australia.

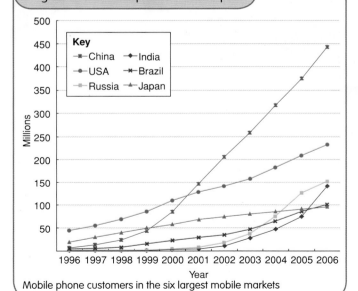

Mobile phone customers in the six largest mobile markets

Ashwini Iyer practises her routine at a rehearsal of the production of *The Merchants of Bollywood* in Maharastra before the show moved to Europe

Figure 2 Examples of India's interdependence with the world economy

How has growing interdependence affected India?

India is the second largest country in the world after China. Its population of 1,132 million people is 17 per cent (or one in six) of the global population. The Indian economy has grown quickly in recent years along with Brazil, Russia, China and Mexico (**BRICM**). As Indians gradually become wealthier they are creating new demand for products. One reason for India's economic growth is due to its interdependence in the global community. Its economy has benefited from recent technological changes and from the interdependence created by flows of people, ideas and investment.

Case study of Tata

Tata is an Indian multinational company that in 2007–8 earned US$62.5 billion of which 61 per cent was from its business outside India. Tata employs 350,000 people worldwide. It owns a large number of businesses, which include steel makers, car manufacturers, chemicals, energy and a hotel chain. Tata owns 38 companies based in the UK which between them employ a total of 47,000 people. Among the most famous brand names employing UK workers are Jaguar, Land Rover and Tetley Tea.

Early in 2008 Tata announced that it was making the world's cheapest mass-produced car. Called the Tata Nano, this small car is expected to sell for just 120,000 rupees which is only £1,400. Incomes in India are much lower than in the UK. For example, a secondary teacher with less than 10 years' experience earns an average of 128,900 rupees (£1,670) a year. So the announcement of an affordable car was treated with excitement in India where car ownership is low.

Tata plans to keep the production costs for the Nano as low as possible by sourcing its parts from India where labour costs are very cheap. As many as 97 per cent of the components used in the car will be provided by European multinational companies who have factories in India. In 2008, about 2 million cars were produced in India but none are as cheap as the Nano.

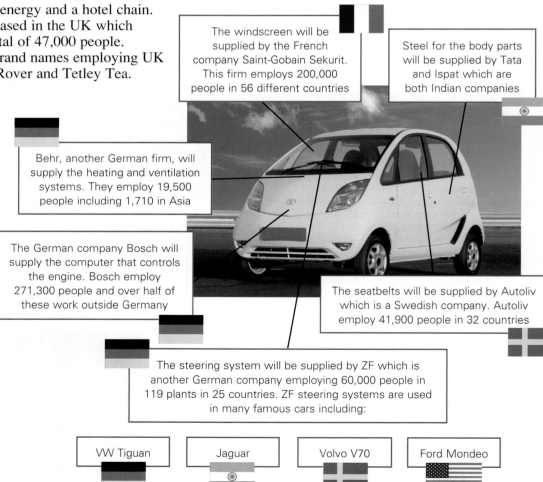

The windscreen will be supplied by the French company Saint-Gobain Sekurit. This firm employs 200,000 people in 56 different countries

Steel for the body parts will be supplied by Tata and Ispat which are both Indian companies

Behr, another German firm, will supply the heating and ventilation systems. They employ 19,500 people including 1,710 in Asia

The German company Bosch will supply the computer that controls the engine. Bosch employ 271,300 people and over half of these work outside Germany

The seatbelts will be supplied by Autoliv which is a Swedish company. Autoliv employ 41,900 people in 32 countries

The steering system will be supplied by ZF which is another German company employing 60,000 people in 119 plants in 25 countries. ZF steering systems are used in many famous cars including:

| VW Tiguan | Jaguar | Volvo V70 | Ford Mondeo |

Figure 3 The new Tata Nano that will sell for around £1,400

Flag indicates ownership of company. Each car may be made in a different country e.g. Jaguar is made in the UK

What are the advantages and disadvantages of the growth of Tata?

Some groups in India oppose the growth of global companies like Tata and have protested against the Nano and plans to build a new factory. The Nano was going to be built in Singur, West Bengal. Twenty of the firms who supply parts for the car were also going to build new factories here. Between them they would have created hundreds of skilled and semi-skilled jobs in this poor region. The local government supported the new development, but after violent opposition in the summer of 2008, Tata decided to pull out. The car is now likely to be built in Maharastra state in western India.

Ratan Tata, Chairman of Tata Motors

I decided to build the Tata Nano some years ago when I observed families riding on two wheelers, the father driving a scooter, his young kid standing in front of him, his wife sitting behind him holding a baby. Surely these families deserve a safe, affordable, all-weather form of transport. A vehicle that could be affordable and low cost enough to be within everyone's reach. Built to meet all safety standards, be low in pollution and high in fuel efficiency.

India's cities are already congested with cars, buses and auto-rickshaws. A cheap car will be very popular and will add substantially to the congestion problem. Exhaust emissions will cause air quality to fall leading to even more health problems for poor people in our cities.

Indian environmentalist

Farm labourer from West Bengal

I protested against the decision to build the Tata factory here along with over 15,000 other people. Three quarters of local people are farmers: we have no experience of working in factories. We argued that the loss of our land would have led to hunger and malnutrition. The state government offered some compensation but it wasn't enough. Women like me would have been worst affected. I have no legal papers for my smallholding so I wouldn't have got any compensation at all.

Tata will produce about 250,000 Nanos per year at first. Demand for the Nano from other developing countries will be huge so Tata expect production to expand to 1 million cars a year. Some of these will be built in India and the rest in other LEDCs. The European companies that are providing the parts are excited about the prospect of their business expanding into more LEDC car markets.

Chairman of Bosch

Figure 4 The advantages and disadvantages of growth at Tata

Activity

1 How might the Tata Nano benefit lower income families?

2 Suggest the possible effect of the Tata Nano on:
   a) India's city streets
   b) levels of pollution in Indian cities.

3 a) Use Figure 4 to explain why some of the people in West Bengal object to the Tata Nano factory.

   b) Use the case study of Tata to complete the following table.

	Benefits for India created by Tata's success	Problems for India created by Tata's success
Economic		
Environmental		
Social		

India

Foreign investment in India

Coca-Cola first opened a bottling plant in India in 1993. Coca-Cola invested US$1,000 million in their Indian business between 1993 and 2003. In 2008 the company employed 6,000 people in India. They claim that a further 125,000 people have indirectly benefited from such jobs as distribution (i.e. lorry drivers who deliver the bottles).

Coca-Cola is one of many foreign owned multinationals that have invested in India in recent years. These investments are further examples of interdependence because money spent by, in this case, an American company is creating jobs in a different part of the world. However, some Indian protest groups are unhappy with the way in which big businesses operate. They claim that big business ignores the needs of poorer communities and disadvantaged groups (like the farmers in West Bengal who would have lost their jobs had Tata built its new factory). In the case of Coca-Cola there have been numerous protests against the soft drinks firm. Most protests have been by local people who claim that their wells are running dry as the drinks company takes water out of the ground for production of the cola. Some have also complained about pollution from the factories. Coca-Cola deny that they have caused any such problems and are trying hard to win over local people by getting involved in local community aid projects.

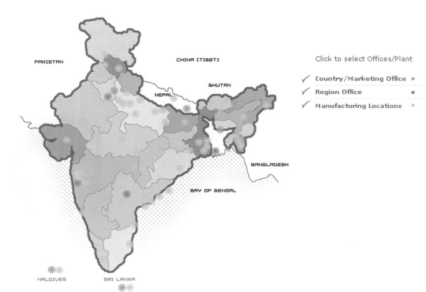

key location

Figure 5 Map of Coca-Cola plants in South Asia

Figure 6 Local people protesting about falling water levels in their wells after Coca-Cola opened a bottling plant in Kerala, India

www.coca–colaindia.com
This is the site of Coca-Cola India. The site has information about its management of water. Read both sides of the issue and make up your own mind where you stand.

Campaign to Hold Coca-Cola Accountable
Coca-Cola Crisis in India

Communities across India are under assault from Coca-Cola practices in the country. A pattern has emerged as a result of Coca-Cola's bottling operations in India.

- Communities across India living around Coca-Cola's bottling plants are experiencing severe water shortages, directly as a result of Coca-Cola's massive extraction of water from the common groundwater resource. The wells have run dry and the hand water-pumps do not work any more. Studies, including one by the Central Ground Water Board in India, have confirmed the significant depletion of the water table.

- When the water is extracted from the common groundwater resource by digging deeper, the water smells and tastes strange. Coca-Cola has been indiscriminately discharging its waste water into the fields around its plant and sometimes into rivers, including the Ganges, in the area. The result has been that the groundwater has been polluted as well as the soil. Public health authorities have posted signs around wells and hand pumps advising the community that the water is unfit for human consumption.

- In two communities, Plachimada and Mehdiganj, Coca-Cola was distributing its solid waste to farmers in the area as 'fertilizer'. Tests conducted by the BBC found cadmium and lead in the waste, effectively making the waste toxic. Coca-Cola stopped the practice of distributing its toxic waste only when ordered to do so by the state government.

- Tests conducted by a variety of agencies, including the government of India, confirmed that Coca-Cola products contained high levels of pesticides, and as a result, the Parliament of India has banned the sale of Coca-Cola in its cafeteria. However, Coca-Cola not only continues to sell drinks laced with poisons in India (that could never be sold in the US and EU), it is also introducing new products in the Indian market. And as if selling drinks with DDT and other pesticides to Indians was not enough, one of Coca-Cola's latest bottling facilities to open in India, in Ballia, is located in an area with a severe contamination of arsenic in its groundwater.

Figure 7 Web extract from India Resource Centre – an organisation that campaigns on behalf of local communities against big companies

Activity

1 Describe the distribution of Coca-Cola manufacturing locations in India.

2 Suggest what benefits are created by foreign multinationals locating in India for:
   a) local people
   b) the multinational company.

3 Outline three different objections that Indian communities have had with local bottling plants.

4 From what you have learned about Tata and Coca-Cola, summarise the advantages and disadvantages of interdependence for India.

Figure 8 Martin Luther King, the black American civil rights campaigner

How have patterns of trade hindered economic progress in the least developed countries?

Speaking in the 1960s, Martin Luther King (Figure 8) reminds us that countries rely on each other for the goods and services that we all need for our daily lives. Since then, faster aircraft, larger ships, and the use of standard-sized containers for moving goods around the world have all contributed to making us rely even more on trade with other countries for our everyday needs.

Goods produced in one country and then sold abroad are **exports.** The goods that a country buys from abroad are **imports.** Countries also buy and sell services.

Comparing the UK and Ghana's trade

Shop in the local supermarket and you can buy a chocolate bar made from cocoa beans grown in Ghana. Ghana doesn't make much chocolate, but it does export a lot of beans and the European Union is its biggest customer. At the same time, people shopping in the supermarkets of Accra, Ghana's capital city, can buy tinned tomatoes or frozen chicken produced in the European Union. Ghana and the European Union trade with each other but, of course, they both trade with a lot of other countries as well.

Ghana imports a lot of manufactured goods whereas a lot of Ghana's exports are raw materials that haven't been processed – like cocoa beans. The UK, by comparison, exports a huge range of different processed and manufactured goods.

Activity

1 Discuss Figure 8 with a partner. What do you think Martin Luther King meant?
   a) Make a list of all the things you have used by breakfast.
   b) Suggest which countries might export these items to the UK.
   c) Using the internet, research the main exporters of breakfast items such as coffee, tea and fresh orange juice.

2 Use Figure 9. Compare Ghana's trade with that of the UK. Pick out the main similarities and differences using connectives:

   whereas   similarly   on the other hand

3 Use the evidence in Figure 10 to explain the advantage of quotas and subsidies for:
   a) consumers in Europe
   b) farmers and businesses in Europe.

4 Explain the likely effect of:
   a) the EU shoe quota for workers in Vietnam
   b) the import of cheap food for farmers in Ghana.

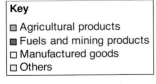

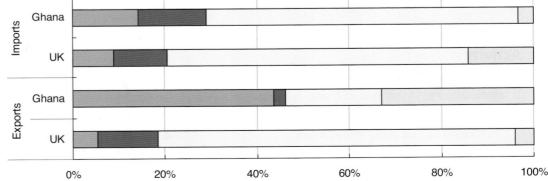

Key
- Agricultural products
- Fuels and mining products
- Manufactured goods
- Others

Figure 9 Comparing the trade of Ghana and the UK by type of import and export (percentage figures)

Should trade be free and uncontrolled?

Free trade, or trade that takes place without any limits or control, is the aim of many countries. The advantage of free trade is that a country can export as many goods as it wants to its trade partners. This is good for the farmers and businesses who produce the exported goods and services. The disadvantage of free trade is that a country can find itself swamped by cheap imports made in countries that have lower labour costs. These cheap imports are good for consumers, but could cause jobs to be lost in similar industries within the importing country. To avoid this problem some countries protect themselves from cheap products. They can do this in one of three ways:

- Placing **quotas** that restrict the amount of these imported goods each year.
- Placing an **import duty** or tax on the imports to make them more expensive.
- Paying a **subsidy** to its own farmers and businesses so that their goods can be sold at a lower price to consumers.

The EU imports billions of pairs of shoes from China and Vietnam. Half of the 2.5 million pairs of shoes sold in the EU were made in China.

Farmers in the EU receive government subsidy to keep the cost of production low so that food is cheap for consumers in Europe. Some of this food is then exported to Africa.

Local farmers find it hard to sell their own tomatoes on this market in Accra, Ghana. Imports of frozen chicken, rice and tinned tomatoes (subsidised in the EU) are cheaper than local food.

EUROPEAN UNION

CHINA

GHANA

In 2006, the EU placed a quota to restrict the number of shoes imported from Asia into Europe. It did this to protect the jobs of 850,000 people working in shoe manufacturing in Italy and elsewhere in the EU. However, the effect on low-paid workers in China and Vietnam could be disastrous.

Ghana's second most important source of foreign exchange comes from the export of cocoa beans. Most are sold to chocolate manufacturers in Europe and the USA.

Prices for primary commodities such as cocoa fluctuate up and down, making it hard for cocoa farmers to plan the growth of their business or even earn a decent wage. The average wage for a cocoa farmer in Ghana is just £160 a year.

Figure 10 The problems created by the international pattern of trade

Ghana and the cocoa trade

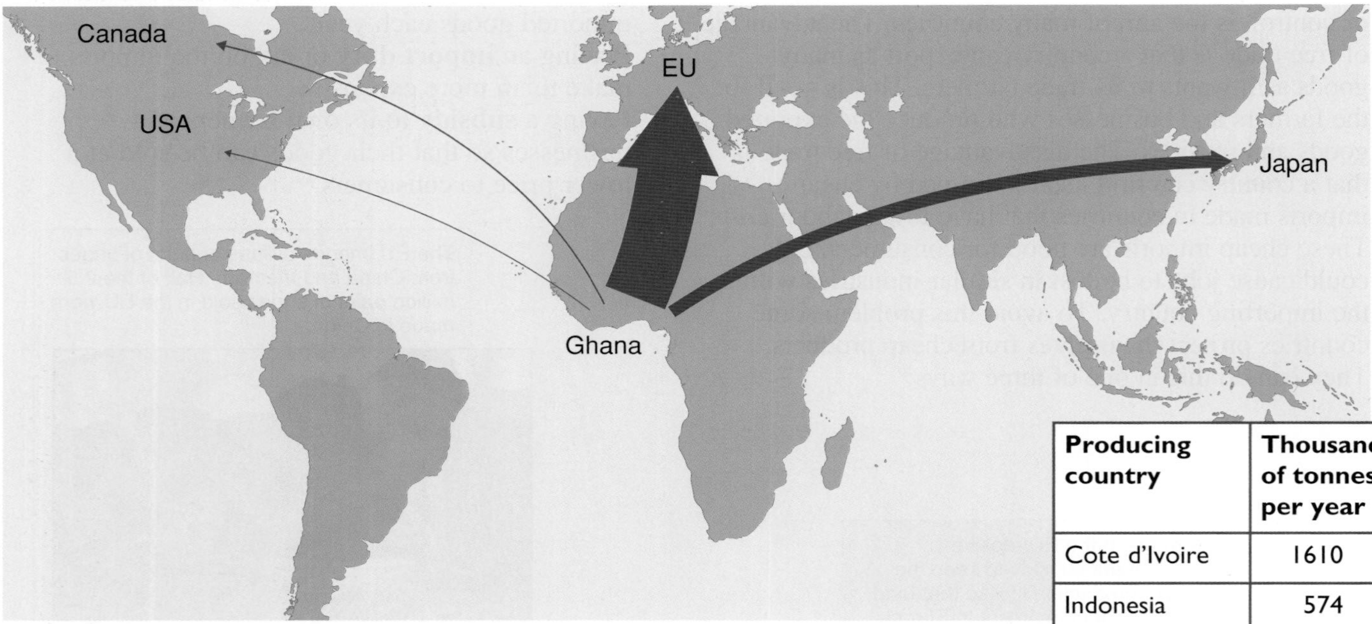

Figure 11 Typical flow of exports of cocoa from Ghana

Almost 90 per cent of all of Ghana's cocoa is grown on smallholdings: tiny farms that are smaller than 3 hectares. About 2.5 million smallholders in Ghana grow cocoa as their main crop. Most of the cocoa is sold for export; only about 5 per cent of Ghana's cocoa crop is processed into chocolate in Ghana.

Currently about 75 per cent of Ghana's cocoa beans are exported to the European Union. The main importing countries are the Netherlands, Germany, Belgium and France. The beans are ground into cocoa powder in these countries. Some of this powder is then exported to other EU countries where the chocolate is made. The main producers of chocolate are in Belgium, Germany, Ireland, the UK and Austria.

The production of cocoa beans goes up and down from year to year. Production depends on a number of factors such as weather conditions, pests and diseases. Figure 14 shows how production (supply) has fluctuated over a ten-year period. Most cocoa beans are processed into cocoa powder (known as grindings) before being used in the manufacture of chocolate. Figure 14 shows how demand for cocoa grindings has changed over the same period. When demand is higher than supply (as in 2007) the price for cocoa bean exports is high.

Producing country	Thousands of tonnes per year
Cote d'Ivoire	1610
Indonesia	574
Ghana	490
Nigeria	212
Brazil	180
Cameroon	129
Ecuador	94
Papua New Guinea	45
Dominican Rep.	44
Malaysia	43
Mexico	37
Colombia	27

Figure 12 The world's top cocoa producers, expected production in 2010

Activity

1 Use Figure 11 to complete the following statement:

   All of Ghana's cocoa exports are sold in LEDCs /MEDCs. ... is the largest buyer of Ghana's cocoa.

2 Use Figure 12.
   a) Choose a suitable technique to illustrate the data.
   b) Compare the amount of cocoa grown in Ghana with that grown in other countries.
   c) If the EU imports more cocoa from other African producers, what would happen to the price of Ghana's cocoa?

One major problem for cocoa growers is that the price they get for their crop is so low. The average income for a cocoa farmer is only about £160 a year. This is because of the way in which primary commodities such as cocoa beans are traded on the world market. Traders in Europe buy cocoa beans on the London Stock Exchange. They shop around and buy the beans from whichever supplier is cheapest. It's a buyer's market. If Ghana's farmers are asking too much for their beans, the buyers will shop around and buy from Côte d'Ivoire or whoever is cheapest. The price can go up or down from day to day, depending on supply and demand. Figure 12 shows that the EU buyers can purchase cocoa from a number of suppliers, but Ghana relies heavily on the EU for selling its cocoa. This fluctuating price makes it very difficult for farmers in Ghana to earn a fair wage for all of their work.

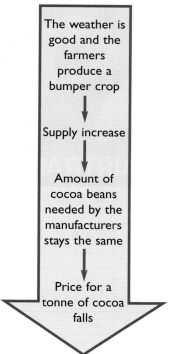

Figure 13 Supply and demand

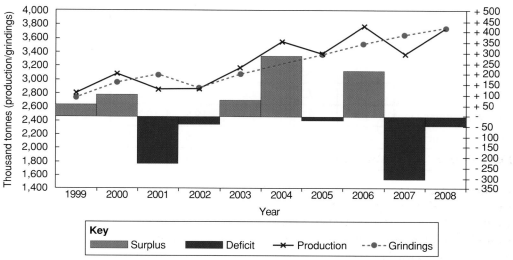

Figure 14 Production (supply) and grindings (demand) of cocoa over a ten-year period.

Activity

3   Study Figure 13. Make a similar flow chart which starts with the following statement:

A disease in many cocoa plantations means that the harvest is poor.

4   **a)** Describe the trend in production over the ten-year period.
    b) Using your understanding of supply and demand, predict in which years the price of cocoa would have been highest and lowest.

5   Look at Figure 15. Suggest what will happen to the price of cocoa beans on the world market for each of these future scenarios.

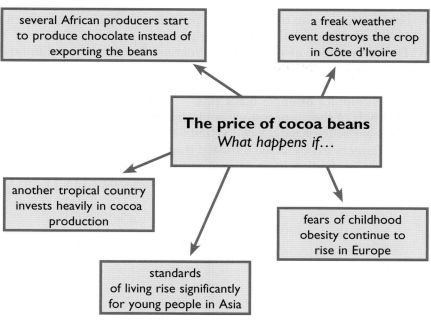

Figure 15 A futures wheel for cocoa

Fair trade

The concept of fair trade has been around for more than 30 years. The Fairtrade Foundation was established in 1992 as an independent certification body that licenses the FAIRTRADE Mark to products that meet international standards that are set by Fairtrade Labelling Organisations International (FLO).

The FAIRTRADE Mark guarantees a better deal for farmers and workers in developing countries so that they can enjoy a better standard of living.

- The farmer receives a payment that is agreed and stable.
- The farmer also receives an additional payment called a **Fairtrade Premium**.
- One of the many aims of Fairtrade is to develop a long-term trading partnership with the producers.

Figure 17 The Fairtrade Mark

	2002	2003	2004	2005	2006	2007	2008	2009	2010	2011
Coffee	23.1	34.3	49.3	65.8	93	117	137.3	160	179.8	194.3
Tea	7.2	9.5	12.9	16.6	25.1	30	64.8	70.3	82.6	86.7
Cocoa products	3.9	7.3	9.6	13.2	16.4	25.6	25.6	44.5	162	217.1
Sugar products	5.7	8.7	14.3	19.5	23.7	50.6	107.7	164.6	384	464.1
Honey products	4.9	6.1	3.4	3.5	3.4	2.7	5.2	3.6	6.8	4.1
Bananas	17.3	24.3	30.6	47.7	65.6	150	184.6	215.5	206.6	208
Flowers	n/a	n/a	4.3	5.7	14	24	33.4	30	27.6	26.3

Figure 16 Estimated UK sales of selected Fairtrade certified products in the UK (£ millions)

The Kuapa Kokoo co-operative of cocoa farmers

www.kuapako
koogh.com
is a website
describing the
co-operative.

Kuapa Kokoo is a co-operative of cocoa farmers in Ghana. The co-operative sells part of its cocoa bean crop to Divine Chocolate Ltd. in the UK who make Fairtrade chocolate products such as Divine and Dubble. The main benefits of this arrangement are:

- Farmers receive an extra US$150 per tonne for their cocoa which is about 10 per cent more than the usual price on the world market.
- The co-operative also receives a Premium that is then used to fund community projects such as the well in Figure 26. 18
- Farmers receive training to help them deal with problems such as pests or diseases that affect the cocoa crop, for example black pod.
- Members of the co-operative can borrow small amounts of money from a micro-credit bank, which is known as the Kuapa Kokoo Credit Union.
- The farmers have elected a trusted member of the village to weigh and record their cocoa beans. This makes trading more official and people more accountable.
- Kuapa Kokoo are shareholders in Divine Chocolate Ltd. Profits from the sale of chocolate bars are invested in projects in Ghana.

Activity

1 **a)** Use the data in Figure 16 to draw line graphs that show the changing number of sales of Fairtrade certified products in the UK.
   b) Compare the trends on your graphs. Which products have been most successful? Suggest the reasons why there has been a growth in the sale of Fairtrade products.

2 Make some notes to show how Fairtrade has helped:
   a) cocoa famers who belong to Kuapa Kokoo
   b) the wider community.

3 Use Figure 19 to make a sketch map of Ghana. Label it using Figure 20 to show how different regions have benefited from Fairtrade.

Figure 18 The Premium is used by the producers for community projects such as this village well

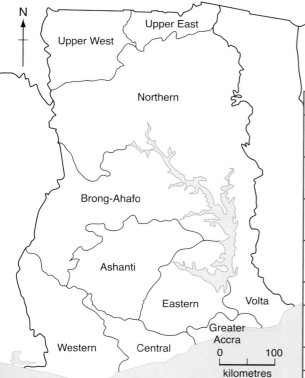

Figure 19 Where cocoa is grown in Ghana

Project	Number of projects in different regions					Total
	Western	Central	Eastern	Brong Ahafo	Ashanti	
Boreholes/ hand dug well	121	11	6	9	27	174
Women's project IGA	1	0	0	0	0	1
School/ education	0	1	1	0	2	4
Corn mills	10	4	3	2	8	27
Construction of latrines	0	0	0	0	2	2
Bridge	0	0	0	0	1	1
Total	**132**	**16**	**10**	**11**	**40**	**209**

Figure 20 How Kuapa Kokoo used the Social Premium, 1993 to 2002

What progress is being made towards achieving the Millennium Development Goals?

The United Nations (UN) is an international organisation supported by 192 different countries. One of the UN's aims is to encourage and assist human development. In 2000, the UN set eight development targets known as the **Millennium Development Goals (MDGs).** The goals use data to measure the development of every country since 1990. The challenge is to meet all of the goals by 2015. The MDGs are described in Figure 21.

P.H.

1 End extreme poverty and hunger:
- Halve the number of people living on less than a dollar a day.
- Halve the number who suffer from hunger.

PE

2 Achieve universal primary education:
- Ensure that all boys and girls complete a full course of primary schooling.

GE

3 Promote gender equality:
- Make it easier for girls as well as boys to access primary and secondary education.

CM

4 Reduce child mortality:
- Reduce by two-thirds the number of children who die before their fifth birthday.

HM

5 Improve health for mothers:
- Reduce by three-quarters the number of women who die in childbirth.

6 Combat AIDS, malaria and other diseases:
- Halt and begin to reverse the spread of these killer diseases.

7 Ensure environmental sustainability:
- Protect the environment, so that future generations can continue to benefit from it.
- Halve the number of people without access to clean water.
- Improve life for 100 million people who live in shanty towns by 2020.

8 Build global partnerships for development:
- Make improvements to aid.
- Boost freedom, justice and democracy.
- Make it easier for the poorest people to have access to medicines.
- Cancel some debts and reduce others.
- Make world trade fairer.

Activity

Use Figure 22.

1 **a)** What was the under fives' mortality rate in sub-Saharan Africa in:
   i) 1990?
   ii) 2006?
   b) What is the target?

2 **a)** What was the ratio of girls to boys in secondary education in South Asia in:
   i) 1990?
   ii) 2006?
   b) What is the target?

3 Which regions are most likely to:
   a) reach both goals
   b) fail to reach both goals
   c) reach only one goal?

Figure 21 The eight Millennium Development Goals

Goal 3: Ratio of girls to boys in secondary school (%)

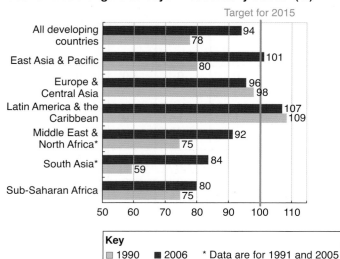

Goal 4: Under 5 mortality rate (per 1,000)

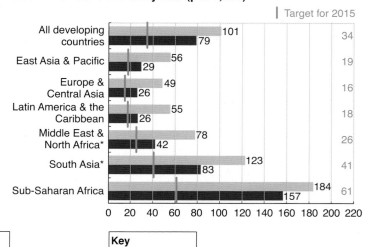

Figure 22 Progress towards goals 3 and 4 MDGs

GIS Activity: World Bank

http://devdata.worldbank.org/atlas–mdg

This interactive world map allows you to check on the progress made towards the MDGs of regions or countries.

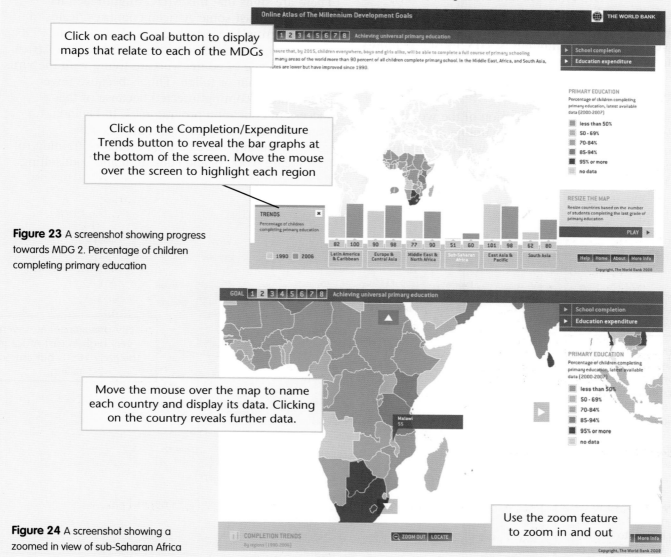

Click on each Goal button to display maps that relate to each of the MDGs

Click on the Completion/Expenditure Trends button to reveal the bar graphs at the bottom of the screen. Move the mouse over the screen to highlight each region

Figure 23 A screenshot showing progress towards MDG 2. Percentage of children completing primary education

Move the mouse over the map to name each country and display its data. Clicking on the country reveals further data.

Use the zoom feature to zoom in and out

Figure 24 A screenshot showing a zoomed in view of sub-Saharan Africa

Activity

1 a) Describe the distribution of countries in Africa that have:
   i)   less than 50 per cent
   ii) more than 95 per cent
   of children completing primary education.
b) Suggest why this is a useful measure of a country's development.

2 a) Use this GIS site to investigate global patterns of:
   i)   child mortality
   ii) immunisation
   iii) maternal (mother) mortality.
b) What are the similarities and differences in these patterns?

6 MDG 6 Combating HIV

Millennium Development Goal 6 has set the target of reversing the spread of HIV, malaria and other diseases by 2015. These diseases result in an early death for millions of people. They are also a major cause of poverty in many communities. HIV most commonly infects people of working age. Deaths among the work force not only cause distress for families but also reduce the earning power of the family.

Sub-Saharan Africa is the region of the world that has been hardest hit by HIV, an incurable disease that attacks the immune system and which eventually leads to AIDS. In 2007, it is estimated that 1.5 million sub-Saharan Africans died of AIDS and more than 11 million AIDS orphans were living in these African countries.

There are signs that this MDG might reach its target in at least some African countries. Rates of infection from HIV reached a peak in the late 1990s. Since then, in most countries of sub-Saharan Africa, the percentage of adults who are living with the virus has levelled out or fallen. This is because fewer people are becoming infected because of the success of education programmes. In Uganda, for example, HIV infection rates fell when the government introduced a programme of training for health care workers and education and counselling for the public.

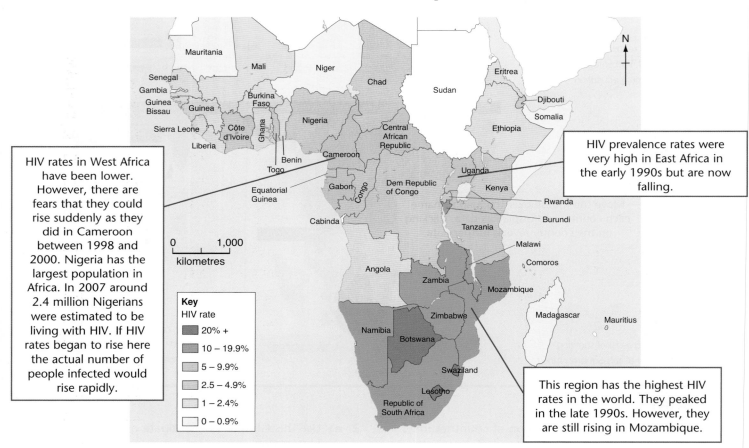

Figure 25 HIV prevalence rate (2007) in sub-Saharan Africa (percentage of adults aged 15–49 who are HIV positive)

Activity

1 Use Figure 25 to describe the distribution of countries with an HIV prevalence rate:
   a) below 2.5 per cent
   b) higher than 10 per cent
   c) higher than 20 per cent.

2 Explain why a slight increase in HIV infections in Nigeria would cause concern.

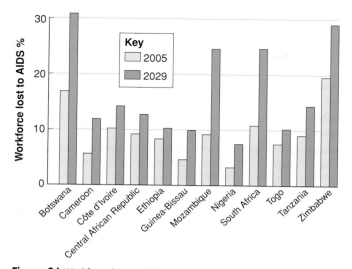

Figure 26 Workforce lost to AIDS in 2005 and estimated for 2029

Activity

3 Explain the links between HIV/AIDS and poverty. Use Figures 26 and 27 to provide evidence for your explanation.

4 a) Choose a suitable graphical technique to process the data in Figure 28.
b) Describe the trends shown on your graphs.
c) Use your graphs and Figure 25 to compare trends in East Africa and Southern Africa.
d) Use your graph to predict what could happen to each country by 2015.

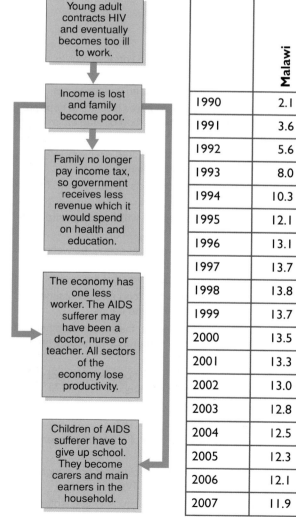

Figure 27 The social and economic consequences of HIV

	Malawi	Mozambique	Uganda	Lesotho	Nigeria	Ghana	South Africa
1990	2.1	1.4	13.7	0.8	0.7	0.1	0.8
1991	3.6	1.8	13.8	1.5	1.0	0.1	1.2
1992	5.6	2.3	13.5	3.1	1.2	0.3	1.9
1993	8.0	2.9	13.1	5.7	1.5	0.7	2.9
1994	10.3	3.7	12.5	9.7	1.9	1.3	4.4
1995	12.1	4.5	11.8	14.2	2.2	1.8	6.2
1996	13.1	5.5	11.1	18.3	2.5	2.2	8.4
1997	13.7	6.5	10.5	21.1	2.7	2.4	10.6
1998	13.8	7.6	9.8	22.8	2.9	2.5	12.8
1999	13.7	8.6	9.1	23.6	3.0	2.4	14.5
2000	13.5	9.5	8.5	23.9	3.1	2.4	15.9
2001	13.3	10.3	7.9	23.9	3.2	2.3	16.9
2002	13.0	11.0	7.4	23.8	3.2	2.2	17.6
2003	12.8	11.5	6.9	23.7	3.2	2.2	17.9
2004	12.5	11.9	6.5	23.6	3.2	2.1	18.1
2005	12.3	12.2	6.1	23.4	3.2	2.0	18.2
2006	12.1	12.3	5.7	23.3	3.1	2.0	18.2
2007	11.9	12.5	5.4	23.2	3.1	1.9	18.1

Figure 28 Trends in HIV prevalence rates (1990–2007)

Glossary

A

Abrasion – Erosion, or wearing away, of the landscape caused by friction. Abrasion occurs when rivers or waves are carrying sand or pebbles. The water uses these materials to do the work of erosion.

Abstraction – When people remove water from either a surface or groundwater store.

Acid rain – Unnaturally acidic rain caused by a high concentration of certain pollutants (especially nitrogen dioxide and sulphur dioxide) in the atmosphere.

Active layer – The upper layer of soil in tundra regions. This layer thaws during the short summer. Buildings may subside as the active layer thaws and moves.

Adult literacy – The percentage of the adult population who can read and write.

Affordable homes – Houses that are either sold or rented at relatively low cost.

Agri-business – Farming combined with commercial activities to maximise production and profits.

Air mass – A large parcel of air in the atmosphere. All parts of the air mass have similar temperature and moisture content at ground level.

Anticyclone – A high pressure system in the atmosphere associated with dry, settled periods of weather.

Aquifer – A large store of underground water usually contained in porous rocks.

Aspect – The direction in which a slope or other feature faces.

Atmosphere – The layer of gases surrounding the earth. The atmosphere is one store in the water cycle.

Attrition – A type of erosion where rocks smash against each other making them smaller and more rounded.

Average life expectancy – The average age to which people can expect to live.

B

Backwash – The flow of water back into the sea after a wave has broken on a beach.

Barrier reef – A long structure in the sea, parallel to the coast, built of limestone by millions of corals.

Baseflow – The normal flow rate of a river caused by groundwater flow.

Beach replenishment – Adding extra sand or gravel to a beach to make it wider and thicker.

Biodiversity – The variety of living things.

Biodiversity hotspot – A region with a particularly great variety of organisms. Central America (or Meso-America) is one such hotspot.

Biofuel – Fuel used in transport or for heating homes that is made from plant material instead of fossil fuel (oil).

Biofuel crops – Crops, such as jatropha, which are grown for their oil content.

Biomes – Very large ecosystems e.g. tropical rainforests or deserts.

Braided – A river pattern made when a shallow river has deposited gravel islands so that the river is split into several smaller channels. From above the river looks a little like plaited (or braided) hair.

Brain drain – The reduction in the number of highly qualified workers due to emigration.

BRICM – **B**razil, **R**ussia, **I**ndia, **C**hina, **M**exico. Large and growing economies that contribute to global patterns of trade and interdependence.

Brownfield site – A development site where older buildings are demolished or renovated before a new development takes place.

C

Canopy – The upper layer of a forest. The canopy receives most sunlight so contains many leaves, flowers and fruit.

Carbon cycle – The flow of carbon between various stores.

Carbon neutral – A product or development (such as a housing estate) that does not add any extra carbon dioxide emissions to the atmosphere over its lifetime.

Carbon sinks – Places where carbon is stored over very long periods of time, for example, in fossil fuels.

Catchment area – The area a river collects its water from. This is also called a drainage basin.

Catchment area (retail) – The area from which a shop attracts its customers.

Circular migration – The flow and return of people between rural and urban areas. People leave the countryside when there are few farming jobs and return at busier times of the year.

Climate – Taking weather readings over long periods of time, and then working out averages, patterns and trends.

Climate change – A long term change in the annual weather conditions. These changes can be natural or caused by human actions.

Clone town – Towns with retail areas that consist mainly of chain stores but have few independent retailers.

Commercial logging – The felling of trees, on a large scale, in order to make a profit on the sale of timber.

Commute – When people who live in rural areas travel every day to jobs in urban areas.

Comparison goods – Items in your shopping that are bought less often, such as washing machines and TVs.

Condensation – The process in the water cycle where water changes state from gas to liquid.

Confluence – The point at which two rivers meet.

Continentality – The climatic condition of large land masses heating up and cooling down very quickly.

Convenience goods – Items in your shopping that are bought regularly, such as bread and milk.

Corrasion – Erosion, or wearing away, of the landscape caused by friction. See abrasion.

Corrosion – The wearing away of the landscape by chemical processes such as solution.

Counter-urbanisation – The movement of people and businesses from large cities to smaller towns and rural areas.

Cycle – A repeating series of events, such as the water cycle or carbon cycle.

Cyclone – A low pressure system in the atmosphere associated with unsettled weather, wind and rain.

D

Debt-for-nature swap – An agreement between poorer nations that owe money to richer nations. The poorer nation agrees to spend money on a conservation project. In exchange the richer country agrees to cancel part of the debt of money that it is owed.

Deforestation – The cutting down or burning of trees.

De-industrialisation – A shift in employment from manufacturing to jobs that provide a service.

Delta – A river landform found at the mouth of a river where deposition causes new land to be formed.

Depopulation – The loss of people due to migration and low birth rates. For example, many of the rural areas of Iceland are suffering from depopulation.

Deposition – The laying down of material in the landscape. Deposition occurs when the force that was carrying the sediment is reduced.

Depression (weather) – A weather system associated with low air pressure. Depressions bring changeable weather that includes rain and windy conditions.

Deprivation – To lack some basic needs of life, such as education, clean water, enough food or equality.

Desertification – When the climate of a dry region becomes even drier. Vegetation dies or is eaten by grazing animals and the soil becomes vulnerable to soil erosion.

Development aid – Help which is given to tackle poverty and improve quality of life over the long term to improve education or health care.

Development gap – The difference in wealth between rich and poor countries.

Discharge – The amount of water flowing through a river channel or out of an aquifer. Discharge is measured in cubic metres per second (cumecs).

Displaced – People who have lost their homes because of conflict, an environmental disaster or a development such as the creation of a new reservoir.

Distributaries – The channels which flow away from the main river channel in the delta of a river after the main river channel divides.

Diversification – Where a wide variety of new jobs and business opportunities are created.

Diversify – Where a much wider variety of new business opportunities and jobs are created in a region.

Drainage basin – The area a river collects its water from. This is also called a catchment area.

Drip flow – Rainwater that falls into vegetation and then drips from the leaves.

Drought – A long period of time with little precipitation.

Dumping – The practice of selling goods cheaply abroad if they cannot be sold at home. For example, tomatoes that cannot be sold in Europe are sold cheaply in Africa.

E

Economic migrant – A migrant who moves in order to find work.

Ecosystem – A community of plants and animals and the environment in which they live. Ecosystems includes both living parts (e.g. plants) and non-living parts (e.g. air and water).

Ecotourism – Small scale tourist projects that create money for conservation as well as creating local jobs.

Emergency aid – Help that is given urgently after a natural disaster or a conflict to protect the lives of the survivors.

Emergent – The tallest trees in a forest that poke out above the canopy.

Emissions – Chemicals released into the atmosphere by industry, such as nitrogen oxide.

Employment structure – The number of people working in the primary, secondary and tertiary sectors of the economy.

Endemic – A disease that is constantly present or a threat in a certain geographical area or amongst a specific group of people. For example, malaria is endemic in many parts of sub-Saharan Africa, including Malawi.

Environmental refugees – People who are forced to leave their homes as a result of some environmental disaster. It is expected that sea level rise due to climate change will create millions of such refugees.

Erosion – The wearing away of the landscape. See abrasion and hydraulic action.

Estuary – The tidal part of a river where it widens into the sea.

Evaporation – Where water changes state from liquid into vapour.

Evapotranspiration – The combined loss of water from plants by both evaporation and transpiration.

Exports – The sale of products from one country to another.

F

FairTrade – An organisation that aims to guarantee that the producer of goods, such as foodstuffs and clothing, gets a fair price for their goods.

Fetch – The distance a wave travels over open sea.

Floodplain – The flat area beside a river channel that is covered in water during a flood event.

Formal occupations – Jobs that receive a regular wage and that are recognised and controlled by the state.

Formal sector – That part of the economy in which workers have a contract which gives them some rights.

Free trade – When countries trade without any limits to the amount of goods that can be exported and imported.

G

Gentrification – The process by which a run-down neighbourhood is improved and becomes more desirable.

Geographical Information System (GIS) – Geographical data that is stored digitally and can be analysed by creating a map.

Glacials – Cold periods in the Earth's history when glaciers have advanced and ice sheets increased in size.

Globalisation – Flows of people, ideas, money and goods are making an increasingly complex global web that links people and places from distant continents together.

Gorge – A steep-sided, narrow valley. Gorges are often found below a waterfall.

Green belt – A government policy used to prevent the spread of cities into the countryside. It is very difficult to get planning permission for new homes in a green belt.

Greenfield site – A plot of land that has not been used before for building.

Greenhouse effect – A natural process in which gases, such as carbon dioxide, trap heat energy in the atmosphere.

Greenhouse gases (GGs) – Gases, such as carbon dioxide and methane, that are able to trap heat in the atmosphere.

Gross National Income (GNI) per person – The average income in a country. It is also known as Gross National Product (GNP) per person.

Groundwater (store) – Water in the ground below the water table.

Groundwater flow – The flow of water through rocks.

Groyne – A type of coastal defence scheme consisting of low walls built into the sea. Groynes trap the sediment that is being moved by longshore drift.

H

Hard engineering – Artificial structures such as sea walls or concrete river embankments.

Heatwave – A long period of hot weather that causes stress for animals, plants and people.

High pressure – Values of air pressure between 1020–1040 millibars. High pressure systems are known as anti-cyclones and bring periods of dry, settled weather.

High-tech industries – The use of advanced technology in manufacturing, such as defence systems and medical equipment.

Honeypot site – A place of special interest that attracts many tourists and is often congested at peak times.

Housing tenure – The legal right to live a house. Housing tenure is usually categorised as either rented or owner occupied.

Hurricane – A tropical storm caused by a low pressure system involving strong winds more than 119km/hr.

Hydraulic action – Erosion caused when water and air are forced into gaps in rock or soil.

Hydro-electric power (HEP) – Electricity generated by water flowing through turbines.

Hydrograph – A line graph showing the discharge of a river over time.

Hydrological cycle – The continuous flow of water between the earth's surface and the atmosphere – more commonly known as the water cycle.

I

Illegal logging – The cutting down of forests for their timber by people who do not own the land or have the legal right to sell the timber.

Impermeable – Soil or rock which does not allow water to pass through it, such as clay.

Import duty – A tax placed on goods brought into a country to make them more expensive.

Imports – The purchase of goods from another country.

Indigenous peoples – Tribal groups who are native to a particular place.

Infant mortality rate (IMR) – The number of children who die before the age of one for every 1000 that are born.

Infiltration – The movement of water from the ground surface into the soil.

Informal sector (informal jobs) – The sector of the economy that includes many types of irregular jobs as well as types of work, such as household chores, child care, and studying.

Informal settlements – Homes where the householders have no legal rights to the land, i.e. they do not have legal housing tenure. Informal settlements are commonly known as shanty towns and squatter settlements.

Inner urban – The central, and usually older, part of a city.

Interception – When water is prevented from falling directly to the ground. For example, the canopy of leaves in a forest intercepts rainfall.

Interdependence – The complex patterns of trade, communication and aid that link different countries together.

Inter-glacials – Warmer periods in the Earth's history when glaciers have retreated and ice sheets have decreased in size.

Irrigation – Supplying farms with water so that they can grow crops.

Isobars – Lines of equal atmospheric pressure.

Isotherms – Lines of equal temperature.

K

Key services – The way in which ecosystems provide benefits for people. For example, mangrove forests act as coastal buffers, soaking up wave energy during a storm and reducing the risk of erosion and flooding.

Knowledge economy – Jobs that require high levels of education or training.

Knowledge Intensive Service (KIS) – Industries such as finance and education.

L

Labour intensive – Work that is still done by hand rather than using labour saving machines.

Lag time – The difference in time between a rain storm and the peak flow of floodwater (the maximum discharge) down a river.

Lateral erosion – The process by which a river can cut sideways into its own river bank.

Leaching – The removal of nutrients from the soil by rainwater washing them away.

Leeward side – The side of a hill or mountain that is sheltered from the wind.

Less Economically Developed Countries (LEDCs) – The countries that are to the South of the Brandt Line in Central and South America, Africa and parts of Asia.

Levees – Banks on either side of a river which contain the flow.

Life expectancy – The average age to which people can expect to live.

Load – The sediment carried by a river.

Local Development Framework – A planning document produced by a local authority after consultation with local residents and businesses.

Long shore drift – A process by which beach material is moved along the coast.

Low pressure – Values of air pressure between 970–990 millibars. Low pressure systems are known as cyclones and bring periods of unsettled weather with strong winds and rain.

M

Managed realignment (retreat) – A coastal management strategy in which holes are made in existing sea defences so that a new coastline is established further inland.

Mangrove forests – A type of tropical forest that grows in coastal regions.

Manufacturing – The production of goods and processed materials by the secondary sector of the economy.

Maritime climate – The climatic condition of land close to sea. The sea moderates temperatures meaning that there are only small variations in temperature.

Mass tourism – A style of tourist development in which massive numbers of holiday makers are encouraged to visit a large resort.

Meander – A river landform. A sweeping curve or bend in the river's course.

Mechanisation – The increased use of machines to replace human labour.

Meltwater – Water flowing from a melting glacier. Melt water rivers are very seasonal, with very low discharges in winter and very high discharges in summer.

Micro-credit – Where small loans are given to businessmen and women who are too poor to qualify for traditional bank loans.

Millennium Development Goals (MDG) – Development targets set by the United Nations with aims to meet by 2015.

More Economically Developed Countries (MEDCs) – The countries that are to the North of the Brandt Line in North America, Europe, northern Asia and parts of Oceania.

Mouth – The point at which a river enters a lake or the sea.

Multi-lateral aid – Funding that involves many donor countries.

Multinational companies (MNCs) – Large businesses, such as Sony, Microsoft and McDonalds, that have branches in several countries. Multi-national companies are also known as trans-national companies.

N

Natural increase – A population increase which is due to their being more births than deaths.

Negative multiplier effect – A downward spiral of decline in the economy. Negative multipliers may be triggered by the closure of a large employer.

Net in-migration – When more people move into the region than leave it.

Net out-migration – When more people leave the region than move in.

Newly Industrialised Country (NIC) – Newly industrialised countries such as India, Thailand or Indonesia have a large percentage of the workforce working in the secondary (manufacturing) sector.

NIMBY – 'Not In My Back Yard'. People who object to a development because they live close by are said to be NIMBYs.

Non-Government Organisations (NGOs) – Non-profit organisations such as OXFAM, ActionAid or Water Aid that are independent of the government.

Nutrient flows – The movement of minerals from one store to another.

Nutrient stores – A part of an ecosystem in which nutrients are kept.

Nutrients – Minerals containing nitrogen and phosphates.

O

Offshore bar – A feature on the sea bed formed by the deposition of sand.

Over-abstraction – When water is abstracted at a faster rate than it is recharged, leading to a store of water decreasing in size.

Overland flow – The flow of water across the ground surface.

Overseas Development Aid (ODA) – Government funding given to many different long term development projects abroad.

P

Pastoral farmers – Farmers who have grazing animals, such as cattle or goats.

Peak discharge – The maximum flow of water recorded in a river during a flood event.

Percolation – A flow in the water cycle. The movement of water out of the soil and into the rocks below.

Permafrost – Soil or rock that has remained frozen for at least two consecutive years. Permafrost is common in the Arctic region.

Permeable – A rock that allows water to pass though it, such as limestone.

Petty commodity production – The production of low value goods or services.

Population density – The number of people per square kilometre.

Porous – A rock which has many tiny gaps within it (pores) that allow it to store water, such as chalk and sandstone.

Positive multiplier (effect) – A positive chain of events triggered by the creation of new jobs in a region.

Post-glacial rebound – An adjustment in the level of the Earth's crust. The crust was depressed by the mass of ice lying on it during glacial periods of the ice age. Since the end of the last glacial period the crust has been slowly rising back to its original level.

Poverty – People who live below a certain income are said to live in poverty.

Poverty line – A level of income. If someone earns less than this amount they are said to be poor.

Precipitation – The movement of water from the atmosphere to the ground. Precipitation may be in many forms including rain, snow and hail.

Prevailing wind – The direction in which the wind most often blows.

Primary commodities – Raw materials that have not been processed. Coal, minerals and unprocessed food stuffs are all examples.

Primary health care – Primary health care is the first point of contact between a health care worker and a patient. It may involve preventative care, such as immunisation.

Primary sector – The part of the economy that produces raw materials such as a food stuffs, timber or minerals.

Private sector – People who are either self-employed or work for a larger company or organisation that is not controlled by the government.

Public sector – People employed by the national, regional or local government.

Pull factors – Reasons that attract migrants to move to a new home.

Push / pull – Reasons for migration.

Push factors – Reasons that force people to move away from their existing home.

Q

Quality of life – A measure of the happiness and contentment of an individual or family.

Quotas – Restrictions on the number of particular goods that can be imported each year.

R

Rain shadow – A climate effect causing an area located on the leeward side of a mountain to have low rainfall.

Rainwater harvesting – The collection of rain water. For example, the collection and use of rain water from the roof of a house.

Recharge – Water that enters an aquifer and refills a groundwater store.

Refugees – People who are in danger and who leave their homes for their own safety. Refugees may move because of a natural disaster, such as a volcanic eruption or because of conflict.

Regional Spatial Strategy – A planning document produced by each regional assembly in England, which considers the need for new housing, roads and schools.

Relief rainfall – Precipitation that is caused when warm, moist air is forced to rise over a mountainous region. As the air rises it cools and the water vapour condenses forming rain clouds. Relief rainfall is also known as orographic rain.

Remittances – The return of money sent by migrant workers to support their families who have remained at home.

Repossession – Repossession is the loss of your home. It occurs when an owner-occupier, who has a mortgage, fails to make their regular repayments to the bank or building society.

Reproduction – A type of economic activity, such as household chores, that does not earn any income.

Reservoir – An artificial lake made by damming the flow of a river.

Retreat – The gradual backward movement of a landform due to the process of erosion. The coastline retreats due to the erosion of a cliff and a waterfall retreats towards the source of a river as it is eroded.

Re-urbanisation – The recent trend for the population of city centres to grow.

Rural depopulation – When the population of a rural region decreases.

S

Sahel – The semi-arid region of North Africa to the south of the Sahara desert. The word means 'shore' in Arabic.

Saltation – The process by which sand-sized particles bounce along the river bed in the flow of water.

Sanitation – The safe disposal and treatment of sewage and waste water.

Savanna – An ecosystem of grasslands with scattered trees and bushes and which has a seasonal wet / dry climate.

Science Park – A group of industrial buildings used for research and design or high-tech processes.

Sea wall – A form of hard engineering used as a coastal defence against erosion and flooding.

Second homes – Houses which are used only for holidays or at weekends. Also called holiday cottages.

Secondary rainforest – Tropical vegetation that grows back after the original trees have been felled.

Secondary sector – The secondary sector is the part of the economy which is involved in processing and manufacturing.

Security of tenure – Where people have no legal right to live in their home and could be evicted at any time.

Sediment – Material carried by a river, glacier or wave in the sea.

Self-employed – People who are their own boss.

Self-help – Improvement projects carried out by ordinary people rather than by businesses or governments. Many homes in informal settlements are improved in this way.

Shanty housing – Homes built by the residents themselves on land that they do not own.

Shoreline Management Plan (SMP) – The plan that details how a local authority will manage each stretch of coastline in the UK in the future.

Social housing – Homes that are rented from a not-for-profit organisation, such as a Housing Association or the Local Authority.

Social landlord – An organisation, such as a Housing Association or Local Council, which rents properties on a not-for-profit basis.

Social premium – A small payment made by Fairtrade companies to their suppliers that is then used to fund community projects.

Socio-economic – A combination of social and economic factors.

Soft engineering – Alternative method of reducing floods by planting trees or allowing areas to flood naturally.

Solar footprint – The amount of the sun's energy that heats each square metre of the earth varies depending on latitude.

Solar furnace – A renewable technology that uses the sun's energy to heat water. The resulting steam is used to turn a turbine and generate electricity.

Solution – The process that dissolves minerals from rocks into water.

Source – The place where a river starts to flow.

Spit – A coastal landform formed by the deposition of sediment in a low mound where the coastline changes direction, for example, at the mouth of a river.

Stakeholder – Any person or group of people who have a vested interest in a planning issue.

Standard of living – A measure of the relative wealth of individuals or families.

Stem flow – Rainwater that falls onto vegetation and then trickles down branches and stems.

Storm surge – The rise in sea level that can cause coastal flooding during a storm or hurricane. The surge is due to a combination of two things. First, the low air pressure means that sea level can rise. Second, the strong winds can force a bulge of water on to the shoreline.

Sub-Saharan Africa – Africa south of the Sahara.

Subsidy – A payment that a country makes to its own farmers and businesses so that their goods can be sold at a lower price to consumers.

Subsistence – A type of economic activity where very little money is used. In subsistence farming the farmer only produces enough food to feed the family. There is very little surplus that can be sold for cash.

Suburban sprawl – When a city expands into the neighbouring countryside. Greenfield sites are used to build new urban homes, offices and retail parks at the edge of the city.

Surface stores – Places where water is found on the surface such as lakes and rivers.

Suspension – The process of transport which carries fine sediment such as silt for long distances down a river.

Sustainable community – A community that is designed to have minimum impact on the environment. Such communities may make use of energy efficiency, renewable technologies and local services in order to reduce transport costs.

Swash – The flow of water up the beach as a wave breaks on the shore.

T

Tele-working – Jobs where most of the working week is spent working from home using personal computers, mobile technology and the internet.

Temperature range – The difference between maximum and minimum temperature.

Tertiary sector – This part of the economy provides services to other industries or to individual consumers like you and me. Retailing, health and education are all examples of the tertiary sector.

Therapeutic food – Food that is high in protein and fat that is given as part of an emergency aid package to treat malnourished children.

Thermal – A column of warm rising air.

Threshold (population) – The number of customers needed before a shop or service becomes worthwhile. For example, a shop selling convenience goods, such as a bakery, needs a smaller threshold population than a shop selling comparison goods.

Throughflow – The downhill flow of water through soil.

Tombolo – A coastal landform made by deposition of sediment joining the coast to an island.

Tourist enclave – A tourist resort that is designed so that tourists are separated from local communities. In this way, the tourist spends more money with the company, and very little with local businesses.

Traction – The process of transport which describes the movement of larger pebbles and cobbles as they roll along the bed of a river.

Trade blocs – Trading partnerships between different countries. The European Union is one example.

Transnational companies (TNCs) – Large businesses such as Sony, Microsoft and McDonalds, who have branches in several countries. Transnational companies are also known as multi-national companies.

Trans-boundary conflicts – Disputes between neighbouring regions or countries. Conflicts can be caused by the use of water from a river that flows from one country to another.

Transpiration – Water loss from plants through pores in the leaves.

Transport – The movement of material through the landscape.

Tributary – A smaller river that flows into a larger river channel.

Tropical rain belt (ITCZ) – A zone between the tropics of Cancer and Capricorn that has a lot of rainfall.

Tropical rainforest – Large forest ecosystems (or biomes) that exist in the hot, wet climate found on either side of the equator.

Tundra – An ecosystem largely found in the Arctic region. The tundra is treeless because the growing season is short and the average monthly temperature is below 10 celsius.

U

Unstable – Warm air that is rising may be described as unstable. Unstable air causes clouds to build up and form rain.

Urban – Larger towns and cities. The United Nations definition is that urban settlements have more than 20,000 inhabitants.

Urban heat island – When a city has temperatures that are warmer than in the surrounding rural area.

Urban micro-climate – The small scale, local climate of a large city that is influenced by its buildings and traffic.

Urban population – The percentage of a country's population that lives in settlements greater than 20,000 people.

Urban sprawl – The growth of towns and cities into the countryside. Sprawl is usually considered to have negative impacts.

Urbanisation – The physical and human growth of towns and cities.

U-shaped valley – A trough shaped valley with very steep sides and a flat bottom that has been eroded by a glacier.

V

V-shaped valley – A valley with sides that slope sharply down to a river which has only the narrowest of floodplains.

W

Water cycle – The continuous flow of water between the earth's surface and the atmosphere - also called the hydrological cycle.

Water stores – A place where water is kept.

Watershed – The boundary of a drainage basin.

Wave-cut notch – A slot with overhanging rocks that has been cut into the bottom of a cliff by wave action.

Wave-cut platform – A coastal landform made of a rocky shelf in front of a cliff. The wave cut platform is caused by erosion and left by the retreat of the cliff.

Weather – Our day-to-day experience of temperature, wind, rainfall and sunshine.

Weather hazards – Weather conditions that could potentially result in harmful or damaging effects.

Weathering – The breaking up of rock by the effects of the weather such as rainfall and temperature change.

Wilderness – Areas that have been left in a wild state and are uninhabited.

Wildlife corridor – Strips of habitat that allow wild animals to migrate from one ecosystem to another e.g. hedgerows.

Windward – The side of a sand dune, hill or mountain that faces into the wind.

Index